MANAGING GENERATION Y @ WORKPLACE

Issues and Challenges

MANAGING GENERATION Y @ WORKPLACE
Issues and Challenges

Editors
Anu Singh Lather
Shalini Garg
Shilpa Jain

BLOOMSBURY
LONDON • NEW DELHI • NEW YORK • SYDNEY

First published, 2013

BLOOMSBURY PUBLISHING INDIA PVT. LTD.
London New Delhi New York Sydney

ISBN: 978-93-82563-47-1

Published by Bloomsbury Publishing India Pvt. Ltd.
VISHRUT Building, DDA Complex, Building No. 3, Pocket C-6 & 7
Vasant Kunj, New Delhi 110 070

Laser Typeset by FORTUNE GRAPHICS
WZ-911/2 Shankarlal Street, Ring Road, Naraina, New Delhi

Printed at Anvi Composers
1 DDA Market, Block A-1B, Pachim Vihar, New Delhi 110 063

Contents

Preface

The workplaces are witnessing a different workforce today. The new entrants in the industry are different in their style of working, expectations and attitudes. They are the generation Y workforce. Generation Yers are often accused of being workplace divas who expect everything to fall into their laps without putting in the required effort. However, many Gen Y enthusiasts counter this view by arguing that they are independent, innovative and creative and ready to engage in companies that are prepared to offer the environments in which they thrive. The Generation Yers are different from their older colleagues. They care much more about having a personal life so they're sometimes seen as slackers. They're willing to work hard and they value work that has an impact, but they also want time to do other things. They're great team players and highly savvy about technology. They resent the traditional organizational structures, and do not want to be bonded by rules. Many managers are reporting issues with the workplace readiness and integration of Generation Y. There is widespread dissatisfaction among employers with the college product, both in hard and soft skills (Bok 2006, Levine 2005b).

Hyper inflated self-esteem and self-importance create difficulties in dealing with the realities of the consequential workplace. If employers are unhappy with Generation Y, workers, Generation Y are the unhappiest on the job. They report the lowest overall satisfaction and engagement levels. They don't think they are making enough money. Many distrust large organizations and refuse to compromise workplace arrangements and workplace style. They are not staying long in jobs with record high rates of turnover, at great expense to employers. Half of younger workers actually report that they feel burned out, and one in four report that they are not only seeking new jobs, but are seeking new careers.

Today's young workers from "Generation Y" are entering the workforce with characteristics and expectations that present unique challenges to those responsible for recruiting, orienting and initiating them into the professional world, as well as those supervising, managing and retaining them once they get there. Understanding typical generational values, traits, preferences and styles can improve recruitment, workplace effectiveness, harmony and employee satisfaction and retention. This book is a compilation of selected papers that focus on the issues and challenges related to generation Y at the workplace. This book provides reader with a better understanding of the development and predictable issues of Generation Y, and describes what organizations and managers can do to help them transition into and be successful in the professional workplace. All the papers are selected for publication through double blind review process, from subject experts.

We take this opportunity to express our sincere thanks to Prof. D.K. Badyopadhyay, Hon'ble Vice Chancellor Guru Gobind Singh Indraprastha University for his enduring guidance and motivation. It is with his vision and support for his pupil in the university we gather the courage to produce such works. We appreciate the efforts of academicians, researchers, and industry practitioners for their valuable contributions in the form of research papers. We also express our gratitude to publishers for enabling us to release the book in public domain for further deliberations and contemplation.

Editors

A Study of Locus of Control and Conflict Resolution Styles of Generation Y in National Capital Region of India

Anu Singh Lather, Shalini Garg and Shilpa Jain

University School of Management Studies, Guru Gobind Singh Indraprastha University, Dwarka, Delhi

ABSTRACT

The aim of the research is to analyse generation Y with respect to their anxiety level, locus of control and conflict resolution styles. The research was conducted on students of undergraduate and post graduate courses of Delhi and NCR. The study consisted of 143 respondents and statistical analysis show that most of the generation Y individuals prefer using Accommodating style of conflict resolution and least preferred style for most of them is Collaborating. Also the results show that most of them have external locus of control. Also the individuals from public schooling background are more competing while the one from private and village schooling are more accommodating.

Keywords: *Conflict Resolution Styles, Locus of Control, Generation Y*

INTRODUCTION

The workplaces are witnessing a different workforce today. The new entrants in the industry are different in their style of working, expectations and attitudes. They are the generation Y workforce. Generation Yers are often accused of being workplace divas who expect everything to fall into their laps without putting in the required effort. However, many Gen Y enthusiasts counter this view by arguing that they are independent, innovative and creative and ready to engage in companies that are prepared to offer the environments in which they thrive. Many managers are reporting issues with the workplace readiness and integration of Generation Y. There is widespread dissatisfaction among employers with the college product, both in hard and soft skills (Bok 2006, Levine 2005b). Hyper inflated self-esteem and self-importance create difficulties in dealing with the realities of the consequential workplace. If employers are unhappy with Generation Y workers, Generation Y are the unhappiest on the job. They report the lowest overall satisfaction and engagement levels. Half of younger workers actually report that they feel burned out, and one in four report that they are not only seeking new jobs, but are seeking new careers. This invokes a need to understand this generation more clearly so that they can be managed well at workplace. The present study is conducted to understand the locus of control and conflict resolution styles of generation Y.

Locus of Control is a dimension of personality indicating how much responsibility does a person takes of his own deeds. An external Locus of Control means the individual does not take responsibility of his own deeds rather throw it on chances and/or other individuals. Contrarily the individuals with the Internal Locus of Control take responsibility of their actions. A person with an external locus of control will always show himself/herself as helpless, will throw responsibilities of his deeds on others, have low self esteem, have casual attitude towards work and others, and will be less creative and innovative. On the other hand, a person with Internal Locus of Control will take responsibilities of his actions; will not keep casual approach to others, possess better self esteem, and will be more creative and innovative.

Locus of control has become an important concept in today's life and has been applied in various fields starting from industrial and organizational psychology, sports psychology, educational psychology and the psychology of religion. Students who tended to be more internally controlled believed that hard work and focus would result oftentimes in successful academic progress and they performed better academically. Those students who were identified as more externally controlled, believing that their future depended upon luck or fate, tended to have lower academic performance levels. Cassandra B. Whyte further researched how control tendency influenced behavioural outcomes in the academic realm by examining the effects of various modes of counselling on grade improvements and the locus of control of high-risk college students.

Another important aspect to understand about generation Y is their conflict resolution styles. Conflict resolution represents an important managerial duty. Research has shown that managers can spend as much as 20% of their time resolving conflicts (Thomas & Schmidt, 1976). As a result of the increase in the time, effort and money spent in resolving conflict, whether seeking employees with "the ability to work with others" or the attributes of a "team player", employers are increasingly emphasizing the ability of their employees to manage or resolve conflict as a key ingredient of future success for both the individual and the firm. Interpersonal or intergroup conflict involves two main issues: the amount of concern people have for their own and for others' outcomes (Bolton, 1986; Fisher & Ury, 1981; Hocker & Wilmot, 1995; Katz & Lawyer, 1992; Polkinghorn & Byrne, 2001; Weeks, 1992). The 'dual concern model' developed by Pruitt and Rubin (1986), and based on the work of Blake and Mouton (1964) and Thomas (1976), suggests five styles of handling conflict: collaborating, compromising, accommodating, controlling and avoiding. The decision to use one style instead of another depends on a number of factors like religion, culture, generational differences etc.

LITERATURE REVIEW

Researchers have indicated that age has a strong relationship with locus of control. It is sometimes assumed that as people age, they will become less internal and more external, but data here has been ambiguous. Bailer (1961) found that locus of control tended to become more internal with age and this developmental process assisted in bringing about specific positive outcomes. Lao (1974) assessed changes in locus of control orientation from youth through adulthood and old age. In her extension of this work, Lao predicted an increase in internality from youth to adulthood (15 to 30-39 yr.); a stabilized sense of internal control in middle age (30 to 59 yr.) ; and a decrease in internality in old age (60 yr. and older). Age-correlated differences in locus of control (LOC) orientation were examined for 306 persons by Robert and Roger (1976) between the age of 13 to 90 years, in three areas of activity: intellectual, social, and physical. On the scales measuring LOC for both physical and social situations, persons over 60 scored more external than adults in the 35–50 age range. On the other hand, Dönmez (1983) stated that there were many studies showing that locus of control might change from being internal to being external or vice verse. Schieman (2001) determined that an individual's locus of control morphs as they age: as an individual gets older, they lose their sense of control. Lachman (2004) in an attempt to find whether locus of control beliefs change in later life, he conducted studies and found that age differences were found most often on the chance and powerful others control dimensions, suggesting that the elderly acknowledge the importance of external sources of control and at the same time preserve their sense of internal control. http://en.wikipedia.org/wiki/Locus_of_control - cite_note-11 Longitudinal data collected by Gatz and Karel (cited in Johnson et al., 2004) imply that internality may increase up to middle age, and thereafter decrease. Noting the ambiguity of data in this area, Aldwin and Gilmer (2004) cite Lachman's claim that locus of control is ambiguous. Indeed, there is evidence here that changes in locus of control in later life relate more visibly to increased externality, rather than reduced internality, if the two concepts are taken to be orthogonal. Evidence cited by Schultz and Schultz (2005), for example Heckhausen and Schulz (1995) or Ryckman and Malikosi, 1975 (cited in Schultz & Schultz, 2005), suggests that locus of control increases in internality up until middle age. These authors also note that attempts to control the environment become more pronounced between the age of eight and fourteen. Tucker, Hamayan and Genesse (2006) also believe that the people become more internal as they get older. Kýralp, Sahin and Dinçyürek (2008) reported that locus of control become more internal as individuals get older. Instead of classifying persons as having internal locus of control or external locus of control, it should be emphasized that locus of control may change in terms of being internal or external (Dinçyürek, Çağlar and Birol, 2010).

Research delineating the effects of gender on locus of control has yielded conflicting results. Archer & Waterman, 1988 found males to be more internally motivated than female adolescents. Cairns, Mc Whirter, Duffy and Barry (1990) found that females were more internally oriented than were males. Susan (1992) undertook a study to examine the relationship between locus of control and gender role. A non-significant trend for the interaction of sex by locus of control was found. Lee and Dengerink (1992) compared locus of control in American college students and Swedish gymnasium students. Swedish women were more externally oriented than Swedish men or Americans of either sex. Aricak (1995) argues that male students have higher levels of internal locus of control. Manger and Eikeland (2000) reported that females have higher levels of internal locus of control in contrast to males. Manger and Eikeland (2001) in a sample of Norwegian 14- and 15-year-old students found no significant relationship between total externality-internality score and level of ability. The analyses of gender differences showed that girls had significantly higher total internal locus of control scores than boys. Schultz and Schultz (2005) point out, significant gender differences in locus of control have not been found for adults in a U.S. population. Sherman et. al (2007) in their article presented a synthesis of research conducted in the last two decades that has explored the relationship of gender to locus of control measures. The research suggested that both males and females are becoming more external. Females, however, tend to be more external than males on most locus of control measures. Gender factors into one's sense of control: women are less likely to possess an internal locus of control than men.

Conflict is a massive growth industry. It is an integral part of the fabric of a postmodern society that is increasingly litigious, competitive, complex and alienating (Bryant 2003, p. 75). Too little conflict results in organizational stasis, while too much conflict reduces the organization's effectiveness and eventually immobilizes its employees (Marquis & Huston 1996). Conflict management refers to the modes used by either or both parties to cope with a conflict. Adler and Towne (1990) identified three possible courses of actions when faced with a conflict: (1) accepting the status quo (i.e. living with the problem); (2) using force and mandating change; (3) reaching an agreement by negotiating. Three types of outcomes result from these approaches to conflict management: Win–Lose approach, Lose–Lose approach and Win–Win approach. Conflict management research focus is centered primarily on the conflict situation and the person–situation interaction (Knapp et al. 1988). However, there is a reason to believe that conflict behaviour is determined by both situational and dispositional influences (Sandy et al. 2000). A number of similar approaches to measuring individual modes of managing interpersonal conflict have been developed (Blake & Mouton 1964, Rahim 1983). The theoretical framework of this study rests on the work of Thomas and Kilmann (1974). The two-dimensional framework and five predominant modes proposed by them are used to define conflict management modes. Thomas and Kilmann (1978) reported reasonable support for the instrument's substantive validity. Internal consistency coefficients are in moderate range with average *a*-coefficient 0.60 and test–retest reliability ranging from 0.61 to 0.68 (Thomas & Kilmann 1978). The findings suggest that the instrument is able to differentiate between conflict management styles. Thomas (1976) suggested the dimensions of Assertiveness and Cooperativeness in classifying his five modes: Avoiding, Accommodating, Competing, Collaborating and Compromising (Figure 1). The instrument was used in earlier nursing studies on conflict management by O'Hearn Woodlti (1987), Barton (1991) and Cavanagh (1991). The Conflict resolution mode represents the one-best-way long-term approach, which emphasizes that contextual variables are changeable and that the ideal organization should be brought nearer by all manner of means. Successful conflict resolution not only removes frustration but also leads to higher effectiveness, trust and openness (Van de Vliert 1998).

OBJECTIVES OF THE STUDY

- To compare the Locus of Control of generation Y (internal v/s external) with respect to their age group, gender, and schooling.
- To compare the conflict resolution styles of generation Y with respect to their age group, gender, schooling and locus of control.

Hypotheses

H1. There is no significant difference in locus of control of generation Y among the various age groups.

H2. There is no significant difference in locus of control of male and female of generation Y.

H3. There is no significant difference in locus of control of generation Y coming from different schooling (Public Schools, Private Schools, Government School, Village School, and Convent School.

H4. There is no difference in the conflict resolution styles of generation Y among the various age groups.

H5. There is no significant difference in conflict resolution styles of male and female of generation Y.

H6. There is no significant difference in conflict resolution styles of generation Y coming from different schooling (Public Schools, Private Schools, Government School, Village School, and Convent School.

H7. There is no significant difference in the conflict resolution styles of generation Y with respect to their locus of control.

Research Methodology

For the study a sample of 200 was targeted out of which 143 valid responses were received with a response rate of 71.5%. The technique of Purposive sampling was adopted for collecting data since the research was focused on generation Y. the data was collected from the students studying in Undergraduate and Post Graduate courses of Delhi and NCR. The research design is given below:

Survey Tools

A three – part questionnaire was used for data collection.

Socio-demographic data concerning name, gender, age group and schooling type (Public School, Private School, Government School, Village School, and Convent School).

Locus of Control (LOC) - Levenson and Miller (1976) multidimensional scale of I-E control was used to measure LOC. It has 24 items related to two sub areas namely internal control and external control. External control has two sub scales i.e. powerful others and chance. The subjects are required to respond to each item on a 5-point scale. The score on the 8 item of each sub-area was used as a score. The higher the score, the greater the subject's degree of expectancy for the particular aspect of locus of control.

Thomas-Kilmann Conflict Resolution Mode Inventory- The two-dimension model derived by Blake and Mouton (1964) is the theoretical foundation for many conflict studies and/or instruments. One of the best known resulting measures, and also the instrument used in this study, is the Thomas-Kilmann Management of Difference Instrument (MODE), initially developed in 1974. Previous research cited in the area suggests that conflict profiles can be measured with success using the Thomas-Kilmann instrument and other factors associated with these profiles readily identified. Reliability data for the Thomas-Kilmann instrument has been reported as ranging from .61-.68 (test-retest) and .43-.71 (Cronbach alpha) (Rahim, p. 47-49) indicating that the instrument is a highly reliable device for such assessments. Originated from the work of Blake and Mouton (1964), the dual-concern model has several variations, all of which assume that individuals choose different modes, strategies, or styles for handling conflict based on some variations of two primary concerns/interests— "concern for self" and "concern for other".

Results and Discussions

The analysis of results shows that 63.6 % individuals of generation Y use Accommodating style of conflict resolution and 74.8% individuals does not prefer to use Collaborating style of conflict resolution (Table 1). The results are quite contradictory to the popular perception about this generation of being straightforward and demanding which indicates towards their being high on assertiveness. However the results here shows that they do not prefer assertion, rather resolves conflict meekly by giving full cooperation. Further the analysis of the locus of control shows that 91.2% individuals of generation Y possess external locus of control. This means most of them throw the responsibility of their own deeds on chances and powerful others. They also do not differ on locus of control across the gender, age and schooling. Thus the hypothesis H1, H2 and H3 are accepted.

Table 3 shows that the individuals differ significantly on their conflict resolution styles with respect to their schooling background on Competing (F= 6.29, p=.00), Compromising (F= 2.68, p= .04), and Accommodating (F= 2.41, p=.05). The table of means (Table 4) show that individuals with public school schooling are highest among the lot on competing followed by government schooling, convent schooling, village schooling and the competing style is least used by the individuals who had their schooling from private schools. Further Table 5 shows that individuals with the private schooling background are significantly lower of competing style of conflict resolution as compared to the individuals coming from the rest of the schooling background.

Table 1: Showing the Percentage Usage of Conflict Resolution Styles by Generation Y

	High	*Average*	*Low*
Competing	25.2	61.5	13.3
Collaborating	4.2	21	74.8
Compromising	18.2	29.4	52.4
Avoiding	28	58	14
Accommodating	63.6	28	8.4

Table 2: Showing the Percentage of Generation Y Individual with Respect to their Locus of Control

Locus of Control	Percentage
External Locus of Control	91.8
Internal Locus of Control	9.2

Table 3: Showing the Analysis of Variance of Conflict Resolution Styles and Locus of Control According to Age Group, Gender, and Schooling

Source	*Dependent Variable*	*Type III Sum of Squares*	*df*	*Mean Square*	*F*	*Sig.*
Schooling	Competing	93.23	4	23.31	6.29	.00
	Compromising	62.05	4	15.51	2.68	.04
	Accommodating	44.16	4	11.04	2.41	.05
Locus of Control	Accommodating	29.09	1	29.09	6.36	.01

Table 4 also shows that individuals with private and convent schooling background are higher than others on Compromising style of conflict resolution followed by individuals from village school, and government school. The individuals coming from public schooling background are scoring least on Compromising style of conflict resolution. Table 6 further shows that individuals coming from private school background are significantly higher on Compromising as compared to individuals coming from public and village school background. For Accommodating style of conflict resolution the individuals coming from village school background are highest followed by individuals with private schooling and individuals with schooling from public school are least accommodating. Also Table 7 shows that the individuals from village schools and private schools are significantly higher on Accommodating style as compared to those from public, convent and government schools. There is no significant difference found in usage of conflict resolution style of individuals from different age groups and gender. Thus hypothesis H4, H5 are accepted, while hypothesis H6 is partially accepted in case of no significant difference in conflict resolution style usage of collaborating and avoiding with respect to schooling and H6 is rejected for Competing, Compromising and Accommodating style of conflict resolution.

Table 4: Showing the Mean Scores of Generation Y from different Schooling Background on Various Conflict Resolution Styles

Dependent Variable	*Public School*	*Private School*	*Convent School*	*Government School*	*Village School*
Competing	6.50	1.75	4.58	6.33	3.88
Compromising	3.36	6.00	6.00	3.37	5.17
Accommodating	6.81	9.75	8.00	7.78	10.00

Table 5: Showing Duncan's Multiple Range Test results on Competing Style of Conflict Resolution with Respect to Schooling of Generation Y

Schooling	*N*	*Subset*	
		1	*2*
Private School	3	1.6667	
Village School	4		4.7500
Convent School	15		4.8667
Public School	79		6.4810
Government School	14		6.5714

Table 6: Showing Duncan's Multiple Range Test results on Compromising style of Conflict Resolution with Respect to Schooling of Generation Y

Schooling	*N*	*Subset*	
		1	*2*
Government School	14	3.3571	
Public School	79	3.5443	
Village School	4	4.7500	4.7500
Convent School	15	5.7333	5.7333
Private School	3		6.6667

The results also emphasize that the individuals with internal locus of control are significantly more accommodating as compared to the individuals with external locus of control. This could be simply attributed to the fact that individuals with internal locus of control take the responsibility of their own deeds and therefore are more understanding. However individuals with the external locus of control throw the responsibility of their own deeds on chance or powerful others thus finding excuses for everything and see others in the same light. Thus hypothesis H7 is partially rejected for Accommodating style while it is accepted for rest of the conflict resolution styles.

Table 7: Showing Duncan's Multiple Range Test Results on Accommodating Style of Conflict Resolution with Respect to Schooling of Generation Y

Schooling	*N*	*Subset*	
		1	*2*
Public School	79	6.812	
Government School	14	7.783	
Convent School	15	8.00	
Private School	3		9.754
Village School	4		10.00

Table 8: Showing Means of Accommodating Style of Conflict Resolution with Respect to Locus of Control of Generation Y

Dependent Variable	LOC	Mean
Accommodating	Internal Locus of Control	8.429
	External Locus of Control	7.391

CONCLUSION

Generation Y bought along with them at the workplaces lot of challenges for the managers to deal with them. To start with managers are facing problems with the lack of hard and soft skills of this generation and then there are issues related to their behaviours of low satisfaction, low engagement, high turnover, job hopping, and disinterest etc. This prompts the need to understand their behaviours more clearly so that the contingent strategies can be devised to manage them at the workplace. As is clearly indicated from the results of this study that most of this generation individuals prefer Accommodating style of conflict resolution while does not prefer Collaborating style. These results though are contrary to the popular notion about this generation of being more assertive, but the results are in line with the most preferred style of conflict resolution of earlier generations of the sub continent well represented through numerous researches. It is interesting to note that most of this generation has external locus of control, and they are not ready to take responsibility of their own actions, thus finding faults with others. This perhaps is the biggest reason for their behavioural challenge at the workplace that leads to their low satisfaction, low engagement levels and similar issues and challenges.

REFERENCES

[1] Adler R.B. & Towne N. (1990), "Looking Out Looking In", Interpersonal Communication. Holt, Rinehart & Winston, Forth Worth.

[2] Aldwin, C.M., Gilman, D.F. (2004). *Health, Illness and Optimal Ageing*. London: Sage. ISBN 0-7619-2259-8.

[3] Arýcak T (1995). Üniversite Öðrencilerinde Saldýrganlýk, Benlik Saygýsý ve Denetim Odaðý Ýliskisi (The relationship between aggressiveness, self-esteem and locus of control in undergraduate students). Unpublished MA Thesis, Ýstanbul: Marmara University, Institute of Social Sciences.

[4] Bailer, I. (1961). Conceptualization of success and failure in mental retarded and normal children. *Journal of Personality, 29,* 303-320.

[5] Barton A. (1991), "Conflict Resolution by nurse managers". Nursing Management 22 (5), 83–86.

[6] Blake R.R. & Mouton J.S. (1964), The Managerial Grid. Gulf Publishing, Houston, TX.

[7] Blake, R. R., & Mouton, J. S. (1964). The managerial grid. *Houston, TX: Gulf Publishing.*

[8] Bolton, R. (1986). People skills: How to assert yourself, listen to others and resolve conflicts. *New York: Simon & Schuster.*

[9] Bryant J. (2003), The Six Dilemmas of Collaboration. John Wiley & Sons Ltd, Chichester.

[10] Cairns, E., Mc Whirter, L., Duffy, U., & Barry, R. (1990). The stability of self-concept in late adolescence: Gender and situational effects. *Personality and Individual Differences, 11,* 937–944. doi:10.1016/0191-8869(90)90275-V

[11] Cavanagh S.J. (1991) The conflict management style of staff nurses and nurse managers. Journal of Advanced Nursing 16, 1254–1260.

[12] Dinçyürek S, Çaðlar M, Birol C (2010). Atýlganlýk ve denetim odaðý düzeyi: gelecek nesillere etkisi (Assertiveness and locus of control: Its effects on the future generations). *H. Ü. J. Educ. Faculty, 39:*142-150.

[13] Fisher, R., & Ury, W. (1981). Getting to yes: Negotiating agreement without giving in. *New York: Penguin Books.*

[14] Hacker, I., & Wilmat, W. (1995). Interpersonal conflict. Madison, *WI: Brown & Benchmark.*

[15] Katz, N., & Lawyer, J. (1992). Communication and conflict resolution skills. *Dubuque, IA: Kendall Hunt.*

[16] Knapp M.L., Putnan L.L. & Davis L.J. (1988), "Measuring interpersonal conflict in organizations: where do we go from here?", Management Communication Quarterly 1, 414–429.

[16] Lachman, M.E. (2004). Locus of Control in ageing research: a case for multidimensional and domain –specific assessment. Psychol Aging, Vol. 1(1), 34-40.

[17] Lao, R. C. The developmental trend of the locus of control. Unpublished paper presented at the meetings of the American Psychological Association, New Orleans, 1974.

[18] Lee, V.K. & Dengerink, H.A.(1992). Locus of Control in Relation to Sex and Nationality: A Cross –Cultural Study. Journal of Cross- Cultural Psychology, Vol. 23 (4), 488-497.

[19] Manger, T. & Eikeland, O.J. (2001). On the relationship between locus of control, level of ability and gender. Scandinavian Journal of Psychology, Vol. 41 (3), 225-229.

[19] O'Hearn Woodlti A. (1987) Deans of nursing: perceived sources of conflict and conflict-handling modes. Journal of Nursing Education 26 (7), 272–277.

[20] Polkinghorn, B., & Byrne, 5. (2001).Between war and peace: An examination of conflict management styles in four conflict zones. *International Journal of Conflict Management, 12, 2346.*

[21] Pruitt, D. C., & Rubin, 1. Z. (1986). Social conflict. *New York: McGraw Hill.*

[22] Rahim M.A. (1983), "A measure of style of handling interpersonal conflict". Academy of Management Journal 26, 368–376.

[23] Sandy S.V., Boardman S.K. & Duetsch M. (2000), "Personality and conflict". In The Handbook of Conflict Resolution. Theory and Practice (M. Deutsch & P.T. Coleman eds), pp. 289–315. Jossey-Bass Publishers, San Francisco, CA.

[24] Schieman, S. (2001). Age, education, and the sense of control: a test of the cumulative advantage hypothesis. Research on Aging vol. 23 (2), 153-178.

[25] Schultz, D.P., Schultz, S.E. (2005). *Theories of Personality* (8th ed.). Wadsworth: Thomson. ISBN 0-534-62402-2.

[26] Sherman, A.C., Higgs, G.E. & Williams R.L. (1997). Gender differences in the locus of construct. Psychology & Health, Vol. 12(2), 239-248. Available Online 19 Dec 2007.

[27] Thomas K.W. & Kilmann R.H. (1974) Thomas-Kilmann Mode Instrument. Xicom, Sterling Forest, NY.

[28] Thomas K.W. & Kilmann R.H. (1978) Comparison of four instruments measuring conflict behavior. Psychological Reports 42, 1139–1145.

[29] Thomas, K. W. (1976). Conflict and conflict management. In M. Dunnette (ed.), *Handbook of Industrial and Organizational Psychology* (pp. 889-935). *Chicago: Rand McNally.*

[30] Tucker, G. R, Hamayan, E. & Genesse, F.H. (2006). Affective, cognitive and social factors in second language acquisition, Canadian Modern Language Review, 32, 214-26.

[31] Van de Vliert E. (1998) Conflict and conflict management. In Handbook of Work and Organizational Psychology, 2nd edn (P.J.D. Drenth, H. Thierry & C.J. de Wolff eds), pp. 351–376. Psychology Press, London.

[32] Weeks, D. (1992). The eight essential steps to conflict resolution: Preserving relationships at work, at home and in the community. *New York: Penguin Books.*

Innovative Strategies in Managing Generation Y at the Work Place

Rahul Bansal and Chhavi Kiran Gupta

Community Medicine, Subharti Medical College, Meerut

ABSTRACT

'Generation y' is a term being popularly used by demographers for those people who were born between early 80's till 2000. It means all the people who are currently between the age group of approximately 15 to 25 years. Most of these people are either on the verge of completing their school/college education or they have just entered jobs in the national/international organizations or are self employed.

Before discussing the management strategies to get the best out of these young minds, let us look at the strengths and weaknesses of this generation.

STRENGTHS OF GENERATION Y

1. **Well informed**: Because of the computer literacy, which is almost universal in this generation, and the easy availability of affordable internet facilities, this generation is well informed about any idea or issue which catches their attention. Due to the current boom of social networking sites, virtual chat rooms and ever expanding national/international media, they have access to any thing happening anywhere around the world with just the click of a mouse.
2. **Highly connectivity**: The distance barriers have crumbled so much in the wake of the 'digital revolution' this generation has witnessed, that they can very easily be termed as 'Global citizens'. They have face book friends in hundreds. They also keep their friends/ relatives well informed about almost anything worth telling through social networking sites.
3. **Confidence**: They have lot of confidence in their abilities, with the result they are 'go getters'; they want to achieve a lot in their lives and they have big dreams for their future. In fact, some of them are literally following the popular maxim 'sky is the limit'.
4. **Better educational opportunities**: This generation has seen wide options in educational opportunities, right from their school days, for example, more number of streams in the schools, options to opt for foreign language learning and newer vocational education. In

the university education also, this generation has been exposed to a wide range of educational opportunities, not only in the government run universities, but also in the established/ emerging private universities, some of which are trying to match international standards.

5. **Higher IQ**: There is some evidence showing that the average IQ of this generation is higher than previous generations. This increased intelligence coupled with information technology, has opened many new doors of opportunity for this generation.
6. **More money and more fun**: This generation has been exposed to better financial resources from childhood, due to the economic reforms in this country. Not only do they have more money in their hands, they also have more things to purchase and enjoy. This generation seems to believe in the motto "earn more and spend more".
7. **Rationalists**: Generation y does not believe in something just because it has been laid down by tradition; be it, religion, norms of society or values of their parents. They want to know the logic behind the dos and don'ts they are asked to follow and if they fail to get a genuine reason they are less likely to follow them. On the other hand if anything appeals to their logical mind they may take strong decisions to change their behavior.
8. **Think out of the box**: This generation can think out of the box in an innovative way provided, they get a positive and supportive environment to do so. A very stressful environment, common nowadays at workplaces, may curb the creativity present in them.

WEAKNESSES OF GENERATION Y

1. **A confused lot:** This generation seems to be quite confused regarding the value systems. They don't know whether to believe in traditional values of their country, or to ape the west. For example according to an article in TOI (Times Of India), "Due to the new found freedom, 'Love' has suddenly become appealing to a group that has traditionally been associated with games and fun, but nursing a broken heart needs maturity. The lack of this maturity makes them doubt relationships and makes them bitter, when the rosy fantasies of future, clash with reality". Also, "materialism, is robbing them of real 'joy'", says another article from TOI (15/11/06). In this article, Naveen Kumar, points out that- "Today's teens have become miniature adults and despite all their expertise at wrangling stuff out of their parents, they are not in control of themselves. Peer perception is all that matters and they get easily bored of their latest acquisitions."
2. **Risk taking:** TOI published an attitudinal survey in private schools of Delhi (27/11/08), which showed that, it is common among adolescents to have drinks in parties (16% boys, 11 % girls), smoking in school premises (33% girls 31 % boys) and trying out new drugs with friends (23% boys, 13% girls). This generation is very pro 'experimentation' such as rash driving and casual sex, especially under the effect of alcohol and other drugs, which in turn makes them quite vulnerable to social misconduct, accidents and sexually/ blood transmitted diseases.

3. **Poor sexual health:** The time tested institution of 'marriage', is being eroded by the western concept of sexual promiscuity, and the results are too obvious to be ignored; sexually transmitted diseases like HIV-AIDS are mostly being seen in the young adults; the .problem of teenage pregnancy (or teenage abortions) is becoming a menace for the parents says article in TOI (24/11/2007); incidences of date raping and other sexual offences are growing by the day; even after getting married, the incidences of divorce are rising very sharply among this generation, one of the reasons being extra marital affairs; Girls pop the morning after pill casually, rather than as an emergency measure; The boyfriends are happy to be carefree and few even bother to find out whether there could be repercussions on the girl's health. All this plays havoc with the emotional health of these young boys and girls which is bound to reflect in their work and conduct at their workplaces.
4. **Poor social support**: The previous generation (generation x) had the luxury of having immense emotional support, not only, from a working father and a home maker mother, but also from '*dada, dadi, 'mama', 'mami', 'fufa', 'mausi, etc.* The earlier generation didn't 'hang out' a lot with friends, but in the times of crisis (physical, mental, financial), had a lot of near and dear ones for help and support. On the other hand, though generation y may have 500-1000 face book friends, there may not even be a single person, who may extend a genuine help when needed.
5. **Poor emotional intelligence**: Due to less interaction with relatives and 'real' friends and also because of the growing popularity of one child norm, this generation has had fewer opportunities to 'share and care' with their siblings and relatives. A lot of sound medical studies are coming out every year, showing a direct relationship between the health status of an individual and the quality of human relations which he/she enjoys with others. The poor emotional intelligence is also reflected in the growing incidences of road rage, violent incidences in school and colleges and out bursts of anger, through violence, in the families.
6. **Unhealthy lifestyle practices**: Because of the vigorous advertising by the multinational food companies and the overall influence of the western media, generation y seems to be going the wrong way, as far as their food preferences are concerned. Fast food has spread like wild fire in this generation, resulting in poor nutrition. The propensity to cut sleep duration for the sake of net surfing, connecting with the virtual friends, checking e mails ever so often, have all resulted in further deterioration of the health scenario. The long sitting hours in front of computer and television has added fuel to the fire. The combined effect of the faulty life style practices is very obvious i.e. early onset coronary heart diseases, diabetes, back pain, high prevalence of hypertension and many more life style diseases.

According to a survey published in TOI (05/11/ 2009), "The 'burger pizza' culture and a sedentary working day is beginning to tell with health issues in corporate Banglore reaching an alarming level. The cost of neglecting health is very high both for the corporate world and for citizens individually. World over, it has been proven that poor health of employees has an adverse impact on corporate productivity".

7. **High level of stress**: This generation seems to be wanting 'too much too fast'. This attitude can push them into gloom of anxiety and lead to growth of suicidal tendencies says an article from TOI (23/04/09), titled, *'Race to Nowhere'*. Those who are working in IT companies, have to meet deadlines on a regular basis, this coupled with unusually high expectations from oneself leads to 'chronic sympathetic hyper stimulation', resulting in all the known hazards of chronic stress, i.e. depression leading at times to suicide, insomnia, poor social behavior leading to relationship problems and higher rates of non communicable diseases like coronary heart disease, diabetes, hypertension etc. A glaring example is the TOI article (01/07/2008) about 'Shinjini' a 16 year old girl who was forced to enter dance competitions in television reality shows by her parents. After losing the competition she slipped into depression, lost her speech and finally went into paralysis. Even many investigations later, no one could find out what was wrong with her medically.
8. **Poor role models:** Perhaps there has been no such time in past 100 years in history of India that the young generation had to bear with such glaring examples of dishonesty and corruption in the public life. They have very few people to chose, amongst the celebrity whom they can take as their role models. This could be the reason for their looking westward for the role models. The unprecedented acceptance for corruption or dishonesty visible in their families and the current society has made them feel that it is 'cool' to be dishonest, which is a worrying sign for the future of our society and the country.

Innovative Solutions for Generation Y

1. **Make them health conscious:** To get the best out of the generation y, most important first step is to make them health conscious and create a healthy environment at the workplace. A lot of productivity is lost due to 'sickness absenteeism'. A latest report from UK shows that young workers are 40% more likely to call in sick due to stress than older employees. Almost 7 in 10 workers between the ages of 18 to 24 have called in sick due to stress in last year (TOI, 07/11/ 12).

   In order to maintain highest level of physical and mental health following areas (habitual physical exercise, diet and stress management) need to be managed in the organization:

   - Sedentariness is a serious threat to health (1, 2, 3) and sitting for long hours (>4 hours) in chair can be a serious health hazard. According to an article published in TOI (23/01/10) titled *'Get up, sitting for long can kill you'* people who spend most of their days sitting are likely to be fat, have a heart attack or even die. Another one entitled *'Sit less, add 2 years to life'* (TOI, 11.07/12), say the same thing in relation to sitting and watching television. Even incidental physical activity can be helpful. Create the culture of physical movement in your work place for yourself and for the employees by encouraging following changes:
     - Walk little steps in your office while talking on phone.

- Don't send e mail to your office colleague for every little thing rather walk up to his/her cabin to discuss.
- Have walking meetings in which everyone is taking little steps in the meeting hall while talking or listening.
- Use staircase instead of elevator; if your office in on the 20th floor get down the lift at 18th and walk up two floors.

Medical science has proved that physical activity also boosts the mood, prevents depression by secreting endorphins and other neurotransmitters, so, walk and talk!

- Junk food can be damaging to the cardiovascular system and overall health (4). Sound studies done in reputed institutions have proved that junk food or fast food is not only hazardous for health of the individual, but also has addicting potential. Let us look at some of the titles which have been published in TOI, Delhi in last 5 years- *'Processed food may lead to lung cancer' (01/01/09), 'Junk food linked to cancer in women' (22/03/07), 'Chips, colas junk I.Q in children' (09/12/09), 'Junk food can hook bingers like heroine' (30/10/09).* A ground breaking study by Dr. T. Colin Campbell, popularly known as *'The China Study'* (there is a book by the same name) has proved that wholesome plant based diet is best for human race in order to prevent cancers, heart attack, obesity, hypertension, diabetes etc. (5,6). Encourage and practice following practices in your organization:
  - Let your canteen/food joints serve healthy snacks like fruit salad, fruits, sprouts, lassi, nimbu shikanjee, green tea etc.
  - Bring fruit salad, poha, upma and the likes in your tiffin.
  - In board meeting serve healthy snacks as mentioned above.
  - All these practices will keep yourself and your young employees fit and healthy which will reflect in increased productivity. Who would like to loose the best brains because of ill health and premature death. Moreover as food is intimately related to health, healthy food will also ensure healthy mind. So, be a sport and start healthy food at your home and office from tomorrow!
- Excessive stress is emerging as a major reason for high sickness rates among young employees. It has been proved scientifically that people can only remain physically healthy when their mind is not unduly stressed. This concept is popularly known as 'Mind Body Medicine'. (7,8, 9,10). Not only health but productivity of an individual is also hampered by excessive stress. Research in behavioral science has shown that up to a moderate level stress may increase the output of persons, but beyond that level stress becomes 'distress' and leads to lower performance by individuals. Try the following measures in your organization to boost the Mind/Body health and harmony:
  - Start the work in your office with 5 deep and slow breaths with awareness.

- Every employee should be given a short training in yoga and pranayama. There are hundreds of well done studies published in leading medical journals proving the role of yoga and pranayama in boosting the mind body health and healing. (10,11,12,13)
- Practice daily meditation at home- mindfulness meditation is one of the best where in one observes his breathing mentally and slowly starts observing his thoughts in a non judgmental manner. With practice one starts witnessing his thoughts which has enormous benefits for the mind/body relaxation. Dr Herbert Benson, the world famous cardiologist has done wonderful work in this field. Some of his best sellers are '*Relaxation Response*', '*Beyond Relaxation Response*' and '*Timeless Healing*'. Their books are written in simple language and should be read by the managers and CEOs, to learn them and their benefits. If possible develop a yoga/meditation hall in your work place where employees can go for short periods during lunch hours or other times.

2. **Develop their Emotional Quotient:** As mentioned earlier, though generation y seems to be more intelligent and faster than previous generations, they lack in emotional intelligence, a term popularized by 'Daniel Goleman' through his international best seller '*Emotional Intelligence*'. In this book he has given scientific evidence (including medical facts) to prove the point that to be successful in life, one needs to develop the ability to observe and manage ones strong emotions and also of others around him. He also says that without E.Q even high I.Q may not ensure success in life. The most important aspect of E.Q is self awareness. All great leaders world over are emotionally intelligent. In order to nurture the E.Q in you and your employees, we suggest following measures:
   - Practice regular meditation
   - Practice regular Yoga and Pranayama
   - Keep daily diary where you write your daily experiences
   - Try to encourage laughter in high pressured meetings
   - Don't discuss any topic with anyone when you or the other one is emotionally charged up. Wait till you and/or other has calmed down and then go ahead with the topic
   - Respect and support your employee when his family is in any crisis. Free him from his office duties and give your moral support to him (and financial, if needed).
   - If possible have a session of group meditation, once or twice in a week.
3. **Develop their Spiritual Intelligence (S.I):** 'Danah Zohar' and 'Ian Marshall', in their famous book '*Spiritual Intelligence- The ultimate intelligence*' have nicely explained the importance of S.I in modern times. According to authors, many young and highly successful persons whom they have met while globetrotting to give lectures are suffering from 'spiritual crisis'. To quote from the same book "We lack an overall context for our lives, a natural flow of meaning of which we can simply be a part. In many ways this spiritual desert has come about as a product of our high human I.Q. We have reasoned ourselves away from

nature and our fellow creatures, and we have reasoned ourselves beyond religion. In our great technological leap forward, we have left traditional culture with the embedded values behind. Our IQ has diminished labor, increased wealth and longevity and invented countless trinkets, some of which threaten to destroy both us and our environment. But we haven't found a way to make it all worthwhile." They further say that "Modern culture is spiritually dumb, not only in the west but also, increasingly, in those Asian countries influenced by the west". By spirituality, the authors mean "The spiritual means to be in touch with some larger, deeper, richer whole that puts our present limited situation into a new perspective. It is to have a sense of 'something beyond', of 'something more' that confers added meaning and value on where we are now". Similar thoughts are expressed by the world famous and best selling author of Man's search for meaning Viktor Frankel-"Man's search for meaning is the primary motivation in his life and not a 'secondary rationalization' of instinctual drives. This meaning is unique and specific in that it must and can achieve a significance which will satisfy his own will to meaning." Those who doubt about the existence of anything spiritual should read the well known books on spiritual health by Dr Larry Dossey, M.D (*Meaning and medicine, Healing Words)* and books on near death experience by Dr Raymond Mody, M.D *(Life After Life)* or scientific work done on reincarnation by Dr Ian Stevenson who was professor of psychiatry in leading American University has written a ground breaking book on the subject- *'Where Reincarnation and Biology Intersect'*- This book provides solid scientific evidence in favor of re incarnation. Even modern physics is strongly hinting at something spiritual about subatomic particles. Moreover there is enough research to prove that physical and mental health is intimately related to spiritual health. (14,15,16). Having developed some conviction about the importance of spiritual intelligence and its role in nurturing physical, mental and emotional health. We can take following steps in that direction:

- Organise workshops on S.I by inviting experts (not essentially the jet set gurus)
- Develop a multipurpose hall at the workplace (as suggested earlier) where people can meditate or pray or read spiritual books from different faiths at lunch breaks or other times of need.
- Expose them, during induction training, to the concepts of 'Self Actualization' as given by Abraham Maslow the well known American psychologist who gave the famous 'Need Hierarchy theory'.
- How a high S.I in your organization can boost productivity can be understood by the example of E.Shreedharan , the 'Metro Man' of India (CEO of Delhi metros). He used to give a copy of 'Bhagwat Gita' at the time of recruitment to all his employees calling Gita a book of management. Shreedharan got out the best from his team members. Another example is A.P.J Abdul Kalam, one of the best examples of a person who has achieved unimaginable heights by balancing I.Q, E.Q and S.Q.

Let us conclude by stating the fact that as we can not separate the person working with us from the 'person' within. Until and unless we take care of the totality of existence of an individual ,i.e. his physical, mental and spiritual well being we can not expect the best from him/her however intelligent he/she may be therefore the key to get the best from generation y is to give an enabling environment where they can balance the I.Q (Intelligence Quotient), E.Q(Emotional Quotient), S.Q(Spiritual Quotient) by following some of the suggestions given in this article.

REFERENCES

[1. Frank B. Hu, MD; Michael F. Leitzmann, MD; Meir J. Stampfer, MD. Physical activity and television watching in relation to risk for type 2 diabetes mellitus in men. Arch inter med 2001;161;1542-1548

[2] Genevieve N. Healy, MPH; David W. Dunstan, PhD; Jo Salmon, PhD. Breaks in sedentary time. Diabtes care, volume 4, april 2008

[3] Claudia Walther, MD, Lauise Gaede, BS; Volker Adams, PhD. Effects of increased exercise in school children on physical fitness and endothelial progenitor cells. Circulation, 2009;120:2251-2259

[4] Jean-Francois Mauger; Alice H Lichtenstein; Lynne M Ausman. Effect of different forms of dietary hydrogenated fats on LDL particle size. American journal of clinical nutrition 2003;78:3705

[5] Gary E Fraser. Associations between diet and cancer, ischemic heart diseases, and all-cause mortality in non-Hispanic White California Seventh-day Adventists. American Journal Of Clinical Nutrition 1999;70(suppl):532S-8S

[6] Position of the American Dietetic Association Vegetarian Diets. Journal of American dietetic association 2009; pg 1260-1276; july, no. 7.

[7] Redford B. Williams, Jr., MD; Thomas L. Haney, MA; Kerry L. Lee, PhD. Type a behavior, hostility, and coronary atherosclerosis. Psychosomatic medicine vol. 42, no. 6

[8] Suzanne G. Haynes; Manning Feinleib; William B. Kannel. The relationship of psychological factors to coronary heart diseases in the frammingham study. American journal of epidemiology 111:37-58, 1980

[9] Johan Denollet, personality and risk of cancer in men with coronary heart disease. Psychological medicine, 1998, 28, 1991-995

[10] Chandra Patel, W.R.S North. Randomized controlled trial of yoga and bio-feedback in management of hypertension. The lancet, july 19, 1975.

[11] Sarang, P. and Telles, S. (2006). Changes in heart rate variability during and after two yoga based relaxation techniques. International journal of stress management, 13(4): 460-475.

[12] Telles, S., Nagarathna, R. and Nagendra, H.R. (1994). Breathing through a particular nostril can alter metabolism and autonomic activities. Indain journal of physiology and pharmacology, 38(2): 133-137

[13] Raghraj, P. and Telles, S. (2003). A randomized trial comparing the effects of yoga and physical activity programs on depth perception in school children. Journal of Indian psychology, 21 (2): 54-60.

[14] Roberto De Vogli; Jane E Ferrie; Tarani Chandola. Unfairness and health: evidence from the whitehall 2 study. Journal of epidemiological community health 2007;61:513-518

[15] KK Aggarwal. Spiritual well being: The evidence and the need to have it as a part of our practice. Indian journal of clinical practice, vol 14, no.3

[16] Jeemy D. Kark, PhD; Galia Shemi, MPH; Yechiel Friedlander, PhD; Oz Martin, MD, Orly Manor, PhD. Does religious observance promote health? Mortality in secular vs religious Kibbutzim in Israel. American journal of public health 1996, vol.86, no.3

[17] Luciano Bernardi; Peter Sleight; Gabriele Bandinelli. Effects of rosary prayer and yoga mantras on autonomic cardiovascular rhythms: comparative study. BMJ 2001:323;1446-1449

A Study of Level of Morale & Trust of Gen Y Managers in BPOs in Delhi-NCR

Puja Khatri and Khushboo

University School of Management Studies, GGS Indraprastha University, Dwarka, Delhi

ABSTRACT

India enjoys certain benefits being the favorite destination for outsourcing as it produces bulk of young, educated and English speaking graduates every year. This young talent is increasingly occupying the managerial positions. Gen Y managers are ambitious, achievement oriented, impatient, team workers, money-oriented and look for continuous growth. They work according to their values and create value for organization if understood correctly. It is not easy to motivate them as they have transformed the definitions of elements of morale and trust. Traditional methods are not useful to motivate them. The present study seeks to understand the perception of employees pertaining to the level of morale & trust with respect to variables like, job security, work-life balance, concern from top management, performance review system etc.. The study was conducted in Delhi NCR region wherein the respondents were selected through multistage sampling (N=100).Data was collected through self-constructed questionnaire (cronbach alpha =0.83).

Contrasting results were also seen between male and female respondents regarding perceptions of different facets of morale and trust. The paper seeks to provide an insight to top management and corporate practitioners of BPOs, who can use advanced techniques to upkeep the level of morale & trust of Gen Y managers.

Keywords: *Gen Y, BPO, Morale, Trust*

INTRODUCTION

Organizations, in recent times are increasingly adopting Business Process Outsourcing. As organizations operate in highly dynamic business environment characterized by fierce competition, emerging technologies and rapid product development, they tend to focus on their core function to maintain the competency and outsource non-core functions (Kim and Won, 2007). In India, BPO industry has grown in the last decade. India enjoys being the favorite offshore destination because of people (manpower) and location. Over 2million students graduate every year in India who are computer literate and can speak English. They are willing to work at nearly 80% less salary than their western counterparts (Raman, Budhwar & Balasubramanian,

2007). The majority workforce of Indian BPOs belongs to generation Y. Generation Y refers to those people who are ambitious, self-centered, demanding, confident and have the ability to change the world (Macleod, 2008). They have grown up in dynamic technical world, are information obsessed and look out for genuine relationships. Generation Y managers' trust in their organization is maintained by respectful treatment, transformational leadership, rich organizational culture and opportunities to continuously learn and grow. The prime reason for joining the BPO sector by young people is the high growth opportunities (Chhabra, 2004). On the other hand, some studies reveal that low level of morale, trust and lack of growth opportunities act as the main reasons for attrition in BPOs (Tiga& Kumar 2003; Ramachandran, 2006; Watson, Ambegaoker and Mishra, 2005). BPO jobs are not considered as long term career option by young managers. The mind-numbing, monotonous tasks and night shifts without any promising career advancement offset the level of morale and trust of young managers in BPOs (Sengupta, Singh & Moses, 2007). Also, BPO doesn't provide any scope for skill up gradation and the work experience of BPOs is not considered to be relevant for other job profiles (Babu, 2004). Due to such reasons, Indian outsourcing industry experiences high level of attrition rate and low level of employee tenure as employees keep looking for better opportunities continuously (Holman, Batt & Holtgrewe, 2007). Another aspect of issues related to BPOs is the disparity between Gen Y male and female managers. Women in this sector are not treated equally with respect to growth opportunities, making initiatives, employer's trust about performing tough tasks, performance review system etc. This creates a difference in the level of morale and trust of female managers in such organizations as perception about the elements of morale & trust differs. This study aims to examine the factors which affect the level of morale and trust of Gen Y managers in BPOs and which lead to disparity between male and female managers.

LITERATURE REVIEW

Amongst all offshore destinations, India possesses the largest pool of talent. This talent base is of young, well-educated and English speaking people (Thite & Russell, 2010). This young talent or Generation Y managers are said to be the complex people who are creative, highly mobile and conscious about the dynamism of industry. They believe in making contacts which makes them the master networkers. Gen Y managers want to be the part of those organizations which have strong values and ethics, effective brands and non-hierarchical environment (Weyland, 2011).On the contrary, Indian BPOs have formal, structured and rationalized HRM systems (Budhwar, Varma, Singh &Dhar, 2006). Being the part of most dynamic industry, young managers sometimes pursue unrealistic goals beyond their capabilities which ultimately remain unfulfilled, this lowers their morale. Reduced level of morale leads to disengagement from job and finally attrition. Employee morale is the basic phenomenon of any business operation. Griffin, Rafferty & Mason (2004) state that the enhanced level of morale results in job satisfaction, incremental rise in efforts, creativity and initiative, a sense of accomplishment and pride, enhanced team spirit and organizational commitment, ultimately leading to enhanced organizational performance. Whereas, low morale coincides with high attrition/turnover, unresolved disputes and disengagement from organization, it reduces the overall performance of organization (Firth, Mellor, Moore & Loquet, 2004).According to Howitt (2002), morale has been considered to be the most crucial component in determining the employee's effort to accomplish a job and thus ascertaining the organization's performance. To upkeep the morale of employees managers need to understand its different indicators and determinants (Linz, Good & Huddleston, 2006). Employee morale can be enhanced by fair treatment at workplace, providing job security and implementing best policies and practices like, following participative form of leadership, strengthening communication channels and recognition of efforts (Sirota, Mischkind & Meltzer, 2005).When organizations upkeep its commitment with the employees like, fair distribution of workload and rewards, it boosts up their morale which enhances the likelihood that employees will behave in the desired manner .Perception about justice and fairness affects the emotional reactions and thus, shape the employee morale and ultimately the performance (Jackson, Rossi, Hoover & Johnson, 2012). Hopkins (1995) opines that there are five ways to enhance the morale level of employees: Social Gatherings, Employee recognition, Employee meetings, Continuing education and Empowerment. Such practices enrich the organizational culture and build trust between the employees and organization. Employees' trust is related to profits, innovation, successful international business and crucial employee behavior and perception (IABC, 2000). According to Mayer, Davis and Schoorman (1995), Organizational Trust is the readiness of one individual to be assailable to the actions of other individual on the basis of assurance that the other will act in favor of the trustier irrespective of the authority of other individual to control the first one. Hoy and Tschannen-Moran (2003) defined organizational trust as an individual's or group's readiness to be vulnerable to other party based on the confidence that the latter party is benevolent, reliable, honest, competent and open. There are three dimensions of organizational trust Openness, Shared values and Autonomy (Kerry, Randall, Joseph & Larry, 1986).The base elements of trustworthiness are: competence, integrity, consistency, benevolence and openness/transparency (Gabarro, 1978). Barber (1983, p. 165) was the first one to put forth this suggestion that two attributes needed to be clearly differentiated with respect to trust in the trustee: whether the person is technically competent and whether he/she is morally responsible. Therefore, the failure to identify one's core competency, aggressive and over-demanding environment, unethical culture and biased policies create an atmosphere of distrust in the organization. Also, resistance to change, poor work-life balance, non-fulfillment of commitments and inefficient mentoring reduces the level of and trust in the organization amongst young leaders (The Economic Times, 2012). The above propositions establish the facts that employee morale and organizational trust are inter-related concepts. There is no doubt that demographics in BPOs have undergone various changes which further determine the level of morale & trust of employees in such organizations. Now, female constitute approximately 30-35% of the total workforce of this sector (Jain, 2011). Women are preferred particularly for call centers as they have pleasant voice, calmer, loyal, more trustworthy and have better interpersonal skills than men (Pradhan and Abraham, 2005). Despite this significant increase women encounter more inhibition for career growth prospects in comparison to their male counterparts. BPO culture compels employees to work round the clock; this worsens the situation for women as they have to fulfill their responsibilities at professional as well as household front (Hyman & Summers, 2004). They are not able to manage their work and life. Female managers are meant to handle administrative tasks only and not given challenging work which inhibits their innovation resulting in difference in their remuneration and advancement in job. Women do not feel secure working in shifts specially, night shifts which further reduces their chances to be promoted as compared to their male counterparts (Pathak & Sarin, 2011). These all factors reduce the morale and trust level of female managers while working in this specific sector which further enhances the attrition rate among the women employees (Gupta, 2012).

When leaders appreciate their teams, treat them as valuable assets of the organization and takes care of their work-life balance, it builds a sense of trust and confidence amongst the employees which enhances the morale level of employees incredibly and thus generates a highly engaged workforce. Not giving enough prospects to grow as a professional is unethical on the part of leaders and it further leads to employee disengagement. Proper and timely communication, positive and constructive feedback techniques can be stated as prime components of morale and trust. An organization like BPO which is characterized by unusual working hours, target oriented jobs, repetitive nature of tasks, pressure from bosses and insufficient time for family develops an urgency to have satisfied and motivated employees which can become the revenue generator for the company (Sengupta, Gupta & Sandhir, 2010).Various surveys have revealed that young employees complain of receiving immediate response for their poor performance but recognition and appreciation for good work is not there. Appreciation and authority of taking important decisions make the employees feel an important part of the organization which builds their trust in their organization and enhances morale. Also, teams constitute the major building blocks of the organizations and transformational leaders can retrieve incredible results out of them which again encourage trust and morale level in employees which further reduces the turnover rate.

OBJECTIVES

- To identify problems experienced by Gen Y BPO managers at workplace.
- To study the level of morale amongst these workers.
- To study the level of trust vested in the organization by Gen Y managers working at BPO.
- To study the difference in level of morale & trust of male and female Gen Y managers.
- To study the factors creating disparity between male & female Gen Y managers.

It has been observed that female executives don't feel comfortable in discussing issues with the supervisors as supervisors' behavior changes towards different genders for various work situations which further enhances the inequality. Sometimes, women complain about their team to be highly manly, antipathetic, combative and self-promoting. It resists women to be a part of any decision making process. Female executives face many constraints because of dual responsibility of office and home, issue of security due to night shifts and unequal treatment at workplace as compared to male executives, giving rise to work-life imbalance. This hampers their morale and trust level with the organization.

HYPOTHESES

H1: There exists a difference in perception of male and female Gen Y BPO managers as regards their level of morale in the organization.

H2: There exists a difference in perception of male and female Gen Y BPO managers as regards their level of morale in the organization.

RESEARCH METHODOLOGY

This research initiative studies the perception of working executives in the Delhi-NCR region regarding their levels of morale & trust in their respective organization. It also tries to probe into gender differences in terms of perception of respondents pertaining to plethora of variables leading to disparity between them in corporate organizations. The research has been carried out with a self-constructed questionnaire. The questionnaire had several items related to the perception of respondents regarding clarity about job expectations, job security, safety of work environment, fairness of review system, support and appreciation extended to employees in corporate organizations. The questionnaire had two parts, part a was purely focused on collecting demographic details and part b mapped the perception of respondents as regards different variables related to morale & trust level of employees like satisfaction with the team-spirit & remuneration, fairness of workload allocation, work-life balance, upkeep of commitment by top management etc. The questionnaire was constructed on a five point likert agreement scale to measure the responses on the decided variables. The questionnaire was subjected to review by experts and their inputs have been incorporated accordingly. Reliability of the same was computed to be Cronbach Alpha .83. According to Nunnally (1978, p. 245) the instruments used in basic research have reliability of about .70 or better.

The sampling was multistage. In the first place it was purposive wherein the researchers drew out a list of 84 IT related BPO organizations in the NCR. The list was generated through the web link *(http://www.fundoodata.com/advance_search_results.php?&new_industry_id[]=18&level_id=1&sector_id[]=1&city_id= 0&criteria=1&search_type=1. Eight companies were shortlisted from the list such that one company each was selected from the east, west, north, south, central, outer Delhi, Gurgaon and Noida region .Questionnaires were administered to about 15 managerial level employees from each of these companies . About 100 completed questionnaires (out of 120) were taken for the study.* The data was subjected to inferential and descriptive analysis.

DATA ANALYSIS

The analysis of Table 1.1 reveals that majority of the respondents have clarity in terms of job expectations (m=4.03, s.d.=0.76) as Gen Y is information obsessed, achievement oriented and aware about the trends of the industry, they have clear aims and goals to achieve. Because young managers possess high sense of self-efficacy and self-belief, many respondents believe that they have been given enough responsibilities in their jobs (m=3.94, s.d.=0.89) however, the perception about the allocation of workload is very low (m=3.34, s.d.=0.99) which results in less satisfaction with the employee review system (m=3.12, s.d.=0.91). Such unjustified practices reduce the morale of employees. Table 1.2 depicts that many respondents have a high level of perception about the job security (m=3.88, s.d.=0.84) and they are quite optimistic about the future of their organization (m=3.82, s.d.=0.74) as BPO industry is at boom and India being the favorite offshore outsourcing destination enjoys certain benefits. However, the perception about the low attrition rate (m=3.4, s.d.=0.91) and satisfaction about the remuneration received for the given contribution (m=3.10, s.d.=0.97) is low. This happens because in BPO sector the salary growth plan for each employee is not well defined and overall compensation structure is not competitive as compared to general market practices. This encourages poaching by other companies. Also, young population keeps striving for better opportunities which results in turnover. Some of the respondents feel that they are able to strike a balance between the family and work(m=3.65, s.d.=0.96) as Gen Y gives importance to socializing practices and takes out time to pursue their hobbies. Table 1.3 was further analyzed to explain that many respondents feel supported, valued and appreciated by their peers (m=3.84, s.d.=0.84) which is one of the main elements of motivation for young managers. However, they are not satisfied with the professionalism and team spirit (m=3.48, s.d.=0.93) as each employee is concerned about their own benefits which reduces their morale level as Gen Y's need for inclusion is very high. They like to perform in teams and get appreciated by members. Few respondents feel that there is enough orientation given to new employees (m=3.51, s.d.=1.01)and their efforts are appreciated and recognized by their superiors (m=3.47, s.d.=0.92).This lowers the level of morale of young managers as Gen Y focusses on continuous learning and looks for immediate feedback from their superiors.

Table 1.4 tells the perception of respondents about the level of trust of young managers. Majority of the respondents believe that they can inform their immediate superior when something is going wrong (m=4.05, s.d.=0.89), they are listened by their superiors (m=3.95, s.d.=0.89) and are free to disagree with their immediate superiors on any issue (m=3.91, s.d.=0.86).This builds up the trust level of young managers as they are full of ideas & opinions and feel confident when listened by their immediate superiors. Though their superiors take care of their professional needs very well the perception about the concern for personal well-being is low (m=3.56, s.d.=0.89). Some of the respondents are of the perception that top management listens to their concern (m=3.69, s.d.=0.75) and upkeep their commitments (m=3.63, s.d.=0.96) but very few believe that the top management is concerned about their well-being (m=3.48, s.d.=0.93). This reveals that the superiors and top management show concern to young managers on the professional front only. This attitude lowers the trust level of such employees as Gen Y managers look for genuine relationships and want to be cared at professional as well as personal front.

For the purpose of testing hypothesis H1 that there exists a difference between male and female respondents as regards their level of morale in their organization caused due to the various individual variables, Levene's t-test for equality of variances (Table 1.5) has been applied. It was found that there exists a difference between perception about morale of male and female about prospects of remuneration in their organization (t=2.054, p<0.05) and perception towards fairness of employee review system (t=2.066, p<0.05). Table 1.6 depicts that male executives have higher level of agreement of satisfaction about remuneration (m=3.22, s.d.=0.85) & fairness of review system (m=3.23, s.d.=0.79). This happens because female executives don't get much challenging tasks to perform owing to certain gender limitations and employers thus prefer male executives giving them better prospects of professional growth thus enhancing difference in remuneration. However, there is no difference in the perception of male and female towards safety of work environment (t=0.270, p<0.05), equal treatment at workplace (t=0.631, p<0.05), work-life balance (t=-0.574, p<0.05), trust in leadership (t=0.745,p<0.05) and supportiveness by peers (t=0.182, p<0.05). This happens because now organizations take care of the needs of female executives specially security and better prospects of advancement. Top management shows concern towards their work-life balance by providing flexible shifts or work from home options. Hence, hypothesis 1 is partially accepted and partially rejected since there exists difference between male and female respondents as regards their perception of morale due to different variables viz. remuneration & fairness of employee review system and there exists no difference on other variables.

Table 1.7 explains the difference in perception of male and female managers as regards their level of trust in their organization with respect to different variables. The analysis of the table reveals that there exists difference towards discussing with supervisors when something goes wrong (t=1.960, p<0.05) and the concern of top management towards employees (t=2.273, p<0.05). It has been observed from Table 1.8 that male Gen Y managers have higher level of perception regarding comfort with supervisors (m=4.05, s.d.=0.78) and concern received from top management (m=4.15, s.d.=0.61). The reason for this difference is that women don't feel comfortable in discussing issues with supervisors openly. They are preferred to perform administrative tasks owing to mobility constraints which reduce the professional concern of top management towards them. However, there exists no difference in the perception of male and female respondents about information regarding the performance evaluation (t=0.340, p<0.05), similarity of values with peers (t=0.302, p<0.05) and concern of immediate supervisor about well-being (t=.048, p<0.05). Supervisors being the part of Gen Y workforce understand the need of hour especially in case of female executives. They try to perform their responsibilities in order to them comfortable at workplace. Therefore, Hypothesis 2 is also partially accepted and partially rejected.

CONCLUSION AND IMPLICATIONS

Gen Y is increasingly occupying positions of responsibility especially in the high growth and knowledge driven organizations globally (Mohapatra and Akhouri, 2011). Young professionals are entering the workforce in BPOs in huge numbers so; it has become crucial to understand their characteristics and expectations from workplace. There needs to be a match between the generation Y employee and employer in order to have a sound and long term relationship. Organizations must try to gain an insight into the behavioral dynamics of Gen Y and its implications for the leaders of tomorrow. There is an urgent need to look into the areas which can build up the morale and trust level of Generation Y managers. The analysis of the data tells that young managers working in BPOs are not satisfied with the leadership shown by the immediate superiors as well as top management. Professional care is not enough for Gen Y to keep them motivated. They are of the opinion that there is much to life than just work. Top management and superiors need to improve their personal working relationships in order to meet their individual needs. Top management must live up to their commitments in order to build trust amongst young managers. Gen Y demands support, recognition and praise from their bosses. Gen Y is highly ambitious, impatient and restless; they need immediate feedback for their work. So, there is a need to keep such systems in place. They don't appreciate unethical or unjustified practices. Unfair allocation of workload, uncompetitive salary structure and unfair review system lessens their morale level leading to disengagement from organization. The jobs situations are needed to be redesigned to motivate Gen Y. Traditional methods are not relevant for them. Advanced technologies like e-learning programs, simulation exercises, motivational training etc. must be used to train them. Women managers need special attention in this sector. Superiors and top management must give them a platform to prove their worth. Challenging work, support system of bright and creative people, team membership, autonomy at workplace, continuous learning and concern for their personal needs can transform the face of working practices for females at BPOs. Family support is also required to enhance the mobility of women managers. Organizations take due care regarding the security of females working in BPOs. This must be accompanied with some autonomy at workplace as well. Also, continuing education courses to keep Gen Y managers updated about the advancements of industry, career development skills training, opportunities for growth and promotion, mentoring and leadership development programs are other avenues which must be considered by the management (Monis & Sreedhara, 2011).

LIMITATION OF THE STUDY AND AVENUES FOR FUTURE RESEARCH

There are certain limitations to this study. It was conducted on the sample of 100 respondents from the BPO organizations in Delhi-NCR. The results so obtained cannot be generalized for whole BPO sector. Time constraint to conduct this study posed another limitation.

BPO culture is characterized by monotonous tasks, rotational shifts, unfair distribution of rewards, stiff competition, stressful jobs and different working practices for male & female managers. The young managers who are part of this industry are ambitious and look out for better opportunities always. The traits of this generation can be studied in some other sector or on a larger scale in the same sector. The spiritual quotient, empowerment and leadership potential of this generation can be studied in link to other parameters.

REFERENCES

[1] Babu, Ramesh P. (2004).Cyber coolies in BPO - insecurities and vulnerabilities of non-standardwork.*Economic and Political Weekly, Vol. 39*, No.05, pp. 492-497.2. Barber, B. (1983). The logic and limits of trust. Rutgers University Press. New Brunswick, NJ.

[3] Budhwar P, Varma A, Singh V and Dhar R (2006b) HRM systems of Indian centres: An exploratory study. *International Journal of Human Resource Management 17*(5):881–897.

[4] Chhabra, Mohit. (2004), "DQ-IDC India survey: BPO E-sat 2004", Retrieved from http://www.dqindia.com/content/top_stories/2004/104110801.5. Firth, L., Mellor, D.J., Moore, K.A. and Loquet, C. (2004). How can managers reduce employee intention to quit?*Journal of Managerial Psychology, Vol. 10* No. 2, pp. 170-87.

[6] Gabarro, J.J. (1978).The development of trust, influence, and expectations in Athos, G. and Gabarro, J.J. (Eds), Interpersonal Behavior: Communication and Understanding in Relationships, Prentice-Hall, Englewood Cliffs, NJ, pp. 290-303.7. Griffin, M.A., Rafferty, A.E. and Mason, C.M. (2004).Who started this? Investigating different sources of organizational change.*Journal of Business and Psychology, Vol. 18* No. 4, pp. 555-70. 8. Gupta, Amrita (2012). Health, Social and Psychological Problems of Women Employees in Business Process Outsourcing: A Study in India. Retrieved from http://paa2012.princeton.edu/papers/121676.9. Hart, Kerry M., Capps, H. Randall, Cangemi, Joseph P., Caillouet, Larry M. (1986). Exploring organizational trust and its multiple dimensions: A case study of General Motors. *Organization Development Journal, Vol 4*(2), pp. 31-39.

[10] Holman D, Batt R and Holtgrewe U (2007). The Global Call Centre Report: International Perspectives on Management and Employment. Report of the Global Call Centre Network (US format). http://www.ilr.cornell.edu/globalcallcenter/upload/GCC-Intl-Rept-US-Version.pdf.

[11] Hopkins, Hampton (1995). A challenge to managers: Five ways to improve employee morale. Executive Development, Vol. 8, Iss.7,pp. 26-28.

[12] Howitt, P. (2002). Looking inside the labor market: a review article. *Journal of Economic Literature, Vol. XL*, March, pp. 125-38.

[13] Hoy, W.K. and M. Tschannen-Moran, (2003). The Conceptualization and Measurement of Faculty Trust in Schools: The Omnibus T-Scale. In: Studies in Leading and Organizing Schools, Hoy, W.K. and C.G. Miskel (Eds.). Information Age Publishing, Greenwich, pp: 181-208.

[14] http://www.ilr.cornell.edu/globalcallcenter/upload/GCC-Intl-Rept-US-Version.pdf.

[15] Hyman, J., and Summers, J. (2004). Lacking balance. Personal Review 33(4): 418–429.

[16] International Association of Business communicators (2000). Measuring Organizational Trust.

[17] Jackson, Erin M., Rossi, Michael E., Hoover, E. Rickamer, Johnson, Russell E. (2012). Relationships of leader reward behavior with employee behavior:Fairness& Morale as key mediators.*Leadership and Organization Development Journal, Vol 33*, Iss. 7, pp.646-661.

[18] Jain, Arjita (2011). Innovative strategies of employee retention. New Delhi: Excel Books.

[19] Kim, Gyeung-Min & Won, Hyun Jung (2007). HR BPO service models for small and medium enterprises.*Business Process Management Journal, Vol. 13*Iss: 5 pp. 694 – 706.

[20] Linz, Susan J., Good, Linda K.&Huddleston, Patricia (2006). Worker Morale in Russia:an exploratory study. *Journal of Managerial psychology, Vol 2,*Iss: 5, pp. 415-437.

[21] Macleod, Dr.Alison (2008). Generation Y: Unlocking the talent of young managers. Executive Summary. Chartered Management Institute. June 2008.

[22] Mohapatra, Mamta&Akhouri, NarendraNath (2011). Young leaders success code. New Delhi: Excel Books.

[23] Monis, Sri. Herald &Sreedhara, Dr. T. N. (2011). Employee Satisfaction with career development practices. *Journal of Arts, Science and Commerce, Vol II*, Iss. 1, pp. 110-122.

[24] Pathak, Sonal & Sarin, Dr. Anil (2011). Management of Stress Among Women Employees in BPO Industry in India : A Contemporary Issue. *International Journal of Management & Business studies, Vol. 1,* Issue 3, September 2011.

[25] Pradhan,J.P. and Abraham, V. (2005). Social and Cultural Impact of Outsourcing: Emerging Issues from Indian Call Centres. *Harvard Asia Quarterly*, *9*(3):22-30.

[26] Ramachandran, Sunder. (2006), "BPO buzz- Creating the leaders of the future", Retrieved from www.bpo.tcp.in.

[27] Raman, S. Raghu ,Budhwar, Pawan&Balasubramanian, G. (2007). People management issues in Indian KPOs. *Employee Relations, Vol. 29*Iss: 6 pp. 696 – 710.

[28] Roger C. Mayer, James H. Davis and F. David Schoorman (1995).An integrative model of Organizational Trust. *The Academy of Management Review, Vol. 20*, No.3, pp. 709-734.

[29] Sen Gupta, Santoshi, Gupta, Aayushi&Sandhir, Vidushi (2010). Relationships among selected Demographic factors and Employee satisfaction level in Indian BPOs. *Tecnia Journal of Management Studies, Vol.5*, No.1, pp. 69-74.

[30] Sengupta, Snigdha, Singh, Shelley & Moses, Nelson Vinod. (2007).BPO industry report - World's Back Office Comes of Age.*Business World*, pp 75-76.

[31] Sirota , David, Mischkind, Louis A. and Meltzer, Michael Irwin (2005). The Enthusiastic Employee. *Business Book Review*, *Vol 23*, No. 31.

[32] The Economic Times (2012). The follies of Young Leaders. The Economic Times, 25 September.

[33] Thite, Mohan and Russell,Bob (2010). Work organization, human resource practices and employee retention in Indian call centers.*Asia Pacific Journal of Human Resources* 48: 356.

[34] Tiga, Pallavi& Kumar, Susheel K. (2006). HR challenges in the BPO industry – A case study in a captive BPO firm. Unpublished Summer project. IIMB, Bangalore.

[35] Watson Wyatt, Ambegaoker Shruti& Mishra, Prince Anuraag. (2005).People Challenges in the IT-ITES sector. HR Best practices Handbook. New Delhi: NASSCOM.

[36] Weyland, Anita (2011).Engagement and talent management of Gen Y. *Industrial and Commercial Training, Vol. 43*Iss: 7 pp. 439 – 445.

APPENDIX

Table 1.1: Perception of respondents regarding level of job expectations, sufficiency of responsibilities, fairness of work allocation & employee review system.

	N	*Minimum*	*Maximum*	*Mean*	*Std. Deviation*
Knowing what is expected in job.	100	1	5	4.03	0.75819
Given sufficient responsibility in my job.	100	2	5	3.94	0.88557
Workload is fairly allocated.	100	1	5	3.3939	0.98787
Fair employee review system.	100	1	5	3.12	0.9132

Table 1.2: Perception of Respondents Regarding Level of Job Security, Optimism About Future of Company, Work-Life Balance, Employee Turnover, Satisfaction with Remuneration.

	N	*Minimum*	*Maximum*	*Mean*	*Std. Deviation*
Job security.	100	1	5	3.88	0.84423
Optimism about the future of the company.	100	1	5	3.82	0.74373
Balance between family life and work life.	100	1	5	3.65	0.95743
Less employee turnover.	100	1	5	3.4	0.9101
Satisfaction with the pay level received for contribution.	100	1	5	3.1	0.96922

Table 1.3: Perception of respondents regarding support from peers, orientation, satisfaction with professionalism & recognition received from supervisors.

	N	*Minimum*	*Maximum*	*Mean*	*Std. Deviation*
Feel supported, valued, and appreciated.	100	1	5	3.84	0.8375
Orientation to new employees.	100	1	5	3.51	1.01
Satisfaction with the professionalism and team spirit.	100	1	5	3.48	0.92638
Recognition and appreciation by superiors.	100	1	5	3.47	0.91514

Table 1.4: Perception of respondents regarding level of trust in their organization.

	N	*Minimum*	*Maximum*	*Mean*	*Std. Deviation*
Free to tell the supervisor when things go wrong	100	1	5	4.05	0.89188
Immediate supervisor listens to issues	100	1	5	3.95	0.89188
Free to disagree with the immediate supervisor.	100	1	5	3.91	0.85818
Top management listens to employees' concerns.	100	2	5	3.69	0.74366
Upkeep of commitment by Top management.	100	1	5	3.63	0.9629
Concern of Immediate supervisor about personal well-being.	100	1	5	3.56	0.88871
Concerned of Top management about employees' well-being.	100	1	5	3.48	0.93203

Table 1.5: Difference in the level of morale of male and female working managers (t-test)Independent Samples Test

		Levene's Test for Equality of Variances		*t-test for Equality of Means*				
		F	*Sig.*	*t*	*df*	*Sig. (2-tailed)*	*Mean Difference*	*Std. Error Difference*
supported, valued & appreciated by peers	Equal variances assumed	0.738	0.392	0.182	98	0.856	0.0345	0.18957
	Equal variances not assumed			0.167	39.816	0.869	0.0345	0.20717
Safe working environment.	Equal variances assumed	0.012	0.913	0.27	98	0.788	0.06038	0.22391
	Equal variances not assumed			0.276	48.66	0.784	0.06038	0.21878
Knowing what is expected in job	Equal variances assumed	0.291	0.591	0.239	98	0.811	0.0411	0.1716
	Equal variances not assumed			0.235	44.884	0.815	0.0411	0.17484
Given sufficient responsibility	Equal variances assumed	0.217	0.643	0.096	98	0.924	0.01928	0.20048
	Equal variances not assumed			0.097	47.549	0.923	0.01928	0.19817
Equal treatment	Equal variances assumed	3.66	0.059	0.631	98	0.53	0.14561	0.23089
	Equal variances not assumed			0.547	36.727	0.588	0.14561	0.26641
Work-life balance	Equal variances assumed	0.065	0.799	-0.574	98	0.567	-0.1243	0.21639
	Equal variances not assumed			-0.552	43.167	0.584	-0.1243	0.2253
Satisfaction with remuneration	Equal variances assumed	3.972	0.049	2.054	98	0.043	0.4414	0.21485
	Equal variances not assumed			1.77	36.413	0.085	0.4414	0.24944
Fair employee review system	Equal variances assumed	4.638	0.034	2.066	98	0.041	0.41806	0.20238
	Equal variances not assumed			1.749	35.59	0.089	0.41806	0.23897
Satisfaction with the professionalism & team spirit	Equal variances assumed	1.38	0.243	1.209	98	0.23	0.25165	0.20818
	Equal variances not assumed			1.098	39.377	0.279	0.25165	0.22912
Employee turnover	Equal variances assumed	5.732	0.019	1.19	98	0.237	0.24353	0.20457
	Equal variances not assumed			1.01	35.664	0.319	0.24353	0.24118
Trust in leadership	Equal variances assumed	1.544	0.217	0.745	98	0.458	0.13902	0.18649
	Equal variances not assumed			0.688	40.35	0.496	0.13902	0.20211

Table 1.6: Group Statistics- Morale (Male & Female Gen Y managers)

	Gender	*N*	*Mean*	*Std. Deviation*	*Std. Error Mean*
Job security	1	73	3.9315	0.805	0.09422
	2	27	3.7407	0.94432	0.18173
Supported, valued & appreciated	1	73	3.8493	0.79357	0.09288
	2	27	3.8148	0.96225	0.18519
Knowing what is expected in job	1	73	4.0411	0.75348	0.08819
	2	27	4	0.78446	0.15097
Safe working environment	1	73	3.9863	1.00683	0.11784
	2	27	3.9259	0.9578	0.18433
Given sufficient responsibility	1	73	3.9452	0.89583	0.10485
	2	27	3.9259	0.8738	0.16816
Equal treatment	1	73	3.8493	0.92303	0.10803
	2	27	3.7037	1.26536	0.24352
Work-life balance	1	73	3.6164	0.93734	0.10971
	2	27	3.7407	1.02254	0.19679
Satisfaction with remuneration	1	73	3.2192	0.85386	0.09994
	2	27	2.7778	1.18754	0.22854
Fair employee review system	1	73	3.2329	0.79093	0.09257
	2	27	2.8148	1.14479	0.22031
Satisfaction with the professionalism & team spirit	1	73	3.5479	0.86668	0.10144
	2	27	3.2963	1.06752	0.20544
Employee turnover	1	73	3.4658	0.80073	0.09372
	2	27	3.2222	1.1547	0.22222
Trust in leadership	1	73	3.6575	0.78562	0.09195
	2	27	3.5185	0.93522	0.17998

Table 1.7: Difference in the level of trust of male and female working executives (t-test)

		Levene's Test for Equality of Variances		*t-test for Equality of Means*				
		F	*Sig.*	*t*	*df*	*Sig. (2-tailed)*	*Mean Difference*	*Std. Error Difference*
Free to tell the supervisor when things go wrong	Equal variances assumed	5.374	0.023	1.96	98	0.053	0.38813	0.19807
	Equal variances not assumed			1.672	35.937	0.103	0.38813	0.23219
Top management listens to employees' concerns.	Equal variances assumed	8.615	0.004	2.273	98	0.025	0.37291	0.16409
	Equal variances not assumed			1.857	33.999	0.072	0.37291	0.20085
Free to disagree with immediate superior	Equal variances assumed	3.803	0.054	1.101	98	0.274	0.21258	0.19309
	Equal variances not assumed			0.943	36.136	0.352	0.21258	0.22544
Information regarding performance evaluation	Equal variances assumed	0.531	0.468	0.34	98	0.735	0.0761	0.22396
	Equal variances not assumed			0.353	50.244	0.725	0.0761	0.21543
Upkeep of commitment by Top management.	Equal variances assumed	0.351	0.555	-0.109	98	0.913	-0.02385	0.21798
	Equal variances not assumed			-0.112	48.777	0.911	-0.02385	0.21273
Similarity of values with peers	Equal variances assumed	0.907	0.343	0.302	98	0.764	0.05682	0.18842
	Equal variances not assumed			0.28	40.815	0.781	0.05682	0.20277
Concern of Immediate supervisor about personal well-being.	Equal variances assumed	0.092	0.762	0.048	98	0.962	0.01015	0.211
	Equal variances not assumed			0.047	44.528	0.963	0.01015	0.21593
Superiors speak positive in front of others	Equal variances assumed	3.965	0.049	0.156	98	0.877	0.03196	0.20525
	Equal variances not assumed			0.139	38.525	0.89	0.03196	0.22915

Table 1.8: Group Statistics- Trust (Male & Female Gen Y managers)

	Gender	*N*	*Mean*	*Std. Deviation*	*Std. Error Mean*
Free to tell the supervisor when things go wrong	1	73	4.0548	0.77979	0.09127
	2	27	3.6667	1.1094	0.2135
Top management listens to employees' concerns.	1	73	4.1507	0.61624	0.07213
	2	27	3.7778	0.97402	0.18745
Free to disagree with immediate superior	1	73	4.0274	0.76326	0.08933
	2	27	3.8148	1.0755	0.20698
Information regarding performance evaluation	1	73	3.5205	1.01529	0.11883
	2	27	3.4444	0.9337	0.17969
Upkeep of commitment by Top management.	1	73	3.3836	0.98079	0.11479
	2	27	3.4074	0.93064	0.1791
Similarity of values with peers	1	73	3.5753	0.79788	0.09338
	2	27	3.5185	0.93522	0.17998
Concern of Immediate supervisor about personal well - being.	1	73	3.6027	0.92406	0.10815
	2	27	3.5926	0.97109	0.18689
Superiors speak positive in front of others	1	73	3.6986	0.84467	0.09886
	2	27	3.6667	1.07417	0.20672

Work Place Health Promotion Among Generation Y – Towards a Healthy Nation

Shabnam Chhabra, Santosh Jain Passi[1] and S.C. Manchanda[2]

Department of Home Science, V.M.L (PG) College, Ghaziabad
[1]Institute of Home Economics (Univ. of Delhi) New Delhi
[2]Formerly Prof. & Head, Cardio-Thoracic Center, A.I.I.M.S., New Delhi

ABSTRACT

The escalating incidence of chronic degenerative diseases, especially coronary artery disease (CAD) looming as the new epidemic, is afflicting Indians at a relatively younger age. A higher mortality is being reported in the developing countries due to the increased life expectancy, altered lifestyles and socio-economic changes associated with urbanization. Cardiovascular risk factors start early, track through the young age and manifest in middle age. Developing comprehensive health promotion programmes for improving the cardiovascular health of the community involves dissemination of information with multifaceted interventions targeting the young generation. Work sites / organizations can offer rich opportunities, since in most of the settings; employers are responsible for the health care costs of their work force. They have capitalized contracts to provide health services to their workers and thus have an additional incentive to prevent / treat the disease. Many employers recognize that they have an obligation to the health and wellbeing of their workforce. Counseling on healthy diet and lifestyle provided to the entire workforce can possibly help in promoting optimum health. Successful implementation of these lifestyle practices will certainly help to achieve a major public health goal and thereby achieve substantial decline in the CAD epidemic, so that well before mid 21st century, our morbidity/ disability/ mortality rates become low, and the war against the chronic disease is won.

Keywords: *Coronary Artery Disease, Risk Factors, Educational Intervention, Diet & Lifestyle Modification, Work Place Health Promotion, Young Generation, Positive Health*

BACKGROUND

Industrialization, modernization, technological advancements and economic up-liftment, have on one hand improved the standard of living of today's youth; and on the other have led to an increase in the incidence of non-communicable chronic degenerative disease, cardiovascular disease (CVD) being the most prevalent one (Hakajima, 2000). *Now days, more and more people below the age of 40 are suffering from heart disease* (Amirthaveni et al, 2003; Chhajer, 2000). The disease rare in early 1900's, has now become a leading cause of death. According to the World Health Organisation (WHO), in the developing region where 80 percent of the world's population lives, CVD is emerging as the major killer and remains the most common cause of early invalidity, professional incapacitation and premature death.

Several studies suggest that diet and lifestyle changes have substantially altered the risk of CVD; and hence, the policies must encompass a wide range of educational as well as regulatory measures, acting through price and non-price mechanisms. The depletion of productive manpower by CVD related deaths / disabilities, which are affecting individuals in the labour force (35-64) years, constitute a strong argument for initiating and implementing effective CVD prevention programmes at a much younger age (Reddy et al, 2005). *The unaffordable demand of an unchecked rise in the risk factors among the present day young generation (Generation Y) calls for the pathways of action towards cost-effective interventions that can provide a comprehensive response to this epidemic in developing countries.*

Diet and nutrition play an important role in the causation of the chronic degenerative diseases and along with physical inactivity; influence many of the biological variables that mediate their risk. The first decade of twenty-first century offers us an opportunity to initiate action to counter these growing epidemics. *The knowledge that is required to provide a comprehensive individual/community health response is readily available; we, however, need an effective application of this knowledge through interventions aimed at youth to reduce the risk of CVD across the life span*

The workplace has been established as one of the priority settings for health promotion into the 21st century since it directly influences the physical, mental, economic and social well-being of youngsters and subsequently the health of their families, communities and society at large. It rather offers an ideal setting and infrastructure to support the promotion of health of a larger audience. The concept that the workplace is an important arena for health campaigns of many kinds, as well as basic occupational health and safety programmes is not yet widely accepted. However, the hypothesis of health promoting workplace (HPW) is becoming increasingly relevant as more private and public organizations are recognizing that future success in a globalizing marketplace can only be achieved with a healthy and motivated workforce. A HPW can ensure a flexible and dynamic balance between customer expectations and organizational targets on the one hand and employee's skills and health needs on the other. This can assist companies and work organizations to compete in the marketplace. For nations, the development of HPW will be a pre-requisite for sustainable social and economic development. Intervention and prevention strategies are being sought to curb the rise in burden of cardiovascular disease in India. Here, the workplace becomes an important location for successful prevention strategies because employees' behaviour can be influenced by providing a supportive environment and leveraging existing infrastructure to offer low-cost but effective interventions (Gottlieb & McLeroy, 1994).

The concept of "Workplace Wellness" needs to be stressed upon as increasingly, Indians are dying of heart diseases in their most productive years, at least 10 years earlier than their counterpart in the West. This imposes not only a blow to the national health but also a huge economic burden on the family and the country. Today, youth is too aggressive at work. Long working hours, junk food and very little physical activity are taking a toll on the heart.

A recent study by the Initiative for Cardiovascular Health Research in Developing Countries, involving over 20,000 people from 10 Indian worksites, showed that workplace interventions could reduce the risk of cardiovascular diseases. The intervention group promoted positive diet and lifestyle changes such as reduced salt intake, increased fruit and vegetable consumption, increased level of physical activity, decreased tobacco use and various other measures to maintain good cardiac health of the employees.

Research has shown that Workplace Wellness Programmes have benefits for both employees and employers – by improving health, productivity and reducing the risk of heart diseases and stroke. A recent study by the World Economic Forum found that Workplace Wellness Programmes could achieve 25 per cent to 30 per cent reduction in medical and absenteeism costs. Apart from diet and lifestyle, the intervention programmes generate harmony at workplace, thereby reducing stress and anxiety among the employees.

BASELINE STUDY

A study was carried out to explore and assess the various diet and lifestyle related risk factors among the known cases of CAD and also test the hypothesis that cumulative benefits of cardiovascular protective therapies result in substantial risk factor modification / reduction when such intervention programmes are applied in practice. Findings related to these issues assisted in envisaging improvised simple and patient friendly multidisciplinary collaborative programmes for successful implementation through educational counseling for leading a better quality life. A *cross-sectional study* at two leading multi-specialty hospitals situated in the outskirts of Delhi (Narender Mohan Hospital, Mohan Nagar, Ghaziabad and Fortis Hospital, Noida) was done where an attempt was made to explore and identify diet/lifestyle related risk factors among the known cases of recently established CAD (n=105); simultaneously enrolling almost a similar number of age and gender matched asymptomatic controls (apparently non-CAD cases; n=111) from the non-cardiac wards of the same hospitals.

As per the inclusion criteria, the known cases of CAD and their more or less age and gender matched asymptomatic controls were aged less than or equal to 55 years. Age wise distribution of the CAD cases indicated that of the one hundred and five subjects, a majority (81.0%) were aged between 45 to 55 years and another 12.4 percent between 40 to 45 years. It was indeed alarming to note that seven of them (6.7%) were as young as less than 40 years of age (youngest being 34 years). Data on educational status / occupation revealed that CAD is inflicting individuals irrespective of all educational and professional fields and that too at a much younger age, especially among the men.

Majority of the CAD cases belonged to nuclear families. An attempt was made to explore and assess the dietary errors (if any) among these CAD cases as well as their asymptomatic controls. Rather than the current dietary data, retrospective technique was employed for estimating the individual's usual dietary intake (past diet history), in view of the fact that the current event could have affected the present dietary pattern/intake of the subjects.

Consequent to urbanization and modernization, practice of consuming food outside home was increasingly popular. Such foods usually included those prepared at restaurants, hotels, grocery stores, fast food service vans, office canteens, dhabas and other non-home locations. Large portion sizes and high energy density were common features of these food items. Most of them, particularly the traditional quick-serve were also high in saturated fat, trans-fatty acids, cholesterol, added sugars, and sodium and low in fibre and micronutrients. As a result, a positive association between frequency of meal consumption at quick-serve restaurants and total energy intake, weight gain, and insulin resistance was demonstrated. Thus, attainment of a healthy diet requires young adults to make wiser choices particularly when they ate food prepared outside home.

Retrospective data gathered on the detailed activity pattern of the subjects from both the groups included information on job profile such as working hours/days, mode of commuting to and back from workplace and distance required to travel each day etc. Further, data were also gathered on their leisure time activity pattern, involvement in household chores, and also their participation in any physical fitness activity, if any, prior to the event (like regular walks, involvement in any indoor or outdoor sport activity and yoga / meditation). In addition, data was gathered on the usual day's activity pattern of the subjects employing 24-hr recall method. Based on data of the various activities undertaken by the subjects, physical activity score was calculated using a modified version of the *Satyanarayan Codes for Physical Activity.* Results indicated that a lesser number of CAD cases were usually indulging in high or moderate physical activity routines as compared to the other group; the practice of morning/evening walks was also lower.

Rapid socio-economic transition in India has resulted in change in occupation and has shifted to formal industry based jobs; the occupational activity has thus declined considerably. Several studies have demonstrated a relation between increased levels of occupational physical activity and risk of myocardial infarction. Since physical activity promotes general health/well being, it should be advised as part of the individual's daily routine.

Wide prevalence of smoking in the subjects (both groups) indicated towards the fact that tobacco use remains an important problem in India and needs to be tackled urgently. Most adults in the present sample began this habit during adolescence/early adulthood, hence important interventions among youth need to be carried out. The data clearly indicates the need of prevention as well as intervention strategies to be implemented and various behavioral treatments, self help approaches and pharmacologic therapies (nicotine replacement therapy) should be offered to those needing help.

Since majority of the subjects were at the peak of their professional careers they reportedly felt that occupational demands accounted for a large proportion of the daily stresses. In view of this, if issues relating to the psychosocial interventions are aimed at the social environment (work sites, neighborhoods, religious settings, schools / colleges) rather than solely at individuals, it shall definitely lead to substantial improvements in their cardiovascular health.

Data relating to anthropometric measurements (BMI, waist circumference and waist-hip ratio) indicated higher mean values in the affected group ($p<0.01$), pointing towards the fact that obesity led to an increased risk of cardiovascular disease, both directly and indirectly, through related co-morbidities. Blood pressure levels (both SBP and DBP) for the CAD group were significantly higher than the asymptomatics ($p<0.001$), once again pointing towards raised blood pressure levels being one of the major risk factors of CAD. Blood glucose (both Fasting and Post Prandial) for the CAD cases indicate a higher mean than the asymptomatic controls. The serum lipid profile indicated a higher mean total cholesterol levels and triglyceride levels for the CAD cases as compared to the asymptomatics.

- The study thus highlighted the prevalence of tobacco smoking, sedentary lifestyle, hypertension, diabetes, obesity, dyslipidemia and metabolic syndrome as the major coronary risk factors among the adult CAD cases.
- Retrospective data indicated a low prevalence of multiple cardiovascular risk factors (unhealthy dietary pattern, smoking, hypertension, lipid abnormalities and diabetes) among the CAD cases during adolescence, but the prevalence of multiple risk factors increased at age-group 20–29 years with an exponential increase in age group 30–39 years. Increasing risk factors correlate with body mass index, waist circumference and waist-hip ratio. A rapid increase in risk factors in young adulthood identifies the target group for interventions.
- The study clearly showed that the increase in risk factors in this North Indian urban population started at about the age of 30 years, aptly *The Generation Y.*
- It was felt pertinent that attempts need to be made to design and offer simple, user friendly and inexpensive programmes comprising of personalized educational interventions to promote diet/ lifestyle changes to the young generation today.

  (Salt, saturated fats, alcohol, and calories; by increasing both work related and leisure time physical activity; by increasing consumption of heart healthy foods such as fruits and vegetables, high fibre cereals, oils containing balanced amounts of poly unsaturated and mono unsaturated fats. Stress management techniques such as yoga and meditation coupled with increased physical activity and appropriate dietary modifications should become part of everyday life.)

PROPOSED RECOMMENDATIONS

The atherosclerosis is assumed to begin early in life and has been linked to elevated levels of plasma lipids/lipoproteins during childhood. Since it takes several years/decades for the fatty streaks to develop into fibrous plaques; the incidence of clinically manifested disease appears to be higher during middle age (Suri, 2003). CHD usually manifests itself after the age of 50, but with heredity predisposition and many other lifestyle factors, it can occur much earlier. With aging, there is a gradual but progressive accumulation of coronary plaques; and this accounts for an increasing risk for CAD with advancing age. Individuals with no other major risk factors for cardiovascular disease in their young adulthood / middle age are at lower age specific risk for death from cardiovascular causes and consequently have greater life expectancy than others in the population. Thus, it is reasonable to assume that low risk status in early adulthood relates to lower health care costs during older age. *With an ever-increasing number of Indians suffering from heart diseases, a drastic change in lifestyle and eating habits is the need of the hour to tackle the alarming situation with a special focus on youth (Gupta et al, 2009).* Data from Delhi hospitals says that the average age of people with heart ailments is coming down to as young as 20 years. Patients under the age of 40 have increased from 10 percent a decade ago to 30 percent today.

According to doctors, many of the young professionals today have odd working hours that lead to *stress*, and not many of them have the privilege of savouring home cooked meals. On top of it, the indulgence in *smoking* and drinking to "reduce the stress" worsens the situation. Such a lifestyle results in *high blood pressure, obesity, diabetes*, etc. leading to heart ailments. Hence, the focus should be on how to educate youngsters to lead a healthy lifestyle. Efforts should be made to stop leading an unhealthy lifestyle which may lead to a cardiovascular disease later. The education and guidance should begin early. Physical exercise, avoiding junk and oily food and not smoking are some of the steps that must be adopted as early as possible (Misra et al, 2009).

World Heart Day was created in Year 2000 to inform people around the globe that heart disease and stroke are the world's leading cause of death, claiming 17.3 million lives each year and the numbers are rising. By 2030, it is expected that 23 million people will die from CVDs annually. The World Heart Federation spreads the news that at least 80 per cent of premature deaths from heart disease and stroke could be avoided if the main risk factors, tobacco, unhealthy diet and physical inactivity are controlled / curbed at an early age.

In recent times, greater levels of awareness have led to a decrease in cardiovascular risk factors among the well-educated (King et al, 2005). Hence, it can be expected that with proper control of diet and lifestyle risk factors, youngsters can advance to higher phases of the epidemiological transition; and while maintaining a modern lifestyle, return to the ancestral low rates of CAD is possible. Developing comprehensive programmes for improving their cardiovascular health involves dissemination of information with multifaceted interventions targeting them as a whole and particularly the organizations and the work sites, since the target population can be aimed at here.

- *Work sites / organizat*ions can offer rich opportunities, since in most of the settings; employers are responsible for the health care costs of their work force. They have capitalized contracts to provide health services to their workers and thus have an additional incentive to prevent / treat the disease. Counseling on healthy diet and lifestyle provided to these high risk employees identified among the entire workforce can possibly help in modifying the CAD risk.

- Identification and aiming interventions to lower the CAD risk in young generation, that are predictive of subsequent development of the disease in adulthood is another suggestive goal. Such programmes comprising of educating the young population can prove highly advantageous for encouraging CVD prevention among the Generation Y.

Many employers recognize that they have an obligation to the health and wellbeing of their workforce. Investing in the health of employees can also bring business benefits such as reduced sickness absence, increased loyalty and better staff retention. In fact, proper attention to workers' health and safety may have extensive benefits:

- Healthy workers are productive and raise healthy families; thus healthy workers are a key for overcoming national poverty.
- Workplace health risks are higher in the informal sector and small industry which are key arena of action on poverty alleviation, where people can work their way out of poverty;
- Safe workplaces contribute to sustainable development, which is the key to poverty reduction;
- The processes of protecting workers, surrounding communities and the environment for future generations have important common elements, such as pollution control and exposure reduction.

For workplace health to be effective, employers need to:

- Track key metrics about employee health and wellbeing - such as levels of sickness absence, so as to identify ill-health among groups of employees and tailor workplace health interventions appropriately.
- Improve the quality of work – such as promoting working practices that offer employee's autonomy, control and task discretion and fostering strong workplace relationships. This helps to protect employees from stress, depression and anxiety.
- Find innovative ways to encourage employees to participate - by providing incentives, such as competitions, prizes or vouchers. This helps to engage employees and make them more receptive to advice about health and wellbeing.

These are important because they help employers take a holistic approach to protecting and promoting employee health and wellbeing. There is strong evidence to support the use of:

- Group counseling sessions and incentives to help employees quit smoking;
- Advice on diet and exercise to help reduce levels of unhealthy cholesterol and protect

against coronary heart disease; and because poor dietary habits and physical inactivity are associated with many adverse health outcomes, most young adults could benefit from interventions designed to improve their eating habits and increase their activity levels.

Such intervention programs fall into three general categories: health promotion, primary prevention, and secondary prevention. The goal of health promotion is to help people establish an active lifestyle and healthy eating habits early in life and to maintain these behaviors throughout their lives. The goal of primary prevention is to help people who have risk factors for chronic disease (e.g., elevated blood pressure or serum cholesterol levels) prevent or postpone the onset of disease by establishing more active lifestyles and healthier eating habits. The goals of secondary prevention are to help people who already have a chronic disease cope with and control these conditions and to prevent additional disability by increasing their physical activity and establishing more healthful eating patterns. Multiple improvements in dietary practices such as lower salt intake, avoidance of high alcohol intake, increased potassium intake, liberal intake of fruits / vegetables, fat-free / low-fat dairy products; and reduced consumption of total fat can favourably influence other major risk factors as well. With the adoption of healthy norms of human behavior, low risk levels can become the rule throughout the adulthood for all strata of population. The same holds true for the other traits contributing to risk of CAD including sedentary lifestyle, tobacco consumption and obesity. Further, improvements in the identification and control of major risk factors such as diabetes and cigarette smoking, especially in younger people is clearly needed. Although newer effective medications for controlling the blood glucose levels, hypertension and dyslipidemia are being introduced, it is pertinent that ways to control the epidemic of obesity are looked into, since that would substantially contribute to the reduced risk of diabetes and its CVD sequel. There is no doubt that the intention of primary prevention and the interventions is to shift health profile of the population in a healthier direction, and small changes in risk factors among the majority who are at moderate risk can have a positive impact in terms of population-attributable risk of disability/death. It was also felt that no amount of knowledge dissemination and awareness would help if the individual is not constantly motivated to change wherever required; and if sustained education programmes and follow-ups are not carried out.

KEY ASPECTS

- Employers face common issues hence improving employee health is a universal workforce issue today. However, employers must tailor their programs, depending on location, specific health issues, and demographics, to develop wellness programs that address local needs.
- Health trends are changing all over the world more so in developing countries especially among the South Asians where the chronic disease and lifestyle-related health issues are increasing and middle class is starting to thrive.

- Employers need to create a culture of health rather than isolated programs. The concept of employee wellness is not new, but focusing on creating an overall culture of health is.
- To help address chronic disease and lifestyle-related issues facing employees, the employers should develop policies, physical facilities, and behavioral standards within the workplace that support healthy living.
- Key performance indicators reflect overall well-being of employees hence identifying a mix of health-related and productivity indicators from the onset helps create a baseline of both individual health profiles and/or the overall health of a facility.
- Employee benefits promote positive change and overall medical, disability, life, and retirement benefits are seen as an integral part of company culture and can contribute, whether directly or indirectly, to a healthier workforce.

CONCLUSION

Benefits of Workforce Health Promotion

Workplace health promotion should support a participatory process to help promote a stronger implementation of occupational and environmental health legislation. It should suggest tools for maintaining or strengthening a national healthy workplace initiative and creation of healthy workplace networks. To be successful, workplace health promotion has to involve active participation of young employees, management and other stakeholders in the implementation of jointly agreed initiatives and should help employers and employees at all levels to increase control over and improve their health.

To the Organization	*To the Young Employee*
a well-managed health and safety programme	a safe and healthy work environment
a positive and caring image	enhanced self-esteem
improved staff morale	reduced stress
reduced staff turnover	improved morale
reduced absenteeism	increased job satisfaction
increased productivity	increased skills for health protection
reduced health care/insurance costs	improved health
reduced risk of fines and litigation	improved sense of well-being

While some health promotion activities in the workplace have focused on a single illness or risk factor (e.g. prevention of heart disease) or on changing personal health practices and behaviours (e.g. smoking, diet), there is a growing awareness that there are multiple determinants of workers' health. In addition to person-focused interventions, workforce health promotion initiatives have moved towards a more comprehensive approach, which acknowledges the combined influence of personal, environmental, organizational, community and societal factors on employee well-being. A health-promoting workplace recognizes that a healthy workforce is essential and integrates policies, systems and practices conducive to health at all levels of the organization. Timely use of preventive cardiology can, thus, help meet an important challenge, fundamentally strategic in nature. This is vital for the years ahead, both to achieve national health goals as well as to tackle the 'bottom line' objective of curbing and ending the CAD epidemic well before mid 21st century.

REFERENCES

[1] Amirthaveni M, Vijaylakshmi P. Effect of fish oil supplementation on hyperlipidemic patients. Abstract book of IX Asian Congress of Nutrition, New Delhi. 2003: 335

[2] Chhajer B. Why heart patients are increasing in number? Reversal of Heart Disease (1^{st}ed). SAAOL Publication Pvt. Ltd, New Delhi. 2000; 24: 122

[3] Gottlieb NH, McLeroy KR. Social health. In: O'Donnell MP, Harris JS. Health Promotion in the Workplace, *2nd ed.* Albany, NY: Delmar Publishers, 1994.

[4] Gupta R, Misra A, Naval K, Kondal D, Gupta S, Agrawal A, Pandey RM *BMC Cardiovascular Disorders* 2009, 9:28

[5] Hakajima. Health Promotion – New Challenges for the future. IUHPE-SEARB. Publications 2000: 15-9

[6] King AC, Jeffery RW, Fridinger F. Environmental and policy approaches to cardiovascular and disease prevention through physical activity: issues and opportunities. *Health Educ Q,* 2005; 22(4):499-511.

[7] Misra A, Chowbey P, Makkar BM, Vikram NK, Wasir JS, Chadha D, Joshi SR, Sadikot S, Gupta R, Gulati S. Consensus Statement for Diagnosis of Obesity, Abdominal obesity and the Metabolic Syndrome for Asian Indians and Recommendations for Physical Activity, Medical and Surgical Management. JAPI. 2009; 57: 163-70

[8] Ranjan S. 'Impact of Yoga and Lifestyle modifications on the prevention of chronic degenerative diseases'. M.Sc. Thesis submitted to the University of Delhi, 2005

[9] Reddy KS, Shah B, Varghese C. Responding to the threat of chronic diseases in India Lancet. 2005; 366: 1744-9

[10] Suri S. Impact of information, education and communication with special emphasis on coronary heart disease - A study among school going adolescents PhD thesis submitted to the University of Delhi, 2003: 38-9

Attracting and Retaining Gen Y: New Trends in Compensation and Benefits

Urvashi Sharma

Department of Management, Maharaja Agarsen Institute of Management Studies, Delhi

ABSTRACT

When it comes to attracting strong talent, it can often be hard to compete with the large businesses, which can offer great compensation and benefit packages. As a result, you are faced with limited access to professional or trade experts.

With thousands of Baby Boomers retiring every year, it has become the younger Generation Y workers, which businesses are focusing on. The paper highlights on the generation Y, who is hard to attract and retain, entering businesses big and small, and advancing quickly through the ranks.

This paper focus on attracting and retaining gen Y and as it may be difficult for a business to compete with the compensation and benefit packages offered by many large organizations but one has the advantage of being able to provide intangible options. By branding the company as a progressive, supportive, creative, and open-minded workplace, and more importantly, living up to that brand, business is sure to get the Gen Y workers you need.

Keywords: *Gen Y, Baby Boomers, Innovation, Flextime, Performance Based Pay, Cafeteria Plan, Work Life Balance*

WHO IS GENERATION Y?

Generation Y (also known as the Millennial Generation, the ME Generation, and Echo Boomers), has different belief and value systems than their parents' generation, the Baby Boomers. Composed largely of individuals born between 1980 and 1995, this generation grew up with more adult supervision than any other. They are used to instant information, instant food, and instant entertainment. They want instant answers or solutions to problems and they expect success to come quickly and easily.

From a retail marketing perspective, Generation Y is well targeted. Thousands of products are successfully sold to them every day. But when it comes to offering attractive work environments, compensation, and benefits for Generation Y workers, employers have been slow to understand what they want. Possibly because it is so different from the priorities of their Baby Boomer parents.

WHY DO COMPANIES WANT TO HIRE GENERATION Y WORKERS?

As more Baby Boomers prepare to depart the workforce, valuable knowledge and skills need to be transferred to the next generations taking over the workforce.

Associate Professor in Management in Maharaja Agarsen Institute of Management Studies (Affiliated to Guru Gobind Singh Indraprastha University, Delhi)

She can be reached at urvashi13@gmail.com

The benefits of the Generation Y worker are that:

- They can build upon the Boomer's knowledge and skills.
- They are comfortable with technology and can use it to improve productivity and therefore profits.
- They adapt to changing markets and demands easily.

However, members of Generation Y are not particularly loyal. If company doesn't offer an appealing work situation you will have a hard time convincing them to work for company. If unhappy, they will simply find a company that caters more to their value and belief systems.

To please Gen Y workers, you must first understand their perspective. Even if you do not hold the same values and beliefs as them you must be prepared to change.

As a small business it is easy for you to change to accommodate the needs of the top Generation Y talent. The key actually knows what they want.

WHAT DO GENERATION Y EMPLOYEES WANT?

Based on what we know about Generation Y individuals, we can assume a few of their wants and needs:

- **Work-life balance.** Gen Y wants flexible work options, compressed workweeks, reduced workweeks, and telecommuting options. Although not a new trend, flexible working is now a necessity rather than a nicc to have.
- **Consistent feedback and recognition.** Generation Y wants daily feedback. They need constant informal reminders that as an individual and/or team they are doing a good job and they want to know how they can improve. They prefer consistent informal feedback rather than annual performance reviews. They expect leaders to take a vested interest in their own individual development and provide clear career paths.
- **Freedom of creativity.** Gen Y individuals look for jobs that allow them the freedom to be creative and autonomous. As a small business you are likely to be able to allow employees to be creative with minimal constraint. Small businesses should use that advantage to attract Gen Y workers.

- **Training and development.** Gen Y craves knowledge. Providing a yearly training and development allowance will help your employees grow with and become invested in the business, while fulfilling their desire for self-improvement.
- **Empower to solve problems.** Generation Y is technologically sophisticated and, if you allow them, they will find efficient, moneysaving ways of doing things. By empowering them to solve a problem and recognizing those solutions as valuable, you will soon have your employees treating your business like it's their own.
- **Give back: Don't just take.** Generation Y was brought up to be aware of others and to care for those less fortunate than themselves. Although you may not have the budget that large organizations have to allocate to volunteering, but you can still support employees by providing them an outlet. That could mean giving them the time to complete a charitable activity. Or it could mean joining with them to do something like the Food Drive. It might cost a little budget, but the engagement, productivity, and positive PR it brings to the business will outweigh the cost associated with it.
- **Say yes to social media – With Boundaries.** Generation Y is fueled by social media. It is part of their life, and a major communications avenue for them. No matter how much you, as an employer, try to suppress their online communication habits, they will find a way to engage in social media.

It may be difficult for you to compete with the compensation and benefit packages offered by many large organizations but you have the advantage of being able to provide intangible options. By branding yourself as a progressive, supportive, creative, and open-minded workplace, and more importantly, living up to that brand, you are sure to get the Gen Y workers you need.

INNOVATIVE COMPENSATION STRATEGIES FOR GENERATION Y

Compensation is the remuneration received by an employee in return for his/her contribution to the organization. It is an organized practice that involves balancing the work-employee relation by providing monetary and non-monetary benefits to employees.

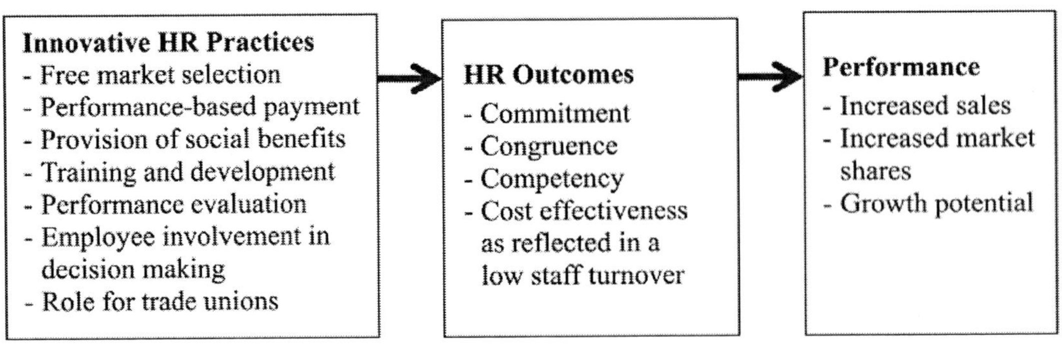

Employee salary in any organization includes basic salary which is the fixed part and apart from it there are certain measures which are given to the employees according to their expenses and performance.

Some of the innovative strategies of compensation for Generation Y are:

1. **An increasing focus on pay for performance.** Employees who get the best results will reap the highest annual raises. "As a result, the gap between high-performing employees and those in the lower-performing categories is widening significantly," says a new Mercer report Generation Y is so much attracted towards this kind of pay where in employee is compensated according to his performance. Gen Y find this kind of pay very much effective because of the reason that they are achievement oriented in nature and believe in doing useful work.
2. **Alignment of compensation with business goals.** The math can be brutally simple in tight times. How much value does each employee add to the organization's work—and bottom line? Gen Y expects the hike and companies seek to its goal and align the compensation package.
3. **Raises send a message.** High performers won't just get raises; they'll get way better raises than others do. HR consultants are advising clients to show their appreciation for MVPs with rises as high as 10%. If that drives off disappointed low performers—who might score a 1% bump—so be it.
4. **Creative budgeting breakouts.** Some companies are splitting pay budgets into two categories: managerial and line employees. It's not to set up a double standard. The division prevents the top brass from dipping into employee pay budgets to line their own pockets.
5. **Flextime.** Gen Y is interested to work in a flexible time framework. A flextime policy allows staff to determine when they will work, while a flexplace policy allows staff to determine where they will work. For example, rather than the strictly structured eight hour work day schedule Monday through Friday, offering flexible work schedules are more attractive to employees as a way to achieve more of a balanced lifestyle. Some employers embrace alternate work arrangements like ten hour work days scheduled four days a week, job sharing between employees and allowing employees to work from home to offer employees added flexibility.
6. **Broader compensation benchmarking.** More organizations will base pay systems on local and industry wide compensation surveys rather than on internal traditions. Business factors—such as recruiting and retention patterns—will be more decisive than how much a position has been worth historically.
7. **Profit-sharing plans.** Profit sharing plans include paying employees a share of the net profit in addition to their wages or salary. It encourages Generation Y to identify themselves more closely with the company by developing a common concern for its

progress and recognize that employees have a moral right to share in the profit they have helped to produce. It increases commitment of employees.

8. **Recalculation of replacement costs.** Conventional wisdom says it costs between 50% and 300% of annual salary to replace an employee. Post-recession, that cost has jumped as high as five times salary. *Reason:* To reduce turmoil in tough times, hiring man—agers and HR want to be absolutely sure a new hire will stick.
9. **Income equivalent payments and reimbursements for incurred expenses**. This broad group of services provides employees with the opportunity for an improved and more enjoyable lifestyle. Thus making them more and more comfortable with the organization and making them feel committed about the organizational goals.
10. **Telecommuting**. It is a *work* arrangement in which employees do not *commute* to a central place of work. A person who telecommutes is known as a "telecommuter", "teleworker", and sometimes as a "home-sourced" employee. Working from home is very attractive to some Gen Y to avoid the daily commute and to complete their work around their own schedule to allow additional time with family.
11. **Part time scheduling**. This is a kind of strategy wherein the organization instead of giving lengthy and boring schedules they divide the working hours so that employee may not get bored or tired of their work. This creates positive impact on the mind of employees about the organization.
12. **Broad banding**. Organizations need to collapse salary grades and ranges into just a few wide ranges or bands, each of which contains a wide range of jobs and salary levels.
13. **A hyper-focus on retention.** Because it costs so much to replace valued talent, employers are going all out to keep their current stars. ***Tip:*** Consider "re-recruiting" your most valuable em—ployees by offering bo—nuses and career advancement—just as you would when wooing an attractive ex—ternal candidate.
14. **Restrictions on extra pay.** While some companies have stopped layoffs and furloughs, many continue to limit overtime. It's approved only if calculations say it will reap a return on the investment.
15. **Better communication with employees.** After three years of pay doldrums, you may have fallen out of practice when it comes to addressing compensation. Warm up for better times to come by meeting with employees to review how your compensation system works. Even if there's nothing new to report, it could improve employee attitudes.
16. **Updated compensation policies.** Left stagnant, compensation policies quickly go out-of-date. That could render your organization less competitive—especially if merit raises still dominate. Dust off your stale pay structure and job descriptions as part of your renewed focus on recruiting and retention of top talent.

17. **Skill-based pay**. It links pay to the level of schemes used in the job and application of additional skills by the persons carrying the job. This kind of pay is very much effective for generation Y because they believe in doing job where they can utilize their efficiencies very well and they feel delighted.

BENEFIT PROGRAMS FOR GENERATION Y

Benefits are indirect monitory and non-monitory payments an employee receives for continuing to work for the company. Due to the family-centric behavior of Gen Y employees, it is very important to provide them various future benefits for their family Due to the reason that Gen Y are very much attention craving and They appreciate being kept in the loop and seek frequent praise and reassurance. This is the reason that organizations are providing spot bonuses to make them recognized in the organization.

Here are some of the benefits which a company should provide to Gen Y workers to motivate, attract and retain them:-

1. **Disability income continuation**. Various disability income continuation components provide weekly or monthly payments in lieu of the regular earned income paycheck. This benefit is essential for the employees to make them feel cared by the organization. It includes continuation of income in case of short-term disability, long-term disability, travel accident, sick leave, and various insurances.
2. **Loss of job income continuation**. they are specially designed to assist generation Y during short-term periods of unemployment due to layoffs and termination to secure employees and their family. This creates positive impression on the mind of Generation Ye as they believe in family values and always wants to make them secure.
3. **Spouse and family income protection**. this type of benefit scheme includes majorly those benefits which are provided directly to the family of employee for their future security and safety. Generations Y is very much interested in these schemes and finds them relevant because it provides betterment of their family. It includes life insurance, retirement plans, Medicare, annuity, accidental death, etc.
4. **Health and accident protection**. It includes all the medical benefits provided to the employee and his family in case of any miss happening. Basic medical coverage includes payments for diagnostic visits to the doctor's office, outpatient X-rays, and laboratory coverage.
5. **Property and liability protection**. It provides employees with personal property and liability protection. These components include group auto, group home, group legal, Fidelity bond insurance, etc.
6. **Performance awards and recognition awards**. They are formal or informal employer-employee exchange programs for appraising the performance of workers in the

organization. It has a positive impact on the performance of the employees as they feel more motivated and confident towards their abilities.

7. **Work-life balance.** Work-life balance is about helping staff to maintain healthy, rewarding lifestyles that will in turn lead to improvements in productivity and performance. Strategies to achieve balance will differ between organizations, partly depending on their function, the types of work roles they offer, and their workforce profile. Implementing work-life balance effectively across an organization is a strategic change management process, and involves culture change. However, the issue is congruent with many organizations' stated values and provides a tangible outlet for modeling those values internally.
8. **Cafeteria plans**. Cafeteria plans are also very much relevant as employees can spend their benefits allowances on a choice of benefits options. It lets the employee put together his or her own benefit package, subject to two constraints.

Many organizations have also added indirect compensation elements focused on employee wellness initiatives. Things like having health clubs on-site with free memberships for employees, offering yoga classes or massage therapy during the work day, offering complementary breakfasts, arranging social outings like sporting events and concerts and by offering free wellness seminars for staff. It is in every company's best interest to concentrate on reducing stress at work and in their employee's personal lives. Wellness initiatives in the workplace can result in less employee absenteeism due to illness and workplace injuries.

And when it comes to the direction actual financial compensation packages are heading, there have been a number of changes in this regard. There has been a shift from pay for job and status to pay for individual employee skills and contributions. As well, discretionary bonuses have been replaced by incentive awards for achieving defined goals and objectives. Innovative compensation programs also include:

* Broad-banding — or reducing the number of pay grades in an organization while expanding the actual salary ranges. The benefit here is being able to expand the actual pay for performance and competency component.
* Competency-based programs — involve identifying the skills employees need to possess in order to meet expectations in a given position. The key benefit here is that the employee continually upgrades their skills and the emphasis is on paying the individual and not the job.
* Incentive compensation — this is paying that is directly connected to the performance of the individual or the team and has been found to increase employee performance in the right environment. The right environment means employees are actually motivated by money, the employee's efforts and results are measurable and the potential rewards are significant.

The final trend in compensation to discuss is stock options, the leading means of compensation for executives and managers in the 1990s. With stock options, the employee owns the option to buy stock in their company at a price that is fixed beforehand and is exercised by a specific date. The goal here would be to motivate the employee to work hard to create the greatest possible value for their company. So when the time came for the employee to buy the stock, they would hopefully earn the expected additional value of the stock by purchasing at the lower price. Some companies are getting away from stock options because of their inherent volatility and are moving towards a more controllable and predictable system that involves providing variable compensation that is tied to medium and long-term strategic goals. Still, stock options remain a component for high-level positions in many organizations. Some feel they are a good avenue for executive staff to share in a company's success and to create value for those professionals who are committed to the company for long-term goals.

All of the various approaches to employee compensation that have been covered are not appropriate for every type of organization. To implement programs that promote wellness initiatives or competency and performance based compensation for example, requires a significant investment of time and resources. While the planning and implementation required is no small task, it can pay large dividends for the organization in the areas of employee development and satisfaction, as well as achieving corporate goals and objectives. In summary, the best compensation system for any organization is one that ties the interests of the employees with that of the company and creates real commitment among staff to work together to strengthen the corporation. The best method is to conduct a complete and thorough analysis of the company to determine what motivates the particular staff members at each level of the organization. Based on this information, the appropriate vehicles for compensation as discussed previously can be implemented. This should create a workforce that is motivated and engaged, which should facilitate the achievement of corporate goals and objectives.

New Trends and Innovativeness in Employee Compensation with the Expectations of Generation Y

In today's day and age, compensation packages have evolved to include perks and benefits that were unheard of a generation ago. Gone are the days of meeting with employees once a year to give them a pat on the back and the standard four percent merit increase. With the world progressing and people's wants and needs shifting, in order to stay competitive, an organization's compensation program must continually change. Merely updating the way a company pays employees may not be enough to keep pace. Because the current marketplace is so competitive, *in order to attract*, retain and motivate the kind of people who are committed to the success of an organization, it may necessitate a complete compensation system overhaul.

There are a number of catalysts present that have strongly influenced the direction and philosophy behind employee compensation packages. Things like the changing business environment including new technology like the Internet, downsizing due to sluggish economic growth, and the transition to flexible or contingency work forces have caused companies to rethink their approach to compensation. As well, the old business model of authority dictating from the top down has been replaced in many organizations with horizontal cross-functional work teams which require a different system to reward performance. And finally, companies today want their compensation programs to help increase productivity and reduce costs. But traditional programs don't reward employees for cutting costs or increasing profits. This creates significant conflict between organizational and employee wants and needs. In my personal experience, when employees see no personal gain for working hard or harder, they have no motivation to embrace continuous improvement.

A new approach to compensation includes new and enticing ways to attract and motivate employees with a wide range of perks designed to enhance individual effort and, in some cases, promote team building and chemistry. While large companies have long touted major corporate perks, including tuition payments and daycare on site, many smaller businesses are now providing plenty of attractive cost-effective perks that are having some very positive results. The following information will attempt to outline the direction employee compensation packages seem to be going, as well as explain some of the reasons these types of modes of compensation are gaining in popularity.

During tough economic times, Gen Y is more likely to settle for a job with a lower salary than older professionals. This is of course due to their inexperience and maybe inability to get a high salary from the start. However, Gen Y does not shy away from asking for raises sooner than older co-workers. Those from Generation Y may be more concerned with gaining experience and getting their feet wet. They may prefer higher salaries over benefits, since many are just starting out, paying back college tuition, and often living paycheck to paycheck between car loans and first apartment rent.

THE NEXT GENERATION WORKFORCE

Generation Y, a much sought-after group, also known as Millennial, represents a generation of ambitious, confident, hopeful and goal-oriented twenty-something employees who are taking corporate America by storm. They are the workforce of the future and they have an entirely new way of interacting and doing business.

What really sets this generation apart from other generations is the way they socialize, communicate and interact with each other. Millennial are more reliant on the internet than previous generations and tend to use it as a mainstream form of communication and networking. They are influenced by their cultural upbringing, and have high-expectations when it comes to their future career and success.

CATERING TO THE WORKFORCE OF THE FUTURE

With Baby Boomers fast approaching retirement age, employers are beginning to tap into resources from younger generations, such as Millennial, to help replace the aging workforce upon retirement which will provide a deficit of positions across a variety of industries and locations. Not only will the Millennial generation be helping to fill positions left behind by retiring Boomers, but their upbringing allows them to bring a fresh, new perspective to the workplace making them valuable to any organization.

Employers can attract and retain skilled workers from the Generation Y by offering competitive salaries, career track, flexible schedules, and making sure individual employees feel challenged and appreciated. However, Millennial are pushing the envelope a step further, and are asking employers to go beyond traditional compensation and benefits to create an environment that is creative, challenging, team-oriented, fun, and financially rewarding. This generation is vocal about their job expectations, and because they are the workforce of the future, employers are beginning to take notice.

To accommodate the wants and needs of the next generation workforce, employers will have to compliment their traditional compensation and benefits packages with unique workplace attributes and company culture. Employers can better attract, retain and motivate millennial workers by incorporating these tips below:

- **Provide leadership and feedback.** Millennial look to their leaders as role models and have a strong desire to learn from them. They work hard to achieve the goals their managers set for them and expect to receive honest and constructive feedback based on their performance. Establishing a clear career track which is supported by a performance review process helps employees understand how they are doing in their job and encourages them to keep improving and moving forward in the organization.
- **Offer unique benefits.** Although this generation wants to be financially compensated for their efforts, they also value non-traditional benefits. Millennial are attracted to organizations that offer unique benefits such as: a game room, an exercise room or healthcare membership reimbursement, peer nominated awards, casual dress or free movie tickets, to name a few.
- **Promote team collaboration.** Millennial like working with people they get along with and enjoy being friends with co-workers. Employers should create an office space that allows co-workers to share ideas and interact with each other and promotes teamwork. Some ideas to encourage employee interaction include: building an office with low cubicles, establishing strategic teams to focus on various projects and tasks or utilizing a company instant messaging system.
- **Give back to the community.** Many members of the millennial generation are showing an interest in community involvement and environmentally-friendly initiatives. When searching for a job, many of these professionals are attracted to employers who have community service projects in place. Employers should establish a community service program that fits within their company culture and make sure to communicate it to potential employees on the company's website, in job ads, interviews and company collateral.

- **Create a fun environment.** This generation wants to look forward to going to work everyday and wants to enjoy a fun, friendly and creative environment in which to work and grow as an individual. Millennial are attracted to organizations that promote company gatherings, such as annual team building events or summer barbeques that give employees a chance to have fun and get to know each other at work.
- **Support growth opportunity.** Make sure individual employees feel challenged and appreciated. This generation wants to learn and likes to participate in projects that allow them to gain valuable hands-on experience.
- **Be flexible.** Millennial like to work hard, but they still desire a life outside of work and are looking for work-life balance. Employers who offer flexibility in employee work schedules such as summer hours, flex-time or work-at-home programs can increase the chance of attracting these workers.

CONCLUSION

It appears that many of the things that keep Gen Y engaged in a role are the same for other generations. However, Gen Y's values, preferences and behaviors are different so their emphasis on certain aspects of work is different... and so, in the future, should be the focus of their employers. If a Gen Y employee does not feel they are getting what they need at work – they will leave to seek the employer that does give them what they need. Unlike Xers and Boomers, they are not remotely daunted by the specter of unemployment.

Gen Y's values, preferences and behaviors are different because of the environment in which they have grown up: a prosperous economy, the many choices and opportunities on offer to them (due largely to technological advance), and the experiences and conditions that give them a different perspective on life (e.g. global warming, the war on terror and connectivity). We also know that the demographic situation is predicted to result in a shrinking workforce which means that, in as little as five to ten years, the majority of an organization's workforce will be Gen Y. The organizations that take steps to understand and implement change based on these two fundamental points will be best-placed to attract, recruit and retain Gen Y.

Now more than ever employers must take the millennial generation into consideration before developing a plan. By getting creative with company benefits, offering flexibility and growth opportunities for employees and promoting teamwork and collaboration, employers will have the best chance of attracting and retaining the workforce of the future. Success is thus repositioned as shared success. Viewed in this way, the greater the investment in people, the greater the benefits for the entire business. By breaking out of rigid compensation and benefits packages focusing on the needs and expectations, employers can cater for Generation Y's desire to take control of their work/life balance and foster a sense of organizational altruism, which ultimately helps them to attract and Retain the best talent.

REFERENCES

[1] Baeten, X. (2010). Global Compensation and Benefits Management: The Need for Communication and Coordination // Compensation & Benefits Review. Vol. 42.

[2] Bloom, M., Milkovich, G. T., Mitra, A. (2003). International compensation: Learning from how managers respond to variations in local host contexts // International Journal of Human Resource Management. Vol. 14.

[3] Core, J. E., R. Guay, W. R., Larcker, D. F. (2003). Executive Equity Compensation and Incentives: A Survey // Economic Policy Review. Vol. 9, No. 1.

[4] Glassman, M., Glassman, A., Champagne, P. J., Zugelder, M. T. (2010). Evaluating Pay-for-Performance Systems: Critical Issues for Implementation // Compensation & Benefits Review. Vol. 42. – http://www.sagepublications.com [2010 09 12].

[5] Hansen, F. (2009). Merit pay produces pay discrimination. – http://www.workforce. com/ section/02/ feature/25/91/53/259165_printer.html [2010 10 10].

[6] Milkovich, G. T. & Newman, J. M. (2008). Compensation. (Ninth edition), McGraw-Hill Irwin.

[7] Moniz, J. (2010). The Basics for Building and Maintaining Incentive Plans at Smaller Firms // Compensation & Benefits Review. Vol. 42. – http://www.sagepublications.com [2010 08 27].

[8] Pfeffer, J., & Sutton, R. (2006). Evidence based management // Harvard Business Review. January, 63–74. – http://www.sagepublications.com [2010 11 04].

[9] Terpstra, D., & Honoree, A. (2005). Employees' responses to merit pay inequity // Compensation & Benefits Review. Vol. 37.

[10] Chip Espinoza, Mick Ukleja, Craig Rusch (2010). Managingthe Millennials: Discover the Core Competencies for Managing Today's Workforce. John Wiley & Sons

[11] Richard I. Henderson, Compensation Management in a Knowledge-Based World, Ninth Edition (2005), Pearson Education, Inc.

Impact of Job Motivators on Job Preference, Organizational Commitment and Intention to Stay: Perceptions of Generation Y

Anu Singh Lather, Shikha Gupta and Archana Singh

University School of Management Studies, GGS Indraprastha University, Dwarka, Delhi

ABSTRACT

In developing countries like India and also in developed countries where Baby Boomers and Generation X employees are about to retire, the attracting, recruiting and retaining young generation is really a tough task. Realizing these challenges; role and importance of the Generation Y as the emerging workforce, the researchers in the present study have tried to find out main attractions for the members of this generation to accept a job. Current study also tried to find out the impact of motivational factors (intrinsic and extrinsic), that acts as attractions for this generation to accept a job, on organizational commitment and intentions to stay. With the data collected from 56 respondents from management students of NCR region, India, these analyses reflect that generation Y perceive extrinsic factors (starting salary; flexi – working – hours; accessibility of workplace form place of stay; workplace environment like physical settings, furnishing; promotions and career advancement opportunities; work – life balance etc.) more appealing than intrinsic factors (interesting job profile; leadership style, superior – subordinate relationship, feedbacks etc.) for accepting a job. These results indicate that over the generations work values have significantly changed. Also it's been revealed from data analyses that those respondents who received extrinsic factors reported higher levels of organizational commitment, and intent to stay with the organization. Though the study has its sets of limitations, but these findings may have practical implications for attraction, recruitment, retention and management of the emerging workforce.

Keywords: *Baby Boomers, Generation X, Generation Y, Emerging Workforce, Intrinsic and Extrinsic Factors, Organizational Commitment, Intent to Stay*

INTRODUCTION

"Gen Y respects those who validate them for who they are now, and who they want to be"

Peter Sheahan

The future and younger generations, the generation Y is going to form the majority of the workforce in the near future. This generation, also known as Millennial Generation, is noticeably different from their parents, the Baby Boomers or Generation X, because of different life experiences such as economic downturn, terrorism, war, growing concern for global warming etc. (A survey jointly conducted by Robert Hall International and Yahoo hot jobs). Members of this group are broadly classified as those who are born between 1979 and 1999 (Sheahan, 2005). The youngest members of this generation are still in schools whereas the forerunners are already in the workforce.

As most of the Baby Boomers are about to retire, Generation X-ers are taking senior executive position. This considerable generation will become a more and more central segment of the workforce. They are the managers, executives and leaders of tomorrow and in context of work related expectations, career concerns and choices they show different job preferences. Thus the organisations need to comprehend the preferences and values of incoming generations and carefully plan their strategies for attracting and retaining this talent as an integral part of their business models.

This generation is confident, independent, and goal-oriented. This segment of generation is born into technology and employees of this age may not even recall a time to spare without personal computers, mobiles, internet, cable television or many more gadgets. This is the generation which often knows more about the digital world than their teachers and parents (D'Netto and a survey jointly conducted by Robert Hall International and Yahoo hot jobs). Their significant time is often spend in online – socializing, online – shopping, instant messaging, chatting, downloading music and movies, job – hunting and doing many more activities those will help in their career building.

Generation Y possesses different work – related values and attitudes from their predecessors. To be on the positive side this generation is being marked as eager and tech – savvy that requires the work to be diversified, fun and challenging and want to be involved in decision – making and soliciting their ideas. On the contrary they have been labeled as generation that are more individualistic, self – focused, over – stimulated, want immediate payoffs such as independence, flexi – hours, an element of fun at work, high – maintenance generation hooked on high gratification (London, 2009; Twenge, 2010; D'Netto). In a survey conducted jointly by Robert Hall International and Yahoo hot jobs when asked to rank eleven factors related to job opportunities, survey respondents marked salary, benefits including health insurance and opportunities for professional learning and growth at the top of the list whereas the organisation's philanthropic activities and the CSR initiates at the bottom. This strengthens the fact that Generation Y prefers extrinsic work values over the intrinsic ones such as work autonomy, work identity etc. This generation considers quality of the workplace environment as an important factor. A survey of more than 2000 office workers found that more than half would work an extra hour a day if they had a better work environment (Pfeffer, 2007). Generation Y enjoy assortment and want jobs that include continued professional learning and career advancement. They are supposed to perform best when their potentials are fully explored and go with challenging task that drives them fully.

Given that the Generation Y is the central segment of young people who are just entered to the job scenario or are to be recruited in the near future, their recruitment is the top priority for the human resource management at many leading organizations (Twenge et. al., 2010). This knowledge of job preferences of Generation Y would be of great value to the recruiters and accordingly they can revise their strategies to suit specifically to this group. Also the members of this generation would be benefitted to begin their career with the organizations that exactly match their preferences (London, 2009; Twenge et. al., 2010). To be successful in the future, it will be important for organisations and managers to understand these new employees and the factors that motivate Gen Y to be satisfied, committed, and willing to stay with the organization.

The present study is conducted with the objective to explore the job characteristics the members of Generation Y prefer. In this process job characteristics have been broadly classified as intrinsic factors and extrinsic factors. Extrinsic factors generally focus on external demand or obtain an externally imposed reward contingency such as income, advancement opportunities and status. In contrast intrinsic factors focus on the process of work—the intangible rewards that reflect the inherent interest in the work, the learning potential, and the opportunity to be creative (Ryan & Deci, 2000).When intrinsically motivated a person is moved to act for the fun or challenge entailed rather than because of external prods, pressures, or rewards. The present study will then test how organizational commitment and intent to stay are affected by extrinsic and intrinsic factors.

LITERATURE REVIEW

Numerous studies have tried to explore what the future generations demand when it comes to job preferences (Yuva, 2007 and Rollsjö, 2008). These studies had found that some of the attractions for Generation Y were pay, job security, work – life balance, job profile, career advancement opportunities, and other benefits. However in a study, London (2009) divided benefits into intrinsic and extrinsic factors to determine which has a greater impact on future generation's job preferences. Researcher studied on 140 undergraduate students from Generation Y the main interactive and interaction effects of the type of rewards (intrinsic vs. extrinsic) and the time frame for which the rewards would be received (short term vs. long term) on job acceptance, satisfaction, organizational commitment and intent to stay. Researcher in the study concluded that the type of reward had significant effect on satisfaction, organizational commitment and intent to stay, while the intent to stay is significantly affected by the time frame.

The study by Twenge et. al. (2010) examines the work values of a nationally representative sample of 16,507 U.S. high school seniors in 1976, 1991, and 2006 representing Baby Boomers, Generation X, and Generation Y. Research findings suggested that that there is a generational shift in the work values and leisure is a salient work value for Generation Y than Generation X and Baby Boomers and there is a decrease in work centrality. Extrinsic values (e.g., status, money) peaked with Generation X but were still higher among Generation Y than among Boomers. Results further revealed that Generation Y does not favor altruistic work values (e.g., helping, societal worth) more than previous generations. Social values (e.g., making friends) and intrinsic values (e.g., an interesting, results-oriented job) were rated lower by Generation Y than by Boomers.

The George Bush School of Government and Public Service conducted a survey to identify and examine the career preferences and public sector perceptions among members of Generation Y so as to assist federal government in devising its recruitment and retention policies. For this purpose 567 undergraduates from the streams of political science and liberal arts were surveyed. Survey findings suggested that among various job related benefits the traditional benefits, salary and health insurance ranked most important while other intrinsic factors such as telecommuting and training opportunities were graded less important. The research further suggested that the vast majority believed that they would be switching sectors during their career and they would be in their initial position less than three years. As per the survey findings the public sector is the preferred place to work because the perceived benefits, job security and societal impact being the strengths of public sector. The results further confirmed that Generation Y considers social network sites a practicable recruitment tool.

Yvonne, Rod, and Shacklock (2012) used generational cohorts to examine similarities and differences in the relationship between supervisor-subordinate communication relationships, nurse's satisfaction with training and development, perceptions of wellbeing and in turn, affective commitment. Researchers in their study concluded that supervisor-subordinate communication relationships are important among all the three generations of nurses as these relationships are important for the satisfaction with training and development and wellbeing, but also significantly impact affective commitment. The findings confirmed that even when there are no significant differences in satisfaction levels (with supervisor-nurse communication relationships or training and development) across the nurses, the impact of other factors (perceptions of wellbeing or affective commitment) was significantly different for Baby Boomers compared with Gens X and Y. The reason for these differences as suggested by researchers is that nurse's generational cohort provides a rational account of the differences in their attitudes and perceptions. This explanation suggested by researchers indicates employer's need of generation - tailored supervision strategies to increase retention of nurses.

Swiggard, S. B. (2011) in Ph.D. thesis examined the relationship between generational cohort and employee commitment of 3 generational cohorts (Baby Boomers, Generation X, and Generation Y). As suggested by researcher the three generations think about, place emphasis on, and relate differently to, contextual issues of employee commitment. Across the three generations financial incentives and compensation are found to be the prime factors that influence people to join the organization and stay with them. Generation X placed relationship with boss at rank one, just slightly higher than the compensation. Relationships with coworkers and relationship with the boss are also dominant subthemes within employer impacts on commitment.

Hurst and Good (2009) conducted a research on 193 Gen Y college students from nine US universities with a purpose to understand the Generation Y's retail career expectations, perceptions of retail careers and career exploration of US retailing industry. Researchers suggested that pre – entry job expectations, perceptions of retail careers and future entitlement perceptions of employee obligations are significant predictors of career exploration.

The study by Solnet and Hood (2008) considers the impact of the Generation Y employees entering the hospitality sector and the paradigm shifts that will be required for the successful recruitment, selection, training, motivation and retention of new generation workforce in order to achieve organisational goals, given the strategic importance of human resource management in creating competitive and sustainable service organizations. Researchers also provide an insight into the Generation Y's work – related values, attitudes and behaviours. Researchers in this study proposed that (i) Gen Y employee's organizational commitment will be directly related to the level of commitment they perceive the organisation has in them personally; (ii) For Gen Y, organisational commitment and retention will have a less significant relationship in comparison to previous generational groups; (iii) Gen Y's job satisfaction will be derived from intrinsic factors, where the opportunity to take ownership and responsibility for a variety of work tasks and meaningful projects with proper support, training and development opportunities will be of high importance; (iv) Gen Y's perception of supervisor support will directly influence their job satisfaction; (v) Hospitality organisations can improve their appeal to potential Gen Y employees and communicate better with existing employees by harnessing Gen Y's innate habit of social networking.

Ching and Kee (2012) in their research paper presented in a conference tried to identify the preferred work values and career commitment of Generation Y teachers in Malaysia, as well as the moderating effect of cultural orientation on the work values-career commitment relationship of Generation Y teachers. The researchers in this study revealed that the preferred work values of Generation Y teachers are environmental (surrounding, association, and relations) and security (independence, economic, way of life, security and prestige). The findings further confirmed that intrinsic work values are correlated to career commitment ($r = .36$), and that intrinsic work values have significant impact on career commitment of individuals and explained 17% of the level of career commitment of Generation Y teachers. It is further confirmed from the study that cultural orientation is significant in explaining the level of career commitment of Generation Y teachers. D'Netto in his study further supported that organisations are likely to explore the full potential of Generation Y if they provide interesting work, greater flexibility, an enjoyable work environment, supportive leadership and offer a good work-life balance.

OBJECTIVES

(1) To determine whether generation Y look more for extrinsic or intrinsic rewards while looking for a job.

(2) To determine whether more extrinsic or intrinsic rewards are able to enhance their organizational commitment.

(3) To determine whether more extrinsic or intrinsic rewards increase their intention to stay in the organization.

HYPOTHESES

Based on review of literature, the following alternate hypotheses can be drawn

(1) Jobs with positive extrinsic factors and negative intrinsic factors will have higher level of preference.

(2) Jobs with positive extrinsic factors and negative intrinsic factors will enhance their organizational commitment.

(3) Jobs with positive extrinsic factors and negative intrinsic factors will lower their intention to stay in the organization.

RESEACH METHODOLOGY

Variables

The variables examined in this study were Motivation Factors (Extrinsic Vs. Intrisic), Job Preferences of Generation Y, Organisational Commitment and Intentions to Stay. Motivation Factors were studied as the independent variables. The dependent variables were Job Preferences of Generation Y, Organisational Commitment and Intentions to Stay.

Sample

To adduce the findings with empirical data, the survey was conducted using a structured questionnaire. The subjects for the study was selected by using random sampling technique. A sample of 56 postgraduate students was used who are going to enter the workforce in next year or two. Respondents were asked to read the scenario they were given. Then they were asked to assume that they were being offered this job and how likely they were to accept this job offer. Suppose they had to accept the job, they were then required to answer the questions based upon their perceptions about the job.

Tools Used

In order to ensure content validity the questionnaire was reviewed by academicians. Reliability of the scale was measured using Cronbach's Alpha test and the value of the coefficient was more than 0.7 in all components of the questionnaire sets thus indicating the goodness of scale measurement. A copy of questionnaire is attached (Appendix B).

Job Preference: Job preference was measured using a single item on five- point Likert-type scale(1=very unlikely, 5=very likely).

Organizational Commitment: Organizational affective Commitment was measured using a 10 item, five-point Likert-type scale(1=strongly disagree,5=strongly agree).The measure was developed by the researchers based on the items from Meyer and Allen(1997) & London(2009).This kind of commitment indicates an employee's emotional attachment and involvement in the organization. Reliability coefficient alpha comes out to be 0.83 (Table 1).

Intention to stay: Intention to stay was measured using a five item,five-point Likert-type scale(1=strongly disagree,5=strongly agree) .The measure was developed by the researchers based on the items from London (2009). Reliability coefficient alpha comes out to be 0.72 (Table 1).

RESULTS AND DATA ANALYSES

Characteristics of Respondents

The sample consisted of 56 respondents out of which 25 (44.6%) were female and 31(55.4%) were male. Their ages vary between 21-24 years and all were postgraduate management students of NCR region..

Type of Motivation Factors and Job Preference

A two - way ANOVA was used to assess the effects of types of motivation factors (extrinsic vs. intrinsic) on job preference. The Levene Statistic p – value = 0.864 is greater than á = 0.05 (Table 4), so we fail to reject the null hypothesis that the variances are all equal. Since the variances appear to be equal and the groups seem to be normally distributed (and we have random/independent samples), we may continue with ANOVA. As clear from the Table 2, there is a significant effect of types of motivation factors on the job preference $\{F(1, 54) = 42.894, p < 0.05\}$. Also it is clear from Table 3 that the mean score of job preference for extrinsic motivation factors are more than the mean scores for the intrinsic factors. This suggests that the hypothesis 1 is supported by the data analysis i.e. jobs with positive extrinsic factors and negative intrinsic factors will have higher level of preference.

Type of Motivation Factors and Organisational Commitment

A two - way ANOVA was used to assess the effects of types of motivation factors (extrinsic vs. intrinsic) on job preference. The Levene Statistic p – value = 0.708 > á = 0.05 (Table 4), so the null hypothesis is accepted that the variances are equal. Since the variances are equal and the organisational commitment for groups seem to be normally distributed, the basic assumptions for two – way ANOVA test are satisfied and hence ANOVA can be applied. It is evident from the Table 2, there is a significant effect of types of motivation factors on the organisational commitment of respondents of Generation Y {$F(1, 54) = 6.64$, $p = 0.013 < 0.05$}. Data analysis also indicates that the mean score of organisational commitment for intrinsic factors are less than the mean scores for extrinsic factors (Table 3). This suggests that the hypothesis 2 is supported by the data analysis i.e. jobs with positive extrinsic factors and negative intrinsic factors will enhance their organizational commitment.

Type of Motivation Factors and Intentions to Stay

The effect of motivation factors (intrinsic vs. extrinsic) on intentions to stay was analysed using two – way ANOVA test. The Levene Statistic p – value = 0.952 > á = 0.05 (Table 4) suggests that the two variances are equal and hence ANOVA can be applied. It is evident from the Table 2, there is a significant effect of types of motivation factors on the intention to stay of respondents of Generation Y {$F(1, 54) = 5.391$, $p = 0.024 < 0.05$}. Data analysis indicates that the mean score of intentions to stay for intrinsic factors are less than the mean scores for extrinsic factors (Table 3). Hypothesis 3 was not supported by data analysis i.e. jobs with positive extrinsic factors and negative intrinsic factors will lower their intention to stay in the organization is rejected.

DISCUSSION

Several other scholarly works tried to find out the job characteristics that are preferred by members of Generation Y. Some of the factors that attract these members of the new brigade to workplace are starting pay – packages, job security, promotions and career advancement opportunities, and many more benefits (Twenge et. al., 2010; D' Netto; Swiggard, 2011). On the other hand some place emphasis on the intrinsic factors (London, 2009; Ching and Kee, 2012). In the light of these findings, the present study has split job preference factors into intrinsic and extrinsic factors to determine which has greater impact on future workforce's job acceptance decision and also its been tried to find the effect of these motivation factors on Generation Y's organisational commitment and intentions to stay.

The current study's results revealed that the type of motivation factors may have an effect on the job preference decisions in Generation Y's future employees. These results are based on the hypothetical job scenerio presented to the respondents, however, the real – life job choices may be different. Respondents were asked to answer some questions based upon the assumption that they have accepted the job.

Findings showed that extrinsic factors such as starting salary, good chances of promotion in the near future, workplace environment, assessibility of the home from the workplace, flexi – timinings etc. would be the main predictors for the job acceptance. Results showed that those respondents who received extrinsic factors reported higher levels of organizational commitment, and intent to stay with the organization. These results are supported by the studies of Twenge, (2010) and Swiggard, (2011). Twenge (2010) in his study concluded that the importance of intrinsic values is declining slightly over the generations and he suggested that the young generations are further not trying to find meaning in their work. The one reason behind these may be the fact that the new generations are to work long hours under stressful conditions and thus they lack work – family balance, peace of mind and good health. This may be the reason of their focus on extrinsic factors and they demand high salaries or the flexi – timings or prefer the workplaces that are closer to their residents.

In contrary to other research findings, the results of the current study suggested that extrinsic factors will determine their intention to stay in an organisation. These results are not supported by the studies of London (2009); Yvonne, Rod, and Shacklock (2012). In her research, London concluded that the respondents who received intrinsic rewards reported inclination to stay with the organisation.

These findings suggest that the recruitment policy makers should focus not only on the intrinsic factors but their attention should be more toward the other side as well and they should accordingly change policies to attract and retain this potential pool of youngesters.

LIMITATIONS AND SCOPE FOR FUTURE RESEARCH

The current study was conducted on a sample of 56 respondents from a Management institute in NCR region. The results of the study cannot be generalized for the entire population. Moreover, these kind of studies need to be replicated in different regions with respondents from different educational backgrounds to focus more on the perceptions of individuals for recruitment, enhancing organisational commitment and finally to reduce attrition.

Based on the findings of the study, several recommendations for future research are offered. First some effort should be made to validate the results of this study among other samples and populations. Second, more scenarios could be created having low extrinsic and high intrinsic factors or scenarios with short term or long term benefits which could be more fruitful for further analysis. Thirdly, to have an extensive outlook of Generation Y's job preferences more of variables such as superior – subordinate relationships, communication, job satisfaction etc. may be included.

REFERENCES

[1] Brown, S., Carter, B., Collins, M., Gallerson, C., Griffin, G., Greer, J., Griffith, R., Johnson, E. and Richardson, K., "Generation Y in Workplace", A Survey Conducted by The George Bush School of Government and Public Service

[2] Ching, S. L. and Kee, D. M. H., (2012) "Work Values-Career Commitment Relationship of Generation Y Teachers in Malaysia", 2012 International Conference on Economics Marketing and Management, IPEDR Vol. 28

[3] D'Netto, B. "Generation Y: Human Resource Management Implications", retrieved from http://www.wbiconpro.com/452-Brian.pdf

[4] Hurst, J. L. and Good, L. K., (2009) "Generation Y and career choice: The impact of retail career perceptions, expectations and entitlement perceptions", Career Development International, Vol. 14 (6), pp.570 – 593

[5] London, A., (2009) "The Impact of Intrinsic and Extrinsic Motivation on Job Choice in Generation Y", Paper Presented in the 4th Annual Siena College Student Conference in Business

[6] Meyer, J., and Allen, N. (1997). Commitment in the workplace. Thousand Oaks, CA: SAGE Publications.

[7] Pfeffer, J., (2007), "Thinking outside the cube", *Business 2.0,* vol. 8(3), pp. 60

[8] Rollsjö, A., (2008) "Attraction and Retention of Generation Y Employees", Unpublished Thesis

[9] Ryan, R. M. and Edward L. Deci, E. L., (2000) "Intrinsic and Extrinsic Motivations: Classic Definitions and New Directions", Contemporary Educational Psychology, Vol. 25, pp. 54 – 67

[10] Sheahan, P., (2005) "Generation Y: Thriving and Surviving with Generation Y at Work", Published by Prahran, Victoria: Hardy Grant

[11] Solnet, D., and Hood, A. (2008) "Generation Y as hospitality employees: Framing a research agenda", Journal of Hospitality and Tourism Management, Vol. 15, pp 59 – 68

[12] Swiggard, S. B., (2011) "Generations and Employee Commitment: An Exploration of the Impact of Changes in Technology, Home and Family Structure, and Employer – Employee Relationships", Unpublished Thesis, retrieved from http/www.proquest

[13] Twenge, J. M., Campbell, S. M., Hoffman, B. J. and Lance, C. E., (2010) "Generational Differences in Work Values: Leisure and Extrinsic Values Increasing, Social and Intrinsic Values Decreasing", Journal of Management, Vol. 36 (5), pp. 1117 – 1142

[14] Yuva, J., (2007) "Corporations Should", Inside Supply Management, pp. 20 – 23.

[15] Yvonne, B., Rod, F. W. and Shacklock, K. H., (2012) "Communication, Training, Wellbeing and Commitment across Nurse Generations", Nursing Outlook, Vol. 60(1), pp. 7 – 15

APPENDIX A

Table 1: Reliability Measures

Construct	*No. of items*	*Cronbach alpha*
Organisational commitment	10	0.83
Intentions to stay	05	0.72

Table 2: Two – Way Analysis of Variance for Test of Type of Motivation Factors

Source	*Job Preference*					*Organisational Commitment*					*Intention to Stay*				
	SS	*df*	*MS*	*F*	*Sig.*	*SS*	*df*	*MS*	*F*	*Sig.*	*SS*	*df*	*MS*	*F*	*Sig.*
TypeM	15.27	1	15.27			199.38	1	199.38			45.51	1	45.51		
Error	19.28	54	0.36	42.89	<0.05	1621.46	54	30.03	6.64	<0.05	455.8	54	8.44	5.4	< 0.05
Total	34.55	55				1820.84	55				501.3	55			

Table 3: Descriptive Statistics for Type of Motivation Factors

Types of Motivation Factor	*n*	*Job Preference*		*Organisational Commitment*		*Intention to Stay*	
		M	*S.D.*	*M*	*S.D.*	*M*	*S.D.*
Extrinsic	44	4.02	0.628	40.18	5.723	19.36	2.93
Intrinsic	12	2.75	0.452	35.58	4.400	17.17	2.79

Table 4: Levene's Test of Equality of Variances

Job Preference				*Organisational Commitment*				*Intention to Stay*			
F	*df1*	*df2*	*Sig.*	*F*	*df1*	*df2*	*Sig.*	*F*	*df1*	*df2*	*Sig.*
0.30	1	54	>0.05	0.141	1	54	>0.05	0.004	1	54	>0.05

APPENDIX B

Questionnaire Used for Research Work

Age:

Gender:

Qualification:

Please study a **hypothetical job description** mentioned underneath and answers the questions based upon how you would feel about such kind of job.

Scenario

Assume that you have received a job offer with the following characteristics:

The job offers you a higher starting salary than you have expected. The company is known to provide regular bonus every year. The company assures good chances of promotion in short duration. The physical settings (i.e. look, design, office furnishings)are very attractive. The work place is easy to access from your residence. There are flexible working hours & it is five days a week. The job profile is not of much interest to you. Your boss has the final say regarding how you have to perform your job tasks. No regular feedback is provided.

Survey	very likely		very unlikely		
How likely are you to accept this job?	1	2	3	4	5

Suppose for any reason you have to join the organization. Answer the following questions based upon your perceptions about the current job. Place a tick in the appropriate box.

Questions	*Strongly Disagree*	*Moderately Disagree*	*Neither Agree nor Disagree*	*Moderately Agree*	*Strongly Agree*
I am very pleased to join current organization					
I will recommend the work place to my friend who is looking for job					
I feel this organization deserves my loyalty.					
I am very sincere in performing my job tasks					
I put my best efforts to serve the organization beyond normally expected for organization success					
I feel emotionally attached to this organization.					
I would accept any type of job assignment to be with the organization					
I can gain a lot by staying in the organization for a long duration					
I feel proud to tell others about my organization					
I feel like "part of the family "at my organization					
It was my mistake to join this organization					
I intend to stay in the organization for long duration					
I intend to stay in the organization until I get another job					
I want to quit the job immediately					
I am very desperately looking for another job					

A Conceptual Paper on the Impact of Knowledge Management Techniques on the Knowledge Sharing Amongst Gen Y in Corporate Scenario

Arushi Sabharwal, Simran Kaur and Bhavneesh Juneja

Master of Business Administration, Delhi Technological University, Delhi

ABSTRACT

This paper hones in on the challenge to inform owners and managers of today's corporate to improve the attraction, motivation and retention of Gen Y employees. A key finding from the literature is that Gen Y employees score lower on those measures where higher scores are seen more favorably (e.g., job satisfaction, engagement, commitment), while conversely, Gen Y employees display higher scores on the constructs that an organization would hope would be lower (e.g., turnover intentions). Employee attitudes are significantly influenced by management policies and practices, as well as organizational culture and climate (Kusluvan, Kusluvan, Ilhan, & Buyruk, 2010; Schneider, 1980; Solnet & Paulsen, 2005). The paper aims to identify the impact of various knowledge management tools/techniques and their importance to the motivation of Gen Y employees who are full of creativity, are being provided the required resources but usually are not inclined towards sharing because of the self centered attitudes.

OBJECTIVE

To analyze various knowledge management initiatives and tools to understand their role and importance in the corporate scenario for Gen Y.

INTRODUCTION

There are various paths by which organizations come to the realization that they must do more to manage their knowledge. For many, it follows in the wake of reengineering and downsizing: with fewer people to do the work, they need to equip each to work smarter. For others, it's a wake-up call from a major customer, taking their business to a more state-of-the-art competitor.

Knowledge management became a buzzword in the 90's and continues to be important in the new century. The concept is based on the idea that firms have both knowledge and physical assets. And, just like physical assets, knowledge assets must be managed.

It is known that much of what a corporation knows resides in documents and between the ears of its employees. Yet we have not had systematic ways of capturing, distilling, and using this knowledge. Knowledge management is an effort to create these systems.

Knowledge is perishable. The shelf life of expertise is limited because new technologies, products, and services continually pour into the marketplace. No one can hoard knowledge. People and companies must constantly renew, replenish, expand, and create more knowledge.

Acc. To Alavi and Leidner: Knowledge is a justified personal belief that increases an individual's capacity to take action. They use the idea due to Churchman that "knowledge resides in the user and not in the collection of information". To them, action refers to: 1) Physical skills and competencies, 2) Cognitive /Intellectual activity. However, Davenport and Prusak argue that knowledge is a fluid mix of experience, values, Contextual Information, and expert insight that provides a framework for evaluation and incorporating new experience and information.

There are certain implications which can be drawn from these definitions: **First**, for one person's knowledge to be used by another, they must communicate it in a form usable by the other person. **Second**, only information that is actively processed can be useful. **Third**, knowledge may be explicit or tacit. These implications are discussed in the following sections.

Key Knowledge Components

Experience: Knowledge is not something that is gained instantly; it develops over time. Experience puts new situations and events into context with respect to what happened before. It allows us to make connections.

Ground truth: Ground truth refers to truth obtained from experience at ground level rather than from theory. Thus, we know what actually worked, not what theory says should work.

Judgment: Unlike data and information, knowledge contains judgment. Judgment is required, in particular, to respond to new situations and new information. When knowledge stops evolving, it turns into opinion or dogma and that is dangerous.

Tacit vs. explicit knowledge: Knowledge comes in two dimensions: explicit and tacit. Explicit knowledge is typically structured and retrievable. It is often written down in books of procedures. Tacit knowledge, on the other hand, is partly or largely inexpressible. It includes the rich, complex, accumulated expertise that resides in people's heads. The best you can do is locate someone who knows, point the knowledge seeker to that person, and encourage them to interact. This idea is behind the use of "yellow pages" in an organization. El Sawy (1998) argues that tacit knowledge and explicit knowledge operate together in a stereo effect. All forms of knowledge have both components. These components are combined holistically and are almost inseparable. They must be managed together but each in its own way. Tacit knowledge transfer can be direct or indirect. Direct approaches include imitation, identification, and learning by doing. Indirect knowledge transfer involves the use of information. Here mass media, manuals, books, computer programs, accounting procedures, among others are used.

Knowledge Management Strategies

McKinsey and Company (1998) argues that as traditional structural advantages decay and companies enter global competition, strategies formed around knowledge can change the rules and create new paths to profitability. Knowledge as an asset differs from physical assets in that it has the characteristics of being leveraged for fetching increasing returns and having uncertain value. Managing knowledge requires the appropriate tools. Here are some navigational aids:-

A north star represents the purpose, sense of identity, and core principles that guide an organization. Knowledge self-organizes around organizational purpose. Monsanto has a director of knowledge management. Dow Chemical has a director of intellectual asset management

An organizational compass consists of guiding principles and strategy. Best-practice companies in knowledge provide a way to expand knowledge by taking an integrated, multi-modal systems approach. **Texas Instruments and Chevron** are noted for sharing best practices, both internally and with benchmarking partners.

The crew. Knowledge is embodied in people. It's impossible to talk about knowledge without addressing the way people work together, learn together, and grow in knowledge individually and collectively. Companies that are serious about knowledge foster an environment and culture that support continuous learning. At **Ernst & Young**, part of each consultant's compensation is based on knowledge sharing activities.

The tools and techniques used for managing knowledge in the corporates entail broadly non IT tools (brainstorming, Peer Assist, Learning Reviews, After Action Review, Storytelling, Knowledge Café, Community of Practice, APO KM Assessment tool) & the IT based tools (Document Management System, Blogs, Social Network Services, VOIP, Expert Locator, Collaborative Virtual Workspaces)

LITERATURE REVIEW

APO KM Assessment Tool

It is based on the APO KM Framework.

The starting point of the APO KM Framework is the understanding of the organizational vision, mission, business goals, and strategic directions. These help the organization to identify and analyze core competencies and capabilities that it has and need to develop. The four accelerators (people, processes, technology, and leadership) can help the organization understand to what extent these drivers and enablers are prevalent in the organization, enabling a successful

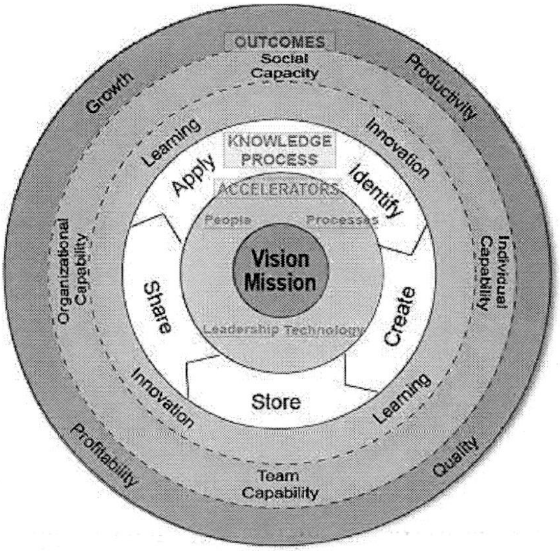

KM implementation. The five core knowledge processes (identify, create, store, share, and apply) provide an initial assessment of existing practices related to KM that can be leveraged on during implementation. Organizations, sometimes, can already be practicing KM without realizing it. The outcomes of KM efforts measure the effectiveness of the knowledge processes supported by the critical success factors (accelerators, vision, and mission). The outcomes must be able to demonstrate enhancement of learning and innovation that build individual, team, organizational, and societal capabilities and, ultimately, lead to improvements in the quality of products and services, productivity, profitability, and growth. The total score of the assessment is then compared against the KM Maturity model shown below. This will show the KM maturity level of the organization.

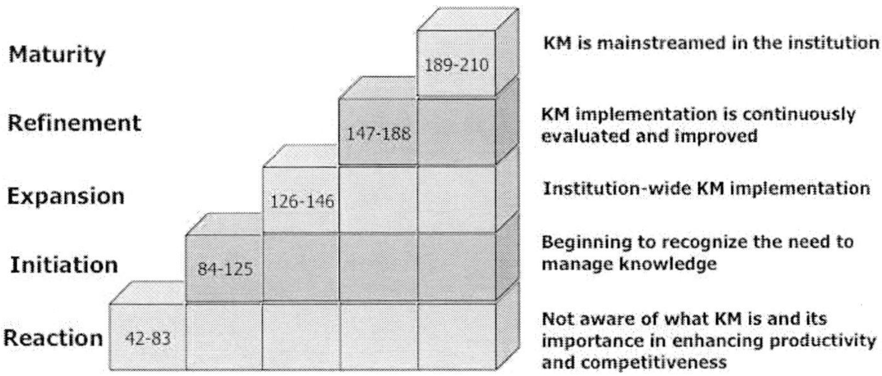

The results of the assessment provide an understanding of the level of KM readiness in an organization. The five levels can be described as:

Reaction Level: The organization is not aware of what KM is and its importance in enhancing productivity and competitiveness.

Initiation Level: The organization is beginning to recognize the need to manage knowledge or may already be initiating a pilot KM project.

Expansion Level: KM is fully implemented and deployed.

Control Level: Implementation of KM is continually evaluated for continuous improvement.

Maturity Level: KM is fully mainstreamed within the organization.

With respect to the Gen- Y context, a **Knowledge Worker Competency Plan** is a personal competency plan for individuals to develop the critical skills required to become an effective knowledge worker viz. awareness and understanding of the knowledge worker skill, the will to apply practice of the knowledge worker skill and the ability to teach others in this competence.

This additional level of competence helps to recognize and create a culture of 'teachers' in the organization. After all, teaching is 'knowledge sharing' and this where organizations face a problem with Gen – Y when their attitudes conflict with the orthodox individuals in the organization. The following table talks of the tools and techniques which are most relevant to the said context of Gen Y personnel.

Tool/ Techniques	*Description*	*USP*
Communities of Practice	A group of people who share a common interest working together over an extended period to explore ways of working in a specific area of knowledge.	For Gen Y, this technique is as cool as social networking.
Peer assist	Gaining input and insight from experts/ other people outside the team to reuse and reapply existing knowledge and experience.	Firsthand knowledge transfer, accessing the organization's knowledge base.
Knowledge café	A group of people having an open, creative conversation in an informal environment on a topic of mutual interest.	Informal learning through dialogue suits Gen Y.
Knowledge Marketplace	Allows the matching of a knowledge requirement with someone with expertise (think of it as a dating service for knowledge).	Starts the connection of people to people, People to documents and documents to people

The following framework is a general purpose tool that can be applied to a variety of problems and solutions and adapted to individual work styles.

Table 1. Sample Rendering of the Framework

Tool				Activity Phase				Activity Level			Agent Type			Artifact Type			Focus		
Name	Practice	Method	Technology	Creation	Retention	Transfer	Utilization	High-level Process	Mid-level Process	Decision or Action	Individual	Automated	Organizational	Explicit	Implicit	Tacit	Agent	Artifact	Process

The framework's theoretical roots focus on the role of knowledge in complex systems and fundamental knowledge interactions. This focus provides a solid foundation that can be built upon, applied and adapted to different contexts. So, while this framework can be used to do highly formalized analysis, it also works for simpler, back-of-the-envelope analysis, or even to sort out a couple of facts. It works for engineers and psychologists and can be used to discuss and describe information policies in neutral language that is neither business-centric nor technology-centric. The framework was designed primarily to support tool classification, hence the term classification framework. It helps individuals identify and differentiate among the roles different tools can play in a knowledge management system. One of the easiest ways to evaluate a tool is to describe its characteristics in terms of its interactions with each of the element subtypes of the framework.

Using the Framework to Identify Knowledge Flow Elements

Underlying the application of the framework in tool classification is the ability to use the framework to identify and classify the individual elements of knowledge flows and their supporting knowledge management systems (i.e. agents, artifacts and behaviors). Mapping knowledge flow elements to agents, artifacts and behaviors raises the level of abstraction and, in effect, simplifies the elements. For instance, in case of e-mail, the following will be the aspects.

Activity Phase — Which Activity Areas Does E-mail Support?

Activity Level — On What Does E-mail Tend to Have the Most Impact?

- On low-level decisions and actions because it is one of the ways (sometimes a primary way) that people engage in one-on-one communication with others, decide priorities, allocate tasks and exchange the small bits of information that drive individual actions

- On mid-level activities because it is not uncommon to see business processes at various project and program levels designed around specific e-mail capabilities and/or specific protocols established for the use of e-mail within the organization
- On high-level business processes because of its well-documented impact on organizational culture, openness, knowledge sharing and structure. For most organizations, the impact of e-mail on strategic processes is fairly low. For businesses with virtual organizations or Internet-based sales and marketing components, however, e-mail is likely to be a critical enabler of core competency.

Agent Type — What Types of Agents Interact with E-mail and How? E-mail tools are automated agents. The primary interfaces tend to be with individuals and not organizations, keeping in mind that organizations cannot type or read.

Artifact Type — How Does E-mail Interact with Each Type of Artifact? E-mail systems inherently accept and reject certain forms of codification and rendering.

Focus — Is E-mail Optimized for Interactions with Agents, Artifacts or Processes?

Tool				Activity Phase				Activity Level			Agent Type			Artifact Type			Focus		
Name	Practice	Method	Technology	Creation	Retention	Transfer	Utilization	High-level Process	Mid-level Process	Decision or Action	Individual	Automated	Organizational	Explicit	Implicit	Tacit	Agent	Artifact	Process
E-mail			X		X	X		X	X	X		X		X				X	

Barriers to Knowledge Sharing While Dealing with Gen Y Employees

Before an organization can develop a successful knowledge management process, the company must understand the barriers to sharing knowledge and develop methods in their planning to overcome them. Barriers can include organizational structure barriers, boundary barriers, management support barriers, and technology barriers.

A study conducted in 1994, to determine why best practices did not transfer well between sections within the same organization, showed a successful method of performing a certain procedure would go unnoticed or shared for years. Once the best practice is identified it would take an average of two years before the method migrated to other sections to use within the company. Gabriel Szulanski, who led the research, stated there were three barriers that caused the delay in identifying and sharing the best practices in the firm. They include the following:

- **"Ignorance":** This means the person with the information didn't think anyone could use it and others in the company did not know anyone had the knowledge.
- **"The lack of preexisting relationships":** The separate sections have no interaction with each other. Normally people acquire knowledge from someone they admire, know or interact with. Seldom will one adapt another person's new process if that person does not have a relationship already established.
- **"Lack of motivation":** The benefit of using the new method and how it can help my department may not be fully understood.

CASE EXAMPLES

McDonald's: The fast food chain works extensively with explicit knowledge in a centralized approach. Its strategy is to identify best practices and drive them across their network of locations. The firm provides specifications for everything, from how to cook hamburgers to how to clean up the store. They have rigid standards for both products and processes. It is not possible to tell whether its value is derived from the brand name or from the shared knowledge. A typical manager receives 1500 to 3000 hours of regional training before going to Hamburger U. in Illinois. Comparable outlets benchmark performance jointly, set operations, and make product mix and service decisions. They are tied together by their management information system that sends sales data to headquarters hourly. Corporate uses MIS to control valuable knowledge that links outlets. (Based on: McKinsey 1998)

Monsanto: Until the mid-1990'sm Monsanto consisted of a chemical group ($3billion/year) and a life sciences group ($5billion/year), Chemicals required low cost and high quality. They were best practices oriented. Life sciences innovation oriented and involved skilled scientists and working with biotech partners. The two groups had different knowledge strategies and different kinds of people. Management decided to spin off the chemicals group to concentrate on the life sciences. Monsanto undertook a Knowledge Management Architecture project in an attempt to codify corporate knowledge. By letting employees share global knowledge locally, the project aimed to combine the diversity and quantity of knowledge of a large firm with the accessibility to knowledge of a small firm. (Based on: McKinsey 1998 and Davenport and Prusak 1998)

Chevron: Chevron claims to have obtained the following tangible benefits from knowledge management: reduced operating costs from $9.4 billion to $7.4billion in seven years; reduced energy costs by $200 million/year, increased the output per employee by 30 barrels per year, and improved safety performance by 50%. Intangible benefits include (according to CEO Derr), making everyone's work more interesting and challenging and making jobs more fulfilling and personally rewarding. These gains were obtained through changes in process, culture, and technology and through adopting best practices.

Chevron improved drilling performance by sharing information among locations from Africa to Australia to Kazakhstan. They use software programs to capture lessons learned from the first wells drilled in an area. Well costs dropped by 20% and cycle time by 40% in some cases. These are big numbers since drilling ships cost $250,000/day. (Velker 1999).

Netscape: Netscape saw its market share erode in 1997 as Microsoft offered a free browser. By 1998, Netscape made the source code to the browser publicly available. They gave away knowledge that had cost them millions to generate and which their competitors guarded closely. They decided that revenue would be generated by server software and by new developments resulting from developers generating products to work with Netscape. Like Linux, they assumed that the efforts of many programs outside the company would turn Netscape into the standard. Initially, most Netscape developers were unknown to them. The extent to which this knowledge strategy worked is not known, since Netscape has been merged into America On Line. (Based on: McKinsey, 1998)

Booz Allen & Hamilton: This well known consulting firm found itself, in 1992, in the position of not having its own knowledge management system and having clients seeking knowledge management help. By 1996, the firm had created its own knowledge management system (called Knowledge On Line(KOL) run on an intranet) that was being accessed each month by 62% of its staff members involved with commercial clients. The system is centralized and relatively small (1.5 Gb), in part because it is text only and in part because it does not reproduce existing databases but gives access to them. The system is not cheap. In 1997, a ¼ million dollars were spent on upgrades and support and ¾ million dollars were spent on content management. With 100 documents per month being added to KOL, content creation is the major cost. They use a specialist to debrief consultants to obtain lessons learned from each engagement. They also fund a dozen consultant "innovation teams" each year to share expertise in a given field.

Ericsson: At Ericsson, KM initiatives focus on information sharing, virtual community building & individual competence development. Current KM initiatives are include Zopps and the web academy which is an internet based competence-boosting network outside the Ericsson firewalls which provides a "playground" for employees & families to interact and share knowledge of the company. Another initiative is Business Intelligence Centre which includes a password protected "executive corner" for top management to share strategic information and general internet portals to external information specifically bought in plus and other information fed in by the staff. Competency Exchange and KNACK (knowledge and competency keys) is also the first of these in the internal web site accessible only from within Ericsson Microwave system. KNACK provides materials, templates, information about internal courses/ programmes as well as job listings and newsletters foe everyone in Ericsson. Stargate is a new initiative growing out of Ericsson Business Consulting; this is an online tool for systematizing both business information and the strategic competence areas of consultants. Another imitative by Ericsson is Experience Engine in which knowledge brokers/ supports the knowledge transfer within and between different customer projects at Ericsson software technology.

Siemens: - Siemens' Information and Communication Networks Division is a global provider of telecommunication solutions, active in more than 100 countries. The company's traditional business used to be quite simple and straightforward: it dominated its home market by means of a close relationship with a regulated national telecom monopoly. Siemens used this position to sell integrated products to other national telecoms around the world. The company was forced to rely more than ever on the front lines of the organization, which are more knowledgeable about the latest developments. Sales people had to act more and more like consultants. Skills like business analysis, business development, network planning, and outsourcing and so on were suddenly in high demand, albeit dispersed globally. Solution selling had become an important value-adding activity. Doing this right meant identifying best practices quickly, sharing them on a global scale and making sure that they were reused for profit in similar settings. The idea of ShareNet as "global knowledge sharing network" was born.

The fundamental paradigm of the ShareNet network is that any reader/user is also a publisher. There is no central or single "source of wisdom". The idea of ShareNet is to gather the collective knowledge of the worldwide community with as little bureaucracy and "barriers to entry" as possible.

LEARNINGS (L)

Successful enterprises have used knowledge sharing to spread the best practices developed in house by analyzing the ground realities. As in the case with Monsanto, the collaborative effort of the two divisions resulted in better synergies and faster pace of knowledge dissemination. At Chevron, it was observed that apart from the tangible benefits of applying knowledge management techniques, there are certain intangibles also achieved which are of much more significance in terms of development of soft skills of the employees. Netscape presents to us a case of a failed knowledge management initiative that had a sound premise but could not deliver fruitful outputs because of the lack of communication. As witnessed in the case of Ericsson, allowing people to commit mistakes and recapitulating is important. The most vital learning from these cases is that it is the vision and the will of the leader that can make or break the knowledge management initiative. Being the leader, one has to set benchmarks for people to follow and the technology will then facilitate put things into the right perspective. Senior members of management team should finalise their own profiles prior to telling others. The idea of ShareNet in case of Siemens is to gather the collective knowledge of the worldwide community with as little bureaucracy and "barriers to entry" as possible. After going through a plethora of text and analyzing the practices observed at multiple organizations, it can be concluded that in order to sustain in modern times, the organizations need to be conscious of the importance of promoting knowledge sharing and knowledge management initiatives because of its impact on the productivity of the Gen Y employees. The level of creativity that we come across in today's environment needs to be tapped and directed well so that it can lead to innovation, the buzz word for survival today.

SUGGESTED ACTION (A)

Based on our analysis of the different scenarios wherein the knowledge management tools and techniques have been deployed, there has been considerable success in cases of strong leadership directing and influencing the Gen-Y. In order to further enhance the knowledge sharing amongst various stakeholders especially Gen-Y, the use of enabling & substantive change management levers right from the initial days needs to be done. Also, the effectiveness of the various tools needs to be audited time to time so that they do not lose their purpose to the disease of obsolescence. Especially for Gen Y, these tools need to be revamped, repackaged, rebranded and reinvented.

PERFORMANCE (P)

With the application of suggested actions, it is hoped that an enhancement in knowledge sharing can be achieved and the increasing trend of job hopping can also be checked. The provision of innovation and facilitating communication through e-tools can lead to better collaboration and a sense of association with the enterprise.

REFERENCES

[1] Angell, I. (2007, July/August). The Knowledge Scam. Information Strategy, 3, 23-24.

[2] Borghoff, U. & Pareschi, R. (Eds.). (2008). Information Technology for Knowledge Management. Heidelberg, Germany: Springer.

[3] Bottomley, A. (2008, July/August). Jumping on the Bandwagon. Information Strategy, 3, 25-26.

[4] Caggiano, C. (1998, January). How're You Gonna Keep 'Em Down On the Firm? Inc. Online, 1-9. Retrieved February 11, 1999 from the World Wide Web: http://www.inc.com/incmagazine/archives/01980701.html

[5] Davenport, T., De Long, D. & Beers, M. (1998, Winter). Successful Knowledge Management Projects. Sloan Management Review (39), 1-2. Retrieved February 9, 1999 from the World Wide Web: http://mitsloan.mit.edu/smr/past/1998/smr3924.html

[6] Davenport, T. & Prusak, L. (1997). Working Knowledge: How Organizations Manage What They Know. Boston, MA: Harvard Business School.

[7] Davenport, T. & Prusak, L. (1998). Know What You Know. Retrieved February 17, 1999 from the World Wide Web: http://www.brint.com/km/davenport/cio/know.htm

[8] Davenport, T. (1998, February 1). Some Principles of Knowledge Management. Retrieved February 11. 1999 from the World Wide Web: http://kman.bus.utexas.edu/kman/kmprin.htm#sharing

[9] O'Dell, C. & Grayson, C.J. (2003). If Only We Know What We Know: The Transfer of Internal Knowledge and Best Practice. New York: Simon & Schuster.

[10] Quinn, J., Anderson, P. & Finkelstein, S. (2004). Managing Professional intellect: Making the Most of the Best. Harvard Business Review on Knowledge Management. Boston, MA: Harvard Business School Publishing.

[11] Sol Common Online newsletter. (2005). Retrieved February 9, 1999 from the World Wide Web: http://learning.mit.edu/com/news/newsletter2.html

[12] Stewart, T. (2011, March 17). Brain Power: Who Owns It ...How They Profit From It. Retrieved February 6, 1999 from the World Wide Web: http://www.pathfinder.com/fortune/1997/970317/cap.html

[13] Stewart, T. & Kaufman, D. (2009, November 27). Getting Real About Brainpower. Retrieved February 7, 1999 from the World Wide Web: http://www.pathfinder.com/fortune/1995/leadedgebrain.htm

[14] A taxonomy of knowledge management software tools: origins and applications: Peter Tyndale

[15] 12 Principles of Knowledge Management By Verna Allee

[16] Generation Y Employees: An Examination of Work Attitude Differences- Solnet David, Kralj Anna, Kandampully J.

Motivational Strategies for Gen Y: An Opinion Survey of Bank Executives

Meenakshi Kansal and Shalini Garg

University School of Management Studies, Guru Gobind Singh Indraprastha University, Dwarka, Delhi

ABSTRACT

The preset opinion survey is concerned with the motivational strategies for the Gen Y with special reference to banking industry. To retain young talent is a big problem for any industry these days. Reasons found are higher expectations, impatience and enormous competive opportunities available in the market. Banking sector is not an exception as it has also been affected by the higher expectations of Gen Y. The purpose of the of the survey was to understand the motivational strategies for bank executives. Motivational and Hygiene factors based on Herzberg's two factor theory have been studied on a sample of 200 and it has been found that the respondents want both the factors as job content .

Keywords: *Motivation, Hygiene, Motivational Strategies*

INTRODUCTION

"Empowered, disappointed, savvy, optimistic, unemployed—for anyone trying to decipher Generation Y (also known as Millennials), it means starting with a fistful of contradictions. With a population estimated at roughly 72 million, Generation Y is the most educated, diverse, tech-proficient, and soon-to-be largest American generation ever. It is also a generation that distrusts traditional advertising and will more likely listen to the opinions of their peers."(Judith Aquino)

What do todays' Gen Y expects from their jobs? Do they want just a higher salary and perks? Or do they want security and a secured future, good relationships with co-workers and management, care for their needs, opportunities for growth and advancement – or something else altogether? This is an important question, because it's at the root of motivation, the base of a job design, the art of retaining young talent, the art of engaging with members of one's team in such a way that they give their very best performance and be satisfied in whatever organisation they are.

An article published in the newspaper Mint 'What I want at work" mentions a study by Meghna Lama and Ankur Gupta that all 20 something employees are too demanding, restless, and on the lookout for instant gratification. Another view expressed by Madhvi Lall, regional head, HR , for India and South Asia at Standard Chartered Bank is that " young employees are committed , prompt about their deadlines, tech savvy and fast learners; but in return they want quick recognition and regular feedback about their contribution to organisational growth".

By 2025, the millennial generation will make up approximately 75% of our workforce. But generation Y's impact on the way we work — and how we think about work — is already being felt. So how does this change the way we need to think about aligning, engaging, and motivating our people? (HR Pulse News Desk, 2012)

Motivation-Hygiene Theory-Job Based Theory of Motivation

The psychologist Fredrick Herzberg asked the same question in the 1950s and 60s as a means of understanding employee satisfaction. He set out to determine the effect of attitude on motivation, by asking people to describe situations where they felt really good, and really bad, about their jobs. What he found was that people who felt good about their jobs gave very different responses from the people who felt bad.

These results form the basis of Herzberg's Motivation-Hygiene Theory (sometimes known as Herzberg's Two Factor Theory.) Published in his famous article "One More Time: How do You Motivate Employees", the conclusions he drew were extraordinarily influential, and still form the bedrock of good motivational practice nearly half a century later.

Herzberg's findings revealed that certain characteristics of a job are consistently related to job satisfaction, while different factors are associated with job dissatisfaction. These are:

Factors for Satisfaction	Factors for Dissatisfaction
Achievement	Company Policies
Recognition	Supervision
The work itself	Relationship with Supervisor and Peers
Responsibility	Work conditions
Advancement	Salary
Growth	Status
	Security

The conclusion he drew is that job satisfaction and job dissatisfaction are not opposites.

- The opposite of Satisfaction is No Satisfaction.
- The opposite of Dissatisfaction is No Dissatisfaction.

Remedying the causes of dissatisfaction will not create satisfaction. Nor will adding the factors of job satisfaction eliminate job dissatisfaction. If you have a hostile work environment, giving someone a promotion will not make him or her satisfied. If you create a healthy work environment but do not provide members of your team with any of the satisfaction factors, the work they're doing will still not be satisfying. (MindTools.com)

According to Herzberg, the factors leading to job satisfaction are "separate and distinct from those that lead to job dissatisfaction." Therefore, if you set about eliminating dissatisfying job factors you may create peace, but not necessarily enhance performance. This placates your workforce instead of actually motivating them to improve performance.

The characteristics associated with job dissatisfaction are called hygiene factors. When these have been adequately addressed, people will not be dissatisfied nor will they be satisfied. If you want to motivate your team, you then have to focus on satisfaction factors like achievement, recognition, and responsibility.

LITERATURE REVIEW

Golshon et al. (2011) found in their study that employees' motivators are related significantly to their intrinsic job satisfaction. However, employees' hygiene factors are not significantly related to extrinsic job satisfaction.According to Judith Aqino (2012), like every other generation, Gen Y has been affected by the recent recession and weak economy.For many members of this group, this has meant difficulty landing their first job or being underemployed.The research by Karefalk A. et al. (2007) has shown that Generation Y have a different attitude towards work than previous organisations. It has also shown that general characteristics of Gen Y are very strong and has conveyed the importance of National Culture values for the motivation of Gen Y

Hong T.T. and Waheed (2011) studied employees in the retail industry and found that hygiene factors were the dominant motivators of sales personnel job satisfaction.Lim H. L. et al (2011) found that Saudi Gen Y regarded Security, Tradition, Conformity, Universalism, and Benevolence as most important life values. To attain these life goals, respondents were most motivated by intrinsic and extrinsic work motivators.According to a research by HR Pulse NewsDesk (2012), generation Y workers have four key expectations:

1. **Global collaboration:** they expect to collaborate with colleagues globally and not to be limited to a small network of contacts within their specific area;
2. **Direct and instant access to management:** They expect more direct and frequent communication with managers. The hierarchical distance that the baby boomer generation recognises as normal is not acceptable to Generation Y.
3. **Co-creation:** They expect to co-create and work transversally in order to to solve real business issues. Executing tasks or isolated parts of a system or process will frustrate them greatly.

4. **Control/personalised work:** they expect to have more control over their work and to be able to personalise their work to suit their personal routine.(HR Pulse news desk)

The above opinions regarding the Gen Y became the basis of this research paper.

Research Design for the Opinion Survey

A small sample of 200 bank employees was drawn as the banks are worst affected by the employees' retention problem.

Objective. The objective of the research is to study the job satisfaction (motivational and hygiene factors) of Gen Y employed in various banks of Delhi and NCR

Hypothesis. To attain the objective, the following hypothesis was formulated.

Hygiene factors score would be greater than motivation factor scores.

Methodology

Sample and sample size. 200 bank employees under thirty yrs of age has been selected randomly from various banks of Delhi and NCR.

Tool used. R.N. Lussiar's 12 statement job satisfaction questionnaire comprising of motivation and hygiene factors has been used for the study. The answer has to be given on a five point scale.

Data collection and analysis. Data has been collected through personal survey. Descriptive statistics-mean, SD and t have been used for data analysis.

RESULTS AND DISCUSSION

Table 1: Mean, SD and t value of Hygiene and Motivational Factors

Factors	*Total score*	*Mean*	*SD*	*t*
Hygiene	498	4.15	1.00	0.234
Motivational	507	4.22	0.98	

As it is clear from the results that total motivation factor score is greater than hygiene factor scores but statistically this difference is non significant according to their t value hence we reject our hypothesis

Table 2: Mean and SD of Hygiene factor scores

Statements	2	5	6	8	9	12
Mean	4.16	4.25	4.15	4.1	3.95	.3.5
SD	0.90	0.85	0.93	0.97	1.05	1.14

Table 3: Mean and SD of Motivation factor scores

Statements	1	3	4	7	10	11
Mean	4.47	4.47	4.05	4.05	4.15	4.1
SD	1.00	1.00	1.05	1.05	0.93	0.97

Table- 2 shows the mean and SD of the hygiene factor scores. It shows that hygiene factors are important for respondents. Table-3 shows the same for motivational factors.

CONCLUSION

The opinion survey concludes that Gen Y is very specific about the job content. They have high expectations regarding their job. They want to work with fun and security. This study can future basis of conducting extensive research on a large sample and can be of help to the corporates and institution builders to design new jobs and the motivational strategies for Gen Y specially in the Banking sector. This is in line with what the nation is believing and doing. According to the Aon Hewitt survey quoted in an article (Mint, Sep.17, 2012) about what the Gen Y wants -it's all about my career and where it is going ; the core of work what I do- my work; I am different –so is my performance; Leaders who inspire me; My manager- a friend, philosopher, guide; A workplace with a buzz; The choice to work my way; I am an entrepreneur-of, by for my organisation. HR departments are realizing that the option of flexible timings suits this generation, and are looking for ways to accommodate them. Rajiv Mehta the managing director of the indian subsidiary of sports apparel brand Puma has created an office space as a living room, as brand ambassador and as a hangout zone according to the expectations of his young team. (TOI, Sep 18, 2012)According to Suniel Goel, director at executive search from GlobalHunt, Leave policies are being increasingly used as a key differentiator in retaining talent .For them in times of economic slowdown, devising innovative leave policy serves as a cost efficient method to retain employees. The new leave policy of ICICI Bank gives "fertility leave" in addition to ' child care' and 'adoption' leave which is a part of the bank's 'Saath Aapka' programme. (TOI, Sep 18, 2012).

The above measures and approaches adopted by the organisations is a wakeup call for the preparedness of the industry in terms of new motivational strategies and job designs for the upcoming Generation Y.

REFERENCES

[1] Aparna P R,"The Eclectic Athlete" , *Mint*, oct. 8, 2012

[2] Golshan N M et al.(2022), Effects of Motivational Factors on Job Satisfaction: An Empirical Study on Malaysian Gen-Y Administrative and Diplomatic Officers , International Business School, University Technology Malaysia2011 3rd International Conference on Advanced Management Science, IPEDR vol.19 (2011).

[3] Herzberg's Motivators and Hygiene Factors - Learn How to Motivate Your Team,- Management training and leadership training, *Mind Tools. Com, online*

[4] Hong T.T. et al. (2011),Herzberg's Motivation-Hygiene Theory and Job Satisfaction in the Malaysian Retail Sector: The Mediating Effect of Love of Money, *Asian Academy of Management Journal*, Vol. 16, No. 1, 73–94.

[5] Judith Aquino "Gen Y- the next generation of spenders", *CRM Magziene*, Feb.2012.

[6] Karefalk A. et al. (2007), How to Motivate GenY with different cultural backgrounds- A cross cultural comparison between China and Swesden , kristianstad University, The Department OF Business Studies, FE6130, Dissertation International Economy, Nov.

[7] Lim H. L. Et al. (2011), Understanding the new Middle-East workforce: Employment expectations of Generation Y professionals in Saudi Arabia, The Petroleum Institute, Abu Dhabi, United Arab Emirates, *Journal of Research in International Business Management* (ISSN: 2251-0028) Vol. 1(9) pp. 262-277.

[8] Lussiar R.N., Human Relations in Organisations : A Skill Building approach, 2nd ed. Homewood, IL: Irwin, 1993.

[9] Namrata S "Cos say We care with fertility leave", *Times of India*, Sep18, 2012.

[10] Nanda P K. Nanda ,"What I want at work" by *Mint* Sep. 17, 2012.

[11] The latest research on generation Y, Culture, Climate & Engagement, Published on Sep. 5, 2012 , HR Pulse News Desk.

Volunteerism as a Route to Employee Satisfaction and Retention for Generation Y

Meenakshi Handa and Monica Mor

University School of Management Studies, Guru Gobind Singh Indraprastha University, Dwarka, New Delhi

ABSTRACT

Employee retention, especially in the case of Gen Y employee, poses a growing challenge for employers in many industries. Various permutations of intrinsic and extrinsic motivational factors are being used to attract, retain and engage this category of employees. This conceptual paper examines the option of volunteerism as a route to employee retention. Several organizations are taking steps to provide opportunities for Gen Y and other employees to express their spirit of community service through concrete action. Such companies have observed an improvement in the attitudes of their employees and the germination of feelings of organizational as well as community bonding. The paper explores the theoretical underpinnings of 'volunteerism' and examines the implementation of volunteerism practices in select organizations. Employees are a critical component to every organization, and their engagement serves as a barometer of organizational health. By examining employee engagement, employers can create an engagement improvement plan to address employee motivation, behaviour, productivity, and subsequently business results (AON Hewitt 2012).

Keywords: *Volunteerism, Generation Y, Employees, Social Cause, Empathy*

INTRODUCTION

Though Generation Y individuals vary by regional, social and economic backgrounds, a common thread, running through this group is the heightened exposure to all types of media and digital technologies. They are more aware and conscious of their surroundings as compared to their seniors. Many of them are willing entrepreneurs with the determination to propound new exciting ideas that can bring about significant changes in the way things work (Lynch, 2008). Companies have been making consistent efforts to get Gen Y employees enthused about various activities within the organisation, almost as if being a part of them would be an added perquisite to remain attached to the organisation.

This paper examines a unique initiative being adopted by many companies across the globe to tap the humanitarian side of their employees and to get them to being more socially responsible. Being a part of some kind of social service has been found to be a great contributor to personal satisfaction and individual self-respect (Bhattacharya, 2007). Invariably companies that have got their employees to be involved in some form of social work have found an improvement in feelings of self-worth among their employees, and such companies hope to lower their attrition rates over time. Companies that have been found to be contributing to the society and environment through some form of philanthropic work being done by their employees are now found to be a part of a growing tribe; to name a few – Infosys, EDS, IBM, Microsoft, McDonald's, GE, Honeywell, Steel Authority of India Ltd. and the TATA group. Certain issues that become pertinent here are: How are the employees made to take some time off their busy work schedules and engage in social service? Different organizations have different plans chalked out for the same. Some give their employees days off to collectively go on a company-sponsored trip to a remote area or children's home & spend a day or so with the underprivileged sections of the society. Often employees have been found to come back and make the inevitable decision to work for a better cause while also working with more enthusiasm for their respective organisations. Companies found a surge in 'employee engagement' after such trips, wherein the employees felt pride in being associated with their company which in turn was associated with a good social cause. Often employees have also taken to the spirit of 'volunteerism' with enthusiasm and turned to working on weekends and after-office hours towards betterment of the world around them. This could take the shape of running helpline services, fundraising for buying ambulances, or opening shelter for the homeless during winter months, or even getting associated with a non-profit organisation. Non-profit organisations have an expressive character. They allow people to demonstrate commitment to social ends and values (Frumpkin, 2001). The corporate sector increasingly sees value in worker volunteer programs and executive participation on non-profit boards.

The term 'volunteerism' is associated with everything non-monetary like NGO & non-compensation. Yet we have seen an increasing number of private and public sector employees turning towards volunteerism to assuage their stressed minds and to bring order to their erratic work schedules. Statistics from across the world point towards an increased participation, formally or informally, in the voluntary sector. In USA, according to the Bureau of Labor Statistics, about 64.3 million people volunteered through or for an organization at least once between September 2010 and September 2011. In UK as well, the Government has identified and has been active in encouraging business organizations to undertake voluntary work in the community (Smith, 1994).

According to Wymer (1998) volunteers cannot be described as a single undifferentiated group as they differ in demographics and possess a wide gamut of experiences and skills. Volunteers operate in numerous diverse organisations in very differing roles. The absence of any standard practice makes it hard to arrive at a definition of a volunteer (Gaskin, 1999). According to Wilson (2000) volunteering involves giving of time freely to help another person, group of persons or a cause. However, according to Unger (1991) there is an element of exchange in volunteering in which volunteers respond to costs and benefits.

LITERATURE REVIEW

Volunteering has been receiving substantial research attention in recent years. The following sections provide an overview of the extant work in some of the areas on this subject.

Motives for Volunteering

Clary et al (1998) listed six functions of volunteerism: values function,(likened to altruism and refers to concern for others and desire to work towards the welfare of society), understanding function (learning and using new knowledge and skills), career function (enhancement of career and opportunities), social function (as a result of normative or reference group pressure), protective function (to overcome the feeling of guilt of being more fortunate than others) and esteem function (enhancement of one's self-esteem). A sense of belonging, the need for affiliation, gaining prestige or self-esteem, or just a way of making friends, are some of the more evident reasons for volunteering. Wilson and Pimm (1994) point to a few other reasons which may cause people to volunteer including the desire to wear a uniform, perquisites received, opportunity to travel or mingle with celebrities. According to Omoto and Snyder (1993) volunteering provides an opportunity for expression of one's intrinsic values. Many a time volunteers end spending some of their most important dates with the community they are volunteering for. Working for others creates a sense of satisfaction, which many say equals none other.

Hibbert et al (2001) found that volunteerism is an example of cooperation and reciprocal altruism. Murnighan et al (1993) suggest that implicit to volunteering is the expectation that in long-term relationships everything will work out evenly in the end on the basis that 'what goes around comes around', although individual acts are rarely driven by expectations of direct reciprocation. Smith (1981) believes that the benefits of individual acts of volunteering are considered to be primarily psychological and essentially altruistic. In a lifestyle analysis of volunteers Schlegelmilch & Tynan (1989) found that all types of volunteers shared a strong liking for group activities. In a study within a college campus McKinne & Halfacre (2008) found that volunteers often contribute to the greater economy, and the stability and cohesiveness of their community. This was found to be true of the communities on college campuses as well. While the benets of volunteerism extend beyond the individual, the benets to the individual, including personal growth, health and well-being are also numerous and potent. They concluded that volunteer-driven sustainability projects more often than not had the potential to be successful endeavours. In a study of literacy volunteers Wymer (2002) found that all reported social or psychological benets and none reported tangible benets from volunteering. Gaskin (1998) reports mixed images of volunteering in UK as being trustworthy, 'caring but also not cool' and 'for wimps and goody goodies'. This could be the image of volunteerism carried in the mind of some Generation Y members as well.

Hankinson & Rochestor (2005) suggested ways of encouraging the spirit of volunteerism amongst the laggards and the latent enthusiasts when it came to marketing voluntary activities:

1. Emphasising on its social purpose: volunteering makes a difference either (a) by providing help to others or (b) by shaping communities to the benefit of all;
2. Emphasising on its benefit to the volunteer as a means of (a) acquiring new skills (both personal and career enhancing) and (b) meeting new people or making new friends;
3. Emphasising on the nature of the activity, (a) the flexibility of engagement (from episodic to regular commitment) and (b) the range of opportunities.

Bussell & Forbes (2001) have suggested a classification model to explain the four Ws of Volunteering (What, Who, Why and Where). According to them volunteers are a very varied group working in very diverse situations and therefore difficult to define. Further according to Bussell and Forbes (2001) volunteering behaviour of individuals and groups may be driven by considerations besides altruistic motives.

Volunteer Demographics

The segment of people who volunteer have been found to be coming from diverse backgrounds and age groups. Most of those who do volunteer have a sense of benefits that would accrue from volunteering and not surprisingly have been found to be educated and well read. Wymer (1998) in his studies found volunteering to be gender specic with more females than males volunteering.

Models on Volunteerism

The model of volunteer behavior proposed by Lee and Brudney (2009) is based on the idea that the benefits of volunteering are likely to be shared by the community, and that people recognize volunteering as a repeated, rather than a one-shot, game. The expected benefits of volunteering increase as people expect that other people will also volunteer and that, as members of the community, they will reap the outcome of others' volunteering.

Govekar & Govekar (2002) have worked on few theories and models to explain the behaviour of volunteers, and we adapt it here for the corporate executives who aim to volunteer. The first model that they proposed – *The Collective Goods model* – assumes that charitable contributions (of time) result from a demand for charitable output by the community as a whole. Volunteering is considered to be a constrained gift; since it's still not clear why individuals would contribute time rather than money (the two are treated as substitutes in the minds of volunteers). This model is based on the concept of opportunity cost, whereby in volunteering, the opportunity cost is the wage or other compensation the person gives up in order to volunteer, and that volunteering is "a conscience good or activity". The *Influence*

& Search model, assumes that the hours volunteered are at least partly dependent on a person's ability to influence output type. This model predicts that hours donated are dependent in part on an individual's ability to influence output or gather information of value. Here donations of money and time are likely to be complements rather than substitutes. The *Private Goods and Skill Development model* states that if one volunteers and makes a contribution to a non-profit organisation with the expectation of feeling good about oneself, this feeling is private (hence a private good) and is not available to others. And a lot of times individuals volunteer in order to acquire job skills easily and to turn those skills into higher future wages. Hence it was stated that volunteering should increase with education and decline with age.

In reality however people in their twenties have been found to be least likely to volunteer in USA and in UK. In India however the statistics of volunteers in the Third sector has not been completely accounted for, so we are not sure of the numbers, which estimably would be atleast 10% among the young workers and maybe lower as the average workers' age increases. The concept of volunteering while working is in a nascent stage in India, despite the fact that we have 1.2 million charities and about half a billion people productively employed, all over the country. One of the main reasons could be the lack of awareness amongst the working population and another could be lack of an inherent desire to go that extra mile. For sure it would call for a reduction in self-time put aside after work for family and friends or even for themselves. This may not seem very promising and exciting to those who work long hours and probably consider themselves to be a part of the 'corporate rat-race'. Nevertheless organisations can work around the BCOS factors, explained below, to encourage their employees, especially the Generation Y to pick up the slate and go teach the underprivileged kids, to plant more trees, or to even pick up the broom and clean the streets they live on.

BCOS Factors

Andreason (1995) focused on four behavioural drivers which explain the behaviour of volunteers. In the BCOS approach the first two factors – *benefits & costs* – emphasize the role of exchange as the relationship with volunteers. The way to achieve success is to offer superior *value propositions* that will lead to better volunteer relationships. For volunteers the realisation has to be that they are benefiting by giving up some costs. The costs would be say, extra time to be devoted to social service or moving out of comfort zones and familiar surroundings and stepping into unfamiliar and unchartered territories. The benefits would be inculcation of feelings like empathy and compassion for manhood, a sense of being worthwhile for the needy, or even a cause that ends being close to the heart enough to be taken up seriously.

The other two factors are "*others*" and "*self-assurance*". Behaviours can be and are strongly influenced by *others* in the environment. Many employees in organisations have taken up the cudgels for the homeless in the society because their bosses and peers had done so. Organisations need to encourage group behaviour amongst their employees when it comes to volunteerism. Often people working alone may get disheartened by the squalor of the slums or the sickness of the slum dwellers. In times like these, support of co-workers would serve as stimulants towards finishing the task once begun. Sometimes it's the journey that matters rather than the destination, and if the journey is arduous enough then the presence of others like friends and team-members make the destination seem much closer than it may be.

Even if benefits exceed the costs and even if social pressures are favourable, people may still not act. *Self-assurance* or the individual's belief can actually make the behaviour happen. To achieve this, organisations need to instil in each of their employees a sense of belonging and capability. A can-do attitude would go a long way in working as a motivational factor. Organisations that have regular sessions for their employees where they are driving in the message of leadership and competency will see amongst their employees a greater degree of self-efficacy. Self-assurance or self-efficacy is that factor that can spur people towards the greater good, and in this case impelling them to be a part, however minor, of the social sector.

VOLUNTEERING AT THE WORKPLACE

Keeping in mind the ongoing research in volunteerism, organisations have tried to seek answers to the following questions - How should executives be motivated towards volunteering; where should they go to perform community services; should there be any compensation for days or hours spent on voluntary work. Around all of this and more, organisations have tried to develop frameworks of policies.

Employer supported volunteering tends to be employee-led, usually in the employee's own time, un-paid, encouraged and supported by the employer but not compulsory. Employer directed involvement is employer-led, in work time with projects chosen to match the organisation's needs and used as a personal development tool. Both types of voluntary work are on the increase.

Empirical Studies on Employee Volunteerism

While going through literature in this area we came across results of a few studies conducted in different countries by scholars and research organizations. Works of some are highlighted below.

Deloitte's Volunteer IMPACT 2011 survey found several strong links between employee volunteerism and employee engagement in the workplace. This report compared *millenials* (moniker for Generation Y) aged 21- 35 who participated in employer sponsored volunteerism and those who did not. The research found that those who participate in employer sponsored volunteerism were 52% more likely to feel very loyal toward their company than those who did not participate. The report also found that 70% millenials want to work for a company that is committed to its community.

In a cross-sectional study conducted across 5 states in USA by Madison et al (2012) that examined the association of employees' organizational commitment and employer sponsored volunteerism, the results indicated that employees who volunteered as a result of encouragement by corporate employers, governmental employers, or not for profit organizations reported increased organizational commitment to the organizations encouraging them to participate in the program.

Turker (2009) reports a link between CSR and organizational commitment which occurs to the extent that socially responsible activities by the organization, including employers encouraging employee volunteerism, enhance the individual's perception of the organization, thereby enhancing the social identity of the employee as a member of the organization. Turker suggests that social identity theory (SIT) provides an explanation for the link between

CSR and Organizational Commitment

Closer home NASSCOM conducts studies in India amongst its member companies, and according to the NASSCOM Foundation's Catalys-ing Change 08-09 report, a study evaluating and defining a CSR matu-rity model for the Indian IT & BPO industry, employee volunteering has been a growing trend within NASSCOM member companies, which today rep-resents over 1200 IT and BPO com-panies in India. Around 93 per cent of NASSCOM members have employee volunteering programs. In order to foster and grow em-ployee volunteerism NASSCOM Foun-dation, the CSR arm of NASSCOM, launched www.MyKartavya.com. It is a portal designed to connect employ-ees to a wide spectrum of innovative as well as regular volunteering opportunities posted by NGOs.

Hackl, Halla & Pruckner (2007) state that the share of the population oering formal voluntary labour varies strongly across countries. Sweden exhibits the highest participation rate in Europe with a share of 59 percent of all employed people who supply voluntary labour. It is followed by Slovakia (55 percent) with a participation rate above 0.50.Denmark, Greece, Great Britain and The Netherlands show participation rates between 0.41 and 0.49. Italy, Luxembourg, Iceland, Malta, Slovenia, Austria, Czech Republic, Ireland, Belgium and Finland have values between 0.31 and 0.39. In Germany, Estonia, Spain, Belarus, Northern Ireland, Bulgaria, Croatia, Romania, Latvia and France at least 21 percent of all employed people participate in voluntary labour.

Benefits of Employee Volunteerism

A 1993 report by the Conference Board, New York indicated that volunteer programs help companies attract & retain good employees. Volunteer activities develop characteristics such as creativity, trust, teamwork & persistence. They build skills & attitudes that foster commitment, company loyalty & job satisfaction. Through community service, employees can develop contacts with government & business leaders. And it was also found that there did exist a clear link between volunteerism & profitability.

A study conducted by IBM & Graduate School of Business at Columbia University showed a positive correlation between community involvement & return on assets, return on investments, & employee productivity. Thus, a company with a high community involvement score was also likely to score high on employee morale & profitability.

Volunteerism increasingly is also being used as a staff development tool. It's found to be way of developing and honing business skills such as soft skills, leadership skills, project management & presentation skills. Many business leaders find that purpose-driven work through cause is linked to boosted morale and productivity, which inevitably affects corporate bottom lines. Organizations are realizing that if you give employees the opportunity to give back, they'll have a renewed appreciation for the importance of their jobs.

A corporate volunteerism report by Deloitte showed that workplace volunteer programs are important even to those who don't typically volunteer in their private time; 61% of millennials who rarely or never volunteer would consider a company's commitment to the community when making a job decision.

Other than benefits to the organisation and its employees, corporate volunteerism has its positive fallouts in society as well. The community brought under the welfare umbrella of the organisation involved would surely gain out of the entire voluntary program for employees. If the company is focusing on education, then children and illiterate adults stand to be beneficiaries; if the company is focusing on environmental protection, then the society as a whole benefits. Moreover recent trends suggest that organisations espousing charity and philanthropy have a positive image in the minds of their customers. Many customers feel gratified by simply buying products from companies that are involved in causes for humanity and environment. It's their indirect contribution to charitable causes.

There surely would be a domino effect if companies adopt employee volunteerism as a way to motivate the Millenials to remain with the company.

Instances of Organisations in India that Encourage Volunteerism

Below are voluntary activities that are conducted in few organisations in India. These organisations have been doing a lot of work in this area in their international centres. The examples quoted here are from the work they do in India. These companies have rigorously worked on creating windows of opportunities for their employees to take up volunteerism and while doing so the companies have made an attempt to effectively engage them as well.

1. "Month of Service" at SAP, India

SAP Labs India, which initiated a week of service in 2006, and enhanced it to the month of service in 2010, participated in a bouquet of more than 42 charitable initiatives, across various cities including Bangalore, Delhi, Mumbai, Chennai and Pune, aimed at sowing seeds of equality in the discriminatory socio-economic terrain of India. Some of their projects included:

- Spending time with the underprivileged children in an orphanage
- Listening to stories at an old age home
- Packing school bags for 1000 underprivileged children
- Packing food boxes for the underprivileged children
- Constructing a playground for children of a primary school
- Building a road to help the villagers
- Planting trees
- Playing with differently abled children at the Spastic Society and Gerezim, Bangalore.

2. Corporate Community Relations at IBM

As a global company, IBM's philanthropic goal is to use their expertise and technology where they can make the biggest difference in communities around them. In India, they partner with the Government and NGOs to implement Community Programs focusing on Primary Education and Healthcare. They also have an active volunteering community that leverages IBM's technical resources to better the lives of the underprivileged and make a difference in their own quaint way. Some of the programs run in India by Corporate Community Relations are:

- KidSmart
- On-Demand Community
- Reinventing Education
- Reading Companion
- Accessibility
- TryScience
- SME ToolKit

IBMers (as the employees of IBM like to call themselves proudly) are also given an opportunity to contribute to the Community through the 'On Demand Community', a program that encourages IBMers to volunteer. The flexible office hours clubbed with tools on the website and grants enable IBMers to effectively manage their time and enhance their skills. IBM further recognises its employees' contribution through certificates and awards.

3. Helping Hand at HSBC

Employees at HSBC are encouraged to participate in various community projects. HSBC launched Employee Volunteering in India in 2007 to enhance volunteering participation. The programme has been named '**Catalyst**' and has been deployed across HSBC branches and Group Companies in India. The various activities that come under its purview include:

- Annual Helping Hands Mela
- HSBC Climate Champions

- Volunteering Action Fortnight
- Breaking Barriers – Celebrating with a Difference
- World Environment Day

4. *Social Contract at Infosys*

Infosys' social contract inspires employees to contribute to community welfare, environment sustainability and digital literacy. In 2011-12, Infosys organized several programs, enabling employees to give back to the society:

- Sabbatical for volunteering
- Emergency Aid to facilitate work at remote areas for health and welfare of rural people
- Employee engagement with a number of external forums such as World Business Council for Sustainable Development (WBCSD); Business Action for Sustainable Development (BASD)
- Infosys also runs a foundation where their employees work with a number of NGOs in India.

5. *Corporate Citizenship at Microsoft*

Microsoft aims to be the global leader in corporate responsibility through its various social responsibility initiatives. One such initiative of theirs is the **Employee Volunteer Program (EVP) and Giving Campaign. These campaigns in** line with the development goals of the Indian government and country's commitment to Millennium Development Goals, have had a strategic focus on 'Promoting Inclusive Growth through Education' since 2006. Choosing the right NGOs for both financial contribution and volunteering activities being critical for the success of the program, MS India also instituted a strong process to select and validate the NGOs. The concentrated approach has steadily showed results with an overall volunteering rate from less than 1% in FY09 to 6.9% in FY10. The results of giving campaign of FY09 convinced more people to join the campaign in FY10. Till date the program has raised more than USD 750 K. Important highlights of the Employee Volunteer Program include the design of simple software by the employees to track the educational achievement of children of jail of inmates for a premier NGO working with prison reforms and facilitating development of platform for a pilot to deliver TB related messages to train rural health functionaries via mobile.

6. *Employee First Council at HCL Technologies*

EFC is a unique platform for HCLites to lead change. It is a participative and democratic forum developed for HCLites and run by HCLites. The Employee First councils provide opportunities to a diverse group of individuals to come together and work towards a common cause that they are passionate about. Employee First Councils have nearly 2,500+ active members who have been instrumental in organizing over 5,670 engagements. HCL's community outreach program is spearheaded by 272 members from this council. One of their key activities is to inculcate social responsibility among HCLites. The meaningful volunteer experiences focused on assisting individuals and families achieve their human potential through education, income stability and healthy lives.

7. Volunteerism at TATA Group Companies

At the various offices of every TATA division, employees are provided with a basket of options to choose from to engage in voluntary activities. Community activities in fact are strategically devised to craft a coherent, focused programme that maximises impact, motivates employees, and encourages participation at all levels. Whether its Indian Hotels or TATA Steel, the company has a matrix that describes the profile of volunteers, and that is developed to match their skills with corresponding activities. The focus is on building livelihood for communities around them, facilitating entrepreneurship amongst rural women, providing engineering trainings to poor students, running immunisation and AIDs awareness camps.

Senior managers at TATA Group have claimed to have seen massive improvements in attitudes and professional skills of those employees who have actively engaged in voluntary activities. Some HR heads have even observed that their employees have not only found volunteerism to be great motivators in every sphere of their lives but that they have also found a unique type of joy in giving. Especially the Indian Hotels division where the employees are surrounded by luxury in their work hemisphere, working with the underprivileged has succeeded in sensitising the employees to the realities of life.

CONCLUSION

There is a growing culture of volunteerism that is spreading through organizations and gradually enhancing the spirit of bonding. Employers want to use it as a tool to not only retain their workforce but to also make them better rounded human beings. While the Human Resources team is working on many human resources related activities to address the apathetic attitude of their employees, it is the CSR (Corporate Social Responsibility) division of most of these companies that have taken this huge leap of faith towards enhancing their employees' satisfaction and well-being. While the government has set a mandate for organisations to put in place their CSR activities, the organisations themselves have lunged ahead with innovative ideas and practices to garner greater commitment and sincerity from their employees, especially the fast track 'Gen Y'.

Moreover there are other sundry benefits to corporate philanthropy, and one of the major one being the good PR that gets generated amongst the organisations' stakeholders, from management to citizen groups to the customers. Employees who do get involved in volunteerism while deriving pleasure, invariably seek a connection with their organisation that could manifest into a bond that might get them to exhibit loyalty towards the same. Generation Y when spoken to would be in denial to the allegations levelled against them, and would surely try to give rational explanations to their restlessness. From the multitude of opportunities in the corporate world, to the innumerable hobbies and past time activities they indulge in, this generation is also surprisingly seeing an upsurge in taking up charge when it comes to civil society welfare. They have been conclusively found to being generous donors for philanthropic causes as mentioned in the India Philanthropy Report published by Bain Consulting in 2012. They have also been found to be comfortable in working in groups, which is a fortunate prerequisite for volunteerism. Steering this generation towards not only making donations towards social welfare but also towards participating in the voluntary sector actively should hopefully channel their faculties in the right direction, that being remaining true to the organisation that gets them their bread & butter. An enthusiastic worker is not only a good performer but is also dedicated to his or her organisation of employment. Studies show that employee satisfaction with volunteerism is greatly enhanced if the volunteer opportunities are carefully matched with the talents and interests of the employee, if the volunteers receive timely and appropriate training, feedback and guidance for performing their duties, and if the volunteers are made to feel responsible for the success of the endeavour and the benefits conferred. Organisational structure may also affect the experience a volunteer has. Robinson (1994) argues that the matrix system may be the most appropriate, although Courtney (1994) stresses the value of a small, at, accessible structure.

It is with these lessons that companies are trying to wield the magic wand of volunteerism to get their restive Generation Y workers to adopt an attitude of restfulness and steadfastness to their respective organisations. According to the Deloitte 2007 Volunteer IMPACT survey, 62 per cent of the Generation Y respondents reported they would prefer to work for companies that give them opportunities to contribute their skills to nonprofit organizations. And companies have set the ball rolling to do the same in a wider scale, across all branches in different countries.

REFERENCES

[1] Albro, Walt (2012); "Community leadership on Display"; ABA Bank Marketing, September Issue, pp 32-36

[2] Andreason, Alan (1995); "Marketing Social Change"

[3] Ashforth, E. Blake & Mael, Fred (1999); "Social Identity theory & the Organization"; academy of Management Review, Vol 14 (1), pp 20-39

[4] Basil, Z. Debra; Runte, S. Mary; Easwaramoorthy, M. & Barr, Cathy (2009); "Company support for employee volunteering: A national survey of companies in Canada"; Journal of Business Ethics; Vol 85, pp 387-398

[5] Bhattacharya, Saumya (2007); "The new age do-gooders"; Business Today, Vol 16(17), pp 152-153

[6] Bussell, Helen & Forbes, Deborah (2001); "Understanding the volunteer market: The what, where, who & why of volunteering"; International Journal of Nonprofit & Voluntary Sector Marketing, Vol 7(3), pp 244-256

[7] Caudron, Shari (1994); "Volunteerism & the Bottom Line"; Industry Week, February Issue, pp 13-18

[5] Clary, E. G., Snyder, M., Ridge, R. D., Copeland, J., Stukas, A. A., Haugen, J., et al. (1998). "Understanding and assessing the motivations of volunteers: A functional approach." Journal of Personality and Social Psychology,74, pp 1516–1530.

[6] Courtney, R. (1994); 'Directions in voluntary sector management', Management Development Review, Vol. 7, No. 3, pp. 33 –36

[7] Flanders, D. Allan; "The tradition of Voluntarism"; british journal of Industrial Relation, pp 352 – 370

[8] Frumkin, Peter (2001); "Going beyond efficiency"; Nonprofit Quarterly, Vol 8(2), pp 22

[9] Economic News Release, "Volunteering in the United States, 2011"; Bureau of Labor Statistics (http://www.bls.gov/news.release/volun.nr0.htm)

[10] Gaskin K. (1998); *"What Young People Want From Volunteering";* Institute for Volunteering Research: London

[11] Gaskin, K (1999); "Valuing volunteers in Europe: A comparative study of the Volunteer Investment & Value Audit"; Voluntary Action, Vol 2(1), pp 33-49

[12] Govekar, L. Paul & Govekar A. Michele (2002); "Using economic theory & research to better understand volunteer behaviour"; Nonprofit Management & Leadership, Vol 13(1), pp 33-48

[13] Hackl, Franz; Halla, Martin & Pruckner, J. Gerald (2007); "Volunteering & Income – The fallacy of the good Samaritan?"; KYKLOS – International Review for Social Sciences; Vol 60 (1), pp 77-104

[14] Hankinson, Philippa & Rochester, Colin (2005); "The face & voice of volunteering: a suitable case for branding?"; International Journal of Nonprofit & Voluntary Sector Marketing, Vol 10(2), pp 93-105

[15] Hibbert, Sally; Piacentini, Maria & Al Dajani, Haya (2001); "Understanding volunteer motivation for participation in a community-based food cooperative"; International Journal of Nonprofit & Voluntary Sector Marketing, Vol 8(1), pp 30-42

[16] Houghton, M. Susan; Gabel, T. a. Joan & Williams W. David (2009); "Connectiong the two faces of CSR: Does employee volunteerism improve compliance?"; Journal of Business Ethics; Vol 87, pp 477-494

[17] Johnson-Coffey & C. Georgean (1997); "Trends in Voluntarism"; The Bottom Line: Managing Library Finances; Vol 10(2), pp 60-64

[18] Keelan, Emma (2005); "Innovative Giving"; accountancymagazine.com, December issue, pp 50-51

[19] Kotler, Phillip & Andreason, Alan (2009); "Strategic marketing for Nonprofit Organisations", 7th ed; pp 384

[20] Laff, Michael (2008); "The hidden classroom"; T+D, July Issue, pp 16

[21] Lee, Young-Joo & Brudney, L. Jeffrey (2009); "Rational volunteering: A benefit – cost approach"; International Journal of Sociology & Social Policy

[21] Lynch, J. Amy (2008); "ROI on Generation Y Employees: Best practice human capital management of Generation Y"; www.GenerationYexpert.com

[22] Madison, F. Thomas; Ward, Stephanie & Royalty, Kent (2012); "Corporate social responsibility, Organizational commitment, & Employer-sponsored Volunteerism"; Internationl Journal of Business & Social Science, Vol 3 (1). Pp 1-14

[23] McKine, L.Kirstan & Halfacre, C. Angels (2008); ""Growing" a campus native specis garden: sustaining volunteer driven sustainability'; International Journal of Sustainability in Higher Education, Vol 9(2), pp 142 – 156

[24] Murnighan, J.K., Kim, J. W. & Metzger, A. R. (1993); "The volunteer dilemma"; Administrative Science Quarterly, Vol 38 (4), pp 515-539.

[25] Omoto. A. M. and Snyder. M. (1993)'AIDS volunteers and their motivations: Theoretical issues and practical concerns', Nonprofit Management and Leadership, Vol. 4, No. 2, pp. 157–76.

[26] Peloza, John & Hassay, N. Derek (2006); "Intra-organizational volunteerism: Good soldiers, Good deeds & Good politics"; Journal of Business Ethics; Vol 64, pp 357-379

[27] Reza, E. (2009); "Identity Constructs in Human Organizations"; Business Renaissance Quarterly, Fall Vol 4 (3), pp 77-107

[28] Robinson, B. (1994); 'Voluntary bodies as learning organisations', The Learning Organisation, Vol. 1, No. 3, pp. 10 –15

[29] Schlegelmilch, B. & Tynan, C.C. (1989); "Who volunteers: An investigation into the characteristics of Charity Volunteers"; Journal of Marketing Management, Vol 5(2), pp 133-151

[30] Singhal, Madhur & Sheth, Arpan (2011); "India Philanthropy Report"; Bain & Company

[31] Smith D. H. (1981); "Altruism, volunteers & volunteerism'; Journal of Voluntary Action Research, Vol 10, pp 21-36

[32] Smith, D.H (1994); "Determinants of voluntary association participation & volunteering: A literature review'; Nonprofit & Voluntary Sector Quarterly, Vol 23(3), pp243-263

[33] Stebbins, R. (1997); 'Serious leisure and well-being', in Haworth, J. (ed.)'*Work, Leisure and Well-being'*, Routledge, London, p. 117

[34] Turker, D. (2009); "How Corporate Social Responsibility influences organizational commitment"; Journalof Business Ethics, Vol 89, pp 189-204

[35] Unger, L. S (1991); "Altruism as a motivation to volunteer"; Journal of Economic Psychology, Vol 12, pp 71-100

[36] Vian,T; McCoy, S.C.; Richards, P. Connelly & F. Feeley (2007); "Corporate Social Responsibility in Global Health: The Pfizer Global Health Fellows International Volunteering Program"; Human Resource Planning, Vol 30(1), pp 30-35 (http://www.bu.edu/actforhealth/reference/HRP%20Pfizer%20GHF%20Final.pdf)

[37] Wilson, A. and Pimm, G. (1996); 'The tyranny of the volunteer: the care and feeding of voluntary workforces', Management Decision, Vol. 34, No. 4, pp. 24–40

[38] Wilson, John (2000); "Volunteering'; Annual Review of Sociology; Vol.. 26, pp. 215–40

[39] Wymer, W. W. (1998); 'Youth development volunteers: Their motives, how they differ from other volunteers and correlates of involvement intensity', Journal of Nonprot and Voluntary Sector Marketing, Vol. 3, No. 4, pp. 321–336

[40] Ramaswamy, Shobha (2004); "Enriching the future through volunteering"; http://www.tata.com/article

[40] http://www.sap.com/india/about/company/saplabs/csr

[42] http://www-07.ibm.com/in/careers/youandibm

[43] 2012 trends in Global Trends in Global Employee Engagement, AON Hewitt Consulting; http://www.aon.com/attachments/human-capital-consulting/2012_TrendsInGlobalEngagement_Final_v11.pdf

[44] www.deloitte.com

[45] 2011 Deloitte Volunteer IMPACT Survey; http://www.deloitte.com/assets/Dcom-UnitedStates/Local%20Assets/Documents/us_2011DeloitteVolunteerIMPACTSurvey_ExecutiveSummary_060311.pdf

[46] "Making it count: How to measure the impact of Volunteerism" (January 2011); Starbucks Coffee; http://missionmeasurement.com/uploads/documents/Making_It_Count_-_Measuring_Volunteerism.pdf

[47] www.nasscomfoundation.org

[48] http://www.hsbc.co.in/1/2/miscellaneous/about-hsbc/corporate-sustainability/employee-volunteering

[49] http://www.causecast.com/blog/bid/127697/How-Corporate-Volunteer-Programs-Increase-Employee-Engagement

[50] http://www.microsoft.com/india/msindia/msindia_up_education.aspx

[51] http://www.infosys.com/building-tomorrows-enterprise/sustainable-tomorrow/Pages/index.aspx

[52] http://www.hcltech.com/socially-responsible-business/redefining-workplace/employee-first-councils-efc

Mapping Individual Personality with Brand Personality: A Study of Generation Y Preferences for Mobile Brands

Anu Singh Lather, Puja Khatri and Shilpa Jain

University School of Management Studies, Guru Gobind Singh Indraprastha University, Delhi

ABSTRACT

The mobile phone industry has undoubtedly witnessed phenomenal growth in nearly two decades, characterized by increased market competition with fierce battle for share and relevance amongst manufacturers mostly because of its major customers coming from Generation Y, who belongs to the mobile generation and uses mobile 24X7. Consequently, players seek to differentiate their products and services through utilitarian motives. Practitioners view it as a key way to differentiate a brand in a product category , as a central driver of consumer preference, and as a common denominator that can be used to market a brand across cultures Brand personality is a part of the brand image, is seen as a set human characteristics associated with a brand. Personality of a brand is similar to the one of a human, e.g. it possesses characteristics such as age and gender, and human personality traits such as warmth and concern. The study seeks to map the preference of generation y for different mobile brands with distinct and symbolic brand personalities. It also endeavors to study the interrelationships existing between individual personality and the personality of a brand. The preferences that respondents have drawn for brands with distinct personalities were found to be significantly correlated with people who were receptive of changes. However, interestingly no relationship was observed for people with other personality variables measured on the big five personality scale.

Keywords: *Brand Personality, Individual Personality, Generation Y*

INTRODUCTION

Salzer-Mörling and Strannegård (2004) stated that, "with the abundance of products in the western world, the managerial challenge, it seems, has become that of differentiating similar products". This goes true especially in case of mobile industry that too with the perspective of generation Y, who are tech savvy and lives their life on mobile. Unfortunately, differentiating products based on their technical functions or quality has never been more difficult (Dumaine, 1991; Veryzer, 1995). Symbolic meaning provides another way to differentiate products (Govers and Schoormans, 2005). Due to symbolic meaning, otherwise indistinguishable products become differentiated in the eyes of the consumer. In the same vein, Elliot and Wattanasuwan (1998) stated that "in a consumer culture, people no longer consume for mere functional satisfaction, but consumption becomes meaning-based, and brands are often used as symbolic construction and maintenance of identity". The consumer is engaged in a symbolic project where she/he must actively construct identity out of symbolic materials, and it is brands that carry out much of the available cultural meaning (Schroeder and Salzer-Mörling, 2006). Recent studies conducted by Pedersen (2005) and, Katz and Sugiyama (2005) emphasize the importance of expressive and symbolic dimensions of technology stating that these dimensions seem critical in understanding the reception and use of mobile communication technology and that indeed, in some cases they may supersede utilitarian motives in their importance.

However, it is argued that the symbolic use of brand is possible because consumers often imbue brands with human personality traits. Consumers easily can think about brands as if they were celebrities or famous historical figures as they relate to one's own self (Gilmore, 1919; Rook, 1985; Fournier 1994). Brand personality enables a consumer to express his or her own self (Belk, 1988), an ideal self (Malhotra, 1988) or specific dimensions of self (Kleine, Kleine and Kernan 1993).. In this regard, Aaker (1997) developed the Brand Personality Scale (BPS), which suggests that consumers perceive brands as having five distinct personality dimensions: Sincerity, Excitement, Competence, Sophistication and Ruggedness, which are supported by 42 personality traits. This scale provides practitioners with an alternative to the adhoc scales being used. In addition, the scale can be used to compare personalities of brands across product categories, thereby enabling researchers to identify benchmark personality brands (Aaker, 1997).

According to Delgado-Ballester & Munuera-Aleman (2005) creating a strong brand is often a goal for many organizations since it provides several advantages. They state that it helps organizations to be less vulnerable to competitive marketing actions, gain larger margins, as well as create brand extension opportunities. In consumer marketing, brands can provide differentiation among competitors and because of this brands have become more important in corporate marketing strategies. (Opoku, 2006)

The branding cycle is a circle like model which describes a continuous five step process built up of research, brand proposition, marketing mix, communication triggers and the consumer.

Hankinson and Cowking (1993) continue by stating that the first step, research, provides a base of information on which to make decisions for step two, the brand proposition. Hankinson and Cowking (1993) state that the brand proposition consists of positioning and personality, which are factors that should be closely linked. Potential competitors will be discovered when positioning while the personality of the brand helps to differentiate the brand.

A consumer who is about to choose between two different brands is more probable to choose the brand he or she recognizes. If he or she knows both brands, the consumer will choose the one with the most perceived positive attributes (Keller, 1993). These different beliefs about the brand's attributes are its brand image (Kotler *et al.*, 2005) and customers do not interpret brands alike; people have filters such as experience and perceptions (Plummer, 2000). A brand can be described with three different groups of characteristics. The first group is physical attributes, the second is its functional characteristics and the third is characterization. Plummer (2000) describes the characterization aspects as the brand personality.

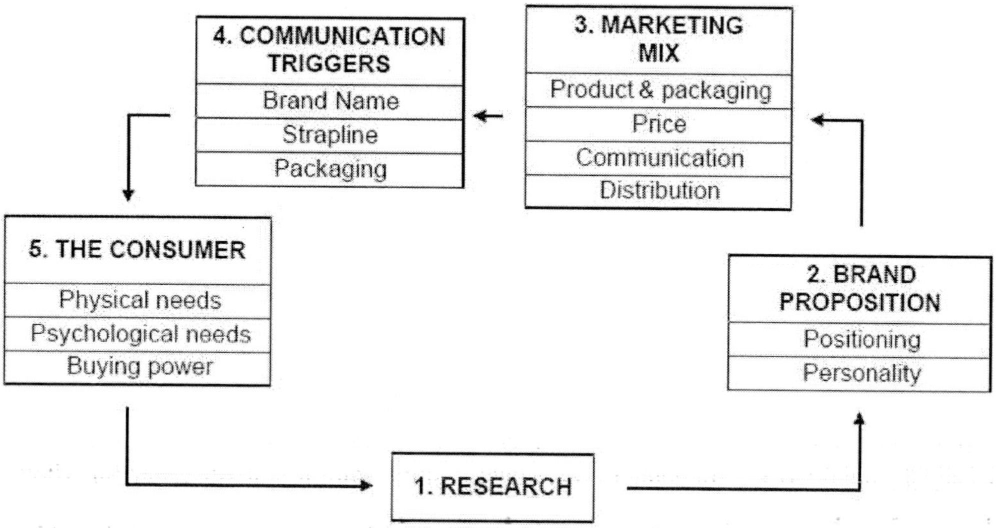

Fig. 1. The Branding Cycle

Source: Adapted from Hankinson & Cowking, 1993, p. 5

The brand personality is a part of the brand image, (Plummer, 2000) and Aaker (1997) defines brand personality as "the set of human characteristics associated with a brand" (p. 347). Aaker (2002) continues by explaining that the personality of a brand is similar to the one of a human, e.g. it possesses characteristics such as age and gender, and human personality traits such as warmth and concern. He also states that brand personality is both consistent, long- term and that everything associated with a brand affects the personality of it. There are both product-related characteristics and non-product-related characteristics. Examples of product- related characteristics are product category, price and attributes. Examples of non-product- related characteristics are symbols, country of origin, celebrity endorser and sponsorships (Aaker, 2002). He also states that a brand personality must be similar to what the target market desires, and that it has to feel important enough to be associated with this personality. (ibid).In traditional area, brand personality and individuals personality are researched, but no clear picture of comparison or relation between brand personality with an individual's personality were found. One reason for this could be that the area is too young for any rules to be developed and confirmed. (Park *et al.*, 2005; Aaker, 1997) While Aaker (1997) states that there is some uncertainty around what brand personality is, and how it should be defined, Sweeney and Brandon (2006) state that the brand personality concept has gained more recognition during the past decade.

Aaker (1997) defines five dimensions of brand personality: sincerity, excitement, competence, sophistication and ruggedness. Brand personalities are related to the self-expressive function that the product fills for the consumer. (Keller, 1993) By seeing brand personality as multidimensional instead of one-dimensional, different types of personalities can be separated from each other, and the ways that different brand personalities appeal to diverse consumer preferences can be better understood. The different dimensions affect people in separate ways, e.g. sincerity, excitement and competence affects the instinctive part of the consumers' personality, but sophistication and ruggedness might try to fulfill a wish of what the consumer would like to be, but is not. (Aaker, 1997)

LITERATURE REVIEW

Aaker (1997) defines brand personality as "the set of human characteristics associated with a brand". If the brand would be a human, a few examples of its characteristics would be: friends, clothes and manner. Another definition is: "Brand personality is the set of human personality traits that correspond to the interpersonal domain of human personality and are relevant to describing the brand as a relationship partner". (Sweeney & Brandon, 2006, p.645)

Plummer (2001) states that brand personality are very important in the consumers' minds when deciding if the product suits him or her. Kim *et al.* (2001) found that brand identification is linked to a higher level of word of mouth, and a larger amount of word of mouth is indirectly connected to higher brand loyalty. Brand identification of the brand personality can help build a long-term relationship between the brand and consumer. Biel (1992) concluded that a brand's personality could help the consumer to filter the large amounts of information on different brands available. Melin (1997) states that the reason for building a brand personality is based on the idea that consumers choose which brands to buy in a similar way that they choose which fellow humans to socialize with. An attractive personality is believed to be strongly connected to a strong and continuous relation between brand and consumer, hence brand loyalty. (Melin, 1997). The stronger the brand's identity fit together with the customer's, the customer will identify him or herself stronger with the brand and thereby have a stronger relationship. (Hankinson & Cowking, 1993) McEnally and Chernatony (1999) state that as personality of brand and consumer come together, the value created is in the form of self-expression for the consumer.

Kim *et al.* (2001) state that "the greater the self-expressive value and the distinctiveness of brand personality are, the greater will be the attractiveness of the brand personality." (p. 198) They continue by saying that when similarities occur between brand personality and the consumer's self-expression, the consumer might see the brand as a human, or even a companion. Consumers also use certain brands to express their personality. Kim *et al.* (2001) explain that consumers have a tendency to classify themselves as members of a specific group. This is called social identification. The research made by Kim *et al.* (2001) showed that the consumers will see the attractiveness of the brand personality more strongly, the more distinct and self-expressive the brand personality is.

Aaker (1997) has developed a Brand Personality Scale (BPS) that shows five key dimensions of the personality of a brand. Each of these dimensions can be described with some adjectives.

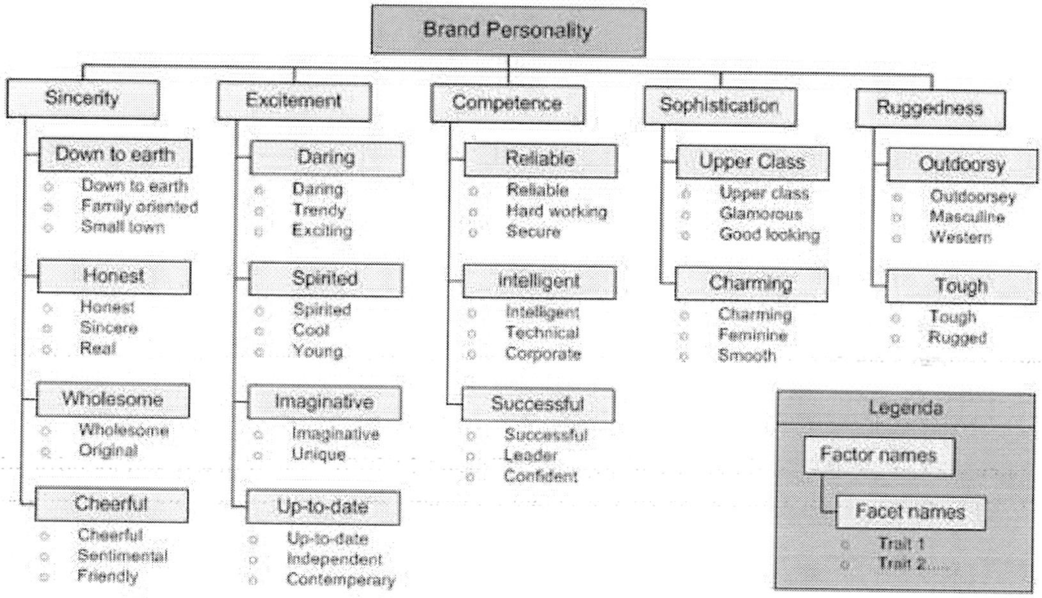

Fig 2. Brand Personality (Aaker, 1997:354)

Source:http://www.vanhaaften.nl/index.php?option=com_content&view=article&id= 78&catid= 48&Itemid=53)

The most important aspect of the brand personality framework is that it is generalizable over different product categories. (Aaker, 1997) The five dimensions in the model have been developed with subgroups consisting of aspects of the dimension to clarify the character and structure of the dimensions. Aaker (1997) states that the five dimensions explain 93% of the studied differences between the competing brands. She continues by saying that the different dimensions influence the consumer in different ways, for example the sincerity, excitement and competence dimensions affects the human's inner personality, while the sophistication and ruggedness dimensions attract consumers who desire this, but do not have it.

According to Sweeney and Brandon (2006) the brand personality research is very young compared to human personality studies. Plummer (2001) raises the question if the same description with adjectives can be made for a brand as with humans. Aaker (1997) states that though some factors may work with brands, as well as humans, others may not. Finally, the brand personality framework developed by Aaker (1997) only includes positive brand attributes, while some brands are not so wholesome. (Sweeney & Brandon, 2006)

Cattell's pioneering work, and the availability of a relatively short list of variables, stimulated other researchers to examine the dimensional structure of trait ratings. Several investigators were involved in the discovery and clarification of the Big Five dimensions. First, Fiske (1949) constructed much simplified descriptions from 22 of Cattell's variables; the factor structures derived from self-ratings, ratings by peers, and ratings by psychological staff members were highly similar and resembled what would be later known as the Big Five. To clarify these factors, Tupes and Christal (1961) reanalyzed correlation matrices from eight different samples, ranging from airmen with no more than high-school education to first-year graduate students, and included ratings by peers, supervisors, teachers, or experienced clinicians in settings as diverse as military training courses and sorority houses. In all the analyses, Tupes and Christal found "five relatively strong and recurrent factors and nothing more of any consequence"

This five-factor structure has been replicated by Norman (1963), Borgatta (1964), and Digman and Takemoto-Chock (1981) in lists derived from Cattell's 35 variables. Following Norman (1963), the factors were initially labeled:

(I) Extraversion or Surgency (talkative, assertive, energetic)

(II) Agreeableness (good-natured, cooperative, trustful)

(III) Conscientiousness (orderly, responsible, dependable)

(IV) Emotional Stability versus Neuroticism (calm, not neurotic, not easily upset)

(V) Culture (intellectual, polished, independent-minded)

These factors eventually became known as the "Big Five" (Goldberg, 1981)—a title chosen not to reflect their intrinsic greatness but to emphasize that each of these factors is extremely broad. Thus, the Big Five structure does not imply that personality differences can be reduced to only five traits. Rather, these five dimensions represent personality at the broadest level of abstraction, and each dimension summarizes a large number of distinct, more specific personality characteristics.

Brand preference refers to the consumers hierarchical prioritization of the brand as a result of their patronage and cognitive comprehension of the brand (Singh, Ehrenberg, & Goodhardt, 2008). Customer merchandise carries much more meaning than their utilitarian, functional, and commercial significance (Terpstra & Sarathy, 1997). Individuals are more likely to buy brands whose personalities intimately match their own self images (Schiffman & Kanuk, 2000) and self expression (Jamal & Goode, 2001). Moreover, consumers express themselves by selecting brands whose personalities are consistent with their own personalities (Aaker, 1999).

Self image or self expression affects consumers product preferences and their purchase intentions (Mehta, 1999). Ericksen (1996) finds a significant relationship between self image and intention to buy an American brand automobile (Ford Escort). In other words, „individuals prefer brands that have images compatible with their perceptions of self (Jamal & Goode 2001: 483). This self image consistency strengthens positive attitude toward products and brands (Sirgy, et al. 1997). Specifically, Graeff (1996: 5) notes that the more similar a consumer's self-image is to the brand's image, the more favorable their evaluations of that brand should be.

In general, consumers have a brand preference toward an established brand during the firms long presence in the market (Dinlersoz & Pereira, 2007) and they tend to show little brand preference toward a particular brand when they are exposed to a new or unfamiliar product category. Research indicates that the greater their shopping experiences and/or information collection, the higher the probability of focusing on a specific brand (Devaraj, Fan, & Kohli, 2006).

Brand personality refers to the set of human characteristics associate with a brand (Aaker, 1997: 347). Contrary to performance-oriented product attributes, brand personality appears to be representative/self-expressive oriented (Keller, 1993; Fennis & Pruyn, 2007). Moreover, it has been suggested that brand personality facilitates a consumer to articulate his/her self (Belk, 1988), an ideal self (Malhotra, 1988), or exact aspects of the self (Kleine, et al. 1993). Additionally, this concept is an essential determinant of consumer preference and usage (Biel, 1993).

Any direct/indirect contact that the consumer has with a brand can influence brand personality (Plummer, 1985). Brand's user imagery is shaped by direct influences or „the set of human characteristics associated with the typical user of a brand (Aaker, 1997: 348), the firm's workers and/or boss, and the brand's endorsers. On the other hand, the indirect influences contain product-related features, product category relationships, brand name, mark or emblem, and other marketing mix elements (Batra, Lehmann, & Singh, 1993).

Customers tend to select and use brands with various salient personality dimensions to highlight certain aspects of their own personality in various situational contexts (Aaker, 1999; Helgeson & Supphellen, 2004). According to Sung and Tinkham (2005), brand personality is a hypothetical construct developed by consumers and it differs from human personality. Individuals possess the human personality traits composed of implicit (perceived) and actual (objective) components, independent of the perceivers characterization. In contrast, no objective personality traits exist in brand. Aaker, Fournier, and Brasel (2004) note that as the connection between brand and the customer interacts, the personality traits have direct influence on this interaction.

RESEARCH OBJECTIVES

Based on the problem discussion, the overall purpose of this thesis is to gain a better understanding of how the personality of a brand is related to an individual's personality.

1. To study the perception of generation Y with respect to their brand association, brand liking, desire to buy, brand referral, purchase intension, sense of pride, trust and brand as reflection of personality.
2. To study individual's personality on the basis of Big Five Model.
3. To relate brand personality with an individual's personality.

Hypothesis

H_1: There exist a significant relationship between one's individual personality and preference for brands with similar brand personality

RESEARCH METHODOLOGY

The main purpose of this research was to gain a deeper understanding of the phenomenon of brand personality. The overall research purpose is mainly descriptive, since the research questions are of descriptive character. In this survey, the primary data was obtained by administering structured questionnaires. The secondary data was collected through various literature reviews and articles. For this study, population is divided into four broad geographical regions: East, West, North, South, Central Delhi and NCR.The second stage was purposive wherein the generation Y (age group 20-30 yrs of age)are drawn from each region. Non-probabilistic convenient Sampling was used. Sample size was taken as 100.

Table 1: Number of Samples

Region	*No. of Samples*
East Delhi	20
West Delhi	15
North Delhi	20
South Delhi	15
Central Delhi	13
NCR	17

RESULTS AND DISCUSSIONS

In this study, generation Y were asked to mark their brand preferences among the following list of brands of mobile phones- Nokia, Samsung, Sony Ericson, HTC, Micromax and iPhone.

Nokia is perceived as the most trusted brand, Samsung as the top brand in customer loyalty, HTC as smart and promising phones, Sony Ericson as stylish but reasonable brand and iPhone as sophisticated, innovative, friendly, stylish brand.

Table 2: Perception of Generation Y Towards Brand Personality

Dimensions	*Attributes*	*Mean*
Sincere	Down to Earth	3.288667
	Honest	4.027333
	Wholesome	4.033
	Cheerful	3.960667
	Overall Mean	3.827417
Excitement	Daring	3.931233
	Spirited	3.910667
	Imaginative	4.0915
	Up-to-date	3.9221
	Overall Mean	3.963875
Competence	Reliable	3.994
	Intelligent	4.033333
	Successful	3.977333
	Overall Mean	4.001556
Sophistication	Upper Class	4.055333
	Charming	3.633
	Overall Mean	3.844167
Ruggedness	Outdoorsy	3.499667
	Tough	3.33
	Overall Mean	3.414833

Table 3: Perception of Generation Y Towards Brand Personality

Dimensions	*Mean*	*Std. Dev*
Sincere	3.8	0.49
Excitement	3.9	1.079
Competence	4	0.933
Sophistication	3.8	0.024
Ruggedness	3.4	0.017

It was found that most of the generation Y preferred the brands which are competent (reliable, intelligent and successful) in nature like Nokia. The next level of preference was for excitement oriented and sophisticated brands such as HTC, iPhone. Many people also prefer the sincere brands of mobile phones such as Samsung, Sony Ericson which are trustworthy and loyal towards customers. The rugged brands are the least preferred brands.

Table 4: Perception of Generation Y about their Own Personality

Dimensions	*Mean*	*Std. Dev*
Extraversion	4.102	0.084
Agreeableness	3.487	0.124
Conscientiousness	4.123	1.01
Neuroticism	2.8994	0.0962
Openness	3.244	0.0446

The perception of generation Y about their own personality was also evaluated and it was found out that most of the people have personalities which have extraversion and conscientiousness characteristics followed by the agreeableness and openness characteristics in their personalities. Neuroticism of was the least perceived dimension of personality among the people researched.

Table 5: Perception of Generation Y Towards the Brand on Different Variables

Perception of Generation Y	*Mean*	*Std Dev.*
Whether the phone brand is refection of individual's personality	3.333	1.286
Whether the phone brand is trusted one	4.033	1.06
Whether the generation Y refer their brand to others	3.5	1.31
Whether the generation Y are associated with their brand	3.183	1.103
Whether the generation Y feel sense of pride for their brand	2.933	1.236
Whether the generation Y have Purchase Intension for their brand	3.2245	1.014
Whether the generation Y like the brand	3.8	0.979
Whether the generation Y desire to know about the brand	4.283	0.754

Maximum number of generation Y preferred the trusted brands such as Nokia and Samsung and also the brands which the customers desire to buy. Most of the people buy those mobile phone brands which they like. A comparable number of people refer their phone brands to others like family and friends. Not many people have purchase intensions for their mobile phone brand. Very few people associate themselves with their mobile phone brands. Also not a large number of people perceive their mobile phones as reflection of their personality and the least number of people buy phones for sense of pride.

Relation Between Brand Personality and Individual's Personality

The personality of different brands of mobile phones as percieved by the generation Y and individual's own personalty on different dimensions of personality were found out.Then, correlation coeffecient between the brand personality traits and individual's personality dimensions was found out.

Table 6: Correlation Between Brand Personality Attributes and Individual's Personality Dimensions

		Sincere	*Excitement*	*Competence*	*Sophistication*	*Ruggedness*
Extraversion	Pearson Correlation	.069	.236	.243	.101	.062
	Sig. (2-tailed)	.601	.069	.062	.445	.639
	N	60	60	60	60	60
Agreeableness	Pearson Correlation	.013	.047	.123	-.031	-.056
	Sig. (2-tailed)	.922	.723	.349	.814	.672
	N	60	60	60	60	60
Conscientiousness	Pearson Correlation	-.035	.057	.064	-.072	.108
	Sig. (2-tailed)	.793	.666	.626	.585	.412
	N	60	60	60	60	60
Neuroticism	Pearson Correlation	-.065	-.006	-.023	-.053	-.126
	Sig. (2-tailed)	.623	.965	.862	.688	.339
	N	60	60	60	60	60
Openness	Pearson Correlation	.195	.357**	.497**	.419**	.174
	Sig. (2-tailed)	.136	.005	.000	.001	.183
	N	60	60	60	60	60

**. Correlation is significant at the 0.01 level (2-tailed).

*. Correlation is significant at the 0.05 level (2-tailed).

Correlation was found out between the individual's personality and brand personality. The above table denotes the Pearson correlation coefficient and significance values of various individual's personality dimensions like extraversion, agreeableness, conscientiousness, neuroticism and openness with the various attributes of brand personality such as sincere, excitement, competence, sophistication and ruggedness. Pearson's correlation coeffecient was found significant only between openness and excitement, openness and competence, openness and sophistication which means that the people who have personality with characteristics of openness (artistic, curious, imaginative, insightful, original, wide interests) prefer the excitement oriented, competent and sophisticated brands of mobile phones like Sony ericsson, HTC, Nokia and iPhone respectively. No significant correlation values were find between other brand personality and individual's personality traits except in the case where respondents were high on the openess variable measured through the big five personality scale. People who were high on openess prefered brands that were promoted on the plank on excitement ($r=.3, p<.01$). The relationship was also high in case of brands promoted on the variable of competence ($r=.45, p<.01$)and sophistication ($r=.45, p<.01$).This can be attributed to the fact that though generation Y as is influenced by new technoligies and symbolic brand images. However interestingly only those of them high on openess were keen to try brands which were positioned on the excitement,competence and sophistication plank . However generation Y with personalities high on concentiousness, agreeableness ,extroversion etc considered other variables apart from brand personilty and positioning for drawing their preferences.Hence the hypothesis H_1 is partially accepted and partially rejected.

CONCLUSION AND IMPLICATIONS

Branding has been one of the most imperative commercial topics over the last decades (Boshoff, Schlechter, &Ward, 2011). The scope of this study focuses only on the brands of the mobile phones and the personalities of the individuals. The findings of this study are consistent with the works of Hellier, *et al.* (2003). Consumers do have significant and diverse brand recognition with perceived value among a variety of brands. „The influence of brand names on quality judgments does exist (Na, *et al.* 2008: 195). In order to retain customers, managers should focus on improving customers' perceived equality of services and goods (Klaus and Maklan, 2007). Consequently, firms shall make the most of highly appraised customer perceived value variable(s) as part of the marketing elements and develop their competitive advantage/s for increasing market share, sales, profit, and brand image (Phusavat and Kanchana, 2008a).

On the subject of what a company is, customers often have various perceptions in brand personality among different brands. "The strongest brands find the appropriate balance between functional and emotional attributes (Bergstrom, 2000: 12; Priilaid & Rensburg, 2010). Functional attributes refer to tangible characteristics such as performance, quality, and price while emotional attributes refer to intangible features such as, how the brand makes you feel (Bergstrom, 2000: 13). The findings of the current study offer additional support to the importance of both attributes and highlight the power of branding in this luxurious product category. For example, 3M is known for its innovation nature, Hallmark is extensively well-known for caring, FedEx is widely famed for its guaranteed speedy delivery service, Disney is drastically associated with fun and family entertainment, and Nike is considerably prominent for individual performance (Davis, 2000). The findings of this study suggest that people who have personality with characteristics of openness (artistic, curious, imaginative, insightful, original, wide interests) prefer the excitement oriented, competent and sophisticated brands of mobile phones like Sony ericsson, HTC, Nokia and iPhone respectively.

These findings can help the marketers to formulate strategies for increasing their sales by selling the brands of products suiting to the personality of the customer.

The prioritization of critical success factors can help practitioners understand their relative importance and develop improvement plans in cases where they lack sufficient resources to deal with all factors simultaneously (Chin, Chan, & Lam, 2008: 437). As advertisements seldom provide any noticeable information related to brand personality, companies may incorporate these findings in their integrated promotional strategies for advertising, such as the creation of brand knowledge in consumers' minds from the firm's investment in various marketing and corporate communication programs (Argyriou, Kitchen, & Melewar, 2006: 575). The efficiency of this advertising approach deserves more research with precision.

REFERENCES

[1] Aaker, D.A., (2002). *Building Strong Brands*, Simon & Schuster UK Ltd: London.

[2] Aaker, J.L. (1997). Dimensions of brand personality, *Journal of Marketing Research*, 34(August), 347-356.

[3] Aaker, J.L. (1999). The malleable self, The role of self-expression in persuasion, *Journal of Marketing Research*, 36(1), 45-57.

[4] Aaker, J.L., Fournier, S., and Brasel, S.A. (2004). When good brands do bad, *Journal of Consumer Research*, 31 (1), 1-16.

[5] Argyriou, E., Kitchen, P.J., & Melewar, T.C. (2006). The relationship between corporate websites and brand equity- a conceptual framework and research agenda, *International Journal of Market Research*, 48(5), 575-599.

[6] Batra, R., Lehmann, D.R., & Singh, D. (1993). The brand personality component of brand goodwill, some antecedents and consequences, Paper Presented in *Brand Equity and Advertising*, Hillsdale, NJ, Lawrence Erlbaum Associates.

[7] Belk, R.W. (1988). Possessions and the extended self, *Journal of Consumer Research*,

[8] Biel, A.L., (1992). How Brand Image Drives Brand Equity, *Journal of Advertising Research*, Vol. 32, Issue 6, p. 6-12.

[9] Boshoff, C., Schlechter, C., & Ward, S.J. (2011). Consumers' perceived risks associated with purchasing on a branded web site, The mediating effect of brand knowledge, *South African Journal of Business Management*, 42(1), 45-54.

[10] Chin, K-S, Chan, B.L. & Lam, P-K. (2008). Identifying and prioritizing critical success factors for coopetition strategy, *Industrial Management & Data Systems*, 108, 437-454.

[11] Davis, S.M. (2000). *Brand Asset Management*. Jossey-Bass Inc.

[12] Delgado-Ballester, E. & Munuera-Alemán, J.L., (2005). Does brand trust matter to brand equity? *Journal of Product & Brand Management*, Vol. 14, Issue 3, p. 187-196.

[13] Denscombe, M., (2000) *Forskningshandboken*, Studentlitteratur: Lund.

[14] Devaraj, S., Fan, M., & Kohli, R. (2006). Examination of online channel preference, Using the structure-conduct-outcome framework, *Decision Support Systems*, 42, 1089-1103..

[15] Ericksen, M.K. (1996). Using self-congruity and ideal congruity to predict purchase intention, an European perspective, *Journal of Euro-Marketing*, 6(1), 41-56.

[16] Fennis, B.M., & Pruyn, A.T.H. (2007). You are what you wear, Brand personality influences on consumer impression formation, *Journal of Business Research*, 60, 634-639.

[17] Hankinson, G. & Cowking, P., (1993). *Branding in Action*, McGraw-Hill: Berkshire. Kapferer, J., (1997) *Strategic Brand Management*, Kogan Page: London.

[18] Keller, K.L., (1993). Conceptualizing, Measuring, and Managing Customer-Based Brand Equity, *Journal of Marketing*, Vol. 57, Issue 1, p. 1-22.

[19] Kim, C.K., Han, D. & Park, S., (2001). The Effect of Brand Personality and Brand Identification on Brand Loyalty: Applying the Theory of Social Identification, *Japanese Psychological Research*, Vol. 43, Issue 4, p.195-206.

[20] Kotler, P., Wong, V., Saunders, J. & Armstrong, G., (2005). *Principles of Marketing, Fourth European Edition*, Pearson Education Limited: Edinburgh.

[21] McEnally, M. & Chernatony, L., (1999) The Evolving Nature of Branding: Consumer and Managerial Considerations, *Academy of Marketing Science*, Vol. 1999, Issue 2. Available at: http://www.amsreview.org/articles/mcenally02-1999.pdf

[22] Melin, F., (1997) Varumärket som strategiskt konkurrensmedel, *Doctoral Thesis*, Lund University.

[23] Plummer, J.T., (2000). How Personality Makes a Different, *Journal of Advertising Research*, Vol. 40, Issue 6, p. 79-83.

[24] Sweeney, J.C. & Brandon, C., (2006). Brand Personality: Exploring the Potential to Move from Factor Analytical to Circumplex Models, *Psychology & Marketing*, Vol. 23, Issue 8, p.639-663.

Role of Social Networking in Managing Generation Y

Guneet Kaur

Department of HMR, Institute of Technology & Management, Delhi

ABSTRACT

Social media communication like Facebook, Twitter etc is an inevitable part of today's generation which is a mixture of some Baby Boomers, more Gen Xers and much of Generation Y. The emerging scenario of organizations is based on the future leadership of Gen Y who is the new workforce these days. More and more organizations are also accepting the social media platforms as a medium for not only brand building but also attracting talent and giving a personal face to the company. Today's employees, be it interns, line personnel to managers, product leaders to executives – are offering innovative solutions for internal effectiveness through social media. Strategy and good administration integrated with social media tools, positively impact an organization. 76 percent of US companies use LinkedIn's 100 million registered users for recruiting. 41% of 2011 university graduates used social media in their job search. Innovative companies are mining connections on key social networking sites, maintaining their organization's reputation online, and watching how their own talent is interacting online. They are also leveraging social media to create talent communities that engage passive candidates and promote their brand.

While a Generation Y employee may have no issues being asked to suddenly use a certain social media tool, a baby boomer may feel overwhelmed and frustrated by such a request. Traditionalists and baby boomers alike prefer face-to-face meetings or phone calls, while Generation X and Y don't necessarily need, or want, face-to-face encounters and would prefer to pick up the phone to send a text versus make a call. Relationship building for this group often occurs through simply "pinging" their social media networks. Implementation of a policy or procedure centred on social media can prove to be challenging with a diverse workforce. One way to better understand how a social media policy change may affect the broader organization is through assessing how each stakeholder group may be affected by the change. Such analysis helps to identify high priority impacts and highlights key stakeholder requirements.

Technology plays an important role in our day to day lives and that is what makes generation Y's view of the social world different to their predecessors, as they haven't lived in a world without it. Gen Y has the need to be connected to some form of technology all the time whether it's via text messaging, instant messaging and any other forms (Clark 2009; Gerger 2007). Many of these young adults describe their mobile phones as a part of themselves and without them they cannot perform any of their daily tasks (Clark 2009). Consider the fact Gen Y loves to collect everything about their lives and share with the world – a highly transparent group! And they know how to document it! While HR recognizes some things are private, it still must collect and capture relevant information and situations taking place at all times. Clearly there exists a linkage between how much Gen Y is addicted to digital mediums, specifically Internet usage, Social media platforms etc. and how much their opinions are affected by connecting to these networks or drawing information from their usage. Given this backdrop, it is imperative that there needs to be a focus on integrating the expectations of GEN Y employees towards their work organizations (which is viewed by them as an extension of their social life), to their psychological needs of expression and acceptance through collaborating on Social Media platforms and connecting to the outside world. With Gen Y rapidly increasing numbers across the workforce, it is time for organizations to take a pause and reflect on their future course of action towards engaging a generation that is highly wired, connected and unconventional.

Keywords: *Generation Y, Social Networking, Millennials*

INTRODUCTION

Generation Y, also known as the **Millennial Generation**, is the demographic cohort following Generation X. These individuals, born around 1980s till 2000 are sometimes called Echo Boomers, due to the significant increase in birth rates during this period. Millennials are mostly the children of Baby Boomers or Gen Xers. The 20th century trend toward smaller families in developed countries continued, however, so the relative impact of the "baby boom echo" was generally less pronounced than the original boom. It is generally marked by an increased use and familiarity with communication, media, and digital technologies. In most parts of the world its upbringing was marked by an increase in a neoliberal approach to politics and economics; the effects of this environment are disputed. Jean Twenge, the author of the 2007 book *Generation Me*, considers Gen Ys along with younger Gen Xers to be part of a generation called Generation Me. This is based on personality surveys that showed increasing narcissism among Millennials compared to the Boomers when they were teens and sometimes in their twenties. Millennials are sometimes called the "Trophy Generation" also, or "Trophy Kids," a term that reflects the trend in competitive sports, as well as many other aspects of life, where mere participation is frequently enough for a reward. It has been reported that this is an issue in corporate environments. Some employers are concerned that Millennials have too great expectations from the workplace. Studies predict that Generation Y will switch jobs frequently, holding far more than Generation X due to their great expectations. To address these new challenges, many large firms are currently studying the social and behaviorial patterns of Millennials and are trying to devise programs that decrease intergenerational estrangement, and increase relationships of reciprocal understanding between older employees and Millennials, while at the same time making Millennials more comfortable.

One of the more popular forms of media use in Generation Y is through social networking. In 2010, research was published in the Elon Journal of Undergraduate Research which claimed that students who used social media and decided to quit showed the same withdrawal symptoms of a drug addict who quit their stimulant.

The term 'Social Media' encompasses a wide variety of internet-based applications that compresses user generated information and allows instantaneous access and exchange across Web 2.0 (Kaplan and Haenlein, 2010). Known for its media richness, strong user content and social presence, this communication medium has been effectively explored and exploited in the marketing domain for its networking capabilities and strong user influence. This powerful communication medium can be exploited by researcher and HR practitioner in relating aspects like loyalty and commitment for the organization.

Social media are the media for social interaction, using highly accessible & scalable publishing techniques. They use web based technologies to turn communication into interactive dialogue allowing creation & exchange of user generated content. Businesses also refer to social media as Consumer Generated Media (CGM). Examples include blogs, social networks like facebook, linkedIn etc. These sites entice users by allowing them to disclose all about themselves through this virtual entity, by way of sharing their happiness, anger, grief and even their trauma. They are platforms that impact users psychologically and are a favourite medium of communication for the net savvy Gen Y.

SOCIAL NETWORKING AND GENERATION Y

Social Media is a HUGE component of a Gen Y individual's life. The soaring application of social networking has eclipsed the relevance of food, clothing, sleep, and social sanity, in exchange for quick Instagram photographs of what we had for breakfast or what we bought for Mother's Day.

Social networking has become a global phenomenon where connectivity and engagement both gets a major facelift, overpowering the sluggish deliverance of message brought by e-mail and the humdrum interface of SMS. Social media has become so unstoppable that employees that belong in the Y-Generation bracket prefer applying for companies that allow its workforce to brag and lounge around in their extensive social media networks.

Microsoft Malaysia shockingly reveals that Y-Generation job seekers prioritize mobile phone and social media access over salary. Younger employees enjoy the absolute freedom given to them during one-hour or fifteen minute breaks, and the kind of respite they're looking for is complete control over their mobile and social life. The changing landscape in today's corporate employment has taken a turn for the good and the bad, whichever way you look at it.

Cisco's Connected World Technology Report of 2011 states that *two in every 5 college students and young employees* treat social media as fundamentally important as air, food, water, and shelter. This twisted belief mobilizes the truth that there is a growing relevance behind social media's pleasure and professional functions. Certainly, these respondents are looking at the big picture, collecting every advantage they can get in their accounts. The Y-Generation isn't really excited of working in a grey-shadowed cubicle with paperwork and curled telephone lines beside their elbows. They want a dynamic workplace. An office that breeds fun and outgoing co-workers and most importantly, a business organization that pays them to do their job while commenting on a friend's Facebook status change or bashing a Tweet. *Generation Y-Facebook users often use their Facebook profiles as an extension of their professional personalities, even as they socialize with family and friends.*

The below figure shows that on average, Gen-Y Facebook users are connected to 16 co-workers via Facebook, although that number is a relatively small percentage (2.3%) of their total average friend count (696):

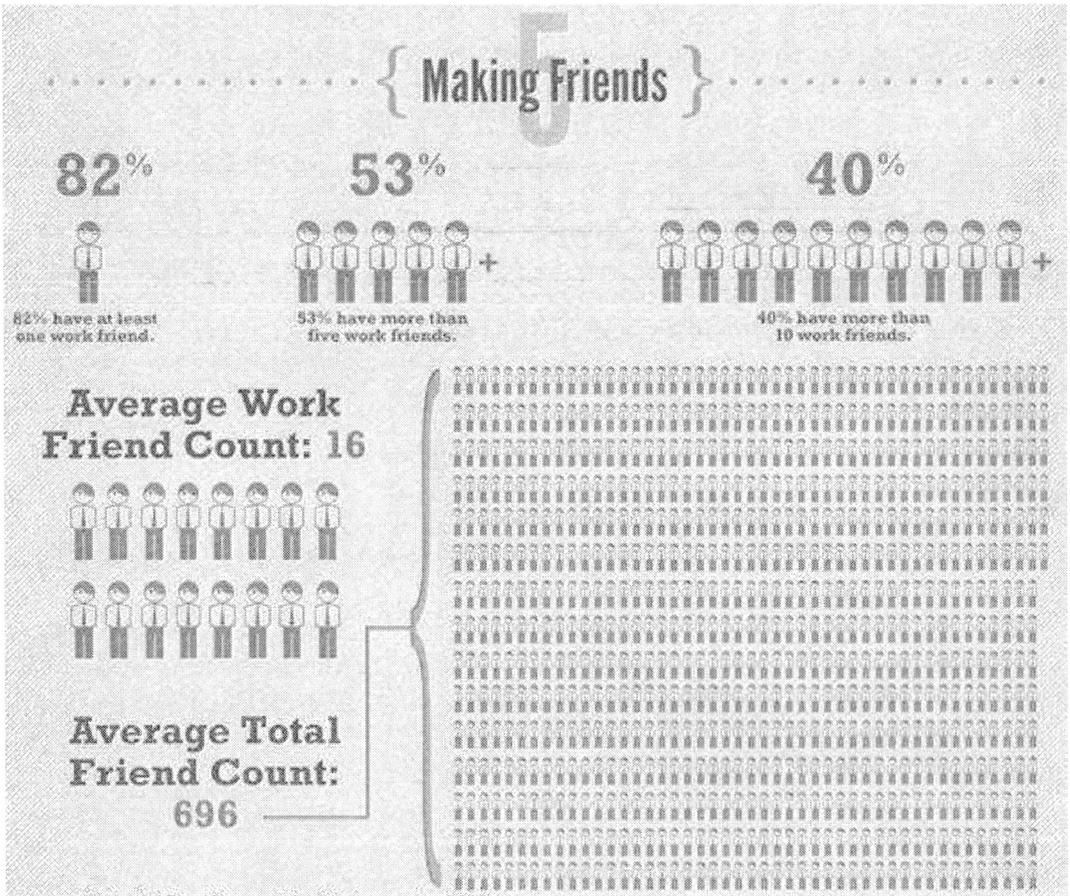

Source: Millennial Branding and Identified.com, Jan 2012

Gen-Y Facebook Users Define Themselves by Colleges, Not Workplaces. Only 36% of Gen-Y Facebook users list an employer on their Facebook profile, whereas 80% list at least one school.

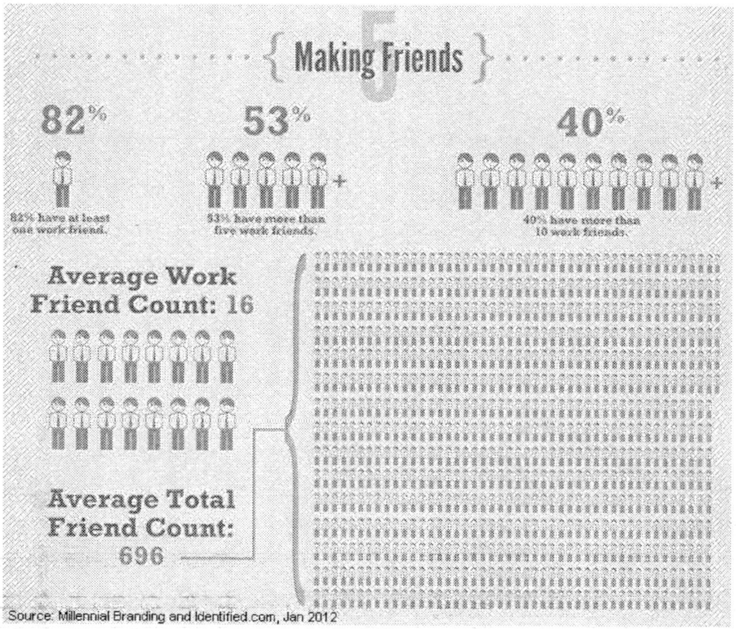

Source: Millennial Branding and Identified.com, Jan 2012

Short work stints are common: Gen-Y Facebook users spend an average of just over 2 years at their first job—and, interestingly, "owner" is the fifth-most popular title among this entrepreneurial generation.

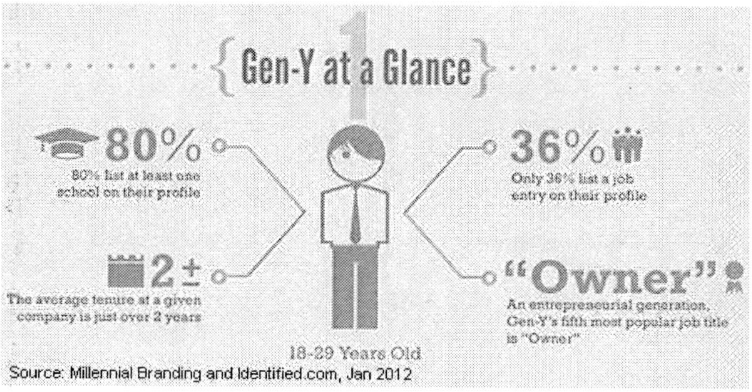

Source: Millennial Branding and Identified.com, Jan 2012

Top Employers

Likely a sign of a down economy, the travel and hospitality industry now employs most Gen-Y Facebook users (7.2%), followed by consumer products companies (6.8%) and the US

Government and Military (4.5%). Moreover, only 7% of Gen-Y Facebook users are employed by a Fortune 500 company, according to the study.

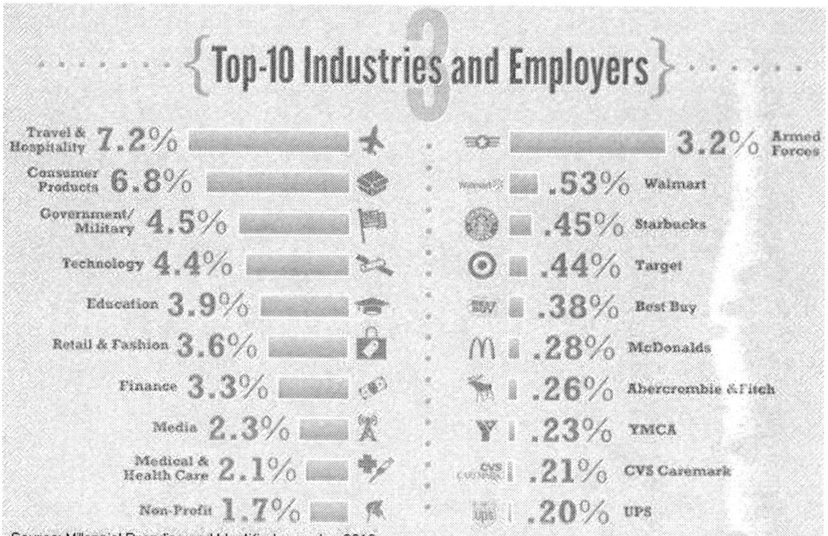

Source: Millennial Branding and Identified.com, Jan 2012

As per the data available for United States, the US Military is the largest Gen-Y employer overall (3.2%), followed by second-ranked Walmart (0.53%) and third-ranked Starbucks (0.45%). Deloitte (0.189%) and Hollister (0.187%) are ranked No. 11 and No. 12, respectively.

IMPACT OF SOCIAL MEDIA ON GEN Y EMPLOYEES

While social media is not reserved to any generation or age, there is no denying that millennials are heavily influencing how organizations operate in the world of digital communication. Millennials are responsible for a culture shift because of their emphasis on social media freedom, quality of work, and collaborative work environments. Because millennials continue to grow both in quantity and quality within the workplace, even the most traditional companies are being forced to adapt and become more collaborative and social by nature.

Reasons why social networking is part of Gen Y's professional portfolio

1. Social networking isn't all about fun and games – The social media sphere is dominated by big names like Facebook, Twitter, Pinterest, and Tumblr. These online avenues continue to generate millions of unique traffic, unparalleled engagement, and business opportunities who are in it for a variety of reasons. However, younger professionals see social networking as an *alternate dimension* wherein they can enhance areas of their craft through communications and resources that are otherwise paid or limited in their location. Social networking platforms like the popular Linkedin and other under-utilized sites like Upspring and Ziggs connect like-minded professionals on a local or international scale, hence users can promote and ask questions directed to industry leaders in their field. These networks are absolutely useful in mining for job prospects that might entail higher pay or extraordinary bonuses (e.g. memberships to elite clubs or free parachute diving lessons are all the rage now, or maybe not.).

2. **Social networks boost morale** – Younger professionals are expected to show signs of weakness whenever they are confronted with pressure at work, and that's absolutely fine. Now let's talk about Facebook and Twitter. From out of nowhere, the two colossal social networks provide emotional comebacks for young employees who are feeling a bit enervated or unmotivated. Social media lights up morale. Publishing a simple I need motivation, help me status change that gets hoarded with hundreds of personal comments and thousands more of Likes from people you barely even know, sparks the dead batteries infusing it with invisible motivation and psychological push. Messages, Tweets, and even Shares (sharing status updates rarely occurs, unless you're some Hollywood hotshot) containing inspiring, but not limited to *you can do it* or *weekend is just around the corner, mush forward* quotes, installs an additional spark plug to an emotionally-stressed employee exposed to higher concentrations of social media toxins.

3. **Social media and the concept of gamification** – Social media provides younger employees the feature to explore the depths of personal achievements and through the concept of *gamification*, unlocking leading some virtual scoreboard is close to being awesome, or *god-like*. Younger employees enjoy this kind of social challenge, and it's a mature way of re-conceptualizing the feeling of being on top of someone for a change.

HR'S CONCERN FOR SOCIALLY ACTIVE GENERATION Y

Generation Y is looking forward to take their social interests to the organizational level and this has engulfed the HR department to take up new initiatives to manage the working of Generation Y. 2/3 of recent college job seekers ask about corporate social media policies in job interviews. 2 in 5 employees of this generation say that they can compromise on a lower salary in exchange for more flexibility in 'device choice', social media access and mobility. 46% say their laptop is the most important technology in their daily lives.7 in 10 facebook users have "friended" a co-worker or superior. 68% of Twitter users "follow" a co-worker or superior. 81% of college students across the globe are accessing Facebook at least once a day. Surprisingly, the US did not have the highest percentage. They strolled in with a 79%. Other countries of note included: UK at 89%, Spain at 84%, Mexico at 91%, and India at 92%. Japan was the lowest percentage bringing up the rear at 46%.

According to a 2011 survey by Robert Half Technology, 54% of firms do not allow employees to visit social networking sites for any reasons while at work. 19% allow access for business purposes only. 16% allow access for personal use and 10% allow access to unlimited personal use. It has also been found that nearly 50% of senior HR Directors are still relying on outdated methods to attract young talent. HR Managers not only handle the Gen Y but the baby boomers and Gen X at the same time. Gen Y has started taking up important roles and profiles and interfering with the traditional styles of management. They tend to move the job towards digital technology, social networks and higher inclination for flexible work environments. They are continuously wired and virtually connected openly displaying their opinions for organizational practices. They are ready to collaborate and exchange information through social communication channels and influence the HR departments to modify existing policies. It's very important for them to know about the leader they are working with and seek to contribute to the organizations through a plethora of ideas, suggestions and informed opinions. HR needs to focus on integrating the expectations of Gen Y employees towards their work organizations, to their psychological needs of expression and acceptance through collaborating on Social Media platforms and connecting to the outside world.

Role of Social Networking in Managing Generation Y

Employee Engagement

It can be used as an important tool for employee engagement in which employee is working towards achieving desired performance through innovation, engaging them emotionally and cognitively also. Gen Y's willingness to dedicate their time to some form of service can be utilized effectively in business as well as fulfilling social responsibility.

Technological Advancement

HR can bring about technological development in the organization through Gen Y's technological savvy nature. They easily communicate with others and access information quickly and instantaneously. For example, Generation Y is just as apt to take a business call at home before dinner as they are to answer a personal e-mail or text message prior to or during a staff meeting.

Workplace Attitude

Technology not only influences the work of Generation Y, but also their workplace attitudes. Unlike their predecessors, Generation Y typically defines themselves by who they are outside of their career, not by their employment. Additionally, members of Generation Y associate less with their employing organization and more with the type of work they do. According to Lloyd (2007), the organization is not the identifier, the work is. They also do not connect long working hours to work quality or devotion to their employer. As previously mentioned, due to technological advancement, this generation believes they can work away from the office and still produce quality results. Technology not only influences the work of Generation Y, but also their workplace attitudes. Social networking among employees gives an insight into their other side, which tells about their attitudes and perception about something. This knowledge can be harnessed by organizations in leading and managing Gen Y.

Flexibility

Generation Y desires work and career flexibility. Generation Y believes they can do more with less; consequently, they feel they deserve the freedom to work fewer hours while still taking jobs that are challenging (Lloyd 2007). However, "doing more with less" does not refer to income, but explains Generation Y's belief that they can accomplish the same task as other generations in less time. Further, with their familiarity with technology, Millennials believe they can work more efficiently. More specifically, they can eliminate what they consider wasted time – the non-essential, face-to-face interaction that occurs within a typical office setting (Erickson 2008).

Continual Learning

Generation Y is continuously looking for feedback and advice from their superiors – most likely a result of their strong ties to and constant feedback from their parents (Cruz 2007; BSG Concours 2007). On the job, Millennials expect frequent direction from managers regarding their performance. They recognize the role knowledge plays in career advancement and look for opportunities to learn from their supervisors and older generations (BSG Concours 2007). Additionally, Generation Y views failure as a motivator and not a deterrent. Thus, they view failure as an opportunity to improve job performance (Blain 2008). Social media is a good channel to provide real feedback with less criticism and open discussions.

Team Orientation & Individualism

While they prefer the flexibility to work outside the office, Generation Y is comfortable in group settings – having worked in teams throughout school – and according to a study by BSG Concours (2007), ¯They understand that a mix of strengths contributes to success. Although Generation Y operates and works comfortably in teams and with other employees, their mentality is slightly different from other generations (Cole, Smith, and Lucas 2002). For example, researchers argue Baby Boomers exhibit a strong teamwork ethic, as they prefer to work as a group of individuals to collaborate and accomplish a single group task (Buanhe and Kovary 2003). Conversely, Generation Y prefers working as a team to accomplish independent tasks as they use the skills, knowledge, and resources of team members to satisfy individual needs (Cole, Smith, and Lucas 2002Karefalk, Petterssen and Zhu 2007). However, when interacting with managers, Generation Y feels more valued if the manager works with them on an individual level (Spiro 2006). Literature explains that Generation Y's team orientation refers to a desire to coordinate and share information with other team members, while their individualism refers to a desire to be mentored and coached as an individual (Buanhe and Kovary 2003; Spiro 2006).

Communication Patterns

One of the most significant challenges facing Generation Y in joining the workforce is their need to communicate effectively with Generation X and the Baby Boomers (Ballenstedt and Rosenberg 2008). Scholars note that differences in values, perceptions, and communication styles among generations can lead to conflict in the workplace (Bassett 2008 Lloyd 2007). Therefore, finding a way to express values clearly between the generations becomes crucial to establishing a coherent and effective workforce. Gen Y is least likely to share information via text message (26 percent compared to 47 percent of those age 55-plus), and least likely to use video conferencing, video chat, and Web conferencing tools. Gen Y is least likely to think meetings are efficient. Only 29 percent of Gen Y workers think meetings used to decide on a course of action are very efficient, compared to 45 percent of older Boomers.

Recruitment Efforts

Generation Y uses social networks in the right way, not only to keep in touch with friends, but also manage their own careers. Around 92% of employers are using or planning to use social networks for recruitment. Some 93 percent of recruiters are using LinkedIn, two-thirds are using Facebook, and 54 percent are using Twitter. 71 percent of recruiters consider themselves moderate to exceptional at using the tools to find candidates, yet only 52 percent consider their recruiting programs to be somewhat successful. It is a method to increase applications and resumes and build brand recognition. Establishing a social recruiting platform like a career site creates a recruiting presence on social networks. For instance, Intel has their Jobs@Intel Blog, where they have links to their Twitter, Facebook and YouTube accounts and categories of posts where they provide career advice and insights. The bloggers are employees from around the world who gives their perspectives on what it takes to build a career at Intel. Another great example of this GE Careers, which allows you to search through their job postings, keep updated with their upcoming career events and learn about the company through the eyes of employees with video and blog content. By having everything in one place, it's easier for the job seeker to find you and for you to stay organized. In addition, you can promote your blog content through your social networks, which will build traffic. If you ask Gen Y what frustrates them the most about the recruiting process, it's that they feel companies ignore them. This is a common feeling because many Gen Y applicants don't receive responses after they submit their resumes. Companies should respond to them on social networks when they have questions. It not only benefits applicants but it also creates goodwill. Two companies with "no comment left behind" policies are Sodexo and Intel.

CONCLUSION

The workforce of 21st Century is a "Multi-Generational" composition, comprising a mix of all generations from Baby Boomers to Generation X, with ongoing inclusion of Generation Y. Generation Y is a generation that knows what it wants, in terms of their space, comfort levels or communication channels. They are open and brash about their expectations and expressions, seeking to collaborate and rapidly exchange knowledge/information, networking for acceptance, thus challenging ways traditional organizations functioned. Many researches indicate that it is important for Gen Y employees to feel connected, updated and involved in an organization. They are also a powerhouse of ideas and new innovations and seek to contribute to the organizational development. They also believe in the concept of instant acceptance and open feedback. They perceive 'workplace environment' as an emotionally engaged place where they socialize, learn and collaborate. They prefer workplaces that are boundary less, colourful and open with breakout spaces, conversation areas and chill out zones that allow them to collaborate, innovate and be creative. Organizations will have to recognize the priority millenials place on flexibility and fulfilling social needs at work, while at the same time setting realistic expectations of career paths and advancement opportunities.

Some Important Points to be Taken Care of While Managing Generation Y

Flatter them: this generation prefers on-the-spot recognition to traditional performance reviews, a whooping 80% of millennials said they would rather receive feedback in real-time, not to mention frequent check-ins to keep a pulse on progress.

Motivate them: motivation of millennials will require coupling structured assignments and frequent feedback with opportunities to learn, grow and contribute in meaningful ways. Millennials want a work environment that is comfortable and inspires them to contribute without fear of being criticised.

Collaborate: millennials are natural collaborators, particularly when the group's purpose and goals are understood. Employers should be clear about deadlines and any business boundaries the group should be aware of.

Companies that do adopt these changes will prove to be successful and leaders within their industry as they will be attracting more talent and bringing that talent to an environment that they can succeed in. As many will tell you, it's not enough to just have social, but to truly succeed in the digital age, you have to BE SOCIAL. The instinctual social nature of Generation Y is preparing them maximize their value by bringing that nature to their employers and driving visible business results across the board. Social media is well-established as a consumer and brand oriented set of tools. Increasingly, social media is being offered as an innovative solution for internal effectiveness. When strategy and governance are integrated with social media tools, they can positively impact an organization. An organization that thoughtfully embraces social media can realize opportunities across four areas:

1. Collaboration: constant, transparent, and effective collaboration with employees, candidates, customers and suppliers
2. Talent Management: top performance delivered through robust and real-time training, development and support

3. Administration: employee-centric Human Resources operations, regardless of where employees are in the world or organization hierarchy
4. Employee engagement: single, unified culture with engaged employees driving business

According to renowned consultancy firm, KPMG, 80% of companies use social media for recruitment and 95% of them use LinkedIn. Many companies that use social media struggle to successfully integrate it into their daily business routines. The challenge is frequently found within the creation, execution, and enforcement of social media policies. Many companies do not establish policies to govern social media usage or can find their policy difficult to enforce due to lack of employee engagement and training on the topic. Given these challenges, it is not surprising that many executives prefer to avoid the topic by saying that they have no need for social media or policies to manage it. However, as companies begin to realize the true value to be gained by social media adoption, consideration of workforce risk is essential for avoidance of loss of employee goodwill, information breaches, and reputational damage. While social media policy creation has challenges, it is not so different from previous challenges such as the adoption of corporate-wide e-mail in the 1990s. Many organizations already have the framework of a policy that governs communications and this framework can provide an excellent foundation to consider where social media might affect the business. Therefore, a good place to start is to create a governance body of key stakeholders. Stakeholders can be defined as any person/group of individuals, internal or external to the organization who will be impacted by the proposed changes, or who could have an impact on the success of the adoption. It's clear that social media tools are transforming the way we work ... and will continue to do so in ways we can only imagine. It is critical for Human Resource professionals to understand what these tools are used for and assess the risks and opportunities they may present to an organization Social media is redefining how companies innovate by connecting people and ideas in ways that have previously not been explored. Organizations now have the ability to utilize knowledge from external audiences around the globe that they could never reach before. It is changing the way we do business today. Additional benefits include the ability to enhance your public image, improve interactions with customers, and promote employee engagement. But it is not without internal and external risk.

BIBLIOGRAPHY

[1] www.sideroad.com
[2] http://socialmediatoday.com/index.php?q=SMC/206771
[3] http://www.robertsgolden.com/services/social-networking-for-employees/
[4] www.ezinarticles.com
[5] http://www.torbenrick.eu/t/r/qkv
[6] http://healthculturesociety.wikispaces.com
  • Social
[7] http://socialmediatoday.com/node/625841

Burn Out Stress Syndrome (BOSS) and Anxiety Among Generation Y – A Study on Call Centres

Indra Nanda and Kusum Tyagi[1]

Department of Home Science, VMLG (PG) College, Ghaziabad
[1]Department of Psychology, VMLG (PG) College, Ghaziabad

ABSTRACT

Call centres are no more a unique or new business organization day to day numbers of BPOs, KPOs and call centres (DSA) are increasing and so the employees. Anxiety and stress are somatic problems unfortunately neglected by the organizers as well as the victims. The present study was undertaken in Delhi and NCR on subjective work experience of call centre agents. Stress and Anxiety among agents was measured with the help of standardised tools. The findings indicate existence of stress and anxiety at initial stages and its exploration with the passage of time. Such somatic disorder affects work performance and well being of these workers.

Keywords: *Call Centres, Anxiety, Stress, Stress Syndrome Inbound, Outbound*

INTRODUCTION

Generation 'Y' a term used for tech savvy, team oriented, Family centric, Achievement-oriented, Attention craving, Nurtured and pampered by parents. It is also addressed as Millennial.

Generation Y is confident, ambitious and achievement-oriented. They have high expectations of their employers, seek out new challenges and are not afraid to question authority. Generation Y wants meaningful work and a solid learning curve. This generation is computer trained and comfortable with spoken English thus BPOs and Call Centres have taken a lead as employment units. Richardson and Marshall, (2000) describes that there are variety of factors, which have led to the increase of telephone services, such as -the development of digital exchanges, intelligent telephone networks and their integration with computer data bases, falling telephony costs and the introduction of toll-free numbers; the high degree of penetration and familiarity of telephone technology; and the ability to communicate complex information by phone in real time. Roy (2004) who has been addressed as father of Indian BPO industry explains- Indian businesses have become self-confident and enterprising today. India has emerged as an important stake holder in the outsourcing arena around the world. Organizers find India as a suitable destination due to availability of skilled English speaking Labour whose wages work out to a fraction of the wage paid in their home country (Chithelen, 2004). Therefore, call centres which are controlling various commercial functions are emerging as the country's new sunshine sector (Babu, 2004).The employees here, are selected on their ability to generate more profits in less time, communication skills, punctuality and basic knowledge of operating computers and other gadgets. Handsome salary and simple selection criteria inspires generation Y to opt these jobs.

Joining a job at early age and no particular training invites anxiety and stress among these employees. Anxiety, in simple words, is an emotional painful, uneasiness of mind concerning some impending or anticipated illness. In the words of eminent psychologists Anxiety may be termed as an effective, Stressful, transitory and highly emotional state, a highly unpleasant condition and all these signal a danger to ego.

Many modern studies of psychologist have focus on degree of anxiety and its critical effects on behavioural aspect. Many western studies Kathy (1998), Kleppa et al (2000) Lewig and Dolland (2003) have shown the impact of anxiety on work performance and arousal of other somatic problems.

Anxiety and stress at work place is related to work place injuries. Mickell Tyrell (1999) stated that the attrition rate of any organization also depends on well being and satisfaction among its employees. It is universally accepted that level of Anxiety at work place is always high initially and as the employee get tuned to the work environment it settles to normal level.

REVIEW OF LITERATURE

The Indian BPO industry needs to compete with international organization in respect to infrastructure. Basant and Rani (2004) stated that during 2003-04, the ITES-BPOs' segment was estimated to have achieved a 54 % growth in the revenues and a rapid rise in employment in IT enabled services. Saradhamani (2005) explains that to gain competitive advantages most of the MNC's are outsourcing their software requirement from India. Narasimhan (2006) said we must be aware about our social and religious values and how one can fit into this unique and new work pattern belonging to European and other countries. Thampson (2001) Houlihan (2002) Lewig and Dolland (2003) addressed the workers of call centres as ***emotional workers or as emotionally exhausted***. The nature of work in a call centre does not result in physical fatigue but mental fatigue after all one is expected to ***smile down the phone*** for 24x7x365as is the punch line of many call centres.

The NASSCAM MCKINSEY study on the BPOs' (2006) summarizes Employment opportunities for 4 million people by the year 2008 in India. Increase by 7% of India's GD Account for 30% of India's foreign exchange India's share of global IT enabled service will be 48% valued at 27,120 cores. It may be satisfying financial sectors but we need to show concern over health issues of the employees in these sectors.

METHODOLOGY

The present study was conducted in year 2008-2009 on call centre agents working in Delhi and NCR

RESEARCH DESIGN

The study is multivariate and based on Pre and Post research design. The study as such has become a multi group and it is related to call centre agents. Anxiety and stress was measured twice as pre and post study to further investigate causes of anxiety and stress.

RESEARCH OBJECTIVES

- To investigate the level of anxiety and stress among the study participants and its effects with passage of time.

THE SAMPLE

The target universe for the study was selected through purposive sampling technique. The youth working in call centres (as agents) were selected from various types of call centres aged 21 to 25 years. Gender was not controlled; however, maximum respondents were female. It was observed that female preferred office jobs in spite of field work. Academic qualifications are not given specific importance. Maximum of the selected sample was under graduates.

Inclusion Criteria for Sample Selection

- Young employees of call centres having at least one year of work experience in the same organization
- The employees engaged in taking a call or making a call not those performing back office assignments or for other technical work.
- The participants with different level of education, gender, and economic status.

Sample Size

150 young respondents from four different types of call centres Inbound and Outbound (n-75 + n-75)

Tool for Measurement of level of Anxiety

Comprehensive Anxiety Test. (2006)

Constructed by R.L.Bharadwaj, H.Sharma, and M.Bhargava

Reliability and validity—The coefficient of reliability has been determined by, test retest method and split-half method. High validity (determined by computing the correlation between scores of other tests)

Description

The tool is reliable and valid to be applied on girls and boy. The tool measures five levels of anxiety as—1.Very high or saturated 2.High 3.Average or normal 4.Low 5.Very low

Tool for Measurement of Level of Stress

Singh Personal Stress Source Inventory (SPSSI) (2004)

Constructed by —Arun K. Singh, Ashish K. Singh and Arpana Singh

Reliability and validity-The SPSS has both test-retest reliability and internal consistency reliability. The test has sufficient degree of content validity and concurrent validity.

Description

The tool is useful for the measurement of the level of stress among working population. The inventory is based on three important sectors of life from which may cause stress. It includes sources of stress related personal life events that are likely to produce stress.

RESEARCH FINDINGS

The work pattern is such that these respondents are at the last hook of a long chain and are answerable to many authorities' thus somatic disorders like anxiety and stress were notices in their behaviour and thus further investigated

Table 1: Level of Anxiety among agents of Call Centres (Pre Study) N-150

Level of Anxiety	*% of respondents*
Very High	9.0
High	13.0
Average	17.6
Low	13.6
Very Low	46.6

Position of Call Center Employee in the Organization

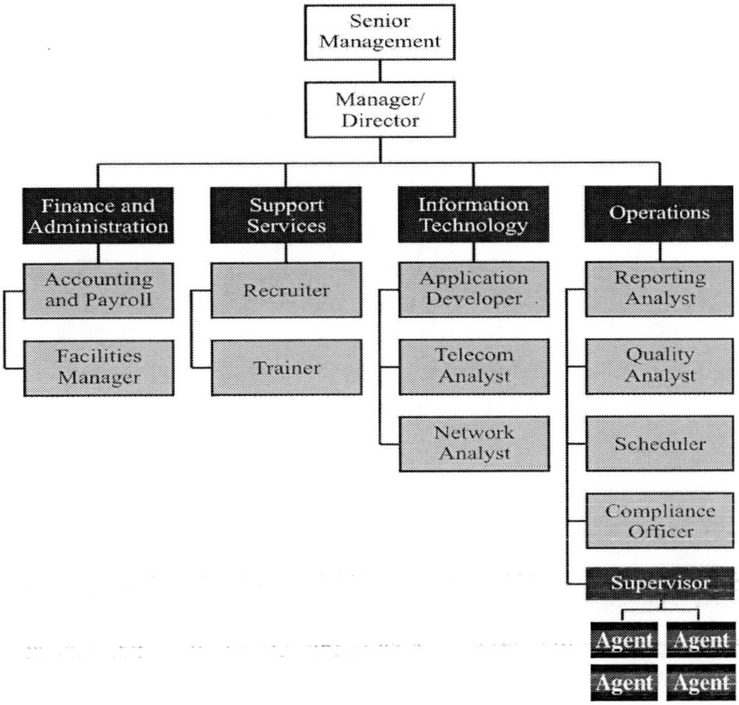

Fig. 1. The Position of Study Respondents in the Organization

Result table 1 explains that 46.4 % of agents felt very low level of anxiety which results lack of interest in the job as well as very slow and faulty output. Only 9% employees expressed very high level of anxiety which again implicit poor performance. Thus rest remaining about 45 % of employees were between low to high level of anxiety, a situation where productivity is not influenced. Thus in a well organised sector the employer did not suffer from low productivity and attrition even at initial period of employment or one can say that employees were accommodated easily in an ergonomically organized environment.

Table 2: Level of Anxiety among Agents of Call Centres (Post Study) N-150

Level of anxiety	*% of respondents*
Very High	25.33
High	9.0
Average	14.66
Low	14.0
Very Low	36.66

The result table 2 explains that with duration of time (post study) the 36.66 % respondents showed very low level of anxiety whereas it was 46.6 % in the pre study. There was no noticeable difference in low, average, and high level of anxiety, but a significant rise is being found in very high level of anxiety which was 9 % in pre study and increased to 25.33 % in post study. Results revel that a person having very high anxiety happens to be tensed, apprehensive, highly worried, dejected, withdrawn and may also report headache frequent abdominal upset and tiredness. They always show lack of confidence in their actions and decisions and do not like to assets in socially interactive situations People having normal anxiety are not disorganized and non adjustive rather they are vigilant, cautious and responsive to disturbing situations. The normal level of anxiety also motivates the individuals to cope with day to day problems. Person Higher level creates negative relationship between creativity and achievements. A person showing very low level of anxiety may be interrupted as none caring, irresponsible and unconcerned with life and environmental situations. They tend to ignore there capabilities and expect others to help them.

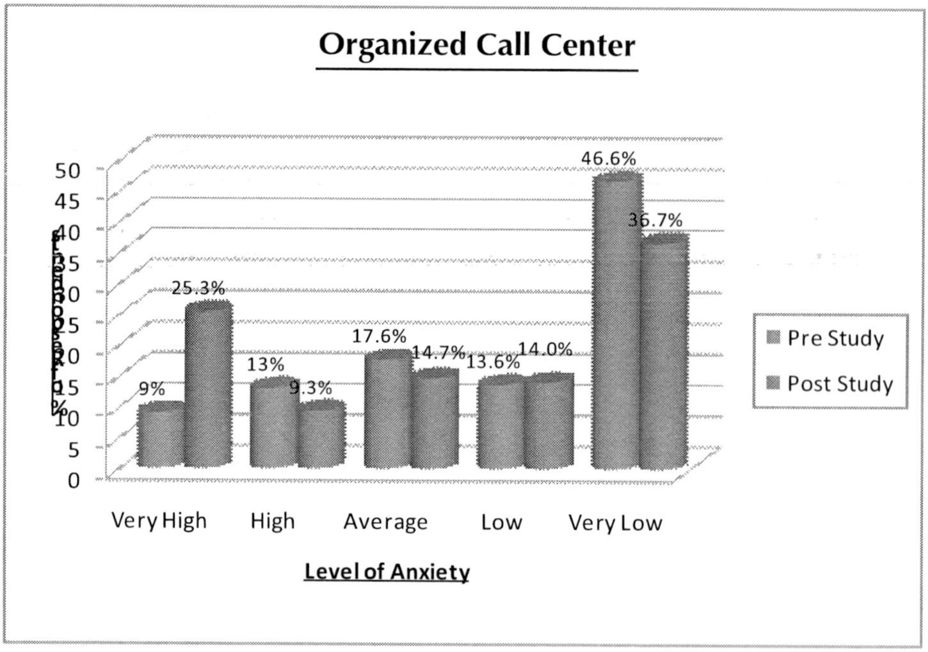

Fig. 2: Level of Anxiety between Two groups (Pre and Post) N-150

Table 3: Significance Level of Anxiety

Call Centre	*N(total)*	*Mean*	*SD*	*t-value*	*Significance Level*
Pre	150	24.69	18.90	4.852	Significant at .01
Post	150	29.80	21.21		

The result table indicates the significant difference at .01 levels between pre and post data of agents working in call centres in respect of the level anxiety.

STRESS

Life would be simple indeed if our needs were automatically gratified. But many obstacles both personal and environmental prevent these. Such obstacles place adjustive demands on us and can lead to the experience of stress. We refer to adjustive demand as stressors and to effects they create within an organism as stress. For many employed in the call centre sector, "the daily experience is of repetitive, intensive and stressful work, based upon Tailors' principles, which frequently results in "burnout". (Brown, 2002) more vividly, characterizes the work as "repetitive brain strain". These descriptions are hardly surprising, in a way, given that call centres are established by organizations to "create an environment in which work can be standardized to create relatively uniform and repetitious activities so as to achieve economies of scale and consistent quality of customer service". This means, *in other words, that workplaces are organized in ways that weaken employee autonomy and enhance the potential for management control, and "a loss of control is generally understood to be an important indicator of work-related stress.* There is almost universal consensus that call centre work is stressful. Even in studies that report the observation that some staff actually enjoys their work, mention of stress is still the norm, and a significant portion of the call centre literature is devoted to detailing the sources of stress.

Table 4: Level of Stress among Agents in Call Centre (Pre Study) N-150

Level of Stress	*% of Respondents*
High	2.6
Moderate	90.3
Low	6.0

The table 4 explains the level of stress among employees in pre study. Results reveals that 90.3 % employees expressed moderate level of stress and 6 % of them showed low level of stress only 2.6 % of the employees felt high level of stress in the pre study.

Table 5: Level of Stress among Agents in Call Centres (Post Study) N-150

Level of Stress	*% of Respondents*
High	6.33
Moderate	91.33
Low	2.33

The table 5 explains a decline in employees with high level of stress from 2.6 % to 6.33 % and an increase in moderate level of stress (90.3% in pre study to 91.33 % in the post study). Moderate level of stress has been considered a motivating factor among agents (Selye,

1976). It promotes and increases healthy competition among workers. The increase in high level of stress indicates nursery stage of (BOSS) the burn out stress syndrome.

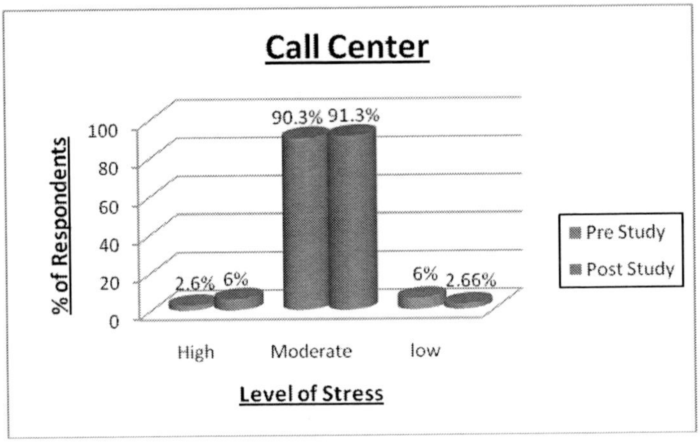

Fig. 3. Level of Stress among two groups of (Pre and Post) N-150

Table 6: Significance Value of Stress Among Employees of Call Centres

Unorganized	*N(total)*	*Mean*	*S D*	*t-value*	*Significance Level*
Pre	150	55.5733	14.4210	6.120	Significant at .01 level
Post	150	61.41	13.74		

The findings reveal a significant increase in level of stress as the work is so repetitive, monitored for time consumes per call and daily performance always bothers the agents

DISCUSSION

The findings reveal that call centre agents have poor task complexity, task variety and job control and higher psychosomatic complaints in contrast to people in comparable, more traditional work places. The work environment of any organization is responsible for physical and mental health of their workers. As observed the ergonomics and infrastructure of call centres are perfect but the work is stressful as one has to express controlled emotions. It is not easy to be polite and humble while we desire to shout and haul. Houlihan (2000) described that the inbound call centres are concerned with 'customer care', or 'keeping customers happy' (providing quality service) Yet these goals are juxtaposed with an ongoing pressure to keep call times down and call volumes up which creates tensions and stress He also address the call centre employees as "exhausting," "robotic," "controlled," and agents discussing the nature of their work often use "machine-like". Anxiety at beginning of any new experience is natural but when it extends

CONCLUSION

The important central stressor in call centre work is its intensity. Leopold (2003) agrees that "As a result of the stress, call centre employees are particularly prone to accidents, workplace injuries and musculoskeletal and psychiatric disabilities, which ultimately lead to an increase in absences and disability claims. Dormann and Zijlstra (2003) on (callnet.com, researches) illustrate that huge teams of people handle a never-ending flow of customers' calls. The agents are described as '21st century sweats shops' and modern-day 'dark satanic mills', while their workers have been called 'battery hens' and 'galley slaves'. It is no wonder some call centre staff report high levels of stress and anxiety. This has been revealed in the findings of present study.

Chakraborty and Nagpal (2005) agree to the number of people between 18-21 years who visit psychiatrists have gone up significantly. Out of which 15 % work in call centres. Many of call centre employees' exhibit symptoms of burn-out stress syndrome (BOSS) like chronic fatigue and insomnia and many more behavioral problems parents are also worried. Shastri, a leading counsellor (2007) said call-centre employees are getting stress and are breaking traditional life style which further leads to stress. They need counselling however anxiety becomes problematic enough to interfere with their ability to function effectively or enjoy everyday life while continuing to work with stress leads to other psychosomatic disorders.

BIBLIOGRAPHY

[1] Agarwal R. (2001), Stress in Life and at work; New Delhi; Sage Publication.

[2] Babu, R. (2004),'Cybercoolies in BPOs', Economic and Political Weekly,39 (2),31January.

[3] Basant,R and Rani (2004).'Labour market Deepening in India's IT: An Exploratory Analysis' Economic and political weekly,39(50) 5317-26.

[4] Belt,V,R. Richardson and Webster,(1999),"Smiling Down the Phone; Work in telephone Call Centers' workshop on call centers march 1999 London; London School of Economics.

[5] Chithelen, I. (2004) Outsourcing to India: Causes, Reaction and prospectus' Economic and Political Weekly, 39(10):1022-24.

[6] D' Cruz P. and Noronha, E.(2006) "Being professional; Organizational Control in Indian Call centers "Social Science Computer Review,24(3);342-362.

[7] Houlihan (2006) A study of inbound call centers and frustrations with 'customer care', or 'keeping customers happy' (providing quality service) published in (NIOH) national institute of occupational health.

[8] Holman D (2003)"Phoning in Sick? An overview of employees stress in call centres" in journal of leadership and organizations Development vol 24 no 3pp123-30

[9] National Association of Software and Service companies (NASSCOM).2007 India ITES-BPOs strategy summit 2007-Background and reference source New Delhi; NASSCOM.

[10] D'Cruz and Noronha, (2007),Technical call centres ; Beyond Electronic Sweatshops and assembly lines in the hand ,Global business review, volume 8 no,1 Jan- June. pp 53-67.

Talent Management Practices: Evidence from Telecom Industry

N. Malati, Ritika Maheshwari, Shubra Ghera and Shruti Saxena

Delhi Institute of Advanced Studies, Delhi

ABSTRACT

Talent in today's world is hard to locate. It is sometimes hidden or overridden by daily pressures of doing business. However it is highly important that this talent is uncovered and utilized to its full potential. In the present scenario where technology has made spectacular progress and revolutionized the work in every field, particularly in the corporate world, it is not physical assets which are gaining importance but talent has emerged as the forerunner in determining the worth of an organization. As such, sourcing for best talent continues to hold prominence for the organizations. After years of paying of lip service to the notion- "our workforce is our greatest asset", organizations are now beginning to take action on the same. It is high time that firms plan and execute talent management for requisite results to survive in this competitive age. The present paper tries to make an attempt to analyze the talent management practices followed in telecom sector.

Keywords: *Talent Management, Strategic Advantage, Employee Satisfaction, Telecom Sector*

INTRODUCTION

Traditionally, organizational growth was driven by hiring more people. However, today's economic environment requires an increase in the productivity of existing workers before a new headcount is considered.

In the previous years, the market appeared to be "buyer's market" with excess talent and few employers. But the situation has reversed with the employee becoming a "seller of his talent" or precisely the market has turned out to be a "seller's market". In this situation wherein the best talent is absorbed by reputed organizations and others who have not developed the reputation of "employer-of-choice" and are not capable of enough to compete with struggle for acquiring and retaining scarce talent resources.

According to a yearlong study conducted recently by Global consultancy (a study involving 77 companies and almost 6000 managers and executives) "the most important corporate resource over the next 20 years would be talent: smart, sophisticated businesspeople, who are technologically literate, globally astute and operationally agile".

However in the modern era, the delicate balance of demand v/s supply conspicuously swings towards the demand side, leaving the companies to always be on the lookout for those rare diamonds from amongst the piles of stones.

The 'talent' in an organization refers to the current employees and their valuable Knowledge, skills and competencies. Talent management is the ongoing process of analyzing, developing and effectively utilizing talent to meet Business needs. It involves a specific process that compares current talent in a department to the strategic business needs of that department. Results lead to the development and implementation of corresponding strategies to address any talent gaps or surpluses.

The implementation of a talent management process that is transparent and equitable is expected to create an environment for people to develop their skills in preparation for a range of future possibilities thereby preparing the workplace for changing roles. The goal of this process is to map the business needs of the HR Community with the potential and career development needs of the people.

Talent signals an ability to learn and develop in the face of new challenges. Talent is about future potential rather than past track record. So talent tends to be measured in terms of having certain attributes, such as a willingness to take risks and learn from mistakes, a reasonable (but not too high) level of ambition and competitiveness, the ability to focus on 'big picture' issues, and an awareness of their own strengths, limitations and impact on others.

Several talent management processes need to be in place on a strategic level in order ensure its success. Such processes/strategies include talent identification, recruitment & assessment, competency management, performance management, career development, learning management, compensation, succession planning etc.

There is now a consensus in the global business community, that acquiring and retaining talent is the biggest challenge facing organizations. There is also an acknowledgment of a global talent shortage across nations and across sectors, and that the shortage is set to increase. Skill shortages have been found to be the number one challenge in China and South East Asia, number two challenge in Japan and number four challenge in India. The Telecommunication Sector is no exception and faces talent management as the biggest challenge.

The telecom industry in India is one of the fastest growing in the world and acts as the primary driver for foreign and domestic telecommunication companies investing into the sector. The sector has witnessed massive investments, both by private and government entities in the recent past.

The telecom industry has witnessed significant growth in subscriber base over the last decade, with increasing network coverage and a competition-induced decline in tariffs acting as catalysts for the growth in subscriber base. The growth story and the potential have also served to attract newer players in the industry. The sector is expected to witness up to US$ 56.3 billion investments and the market will cross the US$ 101 billion mark in five years, according to consultancy firm Boston Consulting Group (BCG). BCG India's Partner and Director, Arvind Subramanian said the industry will continue to grow at 12-13 per cent annually.

With new players coming in, the intensity of competition in the industry has increased, especially over the last four years. The market share of the telecom companies reflects the fragmented nature of the industry, with as many as 15 players. While the private operators hold 88.60 per cent of the wireless market share (based on subscriber base) BSNL and MTNL, the two PSU operators capture 11.40 per cent of the pie. As on July 31, 2012, Bharti telecom led the market with 20.67 per cent share, followed by Vodafone (16.96 per cent), Reliance (14.68 per cent), Idea (12.88 per cent), BSNL (10.81 per cent), Tata (8.52 per cent), Aircel (7.13 per cent), with the remaining share being held by other smaller operators, according to Telecom Regulatory Authority of India (TRAI) database.

LITERATURE REVIEW

Goffee and Jones (2007) define talent as handful of employee whose ideas, knowledge and skills give them the potential to produce the disproportionate vale from the resource they have available from them. Tansley et al. (2006) point out that talent can be considered as a complex amalgam of employees' skills, knowledge, cognitive ability and potential. Employees' values and work preferences are also of major importance. Whilst, Ingham (2006) considers people who are in the key position, the leader team, the individual who has the scarce capability or make particular contribution to the organization is talent. At the same time, talent means the total of all the experience, knowledge, skills, and behaviours that a person has and brings to work. Talent therefore, is used as an all-encompassing term to describe the human resources that organizations want to acquire, retain and develop in order to meet their business goals (Cheese et al., 2008). Lewis and Heckman (2006) conducted a critical review of the talent management literature both in the professional and academic publications, and concluded three primary conceptions of the term. Firstly, talent management is comprised of a collection of typical human resource department practices such as recruiting, selection, development and career and succession management. Secondly, talent management more specifically focuses on predicting the flow of human resources throughout the organization, based on such factors as workforce skills, supply and demand, and growth and attrition. From this perspective, talent management is considered more or less synonymous with human resource or workforce planning, particularly if automated and connected with other organizational databases and systems. Lastly, talent was defined as individuals who have the capability to make a significant difference to the current and future performance of the company (Morton, 2004).

A group of McKinsey consultants coined the phrase the *War for Talent* in 1997 (Michaels et al., 2001; Axelrod et al., 2002), and since then the topic of talent management has received a remarkable degree of practitioner and academic interest. A research paper concluded that there is "a disturbing lack of clarity regarding the definition, scope and overall goals of talent management" (Lewis and Heckman, 2006: 139), a view which also prevails in the practitioner literature. In this regard, a UK survey found that 51 per cent of HR professionals surveyed undertook talent management activities, however only 20 per cent of them operated with a formal definition of talent management (CIPD, 2006). Thus, the field would benefit from a clear and comprehensive definition of the concept. Second, the current state of talent management literature is exacerbated by the fact that, in addition to ambiguities around the definition of the concept, there has also been an alarming lack of theoretical development in the area (for notable exceptions see Boudreau and Ramstad, 2005; 2007; Cappelli, 2008; Lewis and Heckman, 2006).

Further, a recent study of 40 global companies found that virtually all of them identified a lack of a sufficient talent pipeline to fill strategic positions within the organization, which considerably constrained their ability to grow their business (Ready and Conger, 2007).

The Economist Intelligence Unit (2006) found that most CEOs explicitly argued that talent management was too important to be left to HR alone, while a Boston Consulting Group (2007) report identified talent management as one of five critical challenges for HR in the European context. The BCG findings were based not only on those capabilities that executives expect to be most important in managing human capital, but tellingly are also those they perceive their organisations to be weakest at.

The Talent Pulse Survey 2005 of over 1,400 HR practitioners worldwide by Deloitte consultancy, reports that the most critical people management issues are attracting and retaining high-calibre workers. These issues are further heightened by the fact that 54% of the respondents believe that talent issues have an impact on overall productivity and that there is a clear link between talent management and business performance.

Within the Technology, Media and Telecommunication sector, a recent (2008) survey by Deloitte Consulting made similar findings as shown below:

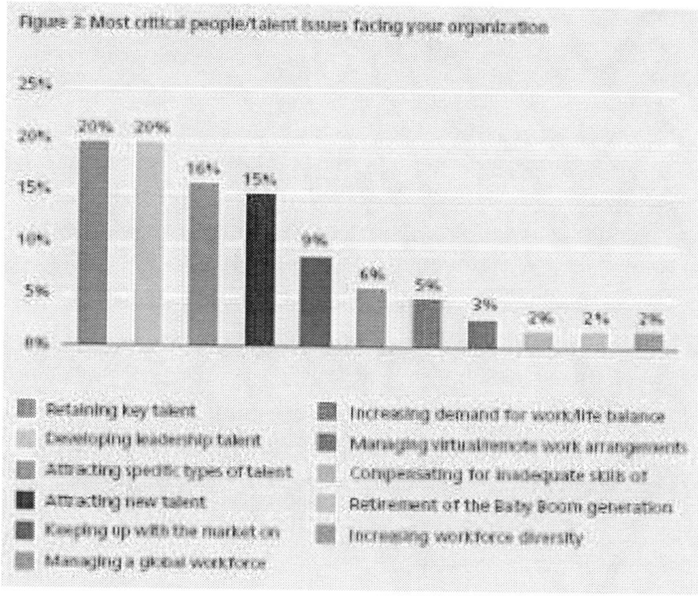

Figure 3: Most critical people/talent issues facing your organization

Deloitte further found that having high quality employees emerged top among a series of factors contributing most to growth of companies.

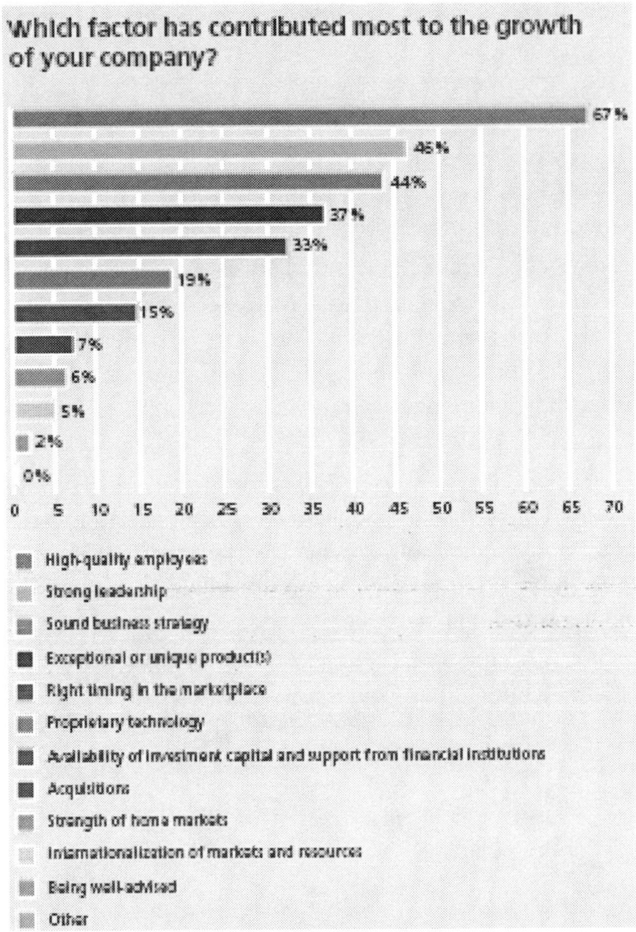

The above findings are interesting and reflect a shift in corporate thinking about people, as the quality of employees now ranks higher than such celebrated factors as sound business strategy (44%), proprietary technology (19%) and investment capital (15%).

The above findings have been corroborated by others from equally internationally renowned institutions. The Harvard Business School for example, identified the ability to spot and develop talent, as the most sought- after attribute among successful CEO's. The Chartered Institute of Personnel and Development (CIPD) UK found "recruiting and retaining best talent" to be in the top five drivers of organizations managing diversity.

So, the message is clear: Talent has become central to business survival; yet that talent is in short supply, and this shortage is set to get worse. Organizations and even nations will do everything to get that talent from anywhere and everywhere, triggering what amounts to a war for talent.

Randall Schuler, 2010 identifies and discusses four drivers that have shaped and are shaping the field of global talent management. More specifically, these are the drivers that impact how organizations attract, develop, retain, and mobilize talent. Major drivers include:

- Shortage of talented workers;
- Changing demographics;
- Changing attitude towards work and structure of work; and,
- Country culture differences.

Tarique & Schuler, 2010 states the impact of the above drivers on Attracting, Developing, Retaining and Mobilizing talent. They say that the above four drivers of factors can strongly impact the need for and content of these global talent management practices and policies:

- Attracting (this includes policies and practices that recruit and select talented individuals);
- Developing (this includes policies and practices that provide job and career related competencies to talented individuals);
- Retaining (this includes practices that prevent talented individuals from leaving the organization); and
- Mobilizing (this includes practices that facilitate the movement of talented individuals across regions or countries).

RESEARCH OBJECTIVES

The objectives of the study are as follows:

- To analyse the talent management practices in Telecom Sector (BhartiAirtel Ltd. , Vodafone Group Plc and Idea Cellular)
- To determine if there is any significant difference in the talent management practices at the 3 organizations.

RESEARCH HYPOTHESIS

The following hypotheses have been framed and tested for the study:

1. **H_1:** There is no significant difference in the Recruitment practices carried for talent management at the organizations.
2. **H_2:** There is no significant difference in the Compensation practices carried for talent management at the organizations.
3. **H_3:** There is no significant difference in the Training and Development practices for talent management at the organizations.

4. **H_4:** There is no significant difference in the Retention Strategies adopted for talent management at the organizations.
5. **H_5:** There is no significant difference in the Succession Planning practices carried for talent management at the organizations.

RESEARCH DESIGN AND METHODOLOGY

The study is exploratory in nature as it investigates the area and provides insights into understanding the problem. A questionnaire constituting five major parameters on Talent Management practices, namely, recruitment, compensation, training and development, retention strategies and succession planning were used to collect the responses of people working in Bharti Airtel Ltd., Vodafone Group Plc and Idea Cellular. Each parameter had a range of 3-4 questions under it. The validity of the questionnaire was checked using the Cronbach's reliability test. The Cronbach's Alpha coefficient has come out to be 0.786 i.e. > 0.6, the questionnaire used for the research has proved to be reliable enough to give accurate results.

A sample of 159 employees was taken of which 55 were from BhartiAirtel Ltd, 57 from Vodafone Group Plc and remaining 47 from Idea Cellular were surveyed. The data was analyzed with the help of Mean response method and One Way Anova test using SPSS 16.0.

DATA ANALYSIS AND RESULTS

The mean responses of employees for the questions on Recruitment Factor - 'Proper process is conducted for the interviews (3.25)', 'High calibre employees are appointed (2.97)', 'Time and energy is given in filling a vacancy (3.11)' and 'Vacancies do not remain open for a long period of time (3.19)' indicate that employees agree to the above mentioned practices being adopted in their respective organizations.

The mean responses of the employees for the questions on Compensation Factor - 'Their organization acknowledge the work of the employees (3.21)' , 'Employees are given variety of incentives (3.18)' and 'External equity is maintained in the compensation (3.11)' indicate that the employees **agree** to the above mentioned practices being adopted in their organization.

The mean responses of the employees for the questions on Training and Development Factor - 'Development needs are continuously assessed for the employees (3.18)', 'Honest feedback is given to employees (3.21)', 'Development opportunities are created for the employees (2.87)' and 'Adequate training is provided to the employees (3.03)' indicate that employees agree to the above mentioned practices being conducted at their organizations to manage talent.

The mean responses of the employees for the questions pertaining to the factor of Retention Strategies - 'Work life balance is maintained (3.07)', 'Employees are satisfied with the talent management system (3.21)' and 'Employee engagement initiatives are undertaken regularly

(3.02)' indicate that employees agree to the above mentioned practices being conducted at their organization to manage talent.

The mean responses of the employees for the questions pertaining to the factor of Succession Planning - 'Employees are aware of the policies and procedures of the organization (3.07)', 'They believe they can help the organization achieve its goals (3.00)', 'Training is provided for the development of employees for further jobs (2.96)', 'Employees are consulted in the process of career planning (2.91)'indicate that employees agree to the succession planning initiatives undertaken at their organizations.

Now, applying inferential statistical tool One Way Anova to determine whether there is significant difference in the talent management practices among the three organizations namely, BhartiAirtel Ltd., Vodafone Group Plc and Idea Cellular.

Recruitment Factor depicts that Sig dif is more than 0.05 for the questions – 'Proper process to conduct interviews is followed', ' High calibre employees are appointed', 'Time and energy is given in filling a vacancy' , ' Vacancies do not remain open for a long period of time'. This indicates that there is no significant difference in the responses of the employees of the three organizations towards talent management practices incorporated to attract talent towards the organization.

From Compensation Factor, it can be inferred that Sig dif is more than 0.05 for the questions – 'Employees are acknowledged for their work', 'Employees are given variety of incentives for their work performed', 'External equity is maintained in the compensation'. This indicates that there is no significant difference in the responses of the employees of the three organizations towards talent management practices incorporated towards acknowledging the work of the employees and rewarding them.

From Training and Development Factor, it can be inferred that Sig dif is more than 0.05 for the questions – 'Development needs are continuously assessed for the employees', 'Honest feedback is given to employees', 'Development opportunities are created', 'Adequate training is provided'. This indicates that there is no significant difference in the responses of the employees of the three organizations towards talent management practices incorporated to train and develop the employees.

From the factor of Retention Strategies, it can be inferred that Sig dif is more than 0.05 for the questions – 'Work life balance is maintained', 'Employees are satisfied with the talent management system', 'Employee engagement initiatives are undertaken regularly'. This indicates that there is no significant difference in the responses of the employees of the three organizations towards talent management practices incorporated towards retaining the employee in the organization.

The factor of Succession Planning depicts that Sig dif is more than 0.05 for the questions – 'Are you made aware of the policies and procedures of the organization', 'Can you help the organization achieve its aims', 'Employees are consulted in the process of career planning', whereas Sig dif is less than 0.05 for the question – 'Training is provided for the development of the employees'. This indicates that overall there is no significant difference in the responses of the employees of the organization towards talent management practices incorporated for succession planning whereas there is a significant difference in providing training for further promotion in the organization and it is further proved by the mean response that Vodafone Group Plc (3.14) and Idea Cellular (3.15) focus more in providing training for further promotion in comparison to BhartiAirtel (2.62).

CONCLUSION

Talent Management has been developed as a platform for corporate world to manage talents of employee, for company benefits. Talent Management for the HR Community is an opportunity for HR professionals to develop in their areas of expertise and in their careers. The goal of talent management is to better understand our people in the HR Community so we can support career development and align individual needs and goals with the business focus of HR. We also want to ensure that we develop people so that we are meeting the future needs of the community and government and our clients. This first broad sweep of the Community provides a foundation on which to ensure leadership continuity, knowledge transfer and service continuity. The initial implementation resulted in a number of important human resource priorities and strategies, such as performance management, leadership and management development, attraction and retention, employee learning and development and culture, all of which are supported by the HR Strategy. The critical next step in the process is the implementation of the Talent Management at all aspects from the Recruitment to planning the career graph of the employee at the organization.

With the growth in the telecom sector i.e. their expansion in the rural areas and also with the 2G and 3G technology the telecom sector is on a growth stage. BhartiAirtel being the market leader wants to grab the first mover advantage and thus rely a lot on its talent pool with other players following the lead. The industry is seeing upto various initiatives taken in recruitment and giving compensation to maintain their position. Though there is no significant difference in the talent management initiatives in the telecom sector and thus so as to enhance their strategic position companies must focus on their talent pool in the organization and take steps that will not only help the organization but also the employees of the organization.

REFERENCES

[1] Axelrod EL, Handfield-Jones H, Welsh TA (2001). War for talent: Part 2. McKinsey Quart., 2, 9 – 12.

[2] Berger, L.A., & Berger, D.R., eds. (2003). TheTalent Management Handbook. New York: TheMcGraw-Hill Companies.

[3] Boudreau JW & Ramstad PM (2005). "Talentship and the Evolution of Human Resource Management: From 'Professional Practices' To 'Strategic Talent Decision Science'" Human Resource Planning 28(2): 17-26.

[4] Cappelli P (2008). Talent management for the Twenty-First century. Harv. Bus. Rev., pp.74 – 81.

[5] Cheese P, Thormas RJ, Craig E (2008). The talent powered organization: strategies for globalization, talent management and high performance. London and Philadelphia: Kogan.

[6] Goffee, R. and Jones, G. (2007): 'Leading Clever People', Harvard Business Review, March, pp 72-79.

[7] Ingham, J. (2006). 'Closing the talent management gap.' Strategic HR Review, Mar/Apr, vol. 5 no.3, pp. 20-23.

[8] Jon Ingham, (2006) "Closing the talent management gap: Harnessing your employees' talent to deliver optimum business performance", Strategic HR Review, Vol. 5 Iss: 3, pp.20.

[9] Julia Christensen Hughes, EvelinaRog, (2008) "Talent management: A strategy for improving employee recruitment, retention and engagement within hospitality organizations", International Journal of Contemporary Hospitality Management, Vol. 20 Iss: 7, pp.743 – 757.

[10] Lewis RE, Heckman RJ (2006). Talent management: a critical review. Hum. Res. Manag. Rev., 16: 139-154.

[11] Michaels, E., Handfield-Jones, H., & Axelrod, B. (2001). The War for Talent. Boston, MA: Harvard Business Review Press.

[12] Morton L (2004). Integrated and integrative talent management: A strategic HR framework. The Conference Board, Research Report, R-1345-04- RR, New York.

[13] Ready, D. A., & Conger, J. A. (2007, June). Make your company a talent factory. Harvard Business Review, 68-77.

[14] Tansley, C., Harris, L., Stewart, J., & Turner, P. 2006. Talent Management: Understanding the Dimensions. In CIPD (Ed.), Change Agenda: 1-16. London: CIPD.

[15] Tony Davis, Talent Assessment, Gower Publications, 2007.

[16] VenkataRatnam, C.S. and Srivastava, B.K. Personnel Management & Human Resource, Tata Mcgraw-Hill publishing company Ltd, 2005.

[17] Nxele Mike, Challenges of Talent Acquisition and Retention in an Era of Brain Drain

[18] http://www.tng.futurestep.com/TMR1_07/tmr20071.pdf

[19] http://45.pisols.com/docs/StratHR_Review_TM_article.pdf

[20] http://www.ncdot.gov/download/performance/Volume7nTalentManagementStrategy.pdf

[21] http://www.ddiworld.com/DDIWorld/media/whitepapers/ninebestpracticetalentmanagement_wp_ddi.pdf?ext=.pdf

ANNEXURE

Factors	*Bharti Airtel Ltd*		*Vodafone Group Plc*		*Idea Cellular*		*Total*	
	Mean	*Standard Deviation*	*Mean*	*Standard Deviation*	*Mean*	*Standard Deviation*	*Mean*	*Standard Deviation*
Proper process to conduct interviews is followed	3.18	1.402	3.19	1.315	3.38	1.226	3.25	1.316
High calibre employees are appointed	3.07	1.317	3.05	1.342	2.74	1.359	2.97	1.338
Time and energy is given in filling a vacancy	3.02	1.326	3.12	1.283	3.19	1.362	3.11	1.315
Vacancies do not remain open for a long period of time	3.35	1.220	2.96	1.180	3.28	1.314	3.19	1.238
Employees are acknowledged for their work	3.20	1.297	3.37	1.096	3.02	1.225	3.21	1.207
Employees are given variety of incentives for their work performed	3.27	1.193	3.19	1.202	3.06	.919	3.18	1.119
External equity is maintained in the compensation	3.05	1.145	3.14	1.217	3.13	1.296	3.11	1.210
Development needs are continuously assessed for the employees	3.09	1.281	3.30	1.281	3.13	1.227	3.18	1.261
Honest feedback is given to employees	3.31	1.275	3.19	1.202	3.11	1.220	3.21	1.228
Development opportunities are created	2.78	1.166	3.04	1.180	2.77	1.127	2.87	1.159
Adequate training is provided	2.98	1.240	3.11	1.277	2.98	1.310	3.03	1.268
Work life balance is maintained	2.95	1.311	3.26	1.247	2.98	1.277	3.07	1.278
Employees are satisfied with the talent management system	3.36	1.238	3.32	1.072	2.91	1.396	3.21	1.239
Employee engagement initiatives are undertaken regularly	3.05	1.224	2.95	1.245	3.06	1.275	3.02	1.240
Are you made aware of the policies and procedures of the organization	2.91	1.281	3.26	1.094	3.02	1.277	3.07	1.218
Can you help the organization achieve its aims	2.87	1.277	3.18	1.151	2.94	1.358	3.00	1.258
Training is provided for the development of the employees	2.62	1.114	3.14	1.141	3.15	1.142	2.96	1.152
Employees are consulted in the process of career planning	3.00	1.202	2.88	1.255	2.83	1.222	2.91	1.221

Factors	*Sig.*
Proper process to conduct interviews is followed	.696
High calibre employees are appointed	.394
Time and energy is given in filling a vacancy	.799
Vacancies do not remain open for a long period of time	.227
Employees are acknowledged for their work	.346
Employees are given variety of incentives for their work performed	.643
External equity is maintained in the compensation	.924
Development needs are continuously assessed for the employees	.655
Honest feedback is given to employees	.706
Development opportunities are created	.398
Adequate training is provided	.839
Work life balance is maintained	.359
Employees are satisfied with the talent management system	.141
Employee engagement initiatives are undertaken regularly	.864
Are you made aware of the policies and procedures of the organization	.293
Can you help the organization achieve its aims	.411
Training is provided for the development of the employees	.023
Employees are consulted in the process of career planning	.765

Retaining Generation Y – A Challenge for the Organisations (Case Study of Real Life Corporate Practices)

Chitra Jha and Meenakshi Kaushik

Delhi Institute of Rural Development, Delhi

ABSTRACT

GEN Y or the millenials, as they are called, are the force to reckon with. They are in their 20's, ready to take on the world, young, energetic, competitive, confident, ambitious. A generation which is very much part of today's workforce. A part of the workforce which the companies cannot ignore and the most important part they won't let, to be ignored.

In the world of dynamic, complex, turbulent business environment and cut throat competition the companies are ever looking after ways to gain edge over each other. After going through the whole process of technological changes, cost cutting programs and various survival strategies, it has been experienced by the companies that people are the key. It is the workforce, the employees working with the organizations, provides the whole meaning to all those processes and strategies, all those innovations and sustenance plans. In a layman's language employees are the lifeline of an organization. A human being would die if there is no blood in his body, similarly an organization can't survive without employees. Employees are the main assets of the organization and it is really important to retain them. And retaining generation y employees is yet another challenge before the companies. Young adults in their 20s. Millennials, also known as Generation Y - think about life and work differently than older boom and gen X employees, and hiring and retaining them requires management that understands their needs and a business environment to match. To extract the best out of them it is important that they enjoy their work and feel attached to the organization.

In this paper we have tried to focus on generation y employees, the working style of generation y and also the paper highlights current initiatives by organizations to retain generation y employees.

Keywords: *Generation Y, Employee Retention, Motivation, Organizational Practices, Attitude, Commitment*

INTRODUCTION

GEN Y or the millenials, as they are called, are the force to reckon with. They are in their 20's, ready to take on the world, young, energetic, competitive, confident, ambitious. A generation which is very much part of today's workforce. A part of the workforce which the companies cannot ignore and the most important part they won't let, to be ignored.

In the world of dynamic, complex, turbulent business environment and cut throat competition the companies are ever looking after ways to gain edge over each other. After going through the whole process of technological changes, cost cutting programs and various survival strategies, it has been experienced by the companies that people are the key. It is the workforce, the employees working with the organizations, provides the whole meaning to all those processes and strategies, all those innovations and sustenance plans. In a layman's language employees are the lifeline of an organization. A human being would die if there is no blood in his body, similarly an organization can't survive without employees. Employees are the main assets of the organization and it is really important to retain them. And retaining generation y employees is yet another challenge before the companies. Young adults in their 20s. Millennials, also known as Generation Y - think about life and work differently than older boom and gen X employees, and hiring and retaining them requires management that understands their needs and a business environment to match. To extract the best out of them it is important that they enjoy their work and feel attached to the organization. So, attracting them and retaining them has become a major task for the human resource management.

The generation of people born during the 1980s and early 1990s. The name is based on *Generation X*, the generation that preceded them. *Members* of Generation Y are often referred to as "echo boomers" because they are the *children* of parents born during the baby *boom* (the "baby boomers"). Because children born during this *time period* have had constant *access* to *technology* (*computers*, *cell phones*) in their youth, they have *required* many *employers* to update their hiring *strategy* in *order* to *incorporate* updated *forms* of technology. Also called millennials, echo boomers, *internet* generation, iGen, *net* generation.

TRAITS OF GEN Y

Tech-savvy: Generation Y grew up with technology and rely on it to perform their jobs better. Armed with BlackBerrys, laptops, cellphones and other gadgets, Generation Y is plugged-in 24 hours a day, 7 days a week. This generation prefers to communicate through e-mail and text messaging rather than face-to-face contact and prefers webinars and online technology to traditional lecture-based presentations.

Family-centric: The fast-track has lost much of its appeal for Generation Y who is willing to trade high pay for fewer billable hours, flexible schedules and a better work/life balance. While older generations may view this attitude as narcissistic or lacking commitment, discipline and drive, Generation Y legal professionals have a different vision of workplace expectations and prioritize family over work.

Achievement-oriented: Nurtured and pampered by parents who did not want to make the mistakes of the *previous generation*, Generation Y is confident, ambitious and achievement-oriented. They have high expectations of their employers, seek out new challenges and are not afraid to question authority. Generation Y wants meaningful work and a solid learning curve.

Team-oriented: As children, Generation Y participated in team sports, play groups and other group activities. They value teamwork and seek the input and affirmation of others. Part of a no-person-left-behind generation, Generation Y is loyal, committed and wants to be included and involved.

Attention-craving: Generation Y craves attention in the forms of feedback and guidance. They appreciate being kept in the loop and seek frequent praise and reassurance. Generation Y may benefit greatly from mentors who can help guide and develop their young careers.

Preferred style of leadership: collaboration with management is expected

Value of experience: for Gen Y experience is irrelevant, as the world is changing so fast

Autonomy : for genYis all about questions, questions, questions

Work life balance: their lives are busy – they need alot of 'me' time

Loyalty: **Y** – already working out their exit strategy

Meaning of money: just something that allows them to maintain their lifestyle

THE GENERATIONS Y IN INDIA

By definition, a Generation is a group a people who, based on age, share not only a chronological location in history, but also the experiences that accompany it. These common experiences, in turn, prompt the formation of shared beliefs and behaviors. Even though there's no direct tie to the population booms of the US, India follows the US with generational titles and timeframes;

meaning Gen Y in India = 1980-2000, Gen X = 1965-1979, etc. In India, the late 1990s and 2000s saw the development of a large middle-class and increased demand for and production of many consumer goods and awareness and access to global goods. The Indian economy grew under liberalization and reform policies, the country was stable and prosperous, and political power changed hands without incident. India became a prestigious educational powerhouse and respected source of IT talent. By 2008, 34 Indian companies, and by 2009, 48 new billionaires were listed on Forbes global list Gen Y's in India share the generation's global sense of immediacy, coupled with the excitement of being part of the country's first wave of broad economic opportunity. As a result, young employees in India tend to share the rapid tempo of GenY's ambitions, but with a greater emphasis on financial reward as a desired outcome. Their mental model is heavily influence by India's rich, complex democracy - they easily accept diversity of opinion, making them strongly suited for global interaction.

Gen Y in India are Open-minded, Energetic, Hardworking, Tech savvy, Ambitious, Positive, Confident, Independent, Competitive, Impatient, Losing Indian culture & values, Selfish.

The shifting focus from Family First to Me First: My work, my friends, my things, and my world

Workplace Values preferred by generation y in India are:

- Money is important but type of work is even more important for achieving growth.
- Company brand and reputation of company matters a lot for Gen Y.
- Most of the work is still focused on business processes and software development and deployment but now slowly the focus is shifting to consulting, research, and innovation.
- Younger employees are desiring for impactful work, higher level of contribution and leadership roles.
- Abundant job opportunities and rising competition is leading to confident and highly competitive workforce.
- Gen Y are educated, open-minded, confident and competitive.
- Entrepreneurship is on the rise and individuals are realizing the value of taking risk in order to grow.
- They are focused on RAPID growth and like to spend.
- They are focused on differentiation: How different, better, smarter and more influential am I compared to others...and the differentiation is achieved in terms of education, money, prestige, reputation, brands and technology.
- Food facilities, café's, entertainment facilities and social engagement spaces at work are considered cool and trendy.
- Work environment is a prime attractor as it enhances employee image and offers prestige.
- It is a refuge from chaotic and polluted outside environments.
- Work environment is a leveler for employees coming from different financial, educational, social, and religious backgrounds.

RETENTION OF GENERATION Y-CURRENT INITIATIVES

Retention of top employees is, of course, an issue for every large organization at HCL Technologies some 60,000 people are employed. . But some categories of employees are tougher to keep in the fold than others — Gen Y, in particular. In this regard, they have had a lot of success with a management approach that they call Employees First, Customers Second or EFCS.

FORGET HIERARCHY, FORGET THE CORPORATE LADDER

The Gen Y group, at least at HCL, approach their work and careers very differently than do members of the generations that preceded them. They have little interest in hierarchy and are not particularly impressed by the titles and positions within the traditional pyramid structure. They don't go about their work in ways that are intended to get them to the next rung of the corporate ladder or win them favor with their bosses. They prefer to get involved in projects and initiatives that fascinate them, that they consider worthwhile and that they see as useful to the world at large.You cannot attract, motivate, or retain such people simply by offering them more money (although they like money as much as any other generation does), a promotion to some essentially meaningless "higher" grade, or by making massages available during work hours or recognizing them at Friday beer bashes (although they also enjoy massages and certainly drink their share of beer.)At HCL, the way to get the most from Gen Y employees is simply to adopt some of their ways of thinking and behaving and apply them to the discipline of management, specifically transparency, mutual accountability, and passion.

TRANSPARENCY IS KEY FOR MANY GEN Y-ERS

The traditional, hierarchical organization has been built on the practice of hoarding of information as a way to gain and maintain power. At HCL, they decided to make a great deal of financial data available for all employees to see. In the old days, only senior managers could know which units and initiatives were doing well or poorly; even within a workgroup, not everyone got to look at the financials. They opened up the books for all to see. Revelation! Suddenly, everyone felt as if they knew the score, understood the circumstances, were trusted with important data. This made Gen Y-ers, who think of access to information as the natural order of things, feel more comfortable at work.

There are efforts to "invert the hierarchy" and "turn the pyramid upside down" in order to make management accountable to those employees who operate in what we call the "value zone" — the interface between employee and customer where real value is created. In fact, what we did by opening up the books was to make accountability two-way: employees remained accountable to their managers (necessary for control and alignment) and managers were also made accountable to employees (necessary to create value.)

INFORMATION BUILDS COMMUNITY

Another way they have achieved this is through an initiative called the Smart Service Desk (SSD), an online portal that enables any employee to create a ticket to report a problem or request information. The ticket is assigned to the department that is best able to address the issue, and a manager in that department becomes responsible for the ticket. Only the employee who opened the ticket can close it once the manager offers a satisfactory solution.

Gen Y employees pursue their interests with a remarkable combination of intensity, focus, and enjoyment. Their preferred way of living goes beyond pursing an "interest" or "getting involved." They want to dig deep and make the absolute most of whatever it is they're working on or playing at. So at HCL they have created hundreds of online communities of passion —

some around business issues, some around everything else under the sun — that enable people to connect with one another, share ideas, create new programs and even products.

These and many other initiatives aimed at increasing transparency, creating two-way accountability, and building passion that have served to put employees first at HCL, including Gen Y employees.

At **Yahoo**, pizza is ordered for the whole work team. Also "employee of the month is selected and it is flashed in the news letter of the company. They also plan off-site activities from time to time like charity walks and miniature golf.

Organizations like **Siemens** and **Essar** have dedicated HR staff for their high-performing and high-potential Gen Y employees. At Siemens, two HR personnel keep in constant touch with the top-notchers while at Essar Group, a 'Gen Essar key talent manager' is deputed for every high performing 'Gen Essar' employee. For such employees the HR manager is just a phone call away, much like in banking, where a personalized manager is deputed for premium accounts. In case a Gen Y employee quits, the resignation letter is flashed off to director-level officials and efforts are made to retain them. Among the few changes that are taking place, the most important is that the new generation wants freedom at work.

"Apart from attraction and retention of talent, the biggest challenge today is communicating with Gen Y. The trend is moving towards Gen Y and our HR strategy is geared to connect with all the three generations," said S Ramesh Shankar, executive vice-president (HR), Siemens, which has started using mass SMSes to connect with employees.

In its own way, every organization is trying to figure out a way of engaging, developing and retaining Gen Y. While *Hexaware Technologies* engages Gen Y in activities like gliding and trekking, HCL Technologies has, what it calls, 'Mad Jam', an initiative that allows even the junior-most employee to think of a new idea and lead it.

At **TCS** , Ajoy Mukherjee, Executive Vice President and Global Head HR highlights the increasing relevance of concepts like social networks and gaming to be used to drive collaboration, creativity and productivity among young employees inside the enterprise. This can help keep GenY professionals engaged and energized through their careers.

CONCLUSION AND SUGGESTIONS

While it's entirely possible to groom this next generation of professionals to be effective leader, it is must to retain them. With so much of energy level, confidence and always ready to challenge, it is very difficult to contain them. But it is hard reality that companies cannot do without them. So the best way is to change according to them even if it means changing organizational culture. The companies should have initiatives to retain them some of it could be:

1. **In-touch always:** As they are in touch with their friends and peers through facebook, twitter, sms. They want to communicate with the management often so make it happen or they will leave! Unfortunately many older generations tend to operate differently. Oftentimes,

they have a hands-off approach to management, but this style clearly does not work well with Gen Y.

2. **Praise culture:** We all need praise from our employers, but Millennials tend to need it more often than older generations. If they are not feeling "valued" on a regular basis, they will leave. So many well-known companies are shifting to a "praise culture" to retain them…and it improves retention of their older employees too.
3. **Having their share:** Gen Y feel that "paying their dues" is just occupying space for no good reason. So if a Millennial employee is truly qualified for a promotion, many companies now offer it to them versus giving the position to someone who has simply been at the company longer. Otherwise give them more responsibility, such as letting them do one or more of the following:
    1. Start, or write for, the company blog
    2. Set-up, or participate in, your company Fan Page on Facebook or other social media presence
    3. Contribute to the company e-newsletter
    4. Research and set-up a new software solution that improves productivity for your company (or department).

    Being creative with increased responsibility can work great. Millennials have fast minds and get bored quickly, but it's your job as their employer to help eliminate the "boredom" factor.
4. **Unleash the shackles:** Gen Y have a very hard time understanding why they need to sit in a cubicle 8-10 hours a day. They want the flexibility to *work anytime, from anywhere*, and many companies are revamping their policies to provide more flexibility, using flex time as a "perk" to attract millennials to their workforce. The upside is that employees from all generations respond favorably to this flexibility and employers actually find that most employees become more productive…and tend to put in longer hours.
5. **Still a child:** Generation Y have grown up with a lot of guidance from their parents, society and teachers. Now, they expect this type of handholding at work. If the company, large or small, doesn't offer a formal (or informal) mentorship program, create one. Mentorship truly means that much to them.
6. **Leadership training:** There is a resurgence of Leadership & Management training programs happening because the gen Y want it, need it and are demanding it. Unfortunately, MANY companies still do not offer these types of programs, much to their own detriment. It's only a matter of time before their genY employees leave to pursue organizations that do offer these programs.

Finally, it's important to remember that generation wants and needs aren't much different from those of older generations; they just have a lower tolerance threshold than generations before them.

REFERENCES

[1] Vineet Nayar is CEO of HCL Technologies, a leading global IT services company and author of *Employees First, Customers Second: Turning Conventional Management Upside*

[2] Smith, M. (2008). Managing Generation Y as They Change the Workforce. Business Wire.

[3] Retrieved May 2009 from http://www.reuters.com/article/pressRelease/idUS129795+08-Jan-2008+BW20080108

[3] Terjesen and Frey. "Attracting and Retaining Generation Y Knowledge Worker Talent." In Vlad Vaiman and Charles M. Vance (ed.) Smart Talent Management: Building Knowledge Assets for Competitive Advantage Cheltenham, UK: Edward Elgar Publishing, Inc., 2008

[4] Namrata singh, times of india/business Yahoo! HotJobs/Robert Half International. What Millennial Workers Want: How to Attract and Retain Gen Y Employees. Retrieved from http://www.hotjobsresources.com/pdfs/MillennialWorkers.pdf. 200 http://www.businessdictionary.com/definition/Generation-Y.

[5] www.steel case.com

On Managing Talent Challenges in Apparel Industry

Japjee Kaur Kohli

Institute of Apparel Management, Apparel House, Gurgaon, Haryana

ABSTRACT

Indian apparel industry is facing talent crunch and talent challenges from employees whether they are shop floor workers or managing personnel. Indian apparel industry is in dire need of a well skilled and trained workforce that imparts strength to industry to face global competition. Vocational and technical education, seen as a solution to industrial problems, aims at imparting skills and training to the youth and preparing them as industry ready professionals. The present study aims to examine the factors fermenting talent challenges in apparel industry, the profile and expectations of the generation Y with focus on talent management by companies. The specific contribution of the paper is in presenting a HRM model for meeting the talent gaps by managing generation Y through strategic HR practices. The new model focuses attention on the manpower demand-supply gap existing in apparel industry, role of academics, need for transforming curriculum, behavioural issues of generation Y and engaging them for retention of talent.

Keywords: *Vocational Education, Apparel Industry, Talent Management, Transforming Curriculum, Generation Y*

INTRODUCTION

Indian Textiles & Clothing (T&C) industry, which comprises of apparel manufacturing industry and textile manufacturing industry, is currently one of the largest and most important industries in the Indian economy in terms of output, foreign exchange earnings and employment (NSDC Report). A document, prepared by ICRA Management Consulting Services Limited (IMaCS), highlights the status of skill development programs running across India and the need for talent management through skill up-gradation and training in apparel industry [1]. According to the Annual Report 2010-11 of the Ministry of Textiles [2], the industry contributes nearly 17% to the country's export earnings, 4% to the GDP and 14% to the industrial production. It provides direct employment to more than 35 million people. Looking at the projected growth statistics by CITI and NSDC [3], the manpower at shop floor level and various levels of management needs to be trained to achieve the targets. A publication of ICRA.

According to Johnson Controls Annual Report 2010 on Generation Y (Gen-Y) and Workplace [4], the Gen-Y makes up more than half of the population in India and is world's largest in Gen-Y category. Bozorg [5] has explained various psychological responses of Gen-Y in relation to global labour environment. Gen-Y, being young and industrially immature, has different perceptions, ambitions behavior and life style than Gen-X which has served for more than a decade longer in industry. In comparison to Gen-X, Gen-Y poses typical talent management challenges due to negativities associated with it and which requires more demanding strategic managerial solutions. Talented manpower is the driver of economic growth and social development of any country. In this competitive era of globalization, countries with higher and better levels of knowledge and skills respond more effectively and promptly to the challenges and opportunities. Various solutions have been suggested to tackle the talent challenges in apparel industry in recent past but due to geographical, socio-economic and cultural difference these solution are not universal.

The role of vocational education becomes pivotal as it improves the functional and analytical ability of workforce and thereby opens up opportunities for individuals to achieve greater access to labour markets and livelihood. However, talent crunch in Indian apparel industry is long standing issue which has not still been handled effectively. Here an attempt has been made to study the issues concerning Gen-Y and based on the findings of the study a new model to be implemented through human resource management for talent management is proposed.

THE STATUS OF APPAREL INDUSTRY IN INDIA

During the last four decades much has been done to improve the quality of education and skills training to make young students capable of competing for jobs at national and international levels. As a result a large number of educated persons enter Indian labour market every year. To identify the right talent and understand the relevance for talent management in apparel industry, it is important to know the value chain of apparel industry. It starts from farms where the raw material grows and ends in retail stores where products are sold to customers. Apparel industry is highly fragmented and consists of the following: vertically integrated units, converters, apparel manufacturers for domestic or exports and freelance workers. The manufacturing value chain involves designing, sourcing, manufacturing, distributing, marketing and merchandising. The risk involved is quite high as the industry works on fashion forecasts and fashion being dynamic, the trends keep changing frequently. To keep pace in the cut throat competitive global apparel industry, the companies need to work on shorter lead times, provide variety, maintain high quality standards, work on competitive cost and an urge to increase operating profits. Such concerns compel apparel and fashion companies to spend their time travelling the world for the best value and sourcing of raw material or finished goods. However tough the circumstances may be, the battle can be fought with right talent at right place in the right time.

Workplaces in apparel industry have undergone dramatic changes in last two decades. The shift from industrial age to knowledge age has transformed the work culture. Workplaces today are experiencing new work styles, locations, patterns, challenges, flexible work contracts, technology and communication systems and this has led to the evolution of complex work environment. It's high time, that the apparel companies should understand the importance of human capital and how their contribution can augment their business and its growth in the long run. Miner [6] claims that the chief cause of the predicted dearth in managerial talent is "no will to manage". Obviously effective implementation of management of resources, whether human or non-human, which takes in to account the dynamics of Gen-Y in particular, is the need of the hour.

The management structure of a typical Indian apparel industry may be represented through a pyramid that explains the kind of manpower requirements at various strategic, and operational

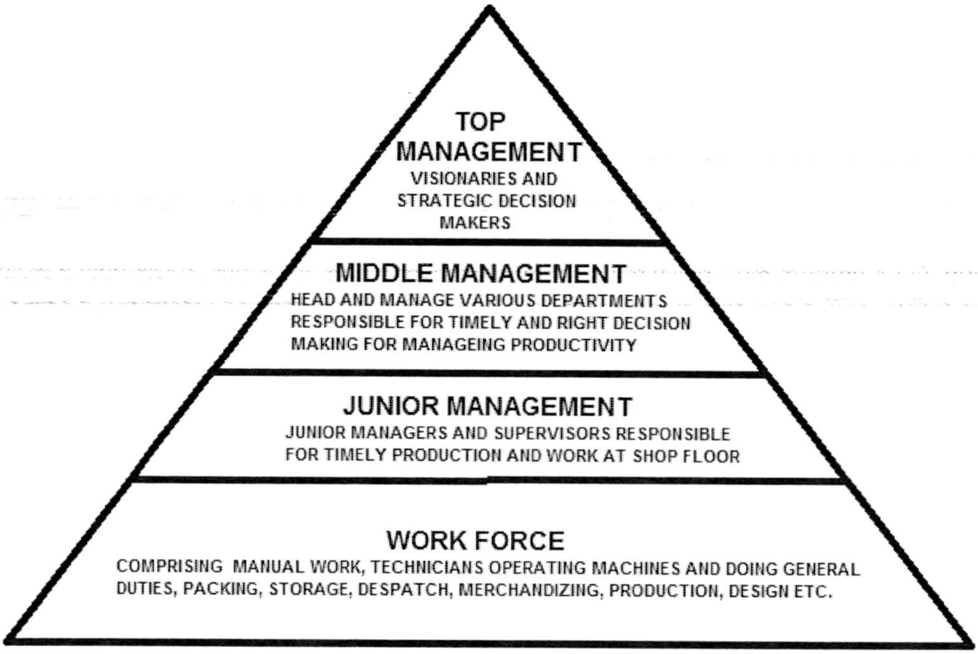

Fig. 1. Structure of Management in a Typical Kashion Apparel Industry

levels. The number of personnel in a segment increases with decrease in managerial duties, powers, responsibilities and nature of work. Gen–Y has penetrated in each segment, down to shop floor where the number of personnel is highest. Therefore, it is essential to consider shop floor personnel as an integral part of the talent employed in sectors of management pyramid in a company. Most talent management challenges come from this section of company.

RESEARCH METHODOLOGY

The present study, on talent management challenges and associated issues in Indian apparel industry, is a part of on-going doctoral work. The methodology has been defined to target specific group of individuals working in apparel industry and therefore, judgment based sampling technique has been used. As Gen-Y is present both in management as well as shop floor workforce, their working, behavioural and perception aspects are studied using survey technique. The population sample of Gen-Y is drawn from middle and junior management personnel beside shop floor personnel. The sample is further divided into two groups comprising 10 personnel from management and 80 personnel from (i) institute pass-outs who just joined workplaces in apparel industry and (ii) in-job workers from apparel industry. The primary data has been collected through in-depth interviews and observation technique. The purpose was to get an overview of the actual working of the apparel industry, the kind of talent required to perform various functions at different levels, availability of talent, talent gap and identify the type of skills, knowledge and attitude that can boost the apparel industry besides talent management challenges from Gen-Y.

FINDINGS OF RESEARCH

Responses recorded from various personnel belonging to Gen-Y and working in apparel industry reveal numerous factors relating to Gen-Y workforce and how Gen-Y talent views the job, work culture, workplace environment, expectation of employer, vocational education, skills learnt, ambitions and many more. Almost 94% of the persons interviewed agree that they feel dissatisfied due to lack of facilities, 67% divulged that structural regulations, restrictions, non-cooperation from seniors make them frustrated, 87% complained that no training programs are run for us, 7% accepted they have quarreled with their supervisory personnel on petty issues, 26% stated that they need to improve their communication skills but there is no facility provided within the unit and 59% disclosed that they would prefer to work in an organization which meets their expectations. 68% informed that they have been insulted by seniors. Analysis of other findings of significance is presented below.

Talent Challenges in Apparel Industry

The study indicates that the issues that need immediate attention for talent management are found at both the managerial level and shop floor level. Extract of information collected from sample population belonging to management group is presented in Table 1.

It is apparent from Table 1 that lack of knowledge and skills is essentially a negativity which needs to be addressed at study level. There is urgent need for establishing ethics, values and work culture in apparel industry and the same are taught during learning stages.

Table 1

Level	*Talent challenge*
Junior Management	Lack fabric knowledge and cannot identify fabrics by touch feel factor
	Lack of oral and written communication skills
	Difficulty in maintaining healthy relations with labour
	Arrogant and abusive
	Wastage of time due to poor coordination of activities
	Ready to stop work when any demand is not met by the management
	Machine Down time and maintenance period
	Inability to meet daily targets due to conflicts, downtime, absenteeism, low morale, sincerity among workers
	Ego clashes
	Non- availability of raw material for work due to problems at supplier's end.
	Making excuses and wasting time
Middle Management	Poor managerial skills- planning, organizing, coordinating , leading
	Lack of knowledge of domain area
	Cannot provide appropriate solution to the problem
	Handling and interacting with buyers
	Lack convincing power and negotiation skills
	Poor coordination between internal as well as external supply chain
	Poor internal communication
	Ego problems
	Passing of inadequate information to other departments
	Achieving targets
	Sourcing new vendors and suppliers for raw material and trims, accessories etc.
	Meeting shipment deadlines
	Maintaining quality standards to avoid rejection of stock
	Delegation of work among juniors
	Managing teams and conflicts
	Un-warranted wastages

Skill Gaps in Shop Floor Personnel

Tables 2 to 4 list out the demand, supply of workforce for apparel industry and the skill gaps observed in three important departments of apparel industry.

Merchandising Department

Table 2

Skill Demand	*Skill Supply*	*Skill Gap*
Thorough fabric knowledge, a must in clothing and textile industry.	Insufficient knowledge and ability to identify and distinguish different fabrics.	Cannot identify common fabrics and lack knowledge w.r.t. their properties like drape, finish, content, count, construction, testing, colour matching, GSM.
Excellent understanding of spec sheet to understand the design and material requirements and calculate consumption.	Brief understanding of spec sheet.	Lack skills to interpret the spec sheet and calculate the consumption requirements for the required order quantity.
Soft skills- written and verbal communication	No inputs on soft skills.	They cannot interact with buyer, seniors and workers due to attitude problems, lack of knowledge of replying to buyer's queries through mails and reply corrections.
Thorough understanding of the roles and responsibilities of a merchandiser.	Theoretical knowledge.	Difficulty in adjusting in industry environment, thus they lose interest and later leave job.

Production Department

Table 3

Skill Demand	*Skill Supply*	*Skill Gap*
Work under pressure: pressure due to daily output required	Academics environment and casual attitude of students towards learning	Get frustrated and lose confidence Exit jobs
Thorough knowledge about the product and its specifications- material, construction and quality.	Only one example taught due to shortage of time to cover entire syllabus.	Insufficient knowledge and skills to understand product requirements for different styles handled in industry and difference in specs of US and EU buyers.
Work in assembly line	Stitch one garment	Do not know the working of assembly line
Knowledge of body types to develop patterns that give accurate fit.	Work on standard dress forms.	Inability to understand different body types. Thus, lack the skill of pattern making and fit.
Team work- to work in planned layouts	Individual working	Inability to work in planned layouts and work stations
Production planning and control	An overview of production planning and control	Do not understand the nitty-gritty of production systems followed in the industry
Digital pattern making, grading and marker making	Use of CAD	Lack skills in manual as well as digital processes

Design Department

Table 4

Skill Demand	*Skill Supply*	*Skill Gap*
Excellent knowledge of fabrics and their properties	Theoretical knowledge with little exposure on fabric handling	Cannot identify fabric and suggest usage based on its properties; cannot understand fabric behaviour
Communication and buyer requirement interpretation skills	Theoretical lectures on business communication.	Cannot interact with buyers/ clients and interpret their requirements. Some cannot even speak properly in hindi and English.
Identifying and understanding current trend forecasts	Study forecast	Interpretation and application of trend forecasts for new product development for season's ahead

Behavioral Aspects

It has emerged from interviews with Gen-Y personnel that in addition to lack of education and skills, talent management challenges posed by Gen-Y come from the followings negativities: Responses from Gen-Y personnel are shown below:

Selfishness (78%) Opportunism (85%)
Ego (67%) Confusion (59%)
Lack of interest (45%) Resistance (37%)
Dissatisfaction (79%) Withdrawal (64%)
Laziness (41%) Criticism (56%)

Apart from above personal requirements at work place, like seating arrangement, lighting, fans and air conditioners, toilets and cleanliness have changed over the years. Still Gen-Y demand better service conditions for efficient working. They find work places uncomfortable, unhygienic, tiresome and controlled. The domain of operations and processes in apparel industry has not changed much despite technological advancement. The resulting dissatisfaction among Gen-Y gives rise to negativities cited above and managerial problems.

Priorities of Gen-Y

During the interviews it has been noticed that for Gen-Y the top three priorities while choosing an employer are opportunities for learning, quality of life and meaningful work. Lack of talent in team is seen by them as an opportunity for bulldozing the team members and even the management. Gen- Y of today is more demanding and challenges management models in use

Contribution of Human Resource Management

Invariably the recruitment of Gen-Y is either direct or through placement agencies. Direct recruitment for keeping industry in business mainly considers individual's skills and salary demand without bothering much about other desirable qualities. When recruitment is through a placement agency, the responsibility of selecting a suitable worker shifts to placement agency. In both the cases factors like workplace environment, work culture, needed skills from industry point of view and individual's industry readiness, character, social back ground and status, criminal record, behavior, ambitions are ignored. In such a case human resource management can contribute much in selection, grooming and welfare of workforce. .

Flow chart of conventional model adopted in most apparel industry is shown below. Here the demand for recruiting workforce is raised by a department and is approved by production manager who nominates some supervisory staff members to recruit man power. Man power requirement, being urgent, supervisory staff selects manpower from what is readily available and newly recruited man power joins industrial units and stars working.

In this model many important aspects relating to both the industrial unit and the man power are ignored. New recruits, in spite of being intelligent and hard working, commit mistakes and create problems for management [7] .. Management ignores the problems in view of urgency in dispatch of consignments. As a result frustration, indiscipline, rough language and quarrels occur frequently. Work environment, work culture, interpersonal relations and production suffer. In view of these limitations the following model is proposed.

The proposed model targets organization, management and workforce simultaneously. The organization structure has to match with its objectives. Their mismatch is likely to retain old perceptions and work culture. Raising of demand must be carried out cautiously, considering purpose, qualification, skills needed, values and ethics besides changes in organizational rules. Implementation of human resource management (HRM) principles and encouragement to creative activities within regulations is necessarily a tool for creating brand value for organization. Search for talent from available supply of workforce in the market is included in responsibilities of manager HRM and he needs to ensure that best of available talent is selected. Proper procedure for selection criteria should be evolved and made known by selectors to the available workforce opting to join the organization. Grooming is proposed to be carried out to bring them at par with the rest of the workforce employed. Periodic review by manager HRM permits him to make changes in regulations and status of the workforce. Training and vocational curriculum are evaluated by manager HRM in association with vocational education program coordinators to enable program coordinators to make amendments in their programs and include what is required in industry.

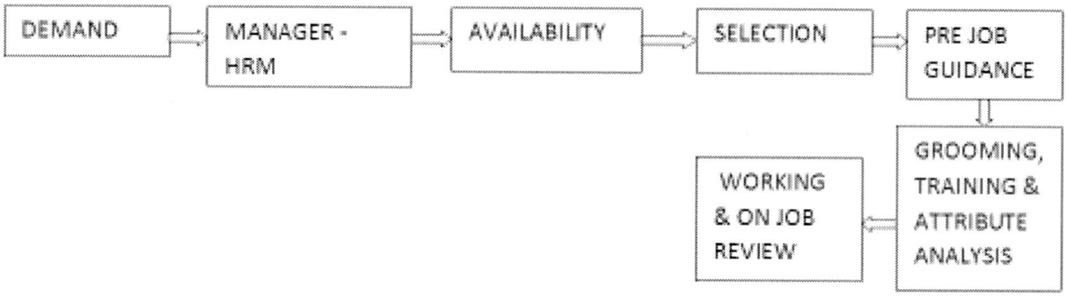

In this model the role of HRM is crucial. The responsibility of recruiting suitable personnel, their training, grooming, attribute analysis and review of periodic performance is entrusted to manager HRM, who enlists qualification, skills, interpersonal qualities, perceptions and expectations to be taken care of during selection process. After wide publicity of posts and calling of applications the candidates meeting selection criteria are short listed and interviewed. During the interview aims, targets, discipline and status of the industrial unit is briefly explained to the selected personnel. The need for training and grooming followed by review of performance is explained.

DISCUSSION AND COMMENTS

Indian apparel industry management frames its organizational policies keeping in view the nature of workforce which is a mix of urban and rural folks. The education, skills and behavior of such a mix of personnel is unique in itself and models as proposed by foreign researchers cannot be directly implemented in apparel industry. However, present study agrees to some of their findings, but cultural and social differences do not match [8]. No doubt the most promising approach is formal training to shape managerial motivation but it varies from industry to industry. Similar approach is suggested here for shop floor work force as illustrated in proposed model. Previously Nxele [9], and Smola and Sutton [10] in their study identified demand and supply factors. The new generation of people (Gen-Y) demands greater work-life balance and wants to work on their terms- when, where and how to work. According to him the pay factor cannot be considered as an approach for luring and retaining talent as many companies cannot win in salary war. Further human resource management plays a crucial role in management and retention of talent within a company. Irde and Ravi [11] suggest the need to recognize, retain and develop the potential of women as workforce to overcome talent crunch. Sharma and Bhatnagar [12] highlight strategic human resource management practices as a means to reduce the talent crunch by building a talent management strategy based on competency profiling. Singh [13] highlights the concept of employee relationship management as a strategic tool for modern business in making employees loyal, motivated, and highly satisfied in order to retain them as talented family for the company. The talent crunch and talent management, in Indian context, requires improved models to be adopted for alleviating talent crunch, maintaining balance and growth of organization, management and workforce simultaneously and the model proposed here caters for these requirements.

From the study it has also come to light that like any other industry, apparel industry also suffers from talent crunch and talent management. The man power problems and general management practices need certain modifications for making them industry specific. At managerial level the personnel possess qualifications which are above diploma or graduation level. Employed personnel with Post-graduate diploma or degree are about 35 % of total strength of the management personnel and remaining with lower qualification. Obviously, under-qualified personnel in spite of skill gaps, continues to serve till they leave the industry. The replacement is not easily available due to shortage of workforce suitably qualified, trained and with ability to take up jobs immediately after studies. Further there is little importance given to human resource management as apparel industry employs a large number of un-organized labour with rural back-ground on temporary or contract basis.

Significance of Education and Skills

Tomlinson [14] has investigated the role of graduates employability and stressed the need for periodic up-gradation of educational curriculum in view of dynamics of labour market. He points out the changing behavioural aspect of new entrants, Gen-Y, to labour market and fluctuations in labour market requirements due to global economic changes. This study high lights the need for education up-gradation in view of variability in curriculum of colleges and institutes, requirements of the apparel industry, and the differences in talent of students passing out from institutes.

Managerial Level

Education required: An eligible candidate should possess a degree or diploma in design, fashion merchandising, apparel marketing and management. A candidate with general management degree may undergo a certificate or diploma programme related to fashion design or merchandising to get knowledge of various aspects of apparel industry. These programmes impart knowledge in the areas of fabric knowledge, costing, production and quality, merchandising, supply chain management in apparel industry, CAD/ CAM, market research, fashion forecasting and garment conceptualization to garment construction. Such courses give an overall and in-depth knowledge of various aspects related to garment manufacturing and marketing in apparel industry. A thorough understanding to these helps boosts the confidence of the candidate and the individual to easily adjust in the work environment in the company. The courses are a mix of theory and project which enable student to get hands on experience of working on live or hypothetical projects. The internship and Diploma Project enable students to work in industry environment to develop an understanding of the various facets of apparel industry functioning. The student works under the mentorship of a company guide and learns various tasks related to a department.

Skill required: To perform a managerial role in an apparel industry, one is expected to be equipped with skills like understand fashion industry terminology, documentation process, interpret buyers expectations, interact with buyers and convince, interpret spec sheets into a garment, manage teams by maintaining healthy inter- personnel relation with subordinates, peers, seniors, excellent oral and written communication skills, decision making, tech savvy, consumer behavior, market understanding, product and process innovation, understanding of local, national and global competitive forces, cost analysis, resource management, time management, new product development, sourcing new suppliers, quality standards for apparel, environmental concerns and issues, implementation of latest government policies, analytical skills, awareness of market prices, coordination with fabric manufacturers and processors, ability to handle multiple accounts, production planning and control, ability to motivate subordinates and workers, coordination with other departments.

Issues due to skill gaps: Skill gaps have resulted in production and quality challenges, delay in delivery, inventory of dead stock, fabric wastage, difficulty in negotiation with vendors and buyers, non- availability of processed fabric for production, difficulty in line balancing, work study and capacity utilization, difficulty in adjusting to long working hours, tensions to meet production targets, job stagnation,

Consequences: This has resulted in unsatisfied buyers, cancellation or delays in shipments, longer lead times, conflicts among employees, wastage of time, energy, low productivity, poor quality, irregular supply of finished fabric due to improper planning, absenteeism, barriers in communication, decrease in profits, loosing buyers, exit jobs, switching to another industry, low motivation, lethargic attitude, irresponsible attitude, arrogance.

Shop Floor Worker Level

Education required: An eligible candidate should possess some kind of training related to various shop floor activities performed in apparel industry. These include measurement interpretation and pattern development, basic reading, writing and mathematical calculation, understanding of fabrics, their properties and fabric behavior, knowledge of body types, garment construction process, knowledge of various stitch types and use, quality standards for garments, types of defects, needle types and specific uses, understanding of different garmenting machines for various parts of garment, threading mechanism, interpreting spec sheets, machine maintenance, planning of work, sampling process, finishing of garment, types of stains and their removal methods, different types of production systems.

Skill required: Soft skills, basic reading, writing and mathematical calculations, taking and checking measurements, basic and specialized stitching, working with different fabrics in one garment, handling different types of fabrics, identifying defects in fit, pattern making skills, pattern grading and marker development for maximum efficiency, fabric consumption, garment inspection, machine maintenance, inter- personnel behavioral skills, cutting skills, garment pressing, work in cross-functional environment, ability to stitch different shapes, colour matching, pattern orientation among various components of a garment.

Issues due to gaps: low efficiency and productivity, poor stitching quality, improper fit, time wastage, inter- personnel conflicts, delay in production, poor knowledge of entire process of stitching a garment, poor finishing of ready product, machine downtime, unable to maintain international quality parameters, inability to work across different machines, inability to handle specialty fabrics, inadequate knowledge of in- line and final quality testing procedures, production bottlenecks.

Consequences: cancellation of orders, delayed shipments, idle time, fabric wastage, increase of alteration work, making several samples before approval, longer lead times, internal conflicts, long working hours, exit jobs, absenteeism, carefree attitude, disrespect for seniors.

SUGGESTIONS

Gen-Y demand parity, choices, openness, flexible timings and growth opportunities, ease and responsibility besides better work environment and work style, importance and dignity. Keeping in view the priorities, Skill gaps and negativities of Gen-Y the following recommendations are proposed for implementation in apparel industry.

- Reduce knowledge and skill gaps through apprenticeships, training in vocational skills
- Implement effective human resource management model as proposed
- Improve work place environment and work culture
- Empower workforce to take decision at working level
- Enhance scope of social responsibility
- Encourage management to respect the sentiments of Gen-Y
- Upgrading of vocational education curriculum to meet industry expectation
- Tackling talent crunch by balancing demand and supply of workforce

CONCLUSION

The study carried out to investigate the talent management challenges and impact of education and skill gaps on working of Gen-Y and their behavioural responses to work place and ambient environment in apparel industry suggests that (i) training and grooming of recruits is needed to synchronize Gen-Y with management expectations and objectives. (ii) education and skill acquired at learning stage influence responses of Gen-Y during service in apparel industry (iii) role of human resource management is crucial to maintain peace, harmony, sincerity, discipline and proficiency (iv) skill gaps should be alleviate by improvements in vocational education curriculum and specialized courses and apprenticeship(v) adopting conducive work-culture and practices.(vi) Tapping overflowing talent by involving Gen-Y in social service activities.

REFERENCES

[1] FICCI, 2010. The Skill Development Landscape in India and Implementing Quality Skills Training. ICRA Management Consulting Services Ltd, New Delhi.

[2] Annual Report 2010-11 of the Ministry of Textiles, Govt. of India, New Delhi. *http://texmin.nic.in/annualrep/ar_10_11_english.pdf*

[3] NSDC, Human Resource and Skill Requirements in Textile Sector (2022) – A report: National Skill Development Corporation. www.nsdcindia.org

[4] Generation Y and the Workplace, Annual Report 2010. Johnson Controls.

(http://www.johnsoncontrols.com/content/dam/WWW/jci/be/global_workplace_innovation/oxygenz/Oxygenz_Report_-_2010.pdf)

[5] Bozorg, S.H.V., (2011). The rise of glocal generation Y: how its personality and psychological contract is affected by global forces and local context. Unpublished Masters Dissertation work, University of Texas, Arlington

[6] Miner, John. B, (1974). The real crunch in managerial power, Harvard Business Review, 51, 6, Nov- Dec 74, pp 146- 158. http://www.eric.ed.gov/ERICWebPortal/search/detailmini.jsp?_nfpb

[7] Yeaton, K. (2008). The influence of the next generation: Recruiting and managing the 'Why' generation. CPA Journal Online. Retrieved Oct. 2012, from *http://www.nysscpa.org/cpajournal/2008/408/essentials/p68.htm*

[8] Twenge et al (2010). Generational differences in work places: Leisure and extrinsic values increasing, Social and intrinsic values decreasing. Journal of Management, Vol. 36, No.5, pp 1117- 1142.

[9] Nxele, M, (2008). Challenges of talent acquisition and retention in an era of brain drain. From www.ituglobalsymposium2008.info

[10] Smola, K.W. & Sutton, C.D., (2002). Generational differences: Revisiting generational work values for the new millennium. Journal of Organizational Behaviour, Vol. 23, Issue, 4, pp 363- 382.

[11] Irde. S and Ravi. M, (2012). Emerging Economy: Emerging talent. In Globalization of Professional Strategies. Springer, pp 203- 210.

[12] Rakesh Sharma, Jyotsna Bhatnagar, (2009) "Talent management – competency development: key to global leadership", Industrial and Commercial Training, Vol. 41 Iss: 3, pp.118 – 132.

[13] Singh, S., (2009). Employee Relationship Management: Strategy to focus on employees. Advances In Management, Vol. 2, Issue 4.

[14] Tomlinson, M. (2007). Graduate employability and students attitudes and orientations to the labour market. Journal of Education and Work, Vol. 20, Issue 4.

APPENDIX

Factors kausing Challenges

Numerous factors precipitate challenges in apparel industry. These factors continue to survive in work place unless properly addressed. Gen-Y is most susceptible to and influenced due to lingering on of issues. The following list provides an over view of factors leading to challenges in talent management in apparel industry.

At Worker Level

1. No or low formal training: The skills acquired by them like stitching, pattern making, quality checking, packing, finishing etc are learnt by them from their family members or 'master ji' who are working or have already worked in fashion apparel industry.
2. Work on daily wages.
3. Low morale resulting in absenteeism and low attendance at workplace.
4. Lack soft skills.
5. Workforce mostly migrated from other states and, therefore, leave job during harvesting time in their states to work in their fields.
6. Arrogant, abusive and adamant behaviour.
7. Lack sincerity and find difficulty in adjusting to long working hours.
8. Semi-literate therefore, cannot read and interpret instructions as mentioned on spec sheet.
9. Difficulty in adjusting to different production systems as one may be expert in one task but not the entire process.
10. Need time to re-skill or up-skill.

At Managerial Level

1. Relatively poor knowledge of the textiles, merchandising, quality, production and documentation process.
2. Lack of interest in studies during graduation and post graduation.
3. Casual attitude towards acquiring knowledge and skill, and life style.
4. Low level of soft and hard skills.
5. High expectations from the company.
6. Prefer doing work that interests them.
7. Inability to take decisions and handling conflicts.
8. Unaware of various managerial tools to enhance work culture and develop positive attitude among peers.
9. Shirk work that they consider is below their level.

10. Difficulty in adjustment to long and tedious working hours.
11. Low engagement level as they prefer flexible working hours.
12. Dependent on Wikipedia and google for problem solving.
13. Ego problems, dissatisfaction and frustration.
14. Lack analytical and mathematical problem solving skills.
15. Wrong perceptions about the functioning of apparel industry.
16. Expect high salaries and hierarchal growth at fast speed.
17. Wrong perceptions regarding work station and air conditioned settings for working.
18. Get irritated and jittery in demanding situations.
19. Misuse of powers and playing politics with sub-ordinates and colleagues.
20. Avoid taking higher responsibility without compensation.
21. Indulge in immoral activities and mal practices.
22. Unauthorized profit sharing with vendors.
23. Approving sub-standard materials.

At Academic Level

1. Outdated curriculum being taught with little industry exposure
2. Poor academic- industry interaction
3. Theoretical approach towards courses being taught
4. Low industry inputs in terms of guest lectures, company visits, case- studies
5. Faculty with little teaching and industry experience.
6. Selection of under qualified/ low experience faculty to maintain low pay budgets.
7. Non- Revision of curriculum
8. Leniency by private institutes in assessing, evaluating and promoting students as students pay heavy fees to get awarded the degree or diploma.
9. No action taken against students who have low attendance or fail in several subjects.
10. Attitude problem among students
11. Casual attitude of students

At Industry Level

1. No time to interact with academics in order to re-vamp the existing curriculum.
2. Quite secretive and do not want to disclose information till one joins the company.
3. Highly unorganized and fragmented
4. Improper recruitment and selection procedure.

5. Highly business oriented and therefore, not interested in training their personnel.
6. New appointee should be kept under observation for understanding his working habits and to be able to provide him with right job as per his talent.
7. Wrong person doing wrong job.
8. Need for proper coordination among various departments within the company for easy flow of work and timely completion.
9. Low pay packages and insecurity of job.
10. Lack of skilled manpower to perform the job.

Recruitment Process Outsourcing: An Effective Solution for Talent Management

Sunita Tank

Maharaja Agarsen Institute of Management Studies

ABSTRACT

Talent acquisition and retaining acquired talent is a competitive edge in today's global scenario. Identification of the right talent with adequate knowledge and matching competencies is a real challenge, but is must to meet the market requirement and the market competition. Employees must posses the necessary skill set to be promoted to positions of greater responsibility and accountability. Therefore in order to ensure that everything is moving as per the organization's strategic planning, effective evaluation of talent in terms of acquisition and retainment is must. Recruitment Process Outsourcing (RPO) is one such process, if adopted, will lead to an effective talent management as a whole. The process will not only identify the manpower gaps in an organization but it further fills those gaps with the right kind of profile with matching competency up to a great extent. The entire process will look up to the whole cycle of the recruitment till the time an employee is associated with the respective organization. RPO manages everything on behalf of the company in terms of staff, technology, methodology and the reporting system. RPO is mainly used in managing talent in those industry where attrition is extremely high, expansion are in the pipeline or profiles are extremely niche to locate. Therefore this paper examines the gaps in talent management, need of talent management and finally the importance of RPO in talent management.

Keywords: *Attrition Factors, Talent Management, Talent Acquisition, and Recruitment Process, Outsourcing*

INTRODUCTION

Talent

"Talent" refers to those employees who have an ability to produce an above-average amount of product or deliver a service. Such talent will separate the winning companies from the rest. In today's knowledge economy, the caliber of a company's talent increasingly determines success in the marketplace (McKenzie war talent 2000 report). According to the report, it was found that having strong talent in key positions creates huge improvements in performance. As per the survey, in a manufacturing company, the best plant managers grew profits 130% while the lowest performing managers achieved no improvement. In an industrial services company, the best center managers grew profits 80% while the lowest performers achieved no improvement. And a study of portfolio managers in a financial services institution showed that top performers grew revenues by nearly 50% while average performers' portfolios remained flat. The success lies with the key to successfully associate the best talent with the organization.

Talent Management

Talent management is the process to effectively hire, retain, deploy and engage talent to the best of its ability that goes well with the organization strategic business planning, growth and expansion plans at all levels. It also ensures organizations have the quantity and quality of people in place to meet their current and future business priorities. The process covers all key aspects of an employee's "life cycle:" selection, development, succession and performance management. To have a successful process a sound talent management plan should be designed in order to identify thc kcy gaps in the organization and the talent required to fill that gap effectively. However the process of talent management is becoming more difficult day by day, as demand for highly skilled people outstrips supply. Companies that recognize the strategic importance of talent and its management reap very large rewards in terms of business growth, expansion and brand promotion.

Key components of an effective talent management process include:

- Understanding the organization current and future business objectives.
- Identification of the key gaps between the talent in place and the talent required to achieve those business objectives.
- Plan to acquire accurate talent, retain the existing talent.
- Linking individual, team and corporate goals to achieve the set business goals
- Regular performance feedbacks and measures to improve the performance.
- Talent development programme to enhance performance in current positions and capability identification for the next level.
- Special emphasis on execution policy and there by measuring the effectiveness of such plan before and after the implementation.
- Following are the six dimensions of talent management
- **Develop Strategy.** Formulating the optimal long-term strategy for attracting, developing, connecting and deploying the workforce.
- **Attract and Retain.** sourcing, recruiting and holding onto the appropriate skills and capabilities, according to organizational business needs.
- **Motivate and Develop.** Verifying that people's capabilities are understood and developed to match business requirements, while also meeting people's needs for motivation, development and job satisfaction.

- **Deploy and Manage** Providing effective resource deployment, scheduling and work management that match skills and experience with organizational needs.
- **Connect and Enable** Identifying individuals with relevant skills, collaborating and sharing knowledge, and working effectively in virtual settings.
- **Transform and Sustain** Achieving clear, measurable and sustainable change within the organization, while maintaining the day-to-day continuity of operations.

Recruitment Process

The process of recruitment can be best explained in the terms that it talks about identifying the workforce gaps across functions in the organization and hiring the same with best of matching competencies and skill set required to fill that gap in a most timely and cost effective manner. The recruitment can take place within or outside of an organization. The process beings with designing of job description, identifying the mode of recruitment publishment, screening the relevant profiles, scheduling of interviews, selection, induction, and finally on boarding.

Recruitment Outsourcing

Recruitment Outsourcing is an act where an organization contract with another company or person to do handle its recruitment functions. The outside firms that are providing such outsourcing services are called third-party service vendors or service providers. Recruitment function is mainly outsourced under the situation where company saves money and time for the other core functions of business.

Recruitment Process Outsourcing

RPO is a form of outsourcing where some or all of an organization's talent acquisition and talent management activities are outsourced to a third party vendor. RPO is counted as a specialized service in Human Resource Outsourcing. An RPO provider leverages the combination of strategy, technology, resources and vendor management to improve the recruitment process. The RPO provider work closely with the client to improve the recruitment efficiencies of quality of hire, speed of delivery and cost containment. Improvements measured and monitored through real-time metrics are then tied to strict service level agreements.

RPO service provider is mainly consulted under three situations in an organization:

- Extreme Level of Attrition
- Expansion in Pipeline
- Profiles are niche to locate.

LITERATURE REVIEW

Recruitment Process Outsourcing as a concept was first realized in 1970's in US with the demand of technical skills going up with high tech companies, mainly Information Technology and manufacturing firms. Hiring cost was growing up in terms of tracking external experts and that time RPO was only used to add greatest value- with greatest difficult technical staff. In 1980's and 1990's companies started realizing the fact of reducing the fixed cost of HR, which was primarily related to recruitments. The earliest academic articles concerning it are from around the mid-2000s. Due to its short history, recruitment process outsourcing has not been extensively researched. Therefore the literature provides a great deal of process-related perceptions and general discussion and applicable data from topics such as human resources outsourcing, but lacks a basic rationale for the process itself. Early 2000 registered a major change in RPO scenario. Further with the introduction of HRO today magazine "The Baker's Dozen Survey- showcases the list of top thirteen RPO vendors in the world" in the year 2002, RPO became a big time business solution to talent management.

Breaugh and Starke (2000) provide a good starting point by going through some of the existing theories related to recruitment, as well as pointing out their limitations. The study stated the fundamental goal for any recruitment outsourcing process, is to attain the best possible candidates for the right positions and as efficiently as possible.

According to a study conducted by FutureStep- A korn/ferry company , RPO: transforming end to end talent acquisition in the year 2005, it was stated that those models which just focus on cost-reduction and process have failed to integrate talent acquisition and management with the strategic imperatives for talent demanded by the business. According to the report, it was stated that while cost and process efficiencies are still a priority, organizations should realize that leveraging talent as a competitive advantage is paramount. HR functions in partnership with their service provider must be more outwardly oriented – i.e., in closely managing and evaluating the various human capital vendors and partners with whom they work and through innovative strategies and tactics that create value while simultaneously driving down cost. The report suggested that an effective RPO provider will work in collaboration to set the talent agenda and then execute by integrating people, process and technology to drive competitive advantage through the appropriate talent solutions. This further will bring a new dimension and a fresh perspective.

According to Talent Management Survey 2009, it was found that a small minority of organizations only take a proactive and strategic approach to talent management even today, factoring in emergent economic conditions. Later the Assessment and Talent Management Survey 2010 – Finding and Analysis report focused on the facts that: Organization talent restructuring is still seen as the top priority for HR. Secondly Performance management, development, identification of high potential employees, team development and succession planning, all areas are capable of improvement. Thirdly, majority of organizations do not re-use their talent management assessment data for complimentary or linked purposes. Lastly and most important aspect was many organizations still continue to find it difficult to differentiate good from average applicants.

Whelan & Carcary (2011) in their study stated Recruitment, whether outsourced or not, deals directly with talent management. The acquirement of talent is linked with the firm's core functions and understanding the impact that talent management may have on RPO is extremely important. Also knowledge management plays a role to some extent and especially when combined with talent management.

Brief Review on the Business Growth of RPO

- In 2007 the global RPO market was worth US$720 million and went up to an increase of by 22% in 2008.
- In 2009 RPO market has surpassed US$1 billion level
- Everest Group PEAK Matrix, published in the April 2012 Recruitment Process Outsourcing (RPO) that the global RPO market continues to witness a rapid growth rate (27.2% year-on-year) to reach US $1.4 billion in actual cash value (ACV).

Although demand comes predominantly from US-based Fortune 1000 companies, the market is growing rapidly in continental Europe, the UK and Asia Pacific.

OBJECTIVES OF THE STUDY

The research paper was undertaken with the following objectives:

- To understand the factor responsible for gaps in talent management.
- To study the need of Talent Management for the survival and growth of the organization.
- To show the importance and effectiveness of Recruitment Process Outsourcing in Talent Management.

RESEARCH METHODOLOGY

It is a cross sectional study which is exploratory in nature. This is a conceptual paper based on the secondary data available through books, magazines, various surveys and research papers. The data is mainly collected from the secondary sources which include articles published in journals, research papers, published interviews of professionals in newspapers, published surveys by various companies and websites of different companies.

SCOPE AND LIMITATIONS

The scope of the study is applicable to the stakeholders in the various companies who are facing difficulties in managing their talent for the business survival and growth. Almost all major industries like Information Technology, ITES, pharmaceuticals, manufacturing, BPO etc are being affected due to gaps in talent management. As is the case with any research, this study is not without limitations. The study is based on the secondary data and thus brings in an element of biasness.

FINDING AND ANALYSIS

"Attracting and retaining the right employees is a challenge for employers globally "and a large majority of companies in the world are struggling to overcome this challenge of retaining top-performing and critical-skill workers. Various studies and survey were taken into consideration in order to find out the gap and to understand the issues in talent management. Attrition across industries was the biggest factor, highlighted by most of the industries. While there are certain other factors as well, mentioned below in detail.

Attrition Review- Attrition Factors

Many employers do not fully understand why workers join or leave an organization which adds to the workforce turnover the most. Out of the moving category of employees, Companies find it difficult to hold on to their young employees as attrition levels stood at 15% for young generation.

A survey conducted by **Team Lease Services Pvt Ltd** (Source – The Hindu, Business Line September 4, 2012) showed that the attrition rate in South India that has a significant concentration of IT and ITES firms have the highest attrition rates. "While on an average, attrition hovers around 8-10% in most organizations, in IT companies and BPOs - where most staffers are in their early 20s - attrition is astonishingly high,". The survey also showed that "better salary" was one of the major reasons for high attrition levels. Majority of the respondents in all of the surveyed cities expressed this view. Junior level profiles having work experience of 1-3 years stole the limelight from across all other hierarchical levels. This segment showed the highest and the fastest growing intent to hire, while middle-level hiring (with 3-7 years of work experience) showed a marginal drop in the data collected from about 8 major cities. The survey spans eight industry sectors and covers small, medium and large companies.

After information technology, the pharmaceuticals industry is grappling with the highest level of attrition rate of 30 to 35 per cent, according to a recent survey of Indian pharmaceutical companies by Interlink Marketing Consultancy. Interlink surveyed a sample of 15 companies in the small, medium and large segments in the Indian pharmaceutical sector. The survey points out that the sector's high churn other than the natural rate of attrition is mainly due to poaching, burnout, high stress at work and inadequate payment. Globally, the rate of attrition in pharmaceutical is only 10 to 12 per cent, says the IBS report. These search reveals that the pharmaceutical industry annually experiences an employee turnover of 30 to40 per cent at the field level and 8 to 10 per cent at the managerial level.

Below are some broad reasons for an employee to leave an organization

- Better pay opportunity elsewhere- money factor,

- Dissatisfaction at workplace- working conditions, organization's culture,
- Opportunities for career growth
- Employee personal reasons

Figure 1. Below showcase the attrition factors from employee's viewpoint and Figures 2. below showcase the attrition factors from employer's viewpoint, of the organizations.

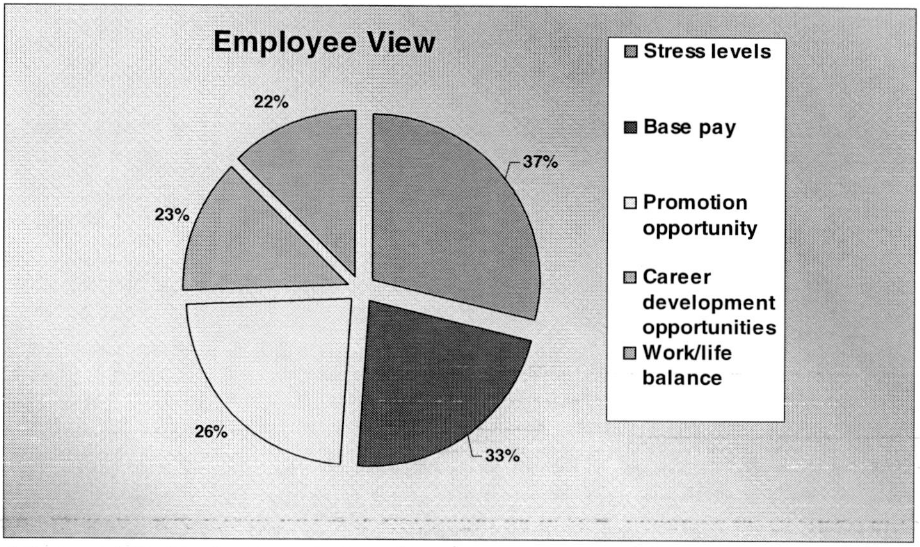

Fig. 1

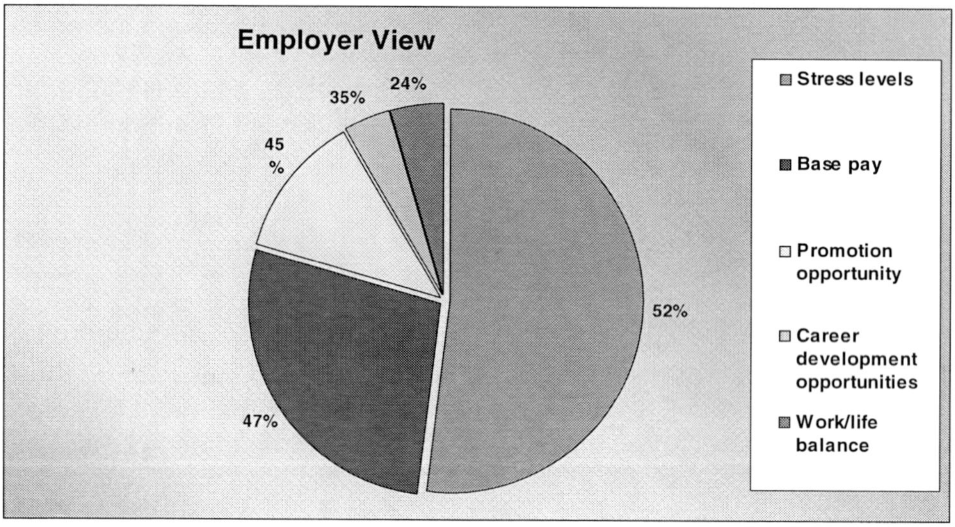

Fig. 2

Talent Recruitment Frequency and Availability of Talent Database

Companies in general only hire when an individual leave or planning to leave an organization. This makes the whole recruitment process a time bound exercise where in an organization in order to avoid business loss at certain point of time compromise on the required competencies of an individual to fill a particular job vacancy. Such gaps results in business losses and gives an opportunity to the competitors to eat the fruits and take an edge, may be for a short period of time. The companies do not maintain a ready pool of candidate database for their key positions. This delays the overall process of recruitment. Companies do not maintain a keen sense of who they are looking for, and at what new places and in what new ways. Companies do not realize that having the right talent is a critical source of competitive advantage. Companies do not spend much time in strengthening the talent pool. According to NorthgateArinso (NGA) (Market-leading global Human Resource Service Provider) Talent Management Survey 2011, it was found that companies have identified 50.7% of talent shortage in their industry. And Industries that are more susceptible for talent shortage are mainly Consulting, Retail, High tech, IT & Telecommunications, Transport. The survey has also suggested that the companies must look 3 years ahead and assess talent management processes in their organization.

Performance Management

Performance is an easiest way to judge an employee as it is directly linked to the initial goals set and the result to be achieved. But in an organization performance-management requires a comprehensive performance-planning process with employees, ongoing coaching, and providing employees with regular updates on the progress that they have made toward performance objectives. The performance in terms of specific goals, or targets to be achieved should be clearly stated to the employees, it should be than measured with the organization selected tools and thereafter the result should be calculated. An Aberdeen Group survey of managerial and technical employees in service organizations found that 99% had some form of performance evaluation. Retail, manufacturing and small businesses are less likely to have performance management systems. In most organizations performance management is primarily an annual event, a form completed prior to the end of the financial year. The form is filed and in most cases will not be touched again until the next review the following year.

Recognition, Rewards and Engagement

An effective reward system in any organization addresses four main areas namely compensation, benefits, recognition and appreciation. Such system further attracts loyalty, longevity and more of participation among employees. The employee with such feeling tends to accomplish their assigned job much more effectively with desired results. It also makes employees aware, as to what is expected out of them in terms of behavior and output. The reward system also strengthens the employer employee contact. It indicates what behavior the organization values. But the problem with reward systems in many businesses today is twofold: They're missing one or more of these elements (usually recognition and/or appreciation), and the elements that are addressed aren't properly aligned with the company's other corporate strategies.

Need of Talent Management

MNC's today are putting extra efforts to retain talent. Talent strategies such as succession planning, more of people involvement and development, building talent communities can be seen in the corporate scenario today. Talent management is must due to the following reasons:

- To make the recruiting process more efficient and effective by using "competency based" recruiting instead of just sorting through resumes.
- To better develop managers and leaders to reinforce culture, instill values, and
- Create a sustainable "leadership pipeline.
- To quickly identify competency gaps in order deliver training, e-learning, or Development programs to fill these gaps as soon as possible.
- To manage people in a consistent and measurable way so that everyone is aligned, held accountable, and paid fairly.
- To identify high performers and successors to key positions throughout the Organization.

CONCLUSION

It is said, organizations are made up of talent, talent that creates value through proven business processes, innovation, customer service, sales, and many other important activities. As an organization strives to meet its business goals, it must make sure that it has a continuous and integrated process for recruiting, training, managing, supporting, and compensating such talent. Therefore such talent management challenges require new processes and systems as well. Those processes that proves to have more integration between the different HR silos and direct integration into line of business management processes. Recruitment Process Outsourcing is one such process which gives an effective solution to all such talent management challenges. RPO combines proven recruitment processes with the ever expanding internet and technology offerings to achieve clear results.

RECOMMENDATIONS

With changes and innovations in the human resource management's strategies, it is possible to reduce attrition across industry with the following tools.

Control over Attrition, proves to be the major advantage for any organization over its competitors. Talent if retained will not only be able to maintain the existing business growth but will also leads to high quality profits, business expansions and adding on to brand value of an organization.

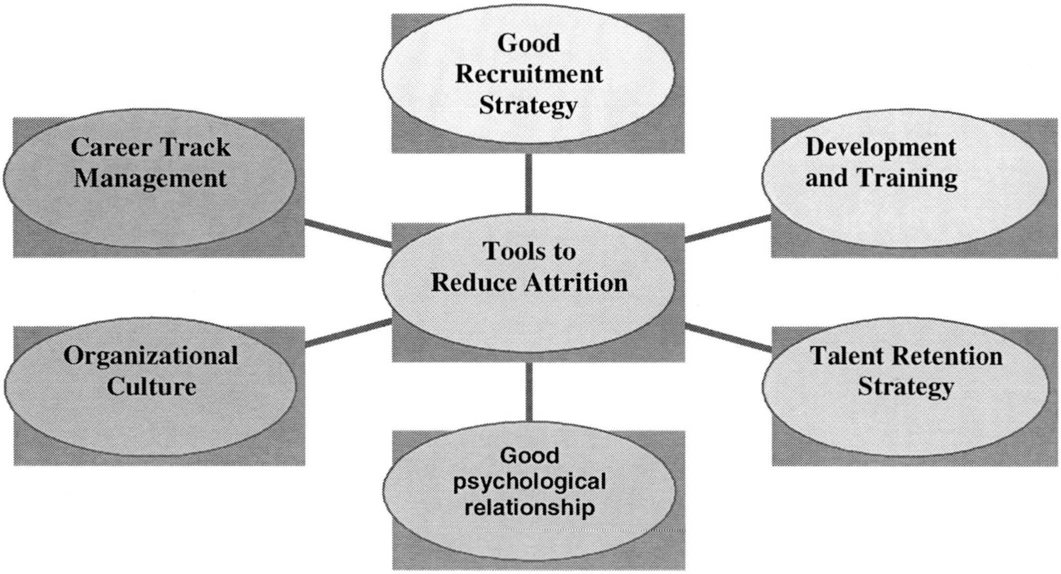

Need of Recruitment Process Outsourcing

According to Recruitment Process Outsourcing (RPO) Annual Report 2012 - Raising the Bar to Sustain Momentum, (RPO) is one of the fastest growing Single Process HRO markets with a growth rate of over 25% to reach US$1.4 billion in annualized spend. The benefits of RPO make the process much more important for its adoption for global survival, growth and expansion.

Operational Benefits of RPO

- **Highly skilled, culturally aligned recruiters** – RPO are not just recruitment consultants rather they are experts in talent acquisition within the client's industry and are well versed with the organizational culture. They will further bring the know how to ensure the talent acquisition process is targeted and streamlined for both one off search led programmes to high volume recruitment campaigns.
- **Costs savings** – Hiring a RPO significantly reduce the overall establishment cost of Human Resource department as the set up is already available with all the relevant resources essential for the recruitment campaigns. RPO is capable of introducing more diverse and innovative sourcing channels, which will further save money on more traditional job advertisements.
- **Quality pool of candidate engagement** – RPO maintains a pool of relevant profiles for all key positions of an organization. RPO provide a highly responsive, direct point of contact for all candidates, ensuring best career opportunities are identified for the most suitable candidates, managing business and candidate expectations carefully.

- **RPO an advisory support** – IT provides the highest level of expert and factual advice to Line Management, saving them time and enabling them to structure and resource their business successfully.
- **Turn around time** – Time to close any open roles is reduced by putting in place the people, processes and technology correctly.

Strategic Benefits of RPO

- **Brand awareness** – partnering with your HR and marketing teams and external brand specialists to identify your employee value proposition by key talent segment. We ensure your EVP is communicated consistently and accurately to your target market across all candidate touch points, dramatically improving candidate awareness of who you are and what you do.
- **Improve resource planning** – RPO helps in understanding short, mid and long term business strategies to facilitate quality based talent pools in line with current and future demands.
- **Develop hiring manager skills** – Continuous interview coaching and training is provided to line Management on both a structured and ad hoc basis to improve interview, selection and recruitment success as well as dramatically enhancing candidate engagement.
- **Employee engagement** – RPO continuously hire managers to identify high performing and high potential internal talent and ensure they are considered for open roles, positively impacting employee engagement in the process.
- RPO should be recognized by all stakeholders as more than just a way to save money. Although costs can be significantly reduced, but RPO's contribution lies with the fact that it emphasize more on improving an organization's resource planning, lifting employee engagement and time to fill and, most importantly, by increasing the quality of your hiring.

Though Recruitment Process Outsourcing (RPO) is one of the fastest growing single process HRO markets with a growth rate of over 25% annually, but there are still many pitfalls to the RPO system. Studies are in the process under the same direction and more research can be done in order to identify the gaps in RPO service and its process and on its improvement strategies.

BIBLIOGRAPHY

Reports

- Multinational Corporations in China: Finding and Keeping Talent. A publication of the Society for Human Resource Management, October 2007.
- Integrated Talent Management, Part-3 – Turning talent management into a competitive advantage: An industry view, a report by IBM Institute for Business Value in partnership with Human Capital Management, August 2008.

- The War for Talent- A report by McKinsey & Company, April 2001.
- Watson Wyatt Survey 2007.
- Northgate Arinso (NGA) Talent Management Survey 2011.
- The Towers Watson M&A Retention Survey, February 2012.
- Rewards Programs- A Report by World at Work October, 2007.
- Aberdeen Group Business at Risk Is employee performance management the antidote? Watson Wyatt Survey March 2004.
- Performance Management- Problems and Potential- 12 key steps to ensure top performance from your staff.

Talent Development in the Travel Industry: Creating a Training Inventory for Generation Y Employees of Travel Agencies in India

Anu Singh Lather, Shalini Garg and Sona Vikas[1]

University School of Management Studies, Guru Gobind Singh Indraprastha University, Delhi
[1]Ansal Institute of Technology, Sector 55, Golf Course Road, Gurgaon

ABSTRACT

Soft skills are increasingly becoming the hard skills of today's work force. It's just not enough to be highly trained in technical skills, without developing the softer, interpersonal and relationship-building skills that help people to communicate and collaborate effectively. These people skills are more critical than ever as organizations struggle to find meaningful ways to remain competitive and be productive. This paper explores the importance of soft skills in the area of travel agency business through a survey of 500 travel professionals across India at various levels viz. top management of the companies and senior level, middle level and junior level of employees, conducted in a span of eight months. Based on industry feedback, a list of twenty-two trainings, including product / technical trainings and soft skill trainings was prepared. This training inventory was administered with both the top management and the employees in the travel companies on a Likert Scale of 5 (very important...unimportant), to understand their importance. Based on the results, it has become very apparent that the survey respondents whole-heartedly feel the necessity to conduct soft skills trainings along with the product/technical trainings. In fact more than the product knowledge, travel professionals feel that it is the behavioral skills that make the difference in tourism, one of the largest service industries in India.

Keywords: *Tourism, Travel Agencies, Training and Development, Soft Skills*

INTRODUCTION

The WTO's Tourism 2020 Vision forecasts that the number of international arrivals worldwide will increase to almost 1.6 billion, and receipts from tourism (excluding transport) are projected to reach US $2 trillion by 2020 (WTO, 2001). Such figures bring to light the fact that tourism is arguably the world's largest and fastest growing industry. Goeldner and Ritchie (2006) have claimed that tourism has virtually embraced all aspects of human society. Not surprisingly, the industry employs in excess of 234.3 million people worldwide (WTTC, 2006), representing around 8.7 percent of the total global workforce. In comparison to tourism's contribution to gross domestic product, foreign exchange earnings, capital investment, or tax contributions, it is the job-creation capacity of the tourism industry that is its most significant feature (Baum, 2006a; Conlin & Baum, 2003; Sharpley, 2002; WTO, 2002; WTTC, 2002). In fact, in a recent employment index survey conducted by the Ascent, Times of India, travel and tourism is one of the top three industries showing growth (February, 2011).

Amongst the various players of the tourism industry, it is the travel agencies that are the most important intermediaries that offer the services provided by the suppliers or vendors (including airlines, car rentals, cruise lines, hotels, railways, sightseeing tours and package holidays) to the clients. Travel agencies are an integral part of the worldwide travel, tourism and transportation industry. A travel agency is a retail business that provides travel – related information and makes arrangements related to transportation, accommodation and travel itinerary of its customers. Nowadays, travel has become both increasingly important and complex in its variety of modes and choices. Travelers depend on travel agencies to guide them honestly and competently. A travel agency takes care of the complete travel requirements of the travelers and sells air, land and sea transportation; lodging accommodations; cruise trips; package tours, travel insurance, visa, foreign exchange services. Travel agents are the backbone of the industry. They play a pivotal role in promoting the country as a tourist destination by making the tourists have a feel of the rich cultural diversity of the country.

The general job profile of a travel agent includes acting as a counselor to the clients, making sales, gathering information, researching travel products and analyzing options and making recommendations. Specifically, some of the many and varied tasks that jobs in the travel industry involve - *Communication* (answer phone calls and respond to email enquiries, talk with a lot of people, translate from one language to another, coordinate for reservations), *Procedural formalities* (prepare travel itineraries for clients and groups, book accommodation and make travel arrangements using industry-specific computer programs, book airline tickets, create and print brochures), *Interaction* (offer clients local, interstate and international travel options; entertain customers with stories about historical, geographical and cultural interest points; lead tour parties; travel to a variety of local, national and international destinations), *Involvement* (organize whiz-bang tourism awards events, recruit and train staff, coordinate educational programs). All these responsibilities focus both on product/technical and soft skills for the employees.

These critical responsibilities demand for both tourism related knowledge (for e.g. tourism products, services, international and domestic ticketing, destinations and general geographical knowledge, fare calculations, computer efficiency, reservation systems, foreign languages etc) as well as business competencies (e.g. customer orientation, selling and negotiation techniques, marketing skills, problem solving, time management etc). To meet the changing demand of travelers, businesses and countries which are competing for tourists, are forced to spend considerable efforts on training and retraining their staff. With emerging areas in tourism like special interest tourism (eco-tourism, rural tourism, heritage tourism, and adventure tourism), recreational tourism (lakes, mountains, spas) and medical tourism, training for these different types is extremely important.

Moreover, the tourism sector across the world is being challenged by a growing demand for customer orientation, increasing international competition, volatile markets in an insecure environment, changing customer demands towards individualization, significant potential in various market segments and an increased dependency on the internet for information and reservations. As the design and delivery of quality tourist experiences remains a key task for tourism professionals (Morgan, 2003), it is only a well-educated and well-trained workforce that can achieve comparative advantage in this highly volatile and competitive global tourism industry.

And it is against this background that the authors discuss the significance of soft skills trainings for travel agencies. While some past studies have been conducted to highlight the significance of trainings in both hotels and airlines, where hotels adopt modern HR techniques to train and develop employees, and airlines were conducting product and behavioral trainings for the cabin crew, airport staff and for their reservations team, it is only in the travel agencies that there is hardly any sign of trainings being conducted for the employees by the management, as a result of which not much of training related research literature is present.

The situation today is that just like the industry itself still does not have a clear and adequate operational framework, the training is largely carried out in a haphazard and uncoordinated manner. There are even concerns about the sub-optimal state of tourism education and training and the associated skills shortages. Many of the students who graduate from tourism colleges are ill-equipped to comprehend the dynamics of globalization and its subsequent effects on the industry. This is despite the fact that improving the skills and knowledge of the workforce can assist destination competitiveness and help to establish and maintain a viable industry. Numerous institutions have sprung up purporting to offer courses at various levels in travel, tourism, catering, hotel and institutional management. However, most of them lack basic training facilities and do not meet acceptable standards. They spew out graduates whose knowledge is questionable as there is no centralized examination or certification. In the face of such expansion, questions have often been raised about the level, scope and quality of tourism training and education in the country. Questions have been often raised on the employability of the students graduating from tourism institutes, leading to a serious problem of talent crunch (Page et al, 2001). The apparent reason for this critical situation, at the first glance, pins down the blame on the education system. Lack of focus on behavioral aspects and soft skills, less of practical training, time constraints leading to limited focus on projects and practical work, lack of correlation and connection with the industry requirements (Lucas, 2004), and the teaching methodologies still comparatively conservative than being experiential—can be attributed as the drawbacks of the tourism educational system, which needs to evolve, be more pragmatic and keep pace with changing times. The growing skills gap reflects the slim availability of high-quality college education in India and the galloping pace of the country's service-driven economy. The biggest challenge is that the academia concentrates on theoretical vs. problem solving skills and analytical skills vs. actual strategy implementation or soft skills encompassing communication, creativity, leadership, innovation, etc. There is a conspicuous gap between skills required and skills acquired, and it neither reflects well on part of the academia, nor does it reflect any industry involvement to help itself rise from the plummeting crisis (Ashraf & Mathur, 2003). There is therefore a need to come up with a uniform curriculum that is not only acceptable to all the industry participants, but which is also competitive both locally and internationally. Therefore, both quality and quantity tourism requires trained personnel to man the various positions in the industry (Foster, 1994). The need for skills, knowledge and vision is being felt more and more today. With new offers and services emerging in tourism, the need for adequately qualified staff becomes even more critical. Thus, training and development plays an important role in developing professionalism in the business of tourism and travel agency operations (Chand & Chauhan, 2003).

Unfortunately, in many parts of the world, the sustainable development of the tourism industry is constrained by unskilled employees and an acute shortage of skilled labour. Today, the tourism industry, particularly in India is besieged by a whole lot of human resource problems including

- *Low wages, high demand for staff flexibility, little training provision, high staff turnover, skill shortages*
- *Qualifications from the tourism sector are much appreciated by other sectors (customer service etc) and qualifications from other sectors are useful for tourism.*
- *Many qualified employees leave the sector and many trained tourism school graduates do not enter the sector, leading to a sheer waste of resources and skills.*
- *Forecasting which skills will be needed in future under conditions of sector volatility and vulnerability*
- *Multi-skilling, newly emerging and hybrid occupations reflect the trends for new types of services and growing demand for flexibility.*
- *Travel SMEs who are the mainstay of tourism, neither have organized practices for human resource management nor do they deploy interventions for human resource development due to their business models of reliance on vendor commissions.*

Training and development amongst the travel companies has not received the kind of importance it deserves. Some major problems for this are cost constraints, time paucity, administrative issues and top management attitude towards training. In fact, training myopia is one key area of concern, since it is the top management of an organization that approves and allocates resources for imparting training to its employees. Pareek (2005) referred this to as hostility towards training which is prevalent in many organizations. According to him, in some cases, the work organization managers in general, and the top management in particular consider training to be a waste of time and may have a hostile attitude towards it. In such cases, the effectiveness of training will be doubtful. Hostility to training may be based on the experience that training is not producing the desired results. However, with such hostility, the results cannot be achieved, and so it becomes a vicious cycle. Instead of looking at the causes of lack of effectiveness of training the managers may not only be indifferent but are also hostile to training. In some cases they tolerate training not because they think it is a useful activity but because historically it is being given some place and budget, and in some cases it may seen as backward if they do not have this function in the organization. Then training loses its real value and is carried out as ritual as even in some case as a necessary evil. With such indifference and hostile attitude towards training those in-charge concerned with training become helpless. Unless the top managers see training as a useful function and support it training cannot function effectively. Another problem related to sending employees for the soft-skills trainings is the management perception that employees should learn on the job, rather than through external instructors. Some of them even feel that these behavioral trainings are not even relevant to their business.

One of the other challenges of conducting these trainings for the travel industry is designing them. The top management feels that these are very complex, and the training companies who conduct such training sessions for other industries are always ready to *customize* them for their industry – there is hardly any company specializing in organizing behavioral trainings only for the travel industry staff. It is difficult to get the precise training content for the travel industry staff. There is a lack of good institutions offering quality travel industry-related trainings. This coupled with the fact that the soft skill trainers currently available in the market are not having in-depth knowledge about the industry, travel processes, functional problems etc, as a result of which they are not able to provide the expertise to handle the day-to-day problems of the employees.

Another problem of these trainings is what trainings to conduct. The management of travel agencies does not have adequate expertise to conduct training need analysis (TNA) for their employees, nor do they hire HR professionals in their organization. In fact, they are ready to spend a lot of their own time and effort in recruiting their employees, doing unorganized appraisals etc, but they are not convinced with the value-add a HR person can be in their organization for streamlining the various employee – related processes. The current industry approach is such that employers take short-cuts in recruitment practices, use contractual and (or) untrained workers to fill shortfall rather than employ permanent workers with prior training. There is also a general lack of commitment on the part of many employers to get workers with some training and then train them as per the specifications of the job that requires to be done. There is high volatility in the labour workforce in the tourism industry due to a fairly large proportion of unskilled occupation and transferability of skills at any level.

So, as a result, there is a desire to obtain workers who are *ready-made*, and can immediately adapt to the challenges of the workforce per force. Employers today are seeking highly skilled workforce who has new ways of thinking, managing, and working. Employers are disappointed with young job applicants because of non- technical, generic employability skills. The companies adopting shortcuts in recruitment practices need to understand that if employability issues are to be seriously considered by industry, then it has to have wider ramifications on the recruitment and training of the workforce. There is a need for ongoing skill development in employees to take account of emerging occupations and changing skill requirements due to technological changes and workplace processes. Job-specific technical skills in a given field are no longer sufficient as employers generate inter-reliant jobs, with emphasis on multi-skilling and multi-tasking. Youth need to possess set of personal attributes and social skills to prepare them for both employment and employability in the context of challenges that the Indian industry is facing. Employers want entry-level employees to have some generic employability skills such as affective skills or personal qualities, e.g. ability to work in teams, the right attitude towards work, following instructions, dependability and responsibility, positive work ethic, punctuality and regularity, and basic skills such as communication and presentation skills.

Despite the non-availability of employee candidates with the desirable skills, the top management of the travel organizations has always been hesitant to invest in the employee development. Amid deadlines, hectic schedules and high work pressure, skill building takes a backseat. With immediate return on investment on training initiatives not visible to them, human resource development is not a priority in the travel companies. And this is one of the most critical hurdles that encourage training. At the heart of this problem is the fact that training outputs are often hard to quantify and that costs are difficult to allocate. Research conducted in hospitality and tourism firms of all sizes has discovered that informality and a relatively unsophisticated management style characterize the approach taken towards recruitment and training (Goldsmith et al., 1997; Price, 1994; Lucas, 1995; Baum, 1995). Research on recruitment and training in small firms in general (Jameson, 1998) has also indicated that an informal approach towards the management of human resources is the norm in these firms.

Another issue in conducting the soft skills trainings is the attitude and perception of employees towards such training initiatives. Most of them take trainings as a distraction away from work. They do not take the training sessions seriously. Some of them even avail the training opportunities and immediately leave for better shores. While there are even some who do not complete the entire duration of the training due to lack of interest. Many of the employees even perceive that trainings do not lead to the development they promise since they are not able to see the visible changes immediately after completion of the training programme. For some employees, training is a time to bond with their colleagues, especially those placed in multiple locations across the country. All these reasons deter the travel agency owners to send their employees for soft skill trainings.

Today, the travel industry is becoming more and more competitive. The amateur stage of the travel agency business is long over. Over the last two decades, the travel companies have transformed their pattern and structure to meet tough challenges in the international tourism market. So, in this volatile business environment, only that travel agency will succeed that will change to meet the competitive threats and opportunities to match the needs of a new travel market, and will bring flexibility, creativity, innovation, determination and professionalism into its operations. Travel agencies need tourism professionals specializing in different operational and managerial functions. Therefore, a company's recruitment policy may not be only to focus on functional expertise but on attitudes and approaches that fit their corporate goals and culture. In a research conducted in 2003 by Chand and Chauhan it was found out that there was hardly evidence to show that any kind of 'HRD' approach was being followed by the travel agencies, forget about training and development initiatives. Even the travel agency literature is silent in this context according to them. According to Batra and Chawla (1995), 'at present, there are no formal training programmes for the personnel in the field of activities of tourism…' This holds good for all kinds of Indian companies, both private and government agencies.

But an interesting trend that has been witnessed in the travel industry is that the management of these companies is always ready to send their employees for trainings conducted by the airlines, CRS (Computerized Reservation System) companies and other vendors. The reasons for this are very simple - because it is a business requirement and does not entail any costs. These technical, product-related trainings are conducted by the vendors free of cost, are of a flexible duration and kept mostly at the convenience of the agencies. These technical trainings keep the employees updated about the latest fare updations, advanced subject – matter trainings, which would enable them to handle the customers more effectively. With technological changes happening at a very fast pace and the fare rules changing very frequently, the management has to send their employees so as to keep their customers updated with the latest information. In this case, the travel agency management has vested interests and hence they have no issues in sending their employees for product training. Knowing the business nuances and keeping their employees updated on the recent happenings, trends and changes is a business imperative for them. They would be ready to take out time somehow for such employee trainings since it has a direct impact on their business.

What the top management does not realize is that even if the employees may have the knowledge and the information, without soft-skills they would not be able to communicate effectively to their customers. This reminds of what Lee Iacocca (former CEO of Ford, famous for reviving the Chrysler brand) said, 'You can have brilliant ideas, but if you can't get them across, your ideas won't get you anywhere.'

Building a business case for a training organization requires overcoming all these hurdles of management myopia, costs and employee perception. In today's world, where the survival of the fittest is the norm, it has become imperative to sharpen both technical and soft skills. Technical skills can be learnt, applied and measured to an established degree. But the same cannot be said of soft skills. According to a Wall Street Journal survey, 'Interpersonal communication and other so-called soft skills are what corporate recruiters crave most but find most elusive in M.B.A. graduates. The major business schools produce graduates with analytical horsepower and solid command of the basics — finance, marketing and strategy. But soft skills such as communication, leadership and a team mentality sometimes receive cursory treatment.'

This underlies the importance and relevance of soft skills and its applicability across all industries, functions and domains. Studies by Stanford Research Institute and the Carnegie Mellon Foundation among Fortune 500 CEOs found that 75% of long term job success depended on people skills and only 25% on technical skills. This is true at other levels as well. For effective performance in the workplace, companies need their employees to have not only domain knowledge, technical and analytical skills, but also the skills to deal with the external world of clients, customers, vendors, the government and public; and to work in a collaborative manner with their colleagues. Training on softer skills is not only beneficial to employees in improving their performance, but is also an effective tool for employee retention. It needs to be viewed as an investment rather than a cost. In a downturn there is a tendency to compromise on training expenses, but this is an error that often committed in a hurry, is subsequently repented for. Training creates qualification, which in turn inculcates professionalism. Professionalism creates service quality, which leads to client satisfaction and loyalty, which are invaluable assets. Moreover, there is a need for stronger integration between training and career path design. When one creates complementary know-how within employees, one should make sure that it leads to results, either in terms of the next career step or enhanced remuneration. If neither happens, people are bound to leave.

It is often asked how these trainings in soft skills are going to help the companies in the long run? The exponential growth of the tourism sector has in turn created the need for technically sound professionals who have the people management skills to be effective managers. Soft Skills as opposed to hard skills (such as technical skills), greatly impact the personality development of employees. Organizations today recognize that the professional development of their employees play an important part in maintaining relationships with their customers and developing a successful business. Organizations that endeavor to be on the path of continuous learning will often find that upgrading the soft skills of their workforce is a necessary part of business. It not only helps improve service but also shows the interest that an organization has in the professional development of their employees, which in turn leads to higher employee retention. With a high turnover crisis being faced by travel agencies today, training their employees on soft skills would assist in reducing the turnover rate. The trainings would lead to improvement in the employee performance, facilitate change management, raising the standards of the employees and thus assisting in better employee retention. Employees do not like to leave organizations which facilitate their development.

Behavioral or soft skills are thus becoming increasingly important, both to cope with the level of change, and to work with a more participatory management style. The increasing emphasis on customer care has further emphasized this. Further, all employees require the skills to interact in a positive manner to be able to create and maintain a safe and dignified working environment. While the continued emphasis on developing core technical and hard skills is essential for the industry, the need for soft skills is increasing and requires attention now to prevent a critical gap arising in the future. The lack of soft skills will impact on the effectiveness of organizations, and ultimately the economy, over the long term (Batra & Chawla, 1995). It is only a Win-Win situation for companies investing in training – they have an edge in developing an employable workforce, who are upwardly mobile, safer and more productive.

DEVELOPING A TRAINING INVENTORY FOR THE TRAVEL INDUSTRY

There are two broad categories of trainings namely, technical trainings and behavioral trainings that are important for all professionals. Specifically related to the travel and tourism industry, the technical trainings cover the product-related aspects of the job and are related to reservation systems, fares, ticketing, itinerary planning, health and travel insurance, visa, foreign language and foreign exchange procedures etc. Knowledge of these products is essential for improved performance of travel agency employees. Behavioral trainings are related to soft-skills trainings in managing business, managing people, managing customers, managing self and some of these are related to sales negotiation skills, leadership, customer service, problem solving and decision making, team building, presentation skills, business communication, stress management, time management. The authors propose some elementary trainings, including both product and behavioral, for the employees of travel agencies, based on their interactions with the travel agency employers and employees. These are given below in Table1.

Table 1. Classification of Trainings

Behavioral or Soft-Skill Trainings	*Product of Technical Trainings*
Telephone Etiquettes	CRS Training
Consultative Selling Skills	Fares
Negotiation Skills	Ticketing (Domestic)
Customer Service	Ticketing (International)
Time Management	Itinerary Planning
Business Communication	Foreign Language
Team Building	Computer Basics
Key Accounts Management	
Customer Relationship Management	
Presentation Skills	
Leadership Skills	
Decision making & Problem solving Skills	
Interviewing Skills	
Finance for Non-finance personnel	
Train- the – trainer	

As Proposed by the Authors

These encapsulate the various possible trainings that can be conducted for the travel agency employees, working at different levels and in various profiles. To maximize their effectiveness, travel and tourism professionals need both the hard technical skills as well as the soft people skills (Negi, 1998). Customers typically want professionals who are effective at listening to their needs, communicating in their language, managing expectations, building trust and resolving issues. In the travel industry, just as it is important to keep technical skills up to date for employability, similarly, for rising in the ranks, it is important to be able to work well with people and know how to lead a team (Swain, 2006). In many cases, managers may not realize that they themselves have room for improvement. Bad interpersonal skills hamper the ability to climb the corporate ladder.

Validation of the Training Kit for Travel Agencies

In order to validate the above list of trainings, an empirical investigation was carried out among top 50 travel companies across India, selected based on their turnover. 500 travel professionals were rendered a structured questionnaire and on a Likert scale of 5 (Very Important to Unimportant), they were asked to indicate their importance. The sample planning is given below-

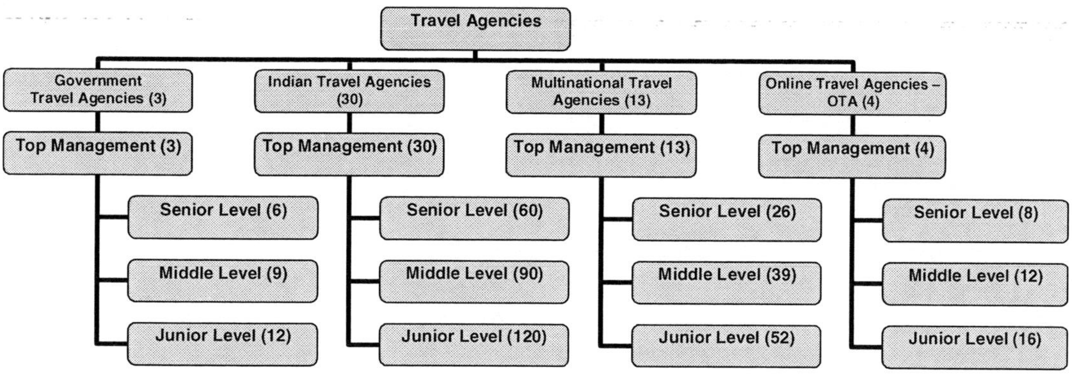

CONCLUSION

The most important element in individuals is their human capital – success does not hinge on scholastic qualifications or technical brilliance alone. The quality of people is of primary importance and a large part of this comes from soft skills. Employers may shortlist candidates based on their technical skills, but they eventually hire them for soft skills (Goel, 2003). Those travel industry professionals who recognize the importance of these soft skills or behavioral skills are miles ahead of their peers.

REFERENCES

[1] Ashraf H. & Mathur, P. (2003) *Human Resource Development in Tourism Industry*, Tourism Industry in India, Excel Books New Delhi

[2] Batra, G. S. & Chawla, A.S.(1995), Tourism Management: A Global Perspective, Deep and Deep Publications India

[3] Baum, T. (1995), Managing Human Resources in the European Tourism and Hospitality Industry ± A Strategic Approach, Chapman & Hall, London.

[4] Baum, T. (2006) 'Reflections on the Nature of Skills in the Experience Economy: Challenging traditional skills models in hospitality', *Journal of Hospitality and Tourism Management*, **13**, 2, 124–135.

[5] Chand M. & V. Chauhan (2003) 'Travel Agency HRD Practices: An Investigation', *Tourism Industry in India*, Excel Books New Delhi

[6] Conlin, M. V., & Baum, T. (2003). *Comprehensive Human Resource Planning: AnEssential Key to Sustainable Tourism in Small Island Settings.* In C. Cooper(Ed.), Classic Reviews in Tourism (pp. 115-29). Clevedon: Channel View.

[7] Foster, D.L. (1994), *An Introduction to Travel and Tourism*, McGraw – Hill Book Co. Singapore

[8] Goel, M.M. (2003) *Essentials for Excellence in Professionals in the Tourism Industry*, Tourism Industry in India, Excel Books New Delhi

[9] Goeldner, C.R. & Ritchie, J.R. Brent (2006). *Tourism: Principles, Practices, Philosophies.* New Jersey: John Wiley & Sons Inc.

[10] Goldsmith, A., Nickson, D., Sloan, D. and Wood, R.C. (1997), *Human Resource Management for Hospitality Services*, International Thomson Business Press, London.

[11] Jameson, S. (1998), "Employment and employee relations", in Thomas, R. (Ed.), *TheManagement of Small Tourism and Hospitality Firms*, Cassell, London, pp. 174-91.

[12] Lucas, R. (1995), *Managing Employee Relations in the Hotel and Catering Industry*, Cassell, London.

[13] Lucas, R. (2004), *Employment Relations in the Hospitality and Tourism Industries*, Routledge Studies in Employment Relations

[14] Negi, J. (1998), *Travel Agency & Tour Operation: Concepts and Principles*, Kanishka Publishers India

[15] Page, S.J, Brunt, P., Busby, G. & Connell, J. (2001), *Tourism: A Modern Synthesis*, Thomson Learning London

[16] Pareek U. (2005) 'Managers as Training Partners', *Indian Journal of Training and Development*, Jul – Sep 05

[17] Price, L. (1994), "Poor personnel practice in the hotel and catering industry: does it matter?", *Human Resource Management Journal*, Vol. 4, No. 4, pp. 44-62.

[18] Sharpley, R. (2002). Tourism: A vehicle for development? In R. Sharpley & D.Telfer (eds), *Tourism and Development – Concepts and Issues.* Clevedon: ChannelView Publications.

[19] Swain S.K. (2006), *Human Resource Development in Tourism: Principles and Practices,* Abhijeet Publications New Delhi

[20] www.timesascent.in

[21] www.unwto.org

[22] www.world-tourism.org

[23] www.wttc.org

A Study of Workplace Attitudes and Behaviours of Generation Y Employees

Puja Khatri and Pragya Gupta

University School of Management Studies, Gru Gobind Singh Indraprastha University, Delhi

ABSTRACT

This paper attempts at studying the characteristic features of the next generation – generation Y workforce and takes a close look at their outlook and behaviours with special focus on their workplace attitudes. The study was conducted in Delhi NCR region where the target population was selected after deciding on a selection of three companies each in the following four industry segments - IT, Finance (Insurance and Banking), Consultancy and Education (N=103). The study specifically targets those employees that have been in the workforce for a few years – employees from lower and middle management level. The data analysis showed varying levels of perceptions related to their technological orientation and the workplace attitudes and employment expectations as well as examines the difference between the perceptions of male and female respondents.

The paper focuses on the challenges and strategies pertaining to managing these employees. The paper also discusses the HR implications of attracting, retaining and motivating the generation Y employees.

Keywords: *Generation Y, Workplace Attitudes, Social Media, Human Resource Challenges*

INTRODUCTION

Globally, the term Generation Y (also called gen next, gen Y, millennials, echo boomers, iGen, etc.) is used to refer to the demographic group of individuals born to the Generation X or 'baby boomers'. So the name is taken after the Generation X that preceded them. Definition of Generation Y as per Oxford Dictionary describes the generation born in the 1980s and early 1990s, comprising primarily the children of the baby boomers and typically perceived as increasingly familiar with digital and electronic technology.

However, assuming that the generations are comparable across geographical and cultural boundaries is absolutely misleading. On one hand, West speaks of generation X and generation Y having more or less standard birthdates for the demographic cohorts ranging between time duration from 1960s to 1990s. Alternatively, in China, Japan and South Korea during the same timespan, there have been respectively 4-6 generational groups which have been defined differently and with different names and birth periods. According to Indian experts, it is difficult to reach consensus on what really comprises of India's Gen X and Y as they are treated as mere euphemisms for the country's youth in general, i.e., they are not separated by decades rather they collapse onto each other. So to assume that gen Y in China or India is equivalent to that of gen Y in the US, Germany or Europe is to oversimplify the matter.

It has been noted that Generation Y makes up 25% of today's workforce, estimated at between 80-90 million in US (as per a study on "Live Births and Birth Rates by Year," www.infoplease.com) and is the most rapidly growing segment of the workforce. So, it is but imperative for the companies to understand the distinctive characteristics of the group and their unique expectations so as to design systems and processes incorporating their needs, desires and attitudes which effectively engages and motivates the employees. Last but not the least, due to the current multigenerational workforce matrix of the organizations it is important to examine the technological knowledge and strengths various generations bring on the table to leverage the same.

LITERATURE REVIEW

There is considerable deliberation regarding the boundaries of Generation Y. Some scholars (CRS, 2008; Erickson, 2008; Hagevik, 1999; Robert Half International, 2008) place the beginning of Generation Y as early as 1977 and as late as 1981 and the cutoff date as early as 1994 and as late as 2002.

Whatever may be the age range but the emergence of Generation Y, people born between mid seventies to end-nineties as a demographic cohort (ref: Wikipedia), is driving dramatic change in practically all fields including education, technology, media and most critically work. It is the first generation to have grown up with undaunted exposure to digital technologies and freely adopted these tools as their primary mechanism for communication, information gathering and sharing. It is also argued to be the most educated generation to date, pursued college and advanced degrees much more than the previous generations (Blain, 2008; Erickson, 2008). The literature review aims at studying the important relevant terminology and understands the background and technological bent of the employees.

Terminology – Generation Y

The term "Generation Y" first came out in the early 1990s. An editorial of a marketing trade magazine, *Advertising Age*, has been attributed with using this term in 1993, as a way to distinguish between the Generation X and Y. Gen Y is also often referred to as "Millennials" and "Echo Boomers."

There is a lot of variations in the definitions of who comprises of Gen Y. Aite Group defines the term as anyone born between 1979 and 1990, or those between ages 21 and 31.

Yet an additional method uses overlapping 20-year periods, such as baby boomers (1945-1965), Gen X (1961-1981) and Gen Y (1979-1999). This definition proposed by Javelin, puts Gen Y consumers between ages 13 and 33 in 2012.

Gen Y's Behaviors and Characteristics

Gen Y is the generation of techno-savvy, digitally inclined twenty to thirty year olds, increasingly dominating the workplace and its workings (Cruz 2007, Trunk 2007, Bassett 2008). They have grown up in a world surrounded by modern gadgets and rapid technological transformation – it took 50 years for radio to reach an audience of 50 million, followed by 13 years for TV and just two years for facebook to reach this milestone. The IT revolution is an integral part of their life and as such the challenges with respect to such a dynamic workforce requires continued efforts by the companies to handle it.

It is important to realise that the Generation Y might bring certain superior skills to the job, especially technology areas but may not necessarily have the wisdom and life experience needed to apply these skills. So, the companies must understand the specific traits of Generation Y which will ensure that their talent is effectively utilized and appreciated and furthermore their skills are spread to older employees.

Tech-savvy: Generation Y is the first generation to be raised amidst technology and have been extensively using various electronic gadgets such as laptops, tablets, cellphones, internet, etc. About 95 percent of them have a facebook profle or other social networking sites like myspace, linkedin, twitter, flickr and so on. They are plugged-in 24 hours a day, 7 days a week. They prefer to communicate through e-mail, text messaging rather than face-to-face contact and prefer webinars and online technology for the professional development as opposed to traditional lecture-based presentations (Javelin, 2009).

Work-life balance: Unlike older generations, the fast-track career does not appeal Generation Y who is willing to swap high pay for lesser number of working hours, flexible schedules and a better work/life balance (Llyod, 2007). They aspire for jobs which provide them flexibility, telecommuting options and the ability to work part time as required. Generation Y professionals have a different visualization of workplace expectations and prioritize family over work; they place high value on self fulfilment.

Financial smartness: Gen Y is attuned to the issues like good healthcare benefits, saving for old-age, and generally being financially secured.

Self-esteem and independence: Gen Yers have a positive, can-do attitude which encourages them to take on responsibility and accomplish anything. They are also comfortable and confident of undertaking independent projects and assuming individual responsibility (BSG Concours, 2007).

Achievement-oriented: Generation Y wants meaningful work and a good professional development curve. They seek out creative challenges and view colleagues as potential resources to gain knowledge. Generation Y is confident, ambitious and goal-oriented and follow speak-your –mind philosophy, i.e. question the authority without any fear (Spiro, 2006).

High expectations of self and of employers: They aim to work sooner and better than their colleagues. Also, they want fair and straight-forward managers who take active interest in their professional development (Nagle, 2009).

Attention-craving: Generation Y craves attention in the forms of feedback, positive reinforcement and guidance. Generation Y seeks to benefit greatly from mentors who can help guide and shape their young careers.

Climate of entrepreneurship, progress and trust: Generation Y wants to operate entrepreneurially within the corporation which must provide them freedom to manage their time, activities and budgets. Gen Y links progress to adapting, creating and experimenting rather than following the tried and tested methods. Many beliefs about progress have roots in Edison's revolutionary notions of innovation, collaboration and competitiveness (Sarah Miller, 2012).

This study of characteristics of Generation Y would remain incomplete without the special mention of the working Gen Y women. As per a study conducted by Accenture (The Path Forward: International Women's Day 2012 Global Research) indicates that more than 69% women researched indicated that flexible work schedule is the primary reason for them to stay with the organization. The Accenture study 2012 also indicated that more men state a lack of opportunity or clear career path while more women cite family responsibilities as barriers to career advancement. Also, more women employees indicated a slowdown of career growth since becoming a parent. Women employees are less likely to speak up for their own careers. As per a survey conducted by the Business and Professional Women's (BPW) Foundation – "*From Gen Y Women to Employers: What They Want and Why it Matters to Business*" (Gen Y Women in the Workplace), there are certain employer characteristics generation Y women seek in a job viz., opportunity for self-manage, emphasis on meeting goals rather than number of hours spent and availability of career advancement opportunities. They evaluate their future with a company based on whether it allows workers to successfully balance family needs and work expectations and how the companies adjust traditional models to meet their expectations. According to Deborah L. Frett, BPW Foundation CEO, "In order for businesses to engage successfully with the workforce of tomorrow, it is imperative that they understand Gen Y women—what challenges them, what inspires them, what motivates them," said.

Social Media Evolution for Generation Y Employees

While the terms Social Networking and Social Media are used interchangeably in the common parlance, there are some fundamental differences between the two. Social media is a way to share information with a broad audience akin to a communication channel like TV, radio, newspaper, etc., whereas social networking essentially is an act of engaging like minded people having common interests through online community building exercise, so it has a two-way communication. Social media can be defined as "a group of Internet-based applications that build on the ideological and technological foundations of Web 2.0, which allows the creation and exchange of user-generated content" (Kaplan & Haenlin, 2010). It is a web-based tool that is optimized solely by the use of its public.

Social media was popularised in 1995, with the onset of Craiglist, an online platform used to promote events and advertisements through online forums and networks (Funk, 2011).This laid the way for a blitz of social media sites which became a rage with the individuals, companies and organizations. Gradually, it became a lifestyle component, so much so that recent studies have shown that the percentage of individuals visiting social media sites is almost equal to those watching TV (Forrester Research, 2010).

Social media is a concept that has colossal impact in the life of a Gen Yer. If we get to relate it to Maslow's Basic Hierarchy of Need, social media may be placed just above the physiological needs (Derek Vicente, 2012). Organizations can no longer ignore the evolution of social media and its internalization in the workplace, especially as it relates to recruiting the younger workforce or Gen Y. The demographic weave of the workforce is undergoing a major shift as baby boomers reach retirement age and more than 80 million millenials are expected to hit the job market around the same time (Sandra Leone, 2012). So, it is imperative for any company to adapt to the new trend and leverage social tools in the workplace to be seen as desirable by the young workforce.

The budding workforce has grown up connecting and collaborating through Social networks like facebook, twitter, linkedin, myspace, youtube, etc. They expect and seek availability of social tools in the workplace. These tools are utilised by the employees to capture knowledge, overcome information gaps, collaborate and communicate with the social communities in real time. Gen Y prefers to collaborate, work in team environment and thereby building strong network relationships with co-workers, departments, throughout company and even globally. Incorporating social media in workplace has enabled an increase in productivity and provides a more efficient workplace. Social business is the way of the future and the younger workforce desires those companies who have adopted enterprise social collaboration tools for daily use.

OBJECTIVE

Objective of this paper is to address the following research questions and critically analyses the popular notions related to generation Y

- To understand the term "Generation Y" employees and their characteristics across different industry segments
- To understand the perception of generation y employees regarding usage and acceptance of role of technology in their lives

- To study the workplace attitudes of generation Y employees and their expectations from the organizations
- Comprehend the role of Social media and its impact on new generation employees
- To analyse the challenges and opportunities faced by the organizations for effective management of generation Y employees

HYPOTHESES

H1: There exists a significant difference between male and female generation Y employees as regards their tech-savviness and use of Social Media

H2: There exists a significant difference between male and female generation Y employees as regards their workplace attitudes and behaviour and employment expectations.

RESEARCH METHODOLOGY

This paper attempts at answering the research questions through Literature review as well as administering survey questionnaire. Based on literature review study, a 75-item questionnaire was developed regarding Generation Y's incline towards tech-savviness, workplace attitudes, job expectations, social media behaviour, etc. as well as demographic information. In short, the questions attempted to test the attitudes, perceptions and characteristics of the individuals; their comfort levels with the technology and also their working life.

The questions were rated on Likert scale of five points ranging from 1 to 5 with 5 being the highest level of response (strongly agree) and 1 being the lowest (strongly disagree). Reliability of the questionnaire was tested to be Cronbach Alpha 0.91.

The target population was a selection of 10 employees in select three companies each across four industry sectors viz., IT, Finance (Insurance and Banking), Consultancy and Education. Researcher contacted HR Managers of all these companies and was handed over the coordinates of 5 employees from Lower management and 5 from middle management level based on convenience sampling and availability. Finally out of 120 solicited participation numbers, 103 complete responses were received and utilised for the analysis, signifying an 85% response rate.

DATA ANALYSIS

The first section of the questionnaire collected the demographic information of the respondents including gender, age, employment history and the industry segment and also their social networking habits.

Demographics

The demographics of the respondents were 68% male and 32% female. The age of the participants indicated that 39.8% were between the ages 25 to 30 years and 36.9% were between 30 to 35 years. The rest of 11.7% population each were less than 25 years and more than 35 years respectively. This essentially captures almost 77% of Generation Y that has been in the workforce longest and must have been able to respond based on their experiences. With respect to employment history, approx. 49.5% are on their first job only, whereas 24.3% are on their second job and 26.2% have already switched multiple jobs. The percentage of respondents from IT, Finance (Insurance and Banking), Education and Consultancy were 39.8%, 28.2%, 18.4% and 13.6% respectively.

General Social Media Usage

The responses showed that 45.6% of respondents used Social Media for personal use only and a meagre 8.7% use it only for business purposes. On the other hand, a substantial 43.7% of participants confirmed the use of social media for both personal and business reasons. About 38.8% respondents reported spending between 30 minutes- 1 hour daily on accessing social media and another 31.1% reported spending between 1-2 hours daily. 15.5% confirmed spending 2-3 hours daily, whereas 6.8% reported remaining online round the clock. As per data, 30.1% confirmed their affiliation with at least one Social networking site, 29.1% were associated with two sites and 27.2% confirmed their active memberships with at least three social media sites. Of all the respondents, almost 99.8% established their presence on the extremely popular facebook and 59.2% admitted to their existence on the business social networking site – LinkedIn. The other popular affiliations were YouTube, Picasa, Google+, etc.

DISCUSSION

The analysis of data indicates that a majority of respondents have their presence on at least one and even more forms of Social media for communication and collaboration (m= 4.02, s.d. = 1.15). On the question of accessing the web for daily utility requirements such as payment of bills, online banking, vacation planning, etc.; a large chunk of respondents admitted to its free and easy usage (m= 3.97, s.d. = 1.17). This ascertains what the findings of Literature review has been suggesting that Generation Y is hooked on to Social Media and extensively uses it for its daily interactions and communication with the outer world. It was found that most of the respondents take keen interest on the information posted by others (m= 3.86, s.d. = 0.94) and feel that they are abreast with the ground rules of the social media used by them (m = 3.81, s.d. = 0.77) as well as the risks associated with its usage (m = 3.78, s.d. = 0.93). This data throws light on the tech-smartness of generation Y who are not only active on Social media but fully prepared for its nitty gritty and the associated threats.

Table 1. Technology Orientation of the Respondents and Social Media Behaviour

	N	*Min*	*Max*	*Mean*	*Std. Dev.*
Multiple social media membership	103	1	5	4.02	1.15
Presence on more than one social media site	103	1	5	3.68	1.11
Freely share and access content on social media	103	1	5	3.44	1.15
Adept to basic fundamentals of usage of social media	103	1	5	3.81	0.77
Keen interest on the information posted by others	103	1	5	3.86	0.94
Risk awareness pertaining to social media	103	1	5	3.78	0.93
Use of social media for 25% of time daily	103	1	5	2.41	1.12
Measurement of popularity in virtual friend circle	103	1	5	2.87	1.27
Stress when unable to access Social Media	103	1	5	2.58	1.19
Use of online access to attend to daily utility requirements	103	1	5	3.97	1.17
Company should allow employees to use Social Media at work	103	1	5	3.40	1.35
Current and potential employers looking at your online activity	103	1	5	3.19	1.26
Seek a job through the social media	103	1	5	3.47	1.36
Prefer use of webinar and online methods for training	103	1	5	3.49	1.12
Loss of productivity due to over- indulgence in Social Media	103	1	5	3.12	1.32
Preference of latest laptops and gadgets to work better and faster	103	1	5	4.15	1.08

The participants disagreed when they were asked whether they felt the need to use social media regularly everyday and feel stressed out or disconnected if they were unable to do so (m= 2.41, s.d. = 1.12). This means that while on one hand generation Yers use the social media frequently, they are aware of the possibility of its addiction (it taking priority over other activities) and also the fact that it could be detrimental on their productivity. A large number of respondents preferred use of latest laptops and gadgets to work faster and better (m = 4.15, s.d. = 1.08) which exhibits clearly that generation Y is hooked on to technology and latest gizmos (Table 1).

For the purpose of testing hypothesis H1 that there exists a significant difference between male and female generation Y employees as regards their tech-savviness and usage of Social media, Levene's t-test for equality of variances has been applied (Table 2).

Table 2. Difference in the Technological Orientation of Male and Female Respondents

		Levene's Test for Equality of Variances		*t-test for Equality of Means*				
		F	*Sig.*	*t*	*df*	*Sig. (2-tailed)*	*Mean Diff.*	*Std. Error Diff.*
Multiple social media membership	Equal variances assumed	0.307	0.582	-0.327	51	0.745	-0.112	0.342
	Equal variances not assumed			-0.318	17.255	0.754	-0.112	0.352
Freely share and access content on social media	Equal variances assumed	3.469	0.068	0.541	51	0.591	0.207	0.383
	Equal variances not assumed			0.64	24.174	0.528	0.207	0.324
Adept to basic fundamentals of usage of social media	Equal variances assumed	3.789	0.057	1.168	51	0.248	0.317	0.271
	Equal variances not assumed			1.43	26.141	0.164	0.317	0.222
Keen interest on the information posted by others	Equal variances assumed	2.543	0.117	-1.269	51	0.21	-0.333	0.263
	Equal variances not assumed			-1.086	14.843	0.295	-0.333	0.307
Risk awareness pertaining to social media	Equal variances assumed	0.37	0.546	-2.379	51	0.021	-0.736	0.309
	Equal variances not assumed			-2.388	18.054	0.028	-0.736	0.308
Use of social media for 25% of time daily	Equal variances assumed	0.063	0.804	1.111	51	0.272	0.415	0.373
	Equal variances not assumed			1.019	16.02	0.323	0.415	0.407
Measurement of popularity in virtual friend circle	Equal variances assumed	0.027	0.869	-0.972	51	0.335	-0.417	0.428
	Equal variances not assumed			-0.935	16.995	0.363	-0.417	0.446
Use of online access to attend to daily utility requirements	Equal variances assumed	5.461	0.023	-1.606	51	0.078	-0.701	0.39
	Equal variances not assumed			-1.472	14.237	0.163	-0.701	0.476
Company should allow employees to use Social Media at work	Equal variances assumed	0.012	0.912	-0.305	51	0.762	-0.14	0.46
	Equal variances not assumed			-0.312	18.566	0.759	-0.14	0.449
Seek a job through the social media	Equal variances assumed	0.263	0.61	-0.541	51	0.591	-0.252	0.466
	Equal variances not assumed			-0.521	17.005	0.609	-0.252	0.484
Use of webinar and online methods for training	Equal variances assumed	1.294	0.261	0.234	51	0.816	0.085	0.365
	Equal variances not assumed			0.269	22.721	0.791	0.085	0.318
Loss of productivity due to over- indulgence in Social Media	Equal variances assumed	3.174	0.081	-2.056	51	0.045	-0.89	0.433
	Equal variances not assumed			-1.809	15.281	0.09	-0.89	0.492
Preference of latest laptops and gadgets to work better and faster	Equal variances assumed	0.027	0.87	-0.155	51	0.877	-0.053	0.34
	Equal variances not assumed			-0.14	15.68	0.89	-0.053	0.377

No difference between male and female respondents was found with respect to presence on multiple social media sites ($t = -0.327$, $p < 0.05$), inclination to freely share/ access content on social media ($t = 0.541$, $p < 0.05$), interest in postings made by others ($t = 1.269$, $p< 0.05$), adept at basics of social media usage ($t =1.16$, $p< 0.05$), seek a job through social media ($t= -0.541$, $p< 0.05$), preference of online methods of training ($t = 0.234$, $p< 0.05$), online utlity services ($t = 1.606$, $p < 0.05$) and preference for latest gadgets ($t= -0.155$, $p< 0.05$). However, it was found that there exists a difference of level of risk awareness pertaining to Social Media in males and females ($t = -2.379$, $p < 0.05$). The reason could be that by nature females are less oriented to risks and therefore presence of the difference. Also, there was a variation in the perception of male and females about the loss of productivity due to over-usage of social media. These differences are present because females are perceived to have lesser opportunity so more sincerity towards their work and have fear of failures therefore aversion to any distracting activities that could be detrimental. Hence, hypothesis 1 is partially accepted and partially rejected as there exists a difference in the perception of technological orientation of male and female respondents as is shown by the variables viz., risk awareness pertaining to social media and loss of productivity due to indulgence in social media.

Further data analysis reveal that a considerable number of respondents prefer their jobs to be interesting and challenging (m = 4.09, s.d. = 1.09) and they prefer informal relationships with their peers (m = 3.92, s.d. = 0.85). This confirms the scholar's views that generation Y wants meaningful work and seeks out creative challenge; they associate less with their employing organization and more with the type of work as is confirmed by the data that they prefer staying with a job as a matter of necessity as much as desire (m = 3.59, s.d. = 0.93). This has forced many companies to realize that good working environments is just what generation Y is looking for which would keep them fresh and motivated (Table 3).

Another factor of great consequence to Generation Y is the feeling that they are making a positive contribution to the environment and society at large. The data shows that a considerable lot of respondents wish their organization to be socially committed (m = 4.16, s.d. = 0.96) and they wish to contribute to society through the organization (m = 4.0, s.d. = 0.96). A major chunk of respondents also prefer to make a contribution towards sustainability and green movement (m = 4.38, s.d. = 0.63). It means that Generation Y get attracted to employers who are not merely socially conscious, but also socially responsible, i.e., such organisations who respect the environment, care about their employees, create meaningful products or services, and give back to the society in their own way (Martin & Tulgan, 2006). Further data analysis also revealed the fact that the respondents are ready to change their jobs if things do not work out for them (m = 4.20, s.d. = 0.72). Gen Y employees are motivated when given the freedom to work as they please and look out for change when they are not satisfied with their job (Table 2).

Table 3. Work-related Attitudes and Employment Expectations of the Respondents

	N	*Min*	*Max*	*Mean*	*Std. Dev.*
Interesting and challenging job profile	103	1	5	4.09	1.09
Informal working relationships	103	1	5	3.92	0.85
Structured and deadline-oriented work environment	103	1	5	3.51	1.28
Formal work environment vs fun at work	103	1	5	2.56	1.27
Prospect of spending career in one organization	103	1	5	3.01	1.39
Comfortable discussing your organization with people outside it	103	1	5	3.53	1.18
Relate to the organization's problems as your own	103	1	5	3.54	1.04
Easy attachment to another organization as you are to this one	103	1	5	3.65	1.13
Feel emotionally attached to your organization	103	1	5	3.38	1.15
Organization has a great deal of personal meaning for me	103	1	5	3.32	1.08
You feel like "member of the family" at this organization	103	1	5	3.34	1.17
Strong sense of belongingness to this organization	103	1	5	3.35	1.16
Staying with your job is a matter of necessity as much as desire	103	1	5	3.59	0.93
Consequences of leaving your job would be the scarcity of available alternatives	103	1	5	2.80	1.17
Organization to be committed to social issues	103	1	5	4.16	0.96
Contribution to social causes through your employer	103	1	5	4.00	0.96
Preference to have green workspace to contribute towards environment	103	1	5	4.38	0.63
Preference to stay with a company for your lifetime	103	1	5	3.01	1.27
Switch job if things do not work out in an organization	103	1	5	4.20	0.72

Data analysis shows that there exists a difference in the perception of male and female respondents towards relating to the organizations' problems ($t = -2.165$, $p < 0.05$) where female score higher than male respondents. This is evident from the fact that the female employees are more emotionally attached than their male peers to the organization they work with and as such they show more association with the problems faced by the organizations. This is also depicted in their loyalty towards the organization as they do not indulge in job-hopping as frequently as the male counterparts. Furthermore, female respondents again show significant difference vis-a-vis the male respondents ($t = -2.239$, $p< 0.05$) as regards to the variable of sense of belongingness to the organization again due to the same reasons as mentioned above. Additionally, on the basis of data analysis, it is clear that there is no difference in the perception of male and female employees towards interesting and challenging job profile

Table 4. Difference in Work-related Attitudes and Employment Expectations of Male and Female Respondents

		Levene's Test for Equality of Variances		*t-test for Equality of Means*				
		F	*Sig.*	*t*	*df*	*Sig. (2-tailed)*	*Mean Diff*	*Std. Error Diff*
Interesting and challenging job profile	Equal variances assumed	2.915	0.094	1.76	51	0.084	0.591	0.336
	Equal variances not assumed			2.143	25.82	0.042	0.591	0.276
Informal working relationships	Equal variances assumed	0.044	0.834	-0.59	51	0.558	-0.226	0.382
	Equal variances not assumed			-0.527	15.538	0.606	-0.226	0.428
Structured and deadline-oriented work environment	Equal variances assumed	0.296	0.589	-0.273	51	0.786	-0.079	0.291
	Equal variances not assumed			-0.256	16.503	0.801	-0.079	0.31
Formal work environment vs. fun at work	Equal variances assumed	0.825	0.368	-1.184	51	0.242	-0.478	0.403
	Equal variances not assumed			-1.362	22.842	0.187	-0.478	0.351
Prospect of spending career in one organization	Equal variances assumed	0.502	0.482	0.31	51	0.758	0.126	0.406
	Equal variances not assumed			0.283	15.908	0.781	0.126	0.446
Comfortable discussing your organization with people outside it	Equal variances assumed	2.673	0.108	-0.308	51	0.759	-0.138	0.448
	Equal variances not assumed			-0.361	23.751	0.721	-0.138	0.382
Relate to the organization's problems as your own	Equal variances assumed	5.567	0.022	-2.165	50	0.035	-0.858	0.396
	Equal variances not assumed			-1.791	12.91	0.097	-0.858	0.479
Easy attachment to another organization as you are to this one	Equal variances assumed	0.379	0.541	-1.714	51	0.093	-0.596	0.347
	Equal variances not assumed			-1.524	15.46	0.148	-0.596	0.391
Organization has a great deal of personal meaning for me	Equal variances assumed	2.397	0.128	-1.591	51	0.118	-0.591	0.372
	Equal variances not assumed			-1.34	14.61	0.201	-0.591	0.441
You feel like "member of the family" at this organization	Equal variances assumed	1.265	0.266	-0.604	50	0.548	-0.217	0.358
	Equal variances not assumed			-0.527	15.195	0.606	-0.217	0.411
Strong sense of belongingness to this organization	Equal variances assumed	0.009	0.926	-2.239	50	0.03	-0.9	0.402
	Equal variances not assumed			-2.31	19.033	0.032	-0.9	0.39
Staying with your job is a matter of necessity as much as desire	Equal variances assumed	0.79	0.378	-0.469	51	0.641	-0.179	0.382
	Equal variances not assumed			-0.415	15.373	0.684	-0.179	0.431
Consequences of leaving your job would be the scarcity of available alternatives	Equal variances assumed	1.067	0.306	-1.253	51	0.216	-0.396	0.316
	Equal variances not assumed			-1.473	23.893	0.154	-0.396	0.269
Benefits at other organization may not match the current one	Equal variances assumed	0.327	0.57	-0.691	51	0.493	-0.264	0.383
	Equal variances not assumed			-0.65	16.53	0.525	-0.264	0.407

($t = 1.76$, $p < 0.05$), informal working relationships ($t = -0.59$, $p < 0.05$), structured and deadline-oriented work environment ($t= -0.273$, $p < 0.05$), prospect of spending career in one organization ($t = 0.31$, $p < 0.05$), comfort in discussing your organization with others ($t = -0.038$, $p < 0.05$) and consideration for overall benefits provided by current organization ($t = -0.691$, $p < 0.05$). Hence, hypothesis 2 gets partially accepted and partially rejected since there is evidence of a difference between male and female employees as regards to their perception towards organisation, i.e., their workplace attitudes manifested through their sense of belongingness to the organization and feeling of being associated with the organizations' problems.

CONCLUSIONS AND IMPLICATIONS

The analysis presented in this paper clearly indicated that Generation Y poses several human resources management challenges for the organizations. Owing to significant differences in the characteristic behaviours and workplace attitudes and their specific needs and aspirations, organizations will have to design unique and innovative strategies to meet these challenges.

Keeping in view the stiff global competition, attraction and retention of capable employees can give a significant competitive edge to the organizations. For developing effective HR strategies, the characteristics of Generation Y needs to studied carefully so as to offer them jobs that are interesting and also offer a good work-life balance.

First of all, adoption of means of recruitment through social media becomes critically important for the companies to successfully recruit promising Gen Y talent. It would be imperative for the organizations to be aware of the fact that Generation Y seeks roles that are ambitious, adequately challenging and complex. They also seek good quality of workplace environment as a highly motivating factor to be more productive at work and also proven by data analysis as shown in Table 3 and Table 4.

Gen Y employees' favours working in real-time, adopting new technology trends and working with social tools in the workplace. The need to offer well-defined career paths, with clear timeframes for progression is the foremost requirement. Also, developing team-work skills and provide mentorship plays a vital role in the retention as it enables them to make positive contribution in the long run. Another motivating factor for Generation Y is feeling that they are making positive contribution towards the environment and the society at large. They get attracted to the organizations that create meaningful products or services, care for the environment and also provide some fodder for their social conscience

The essence is that those Organisations that provide interesting work, greater flexibility, a pleasant work environment, and participative leadership are likely to successfully attract and retain Generation Y employees.

LIMITATIONS

As it remains, survey reports are subject to specific limitations seeing that it is always a fine balance between time investment and thoroughness of research. Although effort was undertaken to minimize the issues by using an exhaustive list of questions incorporating a varied mix of characteristic features, still it has scope for future researchers.

The sample size of 100 is considerably small considering the fact that we are attempting to learn some valuable insights on one whole generation. Also, majority of respondents for this paper belonged to northern part of India, the perceptions, views, behaviours and attitudes of generation Yers in South, West and East India was not captured,. So, future research could be carried out taking into account the geographical diversity to make the research more comprehensive and may even show more authenticated results.

There are still many questions unanswered about Generation Y employees, they are still quite young and comparatively very new to the workforce. We hope that the information and findings presented in the paper serve as stones for foundation for future research work. More studies needs to be directed this way because it is absolutely certain that in the years to come generation Y will bring about big changes in the working world.

REFERENCES

[1] Accenture.com. (2012). *The Next Generation of the Working Woman - 2012 Women's Research—The Path Forward.* Retrieved on 22nd Nov 2012 from http://www.accenture.com/us-en/company/people/women/Pages/insight-womens-research-2012-path-forward.aspx

[2] Barford, I.N. & Hester, P.T.(2011). *Analysis of Generation Y workforce motivation using multiattribute Utility Theory*. Retrieved on 8th Nov 2012 from http://www.dau.mil/pubscats/ARJ_Library/ARJ57/Barford_ARJ57.pdf

[3] Broughton, A., Higgins,T. , Hicks, B. & Cox, A. (2010). *Workplaces and Social Networking: The Implications for Employment Relations*. Acas Research Publications.

[4] Brown, S.; Carter, B.; Collins, M.; Gallerson, C.; Giffin, G.; Greer, J.; Griffith, R.; Johnson, E.; Richardson, K. (n.d.). Generation Y in the Workplace. Retrieved on 20th Nov 2012 from http://www.nslw.org/generation_y.pdf

[5] BusinessDictionary.com (n.d.). *Generation Y: Definition*. Retrieved on 5th Nov 2012 from http://www.businessdictionary.com/definition/Generation-Y.html#ixzz2BJSS6SYY

[6] Cabral, J. (2011). *Is Generation Y Addicted to Social Media?*. The Elon Journal of Undergraduate Research in Communications • Vol. 2, No. 1 . (5 - 14)

[7] D'Netto, B. (20). *Generation Y – Human Resource Management Implications*. Retrieved on 10th Nov 2012 from http://www.wbiconpro.com/452-Brian.pdf

[8] Financial Time Lexicon. (n.d.). *generation Y*. Retrieved on 5th Nov 2012 from http://lexicon.ft.com/Term?term=generation-Y

[9] Funk, T. (2011). *Social media playbook for business: Reaching your online community with Twitter, Facebook, Linkedin, and more*. Retrieved on 16th Nov 2012 from http://www.scribd.com/doc/91012792/Social-Media-Playbook-Reaching-Your-Online-Community

[10] Generation Y (n.d.). Wikipedia, the free encyclopedia. Retrieved on 5th Nov 2012 from http://en.wikipedia.org/wiki/Generation_Y

[11] Hobart, John W. Buddy. & Princeton One (n.d.). *Understanding Generation Y*. Retrieved on 19th Nov 2012 from http://www.princetonone.com/news/PrincetonOne%20 White%20Paper2.pdf

[12] Mann, J.(2006). *Generations in the workplace*. The Bulletin Vol. 74, Issue 1. Retrieved on 10th Nov 2012 from http://www.acui.org/publications/bulletin/article.aspx?issue= 398&id=888

[13] Meier, J. , Austin, Stephen F. , Crocker, M. (2010). *Generation Y in the Workforce: Managerial Challenges*. The Journal of Human Resource and Adult Learning Vol. 6, Num. 1. Retrieved on 20th Nov 2012 from http://www.hraljournal.com/Page/8%20Justin%20Meier.pdf

[14] Ready, Willing & Able (2008). *Gen Y Impact on Strategy*. Retrieved on 6th Nov 2012 from http://www.hrfocus.com.au/HR_Coach_Gen_Y_Impact_on_Strategy.pdf

[15] Robert Half International (n.d.). *Survey Generation Y : A new generation in the workforce*. Retrieved on 6th Nov 2012 from http://www.roberthalf.nl/EMEA/Netherlands/Rich%20Content/Publication%20Library/documents/GeneratieY.pdf

[16] Trunk, P. (2007). *What Gen Y really wants*. Retrieved on 7th Nov 2012 from http://www.time.com/time/magazine/article/0,9171,1640395,00.html

[17] Vicente, Derek (2012). *Why Is Social Media Important To Gen Y Employees?*. Retrieved on 7th Nov 2012 from http://www.onqmarketing.com.au/why-social-media-important-gen-y-employees/

Psychology of Y-Generation

Anju Panwar

MVN Education Society, Palwal

ABSTRACT

This paper is based on the psychology of Y-Generation. Psychology is the science of behavior. Behaviour is an important aspect of the organization which persist employee again & again in their working condition.Next 20 years will be based on this generation so if we study their behavior than we can change our working style of organization.Born between 1977-1998 are generation –Y. Gen Y persons are known as extremely sophisticated, technology wise, immune to most traditional marketing and sales pitches as they not only grew up with it all, they'have seen it all and been exposed to it all since early childhood. Gen Y members are much more racially and ethnically diverse and they are much more segmented as an audience aided by the rapid expansion in TV channels, satellite radio, the Internet, etc. Gen Y are less brand loyal and the speed of the Internet has led the followers to be similarly flexible and changing in its fashion, style consciousness and where and how it is communicated with.The,Gen Y are self-confident and optimistic, independent and goal oriented.They are blunt, confident & contradictory. They are demanding and high-maintenance. Gen Y are loyal,committed employees only so long as their organisations provide them with variety and opportunity. They are entrepreneurial, out-of-the-box thinkers who relish responsibility, demand immediate feedback, and expect a sense of accomplishment hourly. . As we know that psychology is a vast area so I have taken three aspects-Personality,Motivation & Values.

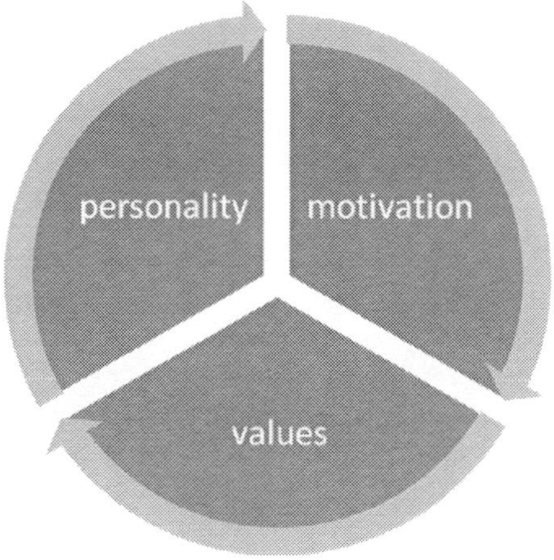

Personality of Y-Generation

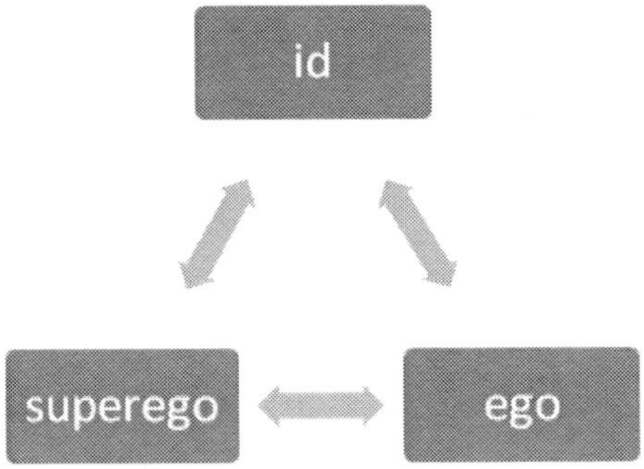

Id in Y-Generation

- According to Freud, we are born with our **Id**
- The id doesn't care about reality;
- based on our pleasure principle;
- the id speaks up until his or her needs are met;
- Id is high in Y-generation.

Ego in Y-Generation

- The ego is based on the reality principle;
- Ego controls higher mental processes such as reasoning and problem-solving;
- Recognizes what is real and understands that behaviors have consequences;
- "I think I am a special person" and "I like to be the center of attention."

Superego in Y-Generation

- The Superego is the moral part;
- Develops due to the moral and ethical restraints placed on us by our caregivers;
- Current **Generation** are much more interested in financial success and less in "a meaningful philosophy of life" than persons were in the 1970s.

AFFECTS OF PERSONALITY TRAITS

Enjoy Life

Generation Y sees work as a means to enjoy life — and life comes first. They have a strong work ethic. Generation Y wants work to be fun and flexible because the line between work and life is faultless. Generation Y also follows a mantra of working smarter, not harder. The key for employers is offering flexible work schedules, adjusting the belief that workers need to "put in the hours at the desk" to be effective, and developing a work culture that is pleasant and positive.

Independence

This generation is very independent and not afraid to challenge. Many in Generation Y want a relationship with their boss like the ones they have with their parents..

Communication

The key for employers is to realize and accept that people communicate differently and to embrace the new techniques while also teaching the Gen Y workers that business sometimes still needs to use traditional methods of communication.Generation Y workers need to use those excellent communications and diversity skills to learn to socialize and communicate with people of all ages and backgrounds.

Want Appreciation

The key for employers is to realize that this generation — at least when they are new to the workforce — need a bit of special care and handling. There's no way they can go months without a review; they need constant (and not too critical) feedback. Generation Y workers need to realize that the reality of the workplace is that it's not like home or college — and that they are expected to do an excellent job without always wanting praise and being told that how good their work is. Finally, Generation Y workers need to tell mom or dad that it's time to stay home so they can learn to fight their own battles.

Job Mobility

Because of more work experiences and greater education, Gen Y workers are simply more mobile, making it easier to move from one employer to another if they are unhappy with the work. They were also raised during a period of great downsizing and rightsizing, and many witnessed the grief and frustration their parents felt when being laid off — and they do not want to experience that emotion. These are also some of the reasons why many Gen Y workers are diligently planning to start their own businesses.

Creative and Fast

While this generation may be more anxious than others to rise quickly to the top, it's less about unrealistic expectations than it is about being better prepared for work than previous generations — with perhaps a touch of the need for instant gratification thrown in. This generation also has no interest whatsoever in working in a cubicle — not because it is beneath them, but because they feel advances in technology should let them be able to choose to work from home, Starbucks, or anywhere there is a Wi-Fi connection. The key for employers is to redesign and rebuild some of the old career ladders that were destroyed with the flattening of organizations and greatly expand telecommuting and remote working arrangements. Gen Y workers need to see a progressive promotion path or they will move on to the next employer.

Technological

Technology has allowed this generation to multitask and find shortcuts in achieving tasks. Texting, instant messaging, social networking, and Web surfing have all made Generation Y workers more competent, efficient, and productive (if not sometimes overwhelmed). The key for employers is to accept that there may be multiple ways for workers to accomplish their tasks. Generation Y workers may need to demonstrate that they are working just as hard as everyone else, but perhaps simply performing the job more efficiently.

Family-Centric

The fast-track has lost much of its appeal for Generation Y who is willing to trade high pay for fewer billable hours, flexible schedules and a better work/life balance. While older generations may view this attitude as narcissistic or lacking commitment, discipline and drive, Generation Y legal professionals have a different vision of workplace expectations and prioritize family over work.

Achievement-Oriented

Nurtured and pampered by parents who did not want to make the mistakes of the previous generation, Generation Y is confident, ambitious and achievement-oriented. They have high expectations of their employers, seek out new challenges and are not afraid to question authority. Generation Y wants meaningful work and a solid learning curve.

Team-Oriented

As children, Generation Y participated in team sports, play groups and other group activities. They value teamwork and seek the input and affirmation of others. Part of a no-person-left-behind generation, Generation Y is loyal, committed and wants to be included and involved.

Motivation of Y-Generation

Technology Advancement

Generation Y grew up with computers and this techno upbringing shapes their work expectations. You can successfully motivate Yers by structuring their work so that it is congruent with their technical competence. For example, allow them to communicate with customers via instant messaging, provide training on-demand in multi-media formats, and give them Internet access for research and resources. Despite what the media says, they are sense only about certain kinds of technology. They can type ten-page memos on the go with their way and will happily program your cell phone for you and seem to spend half their days on social sites, but many of them have only the most primitive experience using corporate software The good news is that they're quick on the uptake and absolutely fearless about learning new technology. The bad news is that they are overconfident and won't ever confess ignorance about how to use a piece of software — not because they're proud, but because it doesn't occur to them that they haven't already mastered it just by clicking a few buttons. Their overconfidence can sometimes cause real confusion so make sure to teach them the basics of productivity software .

Want Immediate Rewards

Y are skeptical of long-term commitments from employers. Many younger workers have seen their parents lose jobs to downsizing and outsourcing and this has led to doubts about their own futures.

Give them Frequent Feedback

In the workplace Generation Y expects supervisors and managers to provide immediate clear feed back just like a ATM. This generation is obsessed with feedback. Half the time, they're not even hungry for new feedback; they just want to hear, over and over again, that the memo they wrote was well done, or that the presentation they gave was effective. What you think of as needy, they think of as a totally natural. And if they're not doing well on the job, they're handing you the perfect opportunity to tell them so, because they do respond well to constructive feedback and mentoring. That hunger for feedback should make your life as a manager easier, even if you find the neediness a bit much in the short run. The challenge for you will be learning how to give feedback to a generation that is used to nothing but gratuitous praise. Give them plenty of clearly defined benchmarks and metrics and milestones so that underperformance is not a surprise to them in their first performance review.

Provide Flexibility in their Work

Yers grew up in flexible times and as adolescents they had a lot of say over their world. They want say in everything from benefits to scheduling to the option of telecommuting. Generation Y expects work to accommodate their personal and family life.

Want Teams

TEAM –Togther empowvering to achieve more . They can't work *without* teams. And if you don't let them work in teams, they'll find a way to build them anyway, without any input from you. They hate making decisions by themselves, and they don't like to do things without getting six or eight or twenty different opinions first. If you don't give them a group to run things by, they'll seek opinions from their workspace mate, their girlfriend, and their dentist. That approach can lead to crummy results, stunt their leadership growth, and paralyze them when they discover that seeking eight different opinions results in eight conflicting suggestions. However, those are all management issues that can be handled if you're aware of them, and the upside is that you can use that preference for teamwork to pair up more senior employees with more junior ones — pairings that everyone says they want, but that many employers don't make a priority.

Be Prepared to Negotiate

Since these young adults could talk, they have been negotiating with a generation of parents who've had a real distaste for imposing rules and who have been loathe to serve as authority figures They've spent their entire college careers negotiating grades and deadlines and feeling entitled to accommodations for anything under the sun... or having their parents do that for them. They do not respond to top-down orders because they haven't encountered them before. You may be the first real authority figure they encounter, and real authority will come as a shock to them. This generation will question anything you ask them to do and expect to be persuaded why they should do what you — their boss — is asking of them. And be prepared for mom and dad to jump in and try to negotiate on your employee's behalf.

Give them Lots of Small Deadlines

They can't get anything done without them, and then they'll wait until the last second to start. They treat their work assignments as if they were college term papers to be written the night before the due date, for professors who often no longer enforce deadlines in the first place. This generation has trouble with longer deadlines and project management, not least because they are used to their parents managing their lives for them. It now falls to you, corporate America, to teach them basic time and project management techniques.

Compliment Desired

They think very highly of themselves. To older generations they seem arrogant and overconfident, and it's true that they have little respect for acquired wisdom, age, or a higher spot on the org chart. They will show up on their first day of work and think they can do your job better than you can. They will also expect management responsibility on their first jobs out of college. However, they are also enormously creative and love to identify and solve problems. If you can see past your initial irritation, you might find them dropping some great ideas in your lap from day one. If you can harness that creativity and penchant for problem-solving, your business will benefit.

Give them flexibility

They are willing to work hard and think nothing of being "findable" at all hours — they are permanently online anyway. In exchange, they don't want bosses to abuse that findability, and they expect the flexibility to mold their work lives around their personal lives. Don't haul them in over the weekend or make them eat their twentieth conference-room dinner in a row unless there's good reason. They will expect to be able to leave in the middle of the day for yoga class and will wonder why there are no vegan offerings in the company cafeteria. Universities have been accommodating their preferences for years, and it will come as a shock to them if your workplace doesn't. That doesn't mean you have to create a meditation room, but understand that they have been spoiled by their schools in that regard, and normal work environments will come as a shock to them.

Teach them How to Work Face-to-face

More experienced workers know that sometimes you need to sit in the same room to get something accomplished, but twenty-somethings would rather just send you a text message. You'll have to insist on a live meeting to get one. They also need to be taught how to interact professionally when meeting with clients and senior colleagues.

Teach them How to Write

Their writing - especially professional writing - is terrible. They are willing to learn if you are willing to teach them. College does not teach them how to write, and it's now your job to do so.

Tell them What You'll do for them

That attitude may drive you crazy, but they think of a "dream job" as their birthright, even in times of high unemployment. If they are employed, they think of whatever current job they have as a temporary stop until they move onto something better. If they're unemployed, they'll hold out for the "perfect job" with their parents' blessing and financing. Many of them will move back home, unemployed, rather than "sell their souls." If you aren't offering their dream job, you may have to pitch them hard, even when they're not currently employed. Believe it or not, many parents are telling them to hold out.

Facilitate their Lives Outside of work

Once they're out in the working world, they are hungry for the intellectual growth and extracurricular opportunities they took for granted in school. Facilitating their continuing education and hobbies goes a long way toward keeping them happy... and on the job.

Values of Y-Generation

1. They value **family, personal connection**, and **loyalty.**
2. They seek out the **genuine** and are repulsed by **phony**.
3. They are famously **optimistic** and believe in the possibility of **change.**

4. They advocate for the **environment** and **social justice**.
5. They treasure **tolerance** and **diversity**, **teamwork** and **balance**.
6. They seek **spirituality** and are open to the possibility of the divine.

CONCLUSION

With the help from Psychology we understand nature of the employee.Technology is the leading way to evolve everyday ways. Technology changes in the blink of an eye from new to enhanced. With technology changing this fast, the Generation Y may forget sometimes where the original ideas came from and its form of recognition. The Generation X has done a great deal of work to form the work industry in every aspect and department possible to exist today. Even though the future lies in the hands of the Millenials who strive to be more and more technologically aware, there is some coaching needed in proper work etiquette to be instilled to completely finish the puzzle. That etiquette can Generation Y is used to refer to people born in the 80s and 90s. Their archetype is the superman generation, Compared to Xers they practically led a charmed life; their parents had ready access to birth control, so they were generally wanted, nurtured children. They were more sheltered by society then their predecessors and their family units were more stable. Gen Y is sometimes known as the Doremon Generation because childhood was so good to them and use gazets that they have a tendency to generates new ideas.Psychological aspects are very important at the time of selection.So we must use psychometric tests based on organizational behavior for future generation.

REFERENCES

[1] Alsop, R. (2008). *The Trophy Kids Grow Up: How the Millennial Generation is Shaking Up the Workplace.* San Francisco, CA: Jossey-Bass.

[2] Armour, S. (2005, November 8). Generation Y: they've arrived at work with new attitude. *USA Today* .

[3] Barrick, M. R., Mount, M. K., & Judge, T. A. (2001). Personality and performance at the beginning of the new millennium: What do we know and where do we go next? *Personality and Performance* , *9* (1-2).

[4] Bimber, B. (1990). Karl Marx and the Three Faces of Technological Determinism. *Social Studies of Science* , *20* (2), 333-351.

[5] Borg, I. (1990). Multiple facetisations of work values. *Applied Psychology: An International Review* , *39* (4), 401-412.

[6] Bottorff, L. M. (2011). *Work Attribute Importance and Loyalty Intention: Millennial Generation Psychological Contract.* CMC Senior Theses.

[7] Cairncross, F. (2001). *The death of distance : how the communications revolution is changing our lives.* Boston: Harvard Business School Press.

[8] Castells, M. (2000). *The Information Age: Economy, Society, and Culture. The Raise of the Network Society.* Wiley-blackwell.

[9] Castells, M., & Cardoso, G. (2006). *The Network Society: From Knowledge to Policy.* Center for Transatlantic Relations, Jhu-Sais.

[10] Cennamo, L., & Gardner, D. (2008). Generational differences in work values, outcom

[11] Chen, P.-J., & Choi, Y. (2008). Generational differences in work values: a study of hospitality management. *International Journal of Contemporary Hospitality Management , 20* (6), 595-615.

[12] Corporate Leadership Coucil. (2004). *Generation X and Y employees.* Washington, DC: Corporate Executive Board.

[13] Cowell, E. L., & Kupritz, V. W. (2007). Human Resources and the future of communication in the workplace: a cross-generational perspective. *College of Commuinication and Information* 29th Annual Research Symposium.

[14] Coyle-Shapiro, J.-M. (2002). A psychological contract perspective on organizational citizenship behavior. *Journal of Organizational Behavior , 23*, 927-946.

[15] Cross, J. (2006). *Informal Learning: Rediscovering the Natural Pathways That Inspire Innovation and Performance.* Pfeiffer.

[16] Dash, M. K., & Panda, B. K. (2010). Comparative Empirical Analysis Of Occupational and Motivational Differences Of Different Generations In Indian Workforce. *International Journal of Business Research , 10* (6).

[17] Day, G. (2006). Community and everyday life. *Psychology Press.*

[18] Deal, J. J. (2007). *Retiring the generation gap: how employees young and old can find common ground.* San Francisco, CA: Jossey-Bass.

[19] Dose, J. J. (1997). Work values and integrative framework and illustrative application to organizational socialization. *Journal of Occupational and Organizational Psychology , 70*, 219-241.

[20] Dries, N., Pepermans, R., & De Kerpel, E. (2008). Exploring four generations' beliefs about career. Is satisfied the new successful? *Journal of Managerial Psychology, , 23* (8), 907-928.

[21] Elizur, D. (1984). Facets of work values: a structural analysis of work outcomes. *Journal of Applied Psychology , 69* (3), 379-389.

[22] Erikson, E. H. (1963). *Childhood and Society.* New York, NY: Norton.

[23] Evans, K. (2004). *Maintaining community in the information age: the importance of trust, place and situated knowledge.* Palgrave Macmillan.

[24] Finegold, D., Mohrman, S., & Spreitzer, G. M. (2002). Age effects on the predictors of technical workers' commitment and willingness to

[25] Florida, R. (2002). *The Rise Of The Creative Class: And How It's Transforming Work, Leisure, Community And Everyday Life.* Cambridge, MA: Basic Books.

[26] Frieze, I. H., Olson, J. E., & Murrell, A. J. (2006). Work values and their effect on work behavior and work outcomes in female and male managers. *Sex Roles , 54*, 83-93.

[27] Govindarajan, V., & McCreary, L. (2010, 11 16). *How U.S. Businesses Can Really Win in India*. Retrieved 11 29, 2011, from Bloomberg Businessweek:

http://www.businessweek.com/managing/content/nov2010/ca20101115_713170.htm

[28] Gursoya, D., Maierb, T. A., & Chi, C. G. (2008). Generational differences: An examination of work values and generational gaps in the hospitality workforce. *International Journal of Hospitality Management , 27.*

[29] Guzzo, R. A., Noonan, K. A., & and Elron, E. (1994). Expatriate managers and the psychological contract. *Journal of Applied Psychology , 79*, 617-626.

[30] Hauw, S. D., & Vos, A. D. (2010). Millennials' Career Perspective and Psychological Contract Expectations: Does the Recession Lead to Lowered Expectations? *Journal of Business Psychology , 25*, 293-302.

[31] Hess, N., & Jepsen, D. M. (2009). Career stage and generational differences in psychological contracts. *Career Development International , 14* (3).

[32] Hofstede, G. (1984). *Cultures Consequences : International Differences in Work-Related Values(Cross Cultural Research and Methodology).* Newbury Park, CA: SAGE.

[33] Hogan, R., Hogan, J., & Roberts, B. W. (1996). Personality Measurement and Employment Decisions. *American Psychologist , 51* (5), 469-477.

[34] Hung, K. H., & Li, S. Y. (2007). A Netnography of Martin, C. (2005). What managers need to know about Generation Y. *Industrial & Commercial Training , 37* (1), pp. 39-44.

[35] Martin, D., & Woodside, A. (2007). Dochakuka: Melding Global Inside Local: Foreign-Domestic Advertising Assimilation in Japan. *JOURNAL OF GLOBAL MARKETING , 21* (1), 19-32.

[36] Maslow, A. H. (1943). A theory of human motivation. *Psychological Review , 50*, 370-396.

[37] May, C. (2002). *The information society : a sceptical view.* Malden, MA: Polity Press.

[38] Meglino, B. M., & Ravlin, E. C. (1998). Individual values in organizations: Concepts, controversies, and research. *Journal of Management , 24*, 351-389.

[39] Moore, R. L. (2005). Generation Ku: Individualism and China's Millennial Youth. *Ethnology , 44* (4), 357-376.

[40] Murphie, A., & Potts, J. (2003). *Culture and technology.* Palgrave Macmillan. Ng, E. S., Schweitzer, L., & Lyon, S. T. (2010). New Generation, Great Expectations: A Field Study of the Millennial Generation. *Journal of Business Psychology , 25*, 281-292.

[41] Pinder, C.C. (1997). *Work motivation in organizational behavior.* Upper Saddle River, NJ: Prentice Hall.

[42] PLearn.net. (2010, 1 19). *How Social Media Changes Authority*. Retrieved 11 29, 2011, from Participatory Learning: http://www.plearn.net/2010/01/19/how-social-media-changes-authority

[43] Putnam, R. D. (2000). *Bowling alone : the collapse and revival of American community.* New York: Simon & Schuster.

[44] Ravlin, E. C., & Meglino, B. M. (1987). Effect of values on perception and decision making: A study of alternative work values measures. *Journal of Applied Psychology , 72*, 666-673.

[45] Rawlins, C., Indvik, J., & Johnson, P. R. (2008). Understanding the New Generation: What the Millennial Cohort Absolutely, Positively Must Have at Work. *Journal of Organizational Culture, Communications and Conflict, 12* (2).

[46] Real, K., Mitnick , A. D., & Mal, W. F. (2010). More Similar than Different: Millennials in the U. S.

[47] Building Trades. *Journal of Business Psychology, 25*, 303-313.

[48] Rhodes, S. (1983). Age-related differences in work attitudes and behavior: a review and conceptual analysis. *Psychological Bulletin, 93.*

[49] Robinson, S. L. (1996). Trust and breach of the psychological contract. *Administrative Science Quarterly , 41*, 574-599.

[50] Robinson, S. L., Kraatz, M. S., & Rousseau, Rokeach, M. (2000). *Understanding Human Values: Individual and Societal.* New York: Free Press.

[51] Ros, M., Schwartz, S., & Surkiss, S. (1999). Basic individual values, work values, and the meaning of work. *Applied Psychology: An International Review , 48* (1), 49-71.

[52] Roudometof, V. (2005). Translationalism, Cosmopolitanism, and Glocalization. *Current Sociology , 53* (1), 113-135.

[53] Rousseau, D. M. (1990). New hire perceptions of their own and their employer's obligations: A study of psychological contracts. *Journal of Organizational Behavior , 11*, 389-400.

[54] Savickas, M. (2002). Career construction: a developmental theory of vocational behavior. In D. (. Brown, *Career Choice and Development* (4th ed. ed., pp. 149-205). San Francisco, CA: Jossey Bass.

[55] Schaeffer, J. (2000). *Kemper Reports (Winter–Spring).* Chicago, IL: Kemper Distributors, Inc.

[56] Schuman, H., & Scott, J. (1989). Generations and collective memories. *American Sociological Review , 54*, 359-381.

[57] Singer, H. A., & Abramson, P. R. (1973). Values of business administrators: a longitudinal study. *Psychological Reports, 33.*

[58] Smith, M. P., & Guarnizo, L. (1998). *Transnationalism from below.* New Brunswick, NJ: Transaction Publishers.

[59] Smola, K. W., & Sutton, C. D. (2002). Generational differences: revisiting generational work Tomlinson, M. (2007). Graduate employability and student attitudes and orientations to the labour market. *Journal of Education and Work, 20* (4).

[60] Trzesniewski, K. H., Donnellan, B., & Robins, R. W. (2008). Do Today's Young People Really Think They Are So Extraordinary? *Psychological Science, 19.*

[61] Trzesniewski, K. H., Donnellan, B., & Robins, R. W. (2008). Is "Generation Me" Really More Narcissistic Than Previous Generations? *Journal of Personality, 76* (4).

[62] Twenge, J. M. (2010). A Review of the Empirical Evidence on Generational Differences in Work Attitudes. *Journal of Business Psychology, 25*, 201-210.

[64] Twenge, J. M., & Campbell, K. (2001). Age and Birth Cohort Differences in Self-Esteem: A Cross-Temporal Meta-Analysis. *Personality and Social Psychology Review, 5* (4), 321-344.

[65] Twenge, J. M., & Campbell, S. M. (2008). Generational differences in psychological traits and their impact on the workplace. *Journal of Managerial Psychology, 23* (8).

[66] Twenge, J. M., Campbell, S. M., Hoffman, B. J., & Lance, C. E. (2010). Generational Differences in Work Values: Leisure and Extrinsic Values Increasing, Social and Intrinsic Values Decreasing. *Journal of Management, 36* (5).

Behavioral Finance in Dividend Decision

Miklesh Prasad Yadav

Chandra Prabhu Jain College of Higher Studies, Delhi

ABSTRACT

Behavioral finance is concerned with psychology of investor. It is crystal clear that evaluation of risk and return are not enough, investor's dreams and fears have also great impact. Investors have certain cognitive and emotional weakness which comes in the way of their investment decision. Psychological obstacles such as this may prevent from putting rational decisions into practice. It combines the individual behaviors and market concepts by using the knowledge of psychology and finance. This approach enables the researchers to concentrate on a new evaluation of differences in risk behavior, framework of information and decision and cognitive errors.

Keywords: *Investor Psychology, Prospect Theory, Mental Accounting, Cognitive Dissonance*

INTRODUCTION

This world is advancing rapidly. In this advancement, decision is backbone of any performance. This needs better insight, and understanding of human nature in the existing global perspective, plus development of fine skills and ability to get best out of investments. In addition, investors' have to develop positive vision, foresight, perseverance and drive. Every investor differ from others in all aspects due to various factors like demographic factors which includes socio-economic background, educational attainment level, age, race and sex. The most crucial challenge faced by the investors is in the area of investment decisions. An optimum investment decision plays an active role and is a significant consideration. In designing the investment portfolio, the investors should consider their financial goals, risk tolerance level, and other constraints. In addition to that, they have to predict the output mean- variance optimization. This process is better suited for institutional investors; it often fails for individuals, who are susceptible to behavioral biases. Understanding the behavioral finance will help the investors to select a better investment instrument and they can avoid repeating the expensive errors in future.

The pertinent issues of this analytical study are how to minimize or eliminate the psychological biases in investment decision process.

The principal objective of an investment is to make money. In the early years, investment was based on performance, forecasting, market timing and so on. This produced very ordinary results, which meant that investors were showered with very ordinary futures, and little peace of mind. There was also a huge gap between available returns and actually received returns which forced them to search for the reasons. In the examining process, they identified that it is caused by fundamental mistakes in the decision-making process. In other words, they make irrational investment decisions. In recognizing these mistakes and means to avoid them, to transform the quality of investment decisions and results, they realized the impact of psychology in investment decisions. Several years ago, the researchers began to study the field of Behavioral Finance to understand the psychological processes driving these mistakes. Thus, Behavioral finance is not a new subject in the field of finance and is very popular instock markets across the world for investment decisions.

BACKGROUND AND EVOLUTION

The Modern Portfolio Theory (MPT), Capital Asset Pricing Model (CAPM) and Arbitrage Pricing Theory (APT) are the quantitative models that underpin the rational expectations based theories. Unfortunately, there is a large amount of research, which could not confirm this theory in the available investment data. For example, Fama and French, (1993, 1996) and others have shown that the basic facts about the aggregate stock market, the cross-section average returns and individual trading behaviour are not easily understood in this framework. The behavioral finance paradigm has emerged in the response to the difficulties faced by the traditional paradigm. In essence, it argues that investment choices are not always made on the basis of full rationality, and it attempts to understand the investment market phenomena by relaxing the two doctrines of the traditional paradigm, that is, (i) agents fail to update their beliefs correctly and (ii) there is a systematic deviation from the normative process in making investment choices.

Schindler (2007) lists three main cornerstones for research in Behavioral finance. (i) Limits to arbitrage- which argues that *"it can be difficult for rational traders to undo the dislocations caused by less rational traders"* (Barberis and Thaler, 2003). So arbitrage opportunities exist which allows investor irrationality to be substantial and have long-lived impact on prices.

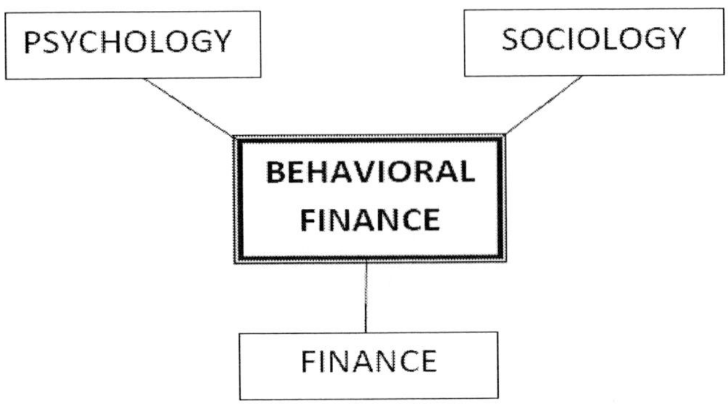

To explain investor irrationality and their decision-making process, behavioral finance draws on the experimental evidence of the cognitive psychology and the biases that arise when people form beliefs, preferences and the way in which they make decisions, given their beliefs and preferences (Barberis and Thaler, 2003) thus bringing us to the second cornerstone (ii) Psychology –research in this area has shown that individuals exhibit certain biases systematically while formulating their beliefs and preferences thus affecting their decisions. (iii) Sociology – which emphasizes the fact that a considerably huge number of financial decisions are a result of social interaction rather than being made in isolation. This contradicts the implicit assumption that individuals reach decisions without external influence

Behavioural Finance Principles and Its Implication

Under the traditional financial theory, the decisions makers are rational. In contrast, modern theory suggests that Investors financial decision-making are not driven by due considerations. The decisions are taken by them are also often inconsistent. Put in another way, human decisions are subject to several cognitive illusions. These are grouped into two and have been depicted in figure 1.

Heuristic Decision Process

The decision process by which the investors find things out for themselves, usually by trial and error, lead to the development of rules of thumb. In other words, it refers to rules of thumb which humans use to made decisions in complex, uncertain environments7. The reality, the investors decision making process are not strictly rational one. Thought the investors have collected the relevant information and objectively evaluated, in which the mental and emotional factors are involved. It is very difficult to separate. Sometimes it may be good, but many times it may result in poorer decision outcomes. It includes:

1. ***Representativeness:*** The investors' recent success; tend to continue into the future also. The tendency of decisions of the investors to make based on past experiences is known as stereotype. Debont (1998)8 concluded that analyses are biased in the direction of recent success or failure in their earnings forecasts, the characteristic of stereotype decisions.
2. ***Overconfidence:*** There are several dimensions to confidence. It can give more courage, and is often viewed as a key to success. Although confidence is often encouraged and celebrated, it is not the only factor to success. The investors who are cautious and analytical can achieve success and others have to withdraw. Yet, confidence, especially self-confidence, is often viewed as a positive trait. Sometimes, the investors overestimate their predictive skills or assuming more knowledge then they have. Many times it leads excessive trading.

3. ***Anchoring:*** It describes the common human tendency to rely too heavily, or 'anchor' on one trait or piece of information when making decisions. When presented with new information, the investors tend to be slow to change or the value scale is fixed or anchored by recent observations. They are expecting the trend of earning is to remain with historical trend, which may lead to possible under reactions to trend changes.
4. ***Gamblers Fallacy:*** It arises when the investors inappropriately predict that tend will reverse. It may result in anticipation of good or poor end.
5. ***Availability Bias:*** The investors place undue weight for making decisions on the most available information. This happens quite commonly. It leads less return and sometimes poor results also.

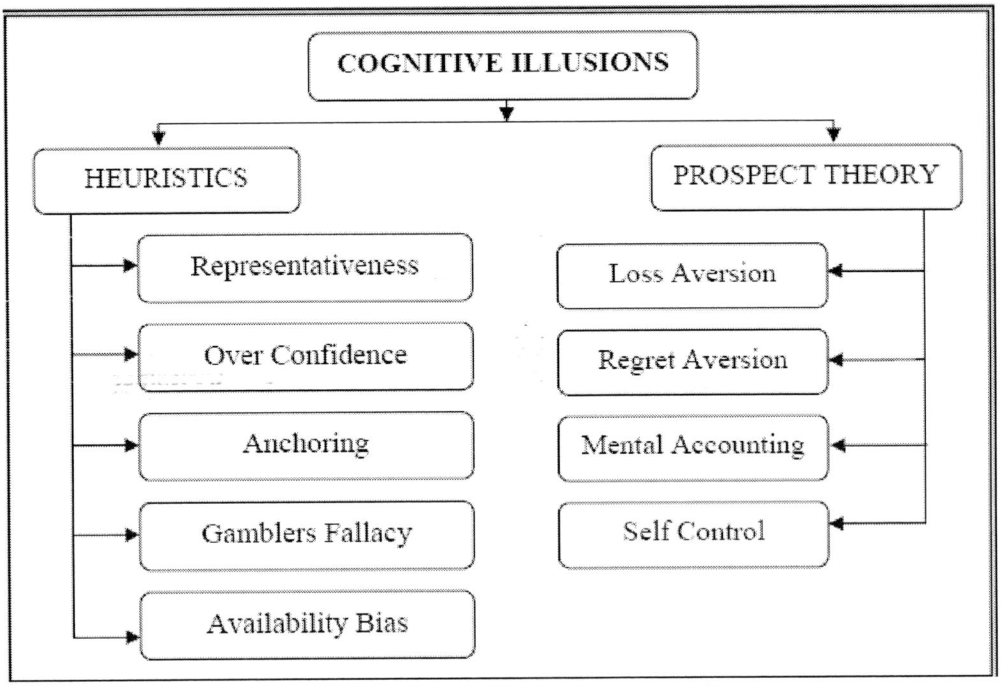

Fig. 1. Classification of Cognitive Illusion

Prospect theory

This theory is developed by Kahneman and Tversky9. The second groups of illusions which may impact the decision process are grouped in prospect theory. He discussed several states of mind which may influence an investors decision making process. The key concepts which he discussed are as follows:

1. ***Loss Aversion***: Loss aversion is an important psychological concept which receives increasing attention in economic analysis. The investor is a risk-seeker when faced with the prospect of losses, but is risk-averse when faced with the prospects of enjoying gains. This phenomenon is called loss aversion10. Ulrich Schmidta, and Horst Zankb11 discussed the loss aversion theory with risk aversion and he aceepted the Kahneman and Tversky views.
2. ***Regret Aversion***: It arises from the investors' desire to avoid pain of regret arising from a poor investment decision. This aversion encourages investors to hold poorly performing shares as avoiding their sale also avoids the recognition of the associated loss and bad investment decision.

   The most central element of the prospect theory is the S-shaped value function depicted in figure below:

   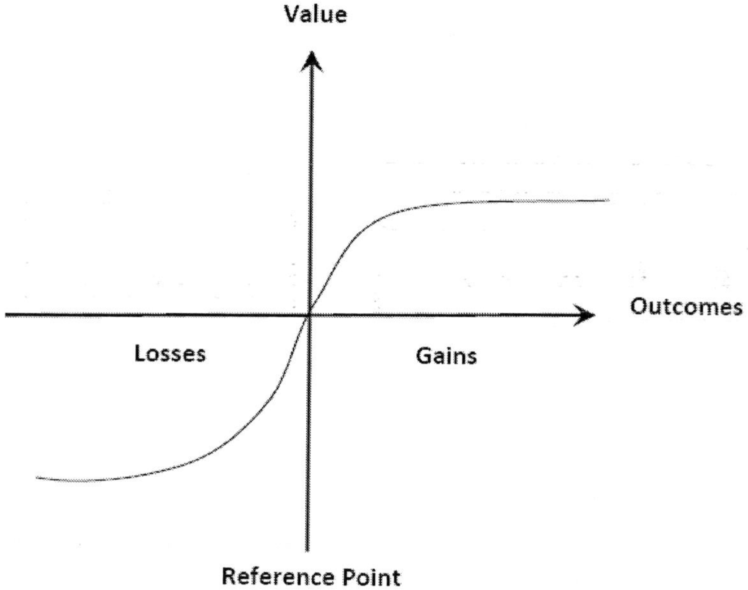

   Regret aversion creates a tax inefficient investment strategy because investors can reduce their taxable income by realizing capital losses.
3. ***Mental Accounting***: Mental accounting is the set of cognitive operations used by the investors to organize, evaluate and keep track of investment activities. Three components of mental accounting receive the most attention. This first captures how outcomes are perceived and experienced, and how decisions are made and subsequently evaluated. A second component of mental accounting involves the assignment of activities to specific accounts. Both the sources and uses of funds are labeled in real as well as in mental accounting systems. The third component of mental accounting concerns the frequency with which accounts are evaluated and 'choice bracketing'. Accounts can be balanced

daily, weekly, yearly, and so on, and can be defined narrowly or broadly. Each of the components of mental accounting violates the economic principle of fungibility. As a result, mental accounting influences choice, that is, it matters.

4. ***Self Control***: It requires for all the investors to avoid the losses and protect the investments. As noted by Thaler and shefrin13 investors are subject to temptation and they look for tools to improve self control. By mentally separating their financial resources into capital and 'available for expenditure' pools, investors can control their urge to over consume.

Role of Behavioral Factor: Analysis

There are numerous identified psychological biases in Behavioral finance literature. Each has implications on financial decision-making and behavior. Table 3.01 shows the nine biases analyzed in this study, their key effects on investors and its consequences.

NAME OF BIAS	KEY EFFECTS ON INVESTOR	CONSEQUENCE
Overconfidence	Too many trades, too much risk, failure to diversify	Pay too much brokerage and taxes, chance of high losses
Representativeness	Tendency to associate new event to a known event and make investments based on it	Purchasing overpriced stocks
Herding	Lack of individuality in decision making	Bubbles, and bubble bursts
Anchoring	Tendency to consider logically irrelevant price level as important in the process of decision making	Missed investment opportunities, or bad entry timing into the market
Cognitive Dissonance	Ignore new information that contradicts known beliefs and decisions	Reduced ability to make rational and fair investment decisions
Regret Aversion	Selling winners too soon, holding losers too long	Reduced returns
Gamblers' Fallacy	Taking too much risk after a lucky win	Chance of high losses
Mental Accounting	Low or no diversification	Irrational and negative effects on returns
Hindsight	The tendency to feel that a past event was obvious when it really was not, at onset	Incorrect oversimplification of decision making

How Biases Affect Investing Behavior

Psychological research has documented a range of biases that can affect decision making. Many of these also affect decisions about money and investing. These biases sit deep within our psyche and as fundamental parts of human nature; they affect all types of investors, both professional and private. Understanding them can help you and your adviser work together to learn to work around them.

Some of the key biases that affect financial decisions include:

- Investing with overconfidence, which can lead to inappropriate or risky investments?
- Investing to avoid loss or regret, at all costs, which can mean we don't invest in way that will truly help us reach our investment objectives.
- Avoiding investing decisions altogether, which can mean we either don't save for the future, or we stick with an inappropriate strategy.
- Avoiding trying to understand complex topics, which can lead us to make uninformed decisions. This can mean we have less chance of meeting investment objectives.

Behavioral Finance and Organizational Behavior

Behavioral finance deals with the overconfidence and optimism tendencies of the decision makers and disadvantages caused by it. Because it will create a great impact on financial decision. This approach provides a very important benchmark for organizational behavior. Organizational behavior field has a tendency for supporting optimistic and confident style and even though there are few exceptions majority of business trends are in favor of optimistic and confident decision maker. Optimism and self confidence brings effectiveness in organizational actions. It provides an opportunity of removing social desirability pressure.

Facing the challenge of interdisciplinary understanding of behavioral finance will not only benefit the field of organizational behavior. Even though field of behavioral finance provides a fresh insight to the workings of the organizations, it lacks the understanding of the management as deep as the field of organizational behavior. Because of their functional importance, corporate leaders affect financial markets by affecting many external groups such as security analysts. Interaction between managers and companies is not limited to the individual level. It is also accelerated by the herding effect. Individually rational behaviors produce group behavior that is irrational. In many of the financial crisis this pattern of behavior was observed. Even at the beginning of the modern economy such behavior was observed. Organizations have a tendency for herding. In the classical finance, it was assumed that all the irrational activities such as herding would be corrected by the efficiency of markets, but in many financial crisis correction was not possible. Inside the organization pressures caused by group think is also another effect that compromises the rationality. It acts as an herding effect inside the organization. Organizational behavior field can offer in-depth studies of groupthink inside the organization but needs the macro level understanding of the behavioral finance to gain a deeper understanding of the herding behavior that occurs between the organizations.

CONCLUSION

One word, which has dominated the world of financial stock markets since 2008, has been 'Volatility'. Extreme movements in global indices and stock prices because of fear and anticipation has, as it is supposed to, made life tough for a rational investor. Market sentiments have been observed to sway wildly from positive to negative and back, in the shortest timeframes like weeks, days and hours. In this context, understanding irrational investor behavior deserves more importance that it has ever had. Behavioral finance - a relatively new field that came into relevance in the 1980s – studies the effect of psychology on financial decision-making. It studies how investors interpret new information and act on it to make decisions under uncertainty. The science does not try to label traditional financial theories as obsolete, but seeks to supplement the theories by relaxing on its assumptions on rationality and taking into consideration the premise that human behavior can be understood better if the effects of cognitive and psychological biases could be studied in context where decisions are made.

The increasing analysis of the human element in the stock market, a market which is much more rational, has quality available data and is more efficient. The study found out that, with the exception of Cognitive Dissonance Bias, investors suffered from all biases in a significant manner. Weighted Scoring Analysis revealed that Regret Aversion, Gamblers' Fallacy and Hindsight bias were seen to be affecting the younger investors only. Anchoring, Gamblers' Fallacy and Hindsight were the three biases, which were seen to affect the younger investor lot in the most significant manner, compared to experienced investors, as suggested by results from Chi-squared tests. Tests had shown that all the investors were affected by the various biases while making investment decisions but it could not be established that one investor group had suffered more losses under the influence of these biases. Results from discriminant analysis suggested that, even though investors were equally prone to committing erroneous decisions owing to being biased, the degree to which each of the biases were affecting them were different in a significant manner to an extent that younger and experienced investors could be separated as two different groups of human beings exhibiting a different behavioral pattern. When asked to reveal financial losses

BIBLIOGRAPHY

[1] Chandra, Abhijeet.2011. *Decision Making in the Stock Market: Incorporating Psychology with Finance*. New Delhi.

[2] Kishore, Rohit. 2004. *Theory of Behavioral Finance and its Application to Property Market*: A Change in Paradigm. Australian Property Journal 38(2): 105-110

[3] Banerjee, Arindam. 2011. *Application of Behavioral Finance in Investment Decisions: An Overview*. The Management Accountant 46 (10) : 869 – 872.

[4] Kristensen, Henrik. and Gärling, Tommy.1997. *Anchor points, reference points, and counteroffers in negotiations*. Göteborg Psychological Reports 27(7).

[5] Monti, Marco and Legrenzi, Paolo.2009. *Investment Decision-Making and Hindsight Bias.* Annual Meeting of the Cognitive Science Society. Amsterdam.

[6] Campbell, J. (2000). Asset Pricing at the Millenium, *Journal of Finance*, 55, 1515-1567.

[7] Daniel, K., Hirshleife r, D., & Subrahmanyam, A. (1998). Investor psychology and security market under- and overreactions. *Journal of Finance*, 53, 1839-1886.

[8] Fama, E. and French, K. (1993). Common Risk Factors in the Returns on Stocks and Bonds. *Journal of Financial Economics,* 33, 3-56.

[9] www.google.com

Globalisation and Gen Y: Transformation in NCR Experience

Naresh K. Vats

University School of Humanities and Social Sciences, Guru Gobind Singh Indraprastha University, New Delhi

ABSTRACT

Things are experiencing a change owing to intensive shift in global scene. The local has been overexposed to the global. This 'glocalization' has affected a major shift in attitude towards the conventional values in educated youth. No doubt, it has also left numerous locals confused about how to respond. Modern economy has left a sizable population in the northern India 'rich and confused'. One and a half century ago, Marx said that capitalism not only produces the object for the subject but it also produces subjects for the object. In today's world of advertisement this is what is actually being done. You are creating human beings who are capable of consuming certain products. The emphasis is no longer on creating the products that are required by the human beings rather creating human beings that are required for the products. This is the new culture. People are being altered to fit the image of the products. This new trend of culture is creating its own atmosphere which, in turn, is affecting every aspect of our life and society. But when we talk of culture, we risk entering a difficult zone. Culture is a social force which is evident where it is significant. Cultures can flow, change, intermingle, cut across and through one another, regardless of national frontiers, and have blurred boundaries. Let us consider the scene in outer Delhi and NCR, the area surrounding Delhi. Blinding development of housing estates with world class luxury, commercial plazas with teeming bars have utterly confused the once poor, hardworking and simple hearted village folk. This heavily reworked local youth feels liberated, inferior and hostile all at the same time.

Keywords: *Glocalization, Culture, Modernity, Consumerism*

INTRODUCTION

One and a half century ago, Marx said that capitalism not only produces the object for the subject but it also produces subjects for the object. In today's world of advertisement this is what is actually being done. You are creating human beings who are capable of consuming certain products. The emphasis is no longer on creating the products that are required by the human beings rather creating human beings that are required for the products. This is the new culture. People are being altered to fit the image of the products. This new trend of culture is creating its own atmosphere which, in turn, is affecting every aspect of our life and society. This also refers to the global interconnectedness, which is termed as globalization. Anthony Giddens defines globalization as 'the intensification of worldwide social relations which link distant localities in such a way that local happenings are shaped by events occurring many miles away and vice versa.' David Held defines it as 'the widening, deepening and speeding up of worldwide interconnectedness in all aspects of contemporary social life, from the cultural to the Criminal, the financial to the spiritual.' This interconnection is multi-aspect and can be viewed from many angles – economic, social, cultural, armament, political, environmental etc.

The most powerful and influential mode of international connectivity is economic. The more powerful a country's economic base, the more influential is its culture. Cultural globalization is not a new phenomenon. It has happened in all the ages with ever increasing passion and intensity. Of late, the intensity of this cultural interconnectedness has risen enormously owing to the growth of mass media and technology. Today's world is the result of crosscutting of interdisciplinary relationships across the globe. The global connectivity opens up new avenues of understanding between cultures. But when we talk of culture, we risk entering a difficult zone. Culture is a social force which is evident where it is significant. Society is complex, with characteristics which are difficult to pin down. Cultures can flow, change, intermingle, cut across and through one another, regardless of national frontiers, and have blurred boundaries.

Sociocultural aspect of globalization is generally viewed as one way flow of patterns (ideological, behavioural and cultural) from west to East – precisely, it is seen as 'flowing down' from the USA to Eastern countries. This representation of the identity of the USA is also termed as Americanization, Westernization, Modernization, McDonaldlization etc. "McDonaldization is the process of global homogenization of culture through five basic principles: efficiency, calculability, control, the substitution of nonhuman for human technology, and the irrationality of rationality." (Samir Dasgupta and Ray Kiely: 2008) Supporters of this view of globalization explain this phenomenon as exposing of the local cultures to the new alternatives of living – to the new ideas about personal space, self, individuality, identity, governance, economics, health, beauty and what not! Life is understood in terms of plans, packages and bits – life insurance, health insurance, retirement plans, tour packages, compensation packages, tariff plans and many more. All these plans have provisions for customization or modification to the individual's needs and interests. When such ideological addressers hail us from all the sides, they have a definite influence on our cognitive world – the result is that even people tend to understand the institution of marriage too in terms of a package which can be customized to the needs of individual likes and dislikes. Today, the idea of marriage and the nature of marital relationship seem to be suspending between cultural conventions and individual conveniences. With times the social dynamics are changing – mainly because of changing equation in family economy. The last three decades have witnessed the economic aspects of power struggle in Indian society.

Globalisation is a socioeconomic concept, which considers economic system based on private property and competition is the most efficient, and the democracy is the best political model in the world. The term 'Globalization' has two parts – 'Global' and 'ization'. The first part implies a single system of connection, and the second part means 'to be' or 'make' or 'make alike' – by implication, it is the phenomenon that operates at and connects all the places at a given time. It produces both cultural fragmentation and homogenization in a connected system. Hegemony is the form of ideology in which the values and interests of the hegemonic group are experienced by the other group as already their own.

Increasing cases of divorce in India and rising popularity of '*Yoga*' and '*Ayurved*' in US best exemplifies Giddens' idea of Globalization – distant localities reshaping/affecting each other. An Indian columnist and novelist Shobha Dé's views about marital relationship pose a clear threat to the hegemonic group of 'male-order'. It is not just divorce; it is the attitude of the individuals towards divorce that matters. This new attitude provides them a considerable degree of 'agency' which is supposed to enable them to fashion their individualities with the freedom as never before– though the nature of the 'freedom', 'agency' and 'individuality' is quite a matter of debate in the society like ours. Shobha Dé talks about the emergent thoughts, values and social structures, and the resultant individual identities that are based on the consumption of the items picked from the global cultural supermarket. We read into and weave stories around these global (American) items (and these stories are not simply unrealistic). The notions of individual identity, space and freedom are now an essential part of our educated upper class psyche. And, not quite surprisingly, the 'alarm reaction' of our society to these new attitudes is getting milder everyday as the meanings of objects and practices are created and recreated continuously. Even a cursory look at the life in metros will testify it. The picking up of these new attitudes from the cultural supermarket may be seen as cultural capital, which raises one's social credit on the rating scale of our 'modern' society. In *Shooting from the Hip* (1994: 172) Shobha De, an Indian writer asserts – "with some amount of economic freedom, women have changed the basic rules somewhat. If a self-sufficient woman with a roof over her chooses to marry, it is because she wants to share her life with someone in the fullest sense, not because she is looking for a lifelong meal ticket. Divorce, too, has got to be viewed in this light. A woman of independent means is not compelled to perpetuate a bad marriage because she has nowhere else to go".

Things are experiencing a change owing to intensive shift in global scene. The local has been overexposed to the global – thanks to cable T.V., Cell-phone, Internet and affordable technology of D.V.D., and, of course, piracy which makes the information available at cheaper cost. This 'glocalization' – the interpenetration of the global and the local – has affected a major shift in attitude towards the conventional values in educated youth. There are some curious news items doing rounds globally – "Actress Sofia Vergara(40), mother of a son(Monalo,

19), wants to freeze her eggs so that she can have children with boyfriend Nick Loeb at some point in the future."(Delhi Times, Mar 16, 2012) "Megan Fox comments tongue-in-cheek about living in a world where losing your phone is more dramatic than losing your virginity. Our phones are storehouses of our dirty laundry – web browsing history, photos, SMSs and, what not? A survey by Confident Technologies Inc indicates that 97% of the respondents have email application running on their mobiles. According to the latest survey by security software company Symantec, the first thing a stranger would do is attempt to access your personal apps, then your photos and then your banking details."(DT: Mar 16, 2012) No doubt, it has also left numerous locals confused about how to respond. Modern economy has left a sizable population in the northern India 'rich and confused'. "A growing band of nouveau riche with an urge to splurge on luxury lifestyle is forcing retailers to redefine marketing in the country by getting staff to converse with customers in local dialect with homely etiquettes. Priya Sachdev Chatwal, Chief Operating Officer and Creative director of TSG International Marketing says – Luxury cannot afford to intimidate." The Economic Times: Mar 15, 2012.

Let us consider the scene in outer Delhi and NCR[1], the area surrounding Delhi. The rapid growth in economy, mainly due to acquisition/selling of land at exorbitant prices, in the adjoining areas of Haryana and UP has left the people 'rich and confused'. Blinding development of housing estates with world class luxury, commercial plazas with teeming bars have utterly confused the once poor, hardworking and simple hearted village folk. This heavily reworked local youth feels liberated, inferior and hostile all at the same time. Two opposing factors are working there simultaneously – development and resentment. Take Gurgaon as a case, 1990s onwards, one part is teeming with development and is dancing on tune global economy, and the other one houses the rural locals soaking in big money without matching education and worldview. The conservative social attitudes make themselves visible in mandatory *parda* clad women and *khaap*[2] brand male mentality. In fact the word *khaap* has become a concept now. I feel it can be seen as a synonymous of 'desperation', which is against everything that wants to break away from 'rigid' and 'conventional'. "A bench headed by chief Justice Vikramajit Sen of Karnataka HC on Tuesday compared thy Army to a khap panchayat for blocking a young officer's bid to marry a 29-year old Sri Lankan woman he's in love with." Times Of India, Oct. 31, 2012. p.1

The farmer turned neo-rich folk, in majority, are surviving on rent income, transport/cab business, utility shops etc. Several low (or almost no) educated people enjoy their life basking in money and doing practically nothing. Participants of the global economy look to them as 'others', giving them inferiority. The recent gang rapes in the area are the result of these two attitudes that are suddenly forced to operate side by side. It's not the shift, but the suddenness and speed of the shift that has confused people off their once simple, comfortable but firm ground. The transition brought about by what we see as global economic phenomenon manifest itself in the increasing number of property related court cases, rising level of animosity within and among families, ambition to consume the top brands (goods as well as ideas) without matching income and disposition, and extreme behavior of slavish acceptance of western cultural artifacts on the one hand and regression into local cultural cocoon on the other. This confusion and mismatch between self-image and reality, which is the socio cultural consequence of globalization, can be confronted with efficient and sincere policies, a mature approach on the part of the society, proper education and, of course, a little patience.

A little of patience, since Gen-Y[3] is in real hurry: they want to grow up fast, be wealthy fast, experience all the possible aspects of life as soon as possible. A great rush has set in. This generation has developed a peculiar world view. I'd like to mention the scene of real estate in NCR. I, during my research interaction, discussed the market scenario with a property dealer. (I would not use the word 'consultant' as it dilutes the real spirit of local property business in the area.) An old property player could not mature a local deal in 'asking amount' of Rs 6200000/- because he found it quite absurd and risky; he was convinced it was not worth more than Rs 5500000/-. Whereas a group of youngsters bought it for Rs 6150000/- and sold it for Rs 6300000/- within three days. It seems the Gen-Y has nothing to lose. The notion of play-it-safe has lost its relevance. But it does not stop just at this. Once started, people keep risking everything – money, relations, life, ... everything.

I can think of three suggestions for solution:

1. Deal the whole thing high-handedly and discipline the chaos, provided the *Generation-correct* is truly disciplined. (A matter of soul searching)
2. Overhaul the entire code-system according to Gen-Y.
3. Whatever is happening, is the solution.

Notes.

1. The National Capital Region of Delhi (NCR), is an area that includes the union territory of Delhi and a few surrounding towns of the neighbouring states like Rajasthan, Haryana and Uttar Pradesh.
2. Loosely defined, Khaap is a group of particular titles in a caste. Today most people know this word from the phrase khaap pachayats, groups of people in villages to give their decisions, especially on caste-issues.
3. Generation-Y, for me, are the people born around and after 1980, and who have had a liberal dose of internet and liberty.

REFERENCES

[1] Dasgupta Samir and Kidy (eds). *Globalization And After.* India. Sage Publication India Pvt. Ltd., 2006.

[2] De Shobha. *Shooting from the Hip: Selected Writings*. New Delhi: UBS Publishers' Distributors, 1994.

[3] Giddens, A. The Consequences of Modernity, Cambridge: Polity Press, 1999.

[4] Gramsci, Antonio. *Selections from the Prison Notebooks of Antonio Grmsci.* Editors and Translators, Quintin Hoare and Geoffrey Nowell Smith. New York: International Publishers, 1971.

[5] Hall, S. and du Gay ,P. (eds). Questions of Cultural Identity. London: Sage, 1996.

[6] Held, D. et. al. Global Transformations: Politics, Economics and Culture. Cambridge: Polity Press, 1999.

[7] Holliday Adrian, Hyde Martin, Kullman John. Intercultural Communication. London: Routledge, 2004.

[8] Jogdand,P. G., S.M. Michael.(eds.) *Glbalization And After Movements: Struggle for a Humane Society.* India: Rawat Publications India Pvt Ltd., 2003.

[9] O'Sullivan et. al. *Key Concepts in Communication and Cultural Studies.* London and New Yark. Routledge, 2000.

Creativity and Locus of Control: A Comparative Study of Age, Gender and Family Type Amongst the Generation Y of Southern India

Anu Singh Lather, Shilpa Jain and Anju Dwivedi Shukla

University School of Management Studies,
Guru Gobind Singh Indraprastha University, Dwarka, Delhi

ABSTRACT

The aim of the research is to analyse and compare locus of control of generation Y with respect to their creativity level, age groups, gender and family type. The research was conducted on students of undergraduate and post graduate courses of university of Mysore. The sample of this study included 450 students. Assessment included socio-demographic details, Abbreviated Torrance Test for Adults and Locus of Control. The statistical analysis evidenced that locus of control was significantly impacted by various creativity levels. The results show that powerful others, chance control and individual control are significantly different according to creativity level. Further it was proved that gender had no significant impact on locus of control, whereas interaction between creativity level and gender had significant impact on locus of control. The results also proved that age group had significant impact on Locus of Control with and on the contrary family type had no significant impact on Locus of Control.

Keywords: *Creativity, Locus of Control, Age, Gender, Family Type, Students*

INTRODUCTION

I could not score well because there was a function next door when I had my exam, or my friend kept on disturbing me during preparation and exam. These kinds of words we hear very often. What does it indicate? It shows that the person using such words has External Locus of Control- a dimension of personality, which means the individual does not take responsibility of his own deeds rather throw it on chances and/or other individuals. Contrarily the individuals with the Internal Locus of Control take responsibility of their actions, so their reaction would be, 'I could not score well because I have not paid attention'. The big question is how does that matter? It does because a person with an external locus of control will always show himself/herself as helpless, will throw responsibilities of his deeds on others, have low self esteem, have casual attitude towards work and others, and will be less creative and innovative. On the other hand, a person with Internal Locus of Control will take responsibilities of his actions; will not keep casual approach to others, possess better self esteem, and will be more creative and innovative.

Locus of control has become an important concept in today's life and has been applied in various fields starting from industrial and organizational psychology, sports psychology, educational psychology and the psychology of religion. Locus of control's most famous application has been in the field of health psychology, specifically mental health, obesity, cancer and diabetes mellitus. Various authors note that data on whether health related behaviors are related to internal health locus of control or external have been ambiguous. For example, they note that some studies found that internal health locus of control is linked with increased exercise, breast self-examination, weight control, non alcoholism, smoking cessation and preventative health behaviors but they also cite several studies that have found only a weak or no relationship. Apart from health, LOC have been correlated with academic success of students enrolled in higher education courses by Whyte in 1970s and 1980s. Students who tended to be more internally controlled believed that hard work and focus would result oftentimes in successful academic progress and they performed better academically. Those students who were identified as more externally controlled, believing that their future depended upon luck or fate, tended to have lower academic performance levels. Cassandra B. Whyte further researched how control tendency influenced behavioral outcomes in the academic realm by examining the effects of various modes of counseling on grade improvements and the locus of control of high-risk college students.

Rotter first proposed the concept of locus of control in 1966 and since then there has been so much of interest in finding out where people locate their cause of events. People have diverse believes regarding who controls their destiny i.e. whether it is controlled by oneself, fate, God or powerful others. Locus of Control is an attribution theory referring to those causes to which individuals attribute their successes and failures" (Forte, 2005, p. 65). Rotter identified two different types of control:

- **Internal:** "Those with a high internal locus believe their will and behaviour is directed by their own internal decisions and thus feel as if they have more influence on their environment" (Jatkevicius, 2010, p. 78).
- **External:** "A personality type guided by high external locus involves the belief that one's behaviour and results are guided by circumstances out of one's control (fate, luck, and so on)" (Jatkevicius, 2010, p. 78).

The internal versus external distinction makes locus of control an attractive concept to explain why some people tend to show more creative ideation in comparison to others. Age also has a strong relationship with locus of control. But there does not exist a consensus on whether locus of control becomes internal or external with age. With regard to locus of control in relation to gender, some scholars believe that females tend to be external in comparison to males others disagree with this and have given the evidence of just the opposite and there exist a third group which states gender does not affect locus of control.

LITERATURE REVIEW

Locus of control has been examined in terms of several variables. In this section an attempt has been made to review the previous literature available in relation to locus of control, creativity, age, gender and type of family.

Researchers have held the view that there are differences in the creative ideation of individuals with internal and external locus of control . Golann (1963) has stated that one of the variables related to the ability to be creative is the presence of an internal source of direction. Torrance (1971) found that creative individuals tended to function more effectively when external reinforcement was not prevalent an indication of locus of control. Erwin and Steinke (1973) conducted a study on ninety 7th, 8th, and 9th grade students, to study the relationship between scores on the Rolter's Internal-External scale, Guilford's Unusual Uses Test and a sorting task which examined their level of abstractness. No trends were seen between locus of control scores, measures of uncommonness and levels of abstractness. Glover and Sautter (1976) found that individuals with internal locus of control scored higher on flexibility and originality subscales of creativity tests. On the other hand, they also found that individuals possessing external locus of control excelled in verbal feedback and scored higher on elaboration subscales of creativity tests. Richmond and De La Serna (1980) and Chadha (1989) found a significant relationship between creativity and internal locus of control.

Age also has a strong relationship with locus of control. It is sometimes assumed that as people age, they will become less internal and more external, but data here has been ambiguous. Bailer (1961) found that locus of control tended to become more internal with age and this developmental process assisted in bringing about specific positive outcomes. Lao (1974) assessed changes in locus of control orientation from youth through adulthood and old age. In her extension of this work, Lao predicted an increase in internality from youth to adulthood (15 to 30-39 yr.); a stabilized sense of internal control in middle age (30 to 59 yr.) ; and a decrease in internality in old age (60 yr. and older). Age-correlated differences in locus of control (LOC) orientation were examined for 306 persons by Robert and Roger (1976) between the age of 13 to 90 years, in three areas of activity: intellectual, social, and physical. On the scales measuring LOC for both physical and social situations, persons over 60 scored more external than adults in the 35–50 age range. On the other hand, Dönmez (1983) stated that there were many studies showing that locus of control might change from being internal to being external or vice verse. Schieman (2001) determined that an individual's locus of control morphs as they age: as an individual gets older, they lose their sense of control. Lachman (2004) in an attempt to find whether locus of control beliefs change in later life, he conducted studies and found that age differences were found most often on the chance and powerful others control dimensions, suggesting that the elderly acknowledge the importance of external sources of control and at the same time preserve their sense of internal control. Longitudinal data collected by Gatz and Karel (cited in Johnson et al., 2004) imply that internality may increase up to middle age, and thereafter decrease. Noting the ambiguity of data in this area, Aldwin and Gilmer (2004) cite Lachman's claim that locus of control is ambiguous. Indeed, there is evidence here that changes in locus of control in later life relate more visibly to increased externality, rather than reduced internality, if the two concepts are taken to be orthogonal. Evidence cited by Schultz and Schultz (2005), for example Heckhausen and Schulz (1995) or Ryckman and Malikosi, 1975 (cited in Schultz & Schultz, 2005), suggests that locus of control increases in internality up until middle age. These authors also note that attempts to control the environment become more pronounced between the age of eight and fourteen. Tucker, Hamayan and Genesse (2006) also believe that the people become more internal as they get older. Kýralp, Sahin and Dinçyürek (2008) reported that locus of control become more internal as individuals get older. Instead of classifying persons as having internal locus of control or external locus of control, it should be emphasized that locus of control may change in terms of being internal or external (Dinçyürek, Çaðlar and Birol, 2010).

Research delineating the effects of gender on locus of control has yielded conflicting results. Archer & Waterman, 1988 found males to be more internally motivated than female adolescents. Cairns, Mc Whirter, Duffy and Barry (1990) found that females were more internally oriented than were males. Susan (1992) undertook a study to examine the relationship between locus of control and gender role. A non-significant trend for the interaction of sex by locus of control was found. Lee and Dengerink (1992) compared locus of control in American college students and Swedish gymnasium students. Swedish women were more externally oriented than Swedish men or Americans of either sex. Aricak (1995) argues that male students have higher levels of internal locus of control. Manger and Eikeland (2000) reported that females have higher levels of internal locus of control in contrast to males. Manger and Eikeland (2001) in a sample of Norwegian 14- and 15-year-old students found no significant relationship between total externality-internality score and level of ability. The analyses of gender differences showed that girls had significantly higher total internal locus of control scores than boys. Schultz and Schultz (2005) point out, significant gender differences in locus of control have not been found for adults in a U.S. population. Sherman et. al (2007) in their article presented a synthesis of research conducted in the last two decades that has explored the relationship of gender to locus of control measures. The research suggested that both males and females are becoming more external. Females, however, tend to be more external than males on most locus of control measures. Gender factors into one's sense of control: women are less likely to possess an internal locus of control than men. Arýcak (1995), Amman, Aykora, Tekin and Kýlýç (2010) and Özerdem (2003) argued that male students had internal locus of control. Amadi (2010) opined in their research findings also that male tends to be more internal than females. Gündüz (1986) and Yasar (2006) Adame, Johnson & Cole, 1989; Kýralp, Sahin and Dinçyürek, 2008; Serin and Derin 2008) state that there is no difference between girls and boys in terms of locus of control. However, the gender gap in regards to locus of control is changing: "as gender inequality in education and life chances decline, we should expect to see gender difference in sense of control to decline as well, because women's and men's life courses are converging" (Slagsvold & Sorenson, 2008, p. 29).

OBJECTIVES OF THE STUDY

- To compare the Locus of Control of students (internal v/s external) with respect to their creativity levels (high, average and low creativity) and age group (18-20 yrs, 21-23 yrs, 24-26 yrs and 26 yrs and above).
- To compare the Locus of Control of students (internal v/s external) with respect to their gender (male and female) and family type (nuclear and joint).

HYPOTHESIS

H1. There is no significant difference in locus of control of high, average and low creative students.

H2. There is no significant difference in locus of control of students among the various age groups.

H3. There is no significant difference in locus of control of male and female students.

H4. There is no significant difference in locus of control of students coming from nuclear and joint families.

RESEARCH METHODOLOGY

This study tries to compare locus of control of students with respect to their creativity levels, age, gender and family type. The sample has been selected on the basis of purposive sampling. The total sample selected consisted of 450 students studying in Undergraduate and Post Graduate courses of University of Mysore. Out of 450, a total of 244 usable responses were obtained with return rate of 53.3%.

The research design is given below:

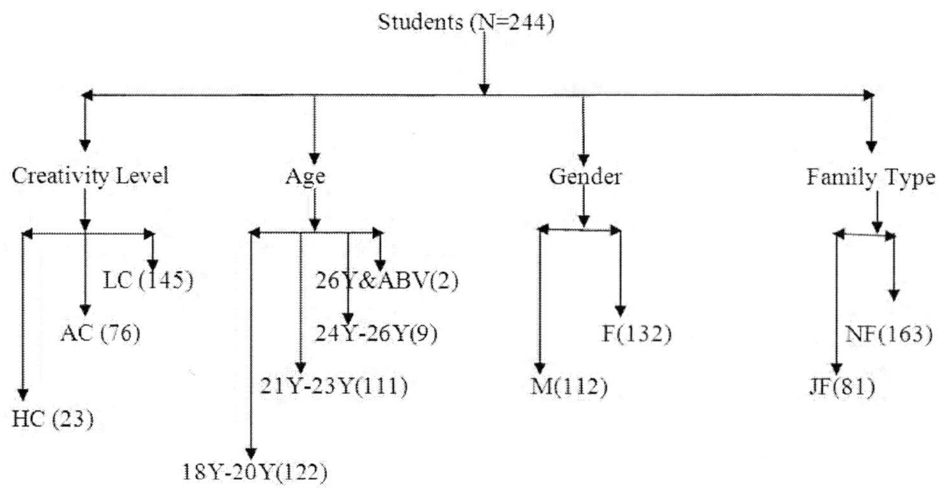

Here,

HC = High Creative AC = Average Creative

LC = Low Creative

18Y-20Y = between the age group of 18 to 20 years

21Y-23Y = between the age group of 21 to 23 years

24Y-26Y = between the age group of 24 to 26 years

26 Y & ABV = 26 years and above age group

F = Females M = Males

NF = Nuclear Family JF = Joint Family

Survey Tools

A three – part questionnaire was used for data collection.

A. Socio-demographic data concerning name, gender, age group and family type (Joint or Nuclear).

B. Abbreviated Torrance Test for Adults (ATTA) - The Torrance Tests of Creative Thinking (TTCT) "is the most widely used and most researched creativity test" (Goff & Torrance, 2002, p. 36).The ATTA was developed from the TTCT and both content and face validity have been established by the Scholastic Testing Service (Goff & Torrance).

The ATTA assessment consists of "four norm-referenced abilities and fifteen criterion referenced creativity indicators" (Goff & Torrance, 2002, p. 1).

The four norm-referenced measures are identified as the following :

- Fluency- the ability to produce quantities of ideas which are relevant to the task instruction.
- Originality – the ability to produce uncommon ideas that are totally new or unique.
- Elaboration – the ability to embellish ideas with details.
- Flexibility – the ability to process information or objects in different ways, given the same stimulus.

The fifteen criterion-referenced creativity indicators included the following (Goff & Torrance, p. 2):

- verbal responses- which included richness and colourfulness of imagery, emotions and feelings, future orientation and humour, conceptual incongruity and provocative questions; and
- figural responses- which included openness and resistance to premature closure, unusual visualization and different perspectives, movement and/or sound, richness and/or colourfulness of imagery, abstractness of titles, context or the environment for object and articulateness in telling story, combination and synthesis of two or more figures, internal visual perspective, expressions of feelings and emotions, and fantasy.

Raw scores from the four norm-referenced measures were converted to normalize scaled score, and were added to fifteen criterion-referenced indicators which received a score ranging from 0 to 2, to create the creativity index (CI).

A seven- point scaled score was developed to interpret the resulting creativity index and Table 1 provides this essential information.

Table 1: The Scaled Score for the Creativity Index, with Added Interpretive Information

Abbreviated Torrance Test for Adult Scoring		
Scaled Score	*Percentage of Adults*	*Meaning*
7	4	Substantial
6	12	High
5	20	Above Average
4	26	Average
3	20	Below Average
2	12	Low
1	4	Minimal

Source : Goff & Torrance, 2002, p. 29.

C. **Locus of Control (LOC).** Levenson and Miller (1976) multidimensional scale of I-E control was used to measure LOC. It has 24 items related to two sub areas namely internal control and external control. External control has two sub scales i.e. powerful others and chance. The subjects are required to respond to each item on a 5-point scale. The score on the 8 item of each sub-area was used as a score. The higher the score, the greater the subject's degree of expectancy for the particular aspect of locus of control.

CONDUCTING RESEARCH

Proper permission was sought to conduct the study from the Head of Departments. Participation in the study was voluntary. The purpose of the study was clearly communicated to all the subjects and they were assured that all the data would be treated as confidential and only the researchers would have access to the data collected .The instructions were provided in their respective class rooms and the completed forms were then collected.

RESULTS

Wilks' lambda is a test statistic used in multivariate analysis of variance (MANOVA) to test whether there are differences between the means of identified groups of subjects on a combination of dependent variables. Wilks' lambda performs, in the multivariate setting, with a combination of dependent variables, the same role as the F-test performs in one-way analysis of variance. Wilks' lambda is a direct measure of the proportion of variance in the combination of dependent variables that is unaccounted for by the independent variable (the grouping variable or factor).

Locus of Control and Creativity

The two way MANOVA (Table 1) revealed that various creativity levels impacted significantly on the combined dependent locus of control variables with Wilks' Lambda = .574, F value = 25.125 and significance value = .000. The further scrutiny of the ANOVA table (Table 2)

Table 1: Summary of Multivariate Tests for the Factors of Locus of Control According to the Gender and creativity levels of students.

Effect		*Value*	*F*	*Hypothesis df*	*Error df*	*Sig.*
Intercept	Wilks' Lambda	.048	1.556E3[a]	3.000	236.000	.000
Creativity_Level	Wilks' Lambda	.574	25.125[a]	6.000	472.000	.000
Gender	Wilks' Lambda	.984	1.306[a]	3.000	236.000	.273
Creativity_Level * Gender	Wilks' Lambda	.933	2.788[a]	6.000	472.000	.011

Table 2: Summary of Analysis of Variance for All Factors of Locus of control According to the Gender of the Students at three Creativity Levels

Source	*Dependent Variable*	*Type III Sum of Squares*	*df*	*Mean Square*	*F*	*Sig.*
Creativity_ level	Powerful_ others	157.668	2	78.834	42.948	.000
	Chance_ control	58.396	2	29.198	16.479	.000
	Indi_ cont	194.448	2	97.224	38.999	.000
Gender	Powerful_ others	4.650	1	4.650	2.533	.113
	chance_ control	4.881	1	4.881	2.755	.098
	Indi_ cont	1.165	1	1.165	.467	.495
creativity_level * Gender	Powerful_ others	16.143	2	8.071	4.397	.013
	Chance_ control	8.181	2	4.091	2.309	.102
	Indi_ cont	15.051	2	7.526	3.019	.051

Table 3: Mean Scores of Creativity for the Factors of Locus of Control

Dependent Variable	*Low Creativity*	*Average Creativity*	*High Creativity*
Powerful others	7.428	6.398	4.525
Chance control	6.516	5.732	4.917
Individual control	5.064	6.651	7.740

according to each variable shows that powerful others, chance control and individual control are significantly different according to creativity level. Analysis of the mean table (Table 3) shows that students who are high on creativity are high on Individual control (Mean=7.740), whereas students who are low on creativity are high on Powerful Others (Mean = 7.428). Post Hoc Tests were applied for further analysis and the Duncan table (Table 3a) showed that low creative students were significantly high on Powerful others (7.4414) in comparison to average creative students (6.5132) whereas high creative students were found to be significantly low on powerful other (4.6957). Duncan table (Table 3b) which showed the relationship of chance

Table 3a: Test of Homogenous Kubset – Powerful Others

Creativity_ Level	*N*	*Subset*		
		1	*2*	*3*
High creativity	23	4.6957		
Average creativity	76		6.5132	
Low creativity	145			7.4414
Sig.		1.000	1.000	1.000

Table 3b: Test of Homogenous Subset – Chance Control

		Subset		
Creativity_ Level	*N*	*1*	*2*	*3*
High creativity	23	4.9565		
Average creativity	76		5.8684	
Low creativity	145			6.5103
Sig.		1.000	1.000	1.000

Table 3c: Test of Homogenous Subset – Individual Control

Creativity_ level	*N*	*Subset*		
		1	*2*	*3*
Low creativity	145	5.0483		
Average creativity	76		6.5395	
High creativity	23			7.6957
Sig.		1.000	1.000	1.000

control on various levels of creativity revealed that students who were high on creativity were significantly low on Chance control (4.9565), average creative students were moderate on chance control (5.8684), and the students low on creativity scored the highest on Chance control (6.5103). Duncan table (Table 3c) which showed the relationship of Individual control on various levels of creativity revealed that students which were low on creativity were lowest on individual control (5.0483), average creative students were moderate on individual control (6.5395), and the students high on creativity scored the highest on Individual Control (7.6957).

Locus of Control, Creativity and Gender

Table 1 shows the results of Two Way MANOVA with gender and creativity as independent variables and factors of locus of control as dependent variable. The two way MANOVA (Table 1) revealed that gender did not impacted significantly on the dependent variable locus of control. Analysis of the mean table (Table 4) shows that female students are high on powerful others and Chance control whereas male students are high on Individual control. The two way MANOVA (Table 1) revealed that interaction between creativity level and gender impacted significantly on the combined dependent variable locus of control with Wilks' Lambda = .933, F value =2.788 and significance value = .011. The further scrutiny of the ANOVA table (Table 2) according to each variable shows that powerful others and individual control are significantly different when creativity and gender interacts. Analysis of the mean table (Table 5) shows that low creative males and females are high on Powerful others (Males = 7.582 and Females = 7.273) and high creative males and females are low on Powerful others (Males = 4.167 and Females = 4.882).It is also observed that high creative males and females are high on Individual Control (Males = 7.833 and Females = 7.647). The result showed no difference between male and female students in regards to locus of control orientation, although females were slightly more externally oriented than males. Similar results were found by Nowicki and Strickland (1973), Adame et al. (1989), Archer & Waterman (1988), Dellas & Jernigan (1987). But MANOVA table revealed that low creative male and female students are high on Powerful others i.e. External Locus of Control whereas high creative male and female students are low on External Control and high on Individual Control i.e. Internal Control. This is supported by findings of previous researchers like Torrance (1971) according to whom individuals who are creative tend to rely on internal locus of control.

Table 4: Mean Scores of Gender for the Factors of Locus of Control

Dependent variable	*Males*	*Females*
Powerful others	5.916	6.317
Chance control	5.516	5.927
Individual control	6.585	6.385

Table 5: Mean Scores of Creativity X Gender for All Factors of Locus of Control

Dependent Variable		*Low Creativity*	*Average Creativity*	*High Creativity*
Powerful Others	Male	7.582	6.000	4.167
	Female	7.273	6.796	4.882
Chance Control	Male	6.456	5.259	4.833
	Female	6.576	6.204	5.000
Individual Control	Male	4.886	7.037	7.833
	Female	5.000	6.265	7.647

Locus of Control and Age

The two way MANOVA (Table 6) revealed that age group impacted significantly on the combined dependent locus of control variable with Wilks' Lambda = .873, F value =3.611 and significance value = .000. The further scrutiny of the ANOVA table (Table 7) according to each variable shows that only powerful other is significantly different as per age – groups. Analysis of the mean table (Table 9) shows that students in the age group 24-26 score highest on Powerful others and if we ignore the students in the age-group of 26 and above (being less in number), we will notice a trend that as the age increases score on Powerful others increase. This means that as the age increases the locus of control shifts from being internal to external, hence losing their sense of control and believing that his fate is determined by the powerful others around him and he has no control on his actions, outcomes and results. Moreover as students grow older they start acknowledging the importance of external sources of control and at the same time preserves their sense of internal control. Post Hoc Tests were applied for further analysis and the Duncan table (Table 9a) showed that students in the age group of 24-26 years were significantly high on powerful others (8.6667) in comparison to other groups of students who reported a lower score (18-20 yrs = 6.6393, 21-23 yrs = 7.0360 and 26 + years = 6.5000). This result shows that as students grow older from 18 to 26 years they start attributing the causes of the events in their life to external forces such as luck, fate, chance or powerful others.

The two way MANOVA (Table 6) revealed that interaction between creativity level and age – group impacted significantly on the combined dependent variable locus of control with Wilks' Lambda = .886, F value =3.208 and significance value = .001. The further scrutiny of the ANOVA table (Table 7) according to each variable shows that powerful others, chance control and individual control is significantly different when creativity and age – group interacts. Analysis of the mean table (Table 10) shows that low creative students in almost all age-groups scored significantly higher on Powerful others (18-20 years = 7.370, 21-23 years = 7.431, 24-26 years = 8.286), whereas High creative students in all age –group scored significantly low on Powerful others (18-20 years = 4.250, 21-23 years = 4.889, 26 +years = 6.500). Low creative students in almost all age- groups scored significantly higher on chance Control (18-20 years = 6.562, 21-23 years = 6.432, 24-26 years = 6.714) in comparison to High creative students of all age group who scored significantly lower on chance control (18-20 years = 4.833, 21-23 years = 5.111, 26 + years = 5.00). As far as Individual control is concerned , it was observed that Low creative students in all age groups scored significantly low on Individual control (18-20 years = 4.945, 21-23 years = 5.031, 24-26 years = 6.286), whereas High creative students of all age groups scored significantly high on Individual control (18-20 years = 7.833, 21-23 years = 7.667, 26 + years = 7.000). The result shows that low creative students of almost all age group scored high on chance control and low on Individual control, in contrast to high creative students of all age group who scored high on Individual control and low on Chance control. This make clear that high creative students irrespective of their age group believe that their action, thoughts and attitudes usually control their destiny in contrast to low creative students across all age groups who believe that their destiny is mostly controlled by external forces such as God, luck or fate.

Table 6 shows the results of Two Way MANOVA with age –group and creativity as independent variables and factors of locus of control as dependent variable. The two way MANOVA revealed that various creativity levels impacted significantly on the combined dependent locus of control variables with Wilks' Lambda = .697, F value =15.389 and significance value = .000. The further scrutiny of the ANOVA table (Table 7) according to each variable shows that powerful others, chance control and individual control are significantly different according to creativity level. Analysis of the mean table (Table 8) shows that students who are high on creativity are Individually controlled. The students who are low on creativity are chance controlled or controlled by powerful others. This means that low creative students feel that whatever happens in their life is controlled by fate, chance or luck or other people around them and they are not in control of their life. Post Hoc Tests were applied for further analysis and the Duncan table (Table 8a) showed that low creative students were significantly high on Powerful others (7.4414) in comparison to average creative students (6.5132) whereas high creative students were found to be significantly low on powerful other (4.6957). High creative students have the belief that they are masters of their fate and are internally motivated to accomplish their goals, they believe less in chance or destiny but more in their efforts and strengths. Duncan table (Table 8b) which showed the relationship of chance control on various levels of creativity revealed that students which were high on creativity were significantly low on Chance control (4.9565), average creative students were moderate on chance control (5.8684), and the students low on creativity scored the highest on Chance control (6.5103). Duncan table (Table 8c) which showed the relationship of Individual control on various levels of creativity revealed that students who were low on creativity were lowest on individual control (5.0483), average creative students were moderate on individual control (6.5395), and the students high on creativity scored the highest on Individual Control (7.6957).

Table 6: Summary of Multivariate Tests for the Factors of Locus of Control According to the Age and Creativity Levels of Students

Effect		*Value*	*F*	*Hypothesis df*	*Error df*	*Sig.*
Intercept	Wilks' Lambda	.126	5.374E2[a]	3.000	233.000	.000
creativity_ level	Wilks' Lambda	.697	15.389[a]	6.000	466.000	.000
age_ group	Wilks' Lambda	.873	3.611	9.000	567.211	.000
creativity_ level * age_ group	Wilks' Lambda	.886	3.208	9.000	567.211	.001

Table 7: Summary of Analysis of Variance for All Factors of Locus of control According to the Age Kroup of the Students at three Creativity Levels

Source	*Dependent Variable*	*Type III Sum of Squares*	*df*	*Mean Square*	*F*	*Sig.*
creativity_ level	Powerful_ others	102.151	2	51.076	30.058	.000
	Chance_ control	26.899	2	13.450	7.739	.001
	Indi_ cont	85.831	2	42.916	17.764	.000
age_ group	Powerful_ others	46.630	3	15.543	9.147	.000
	Chance_ control	11.115	3	3.705	2.132	.097
	Indi_ cont	8.100	3	2.700	1.118	.343
creativity_ level * age_ group	Powerful_ others	19.717	3	6.572	3.868	.010
	Chance_ control	21.724	3	7.241	4.167	.007
	Indi_ cont	25.815	3	8.605	3.562	.015

Table 8: Mean Scores of Creativity for the Factors of Locus of Control

Dependent Variable	*Low Creativity*	*Average Creativity*	*High Creativity*
Powerful others	7.695	7.613	5.213
Chance control	6.569	6.383	4.981
Individual control	5.421	6.369	7.500

Table 8a: Test of Homogenous Subset – Powerful Others

Creativity_ level	*N*	*Subset*		
		1	*2*	*3*
High creativity	23	4.6957		
Average creativity	76		6.5132	
Low creativity	145			7.4414
Sig.		1.000	1.000	1.000

Table 8b: Test of Homogenous Subset – Chance Control

Creativity_ level	*N*	*Subset*		
		1	*2*	*3*
High creativity	23	4.9565		
Average creativity	76		5.8684	
Low creativity	145			6.5103
Sig.		1.000	1.000	1.000

Table 8c: Test of Homogenous Subset – Individual Control

Creativity_ level	N	Subset		
		1	2	3
Low creativity	145	5.0483		
Average creativity	76		6.5395	
High creativity	23			7.6957
Sig.		1.000	1.000	1.000

Table 9: Mean Scores of Age- groups for the Factors of Locus of Control

Dependent variable	*18-20 years*	*21-23 years*	*24-26 years*	*Above 26 years*
Powerful others	5.864	6.395	9.143	6.500
Chance control	5.555	5.973	7.107	5.000
Individual control	6.647	6.214	6.143	7.000

Table 9a: Test of Homogenous Subset – Powerful Others

Age_ group	*N*	*Subset*	
		1	*2*
Above 26 years	2	6.5000	
18-20 yrs	122	6.6393	
21-23 yrs	111	7.0360	
24-26 yrs	9		8.6667
Sig.		.494	1.000

Table 10: Mean Scores of Creativity X Age –group for All Factors of Locus of Control

Dependent Variable		*Low Creativity*	*Average Creativity*	*High Creativity*
Powerful Others	18-20 Yrs	7.370	5.973	4.250
	21-23 Yrs	7.431	6.865	4.889
	24-26 Yrs	8.286	10.000	A
	Abv 26 Yrs	a	a	6.500
Chance Control	18-20 Yrs	6.562	5.270	4.833
	21-23 Yrs	6.432	6.378	5.111
	24-26 Yrs	6.714	7.500	A
	Abv 26 Yrs	A	a	5.00
Individual Control	18-20 Yrs	4.945	7.162	7.833
	21-23 Yrs	5.031	5.946	7.667
	24-26 Yrs	6.286	6.000	A
	Abv 26 Yrs	A	a	7.000

a. This level combination of factors is not observed, thus the corresponding population marginal mean is not estimable.

Locus of Control and Family Type

The two way MANOVA (Table 11) revealed that family type did not impacted significantly on the dependent variable locus of control. The further scrutiny of the ANOVA table (Table 12) according to each variable shows that chance control is significantly different when creativity and family type interacts. The two way MANOVA (Table 3.1) revealed that interaction between creativity level and Family Type did not impacted significantly on the combined dependent variable locus of control.

Table 11 shows the results of Two Way MANOVA with family type and creativity as independent variables and factors of locus of control as dependent variable. The two way MANOVA revealed that various creativity levels impacted significantly on the combined dependent locus of control variables with Wilks' Lambda = .721, F value =14.007 and significance value = .000. The further scrutiny of the ANOVA table (Table 12) according to each variable shows that powerful others, chance control and individual control are significantly different according to creativity level. Analysis of the mean table (Table 13) shows that students who are high on creativity are low on Powerful others.

Table 11: Summary of Multivariate Tests for the Factors of Locus of Control According to family Type and creativity levels of students

Effect		*Value*	*F*	*Hypothesis df*	*Error df*	*Sig.*
Intercept	Wilks' Lambda	.076	9.551E2[a]	3.000	236.000	.000
Creativity_ level	Wilks' Lambda	.721	14.007[a]	6.000	472.000	.000
Family_ Type	Wilks' Lambda	.993	.568[a]	3.000	236.000	.637
Creativity_ level * Family_ Type	Wilks' Lambda	.968	1.297[a]	6.000	472.000	.257

Table 12: Summary of Analysis of Variance for All Factors of Locus of control According to Family Type of the students at Three Creativity Levels

Source	*Dependent Variable*	*Type III Sum of Squares*	*df*	*Mean Square*	*F*	*Sig.*
creativity_ level	powerful_ others	87.194	2	43.597	23.605	.000
	chance_ control	27.898	2	13.949	7.789	.001
	indi_ cont	105.273	2	52.637	20.667	.000
Family_ Type	powerful_ others	1.645	1	1.645	.891	.346
	chance_ control	.380	1	.380	.212	.645
	indi_ cont	1.998	1	1.998	.785	.377
creativity_ level * Family_ Type	powerful_ others	5.128	2	2.564	1.388	.251
	chance_ control	11.636	2	5.818	3.249	.041
	indi_ cont	1.164	2	.582	.229	.796

Table 13: Mean Scores of Creativity for the Factors of Locus of Control

Dependent Variables	Low Creativity	Average Creativity	High Creativity
Powerful Others	**7.454**	**6.866**	**4.543**
Chance Control	6.502	6.225	4.833
Individual Control	5.044	6.504	7.400

Table 14: Mean Scores of Family Type for the Factors of Locus of Control

Dependent Variables	*Nuclear Family*	*Joint Family*
Powerful Others	6.134	6.441
Chance Control	5.779	5.927
Individual Control	6.485	6.147

Table 15: Mean Scores of Creativity X Family Type for All Factors of Locus of Control

Dependent Variable		*Low Creativity*	*Average Creativity*	*High Creativity*
Powerful Others	Nuclear Family	7.282	6.369	4.750
	Joint Family	7.627	7.364	4.333
Chance Control	Nuclear Family	6.615	5.723	5.000
	Joint Family	6.388	6.727	4.667
Individual Control	Nuclear Family	5.103	6.554	7.800
	Joint Family	4.985	6.455	7.000

DISCUSSION

From the research data it becomes clear that no significant difference exist on locus of control between male and female students, though the mean table shows females to be high on external control (powerful others and chance control) and males on internal control (individual control) but it is not significant. Creativity of an individual is influenced by cognitive attributes of an individual. Cognitive processes used in identifying a need for a solution are dependent upon the creative person's perception of the amount of personal control (Pannells & Claxton,2008). The stated finding is shown in the present study also, that a student having internal locus of control are higher on creativity levels in comparison to students having external locus of control. Results show that as the age increases the locus of control shifts from being internal to external this may be as a result of changed interests of the students as they come closer to being a graduate and post graduate. In other words, as students complete their studies, their interest shifts to areas which are considered uncontrollable such as finding a good job, a nice life partner and a progressive career. Hence, some part of externality may be a result of shift in interest to other life dominies. The results show that whether the student coming from joint family or nuclear family neither differ on their level of creativity nor on their locus of control.

REFERENCES

[1] Adame, D. A., Johnson, T. C., & Cole, S. P. (1989). Physical fitness, body image, and locus of control in college freshman men and women. Perceptual and Motor Skills, 68, 400-402.

[2] Aldwin, C.M., Gilman, D.F. (2004). *Health, Illness and Optimal Ageing*. London: Sage. ISBN 0-7619-2259-8.

[3] Amadi, M. (2010). Affective Determinants of ESL Success, Unpublished M. Ed Project, Department of Teacher Education, University of Ibadan.

[4] Amman T, Aykora E, Tekin C, Kýlýç M (2010). Açýk ve kapalý alan rekreasyoncularýnýn denetim odaðý ve benlik tasarýmý açýsýndan karsýlastýrýlmasý (Comparison of outdoor

and indoor recreation participants considering self-concept and locus of control). Turkiye Kickboks Federasyonu Spor Bilimleri Dergisi (Turkish Kick Boxing Federation Journal of Sports Science), 2: 1-13.

[5] Archer, S. L., & Waterman, A. S. (1988). Psychological individuation: Gender differences or gender neutrality? Human Development, 31, 65-81.

[6] Arýcak T (1995). Üniversite Öðrencilerinde Saldýrganlýk, Benlik Saygýsý ve Denetim Odaðý Ýliskisi (The relationship between aggressiveness, self-esteem and locus of control in undergraduate students). Unpublished MA Thesis, Ýstanbul: Marmara University, Institute of Social Sciences.

[7] Bailer, I. (1961). Conceptualization of success and failure in mental retarded and normal children. *Journal of Personality, 29,* 303-320.

[8] Bradley, R.H. & Webb, R. (1976). Age-Related Differences in Locus of Control Orientation in Three Behavior Domains. Hum Dev, Vol. 19, 49-55.

[9] Bulut Serin, N., Derin, R. (2008). Ilkogretim ögrencilerinin kisilerarasý problem çözme becerisi algýlarý ve denetim odagý düzeylerini etkileyen faktörler. *Uluslararasý Insan Bilimleri Dergisi*, 5 (1),1-18.

[10] Cairns, E., Mc Whirter, L., Duffy, U., & Barry, R. (1990). The stability of self-concept in late adolescence: Gender and situational effects. *Personality and Individual Differences, 11,* 937–944. doi:10.1016/0191-8869(90)90275-V

[11] Carton, J.S. & Stephen, N. J. (1994). Antecedents of Individual Differences in Locus of Control of Reinforcement : a Critical review. Genetic , Social, and General Psychology Monographs, Vol. 120.

[12] Dinçyürek S, Çaðlar M, Birol C (2010). Atýlganlýk ve denetim odaðý düzeyi: gelecek nesillere etkisi (Assertiveness and locus of control: Its effects on the future generations). *H. Ü. J. Educ. Faculty, 39:*142-150.

[13] Erwin, J. & Steinke, J. (1973). Internal-external control, divergent thinking and levels of abstractness. *Psychological Reports, 32* , pp. 1035-1041.

[14] Forte, A. (2005, April/May). Locus of control and the moral reasoning of managers. Journal of Business Ethics, Vol. 58, 65-77.

[15] Freedman, S.A. (1992). Sex, Gender and Locus of Control in College Students. Paper presented at the Annual Convention of the American Psychological Association (100th, Washington, DC, August 14-18, 1992).

[16] Glover, J. A. and Sautter, F. (1976).An investigation of the relationship of four components of creativity to locus of control. *Social Behavior and Personality* **4** , pp. 257-260.

[17] Gündüz, Z. (1986). Okul basarýsý ve ortaokul birinci sýnýf öðrencilerinde denetim odaðý (Achievement and secondary first-graders' locus of control). Unpublished MA Thesis, Ankara: Ankara University, Institute of Social Sci.

[18] Jatkevicius, J. (2010). Libraries and the lessons of abilene. Library Leadership & Management (Online). 24(3), 77-81.

[19] Lachman, M.E. (2004). Locus of Control in ageing research: a case for multidimensional and domain –specific assessment. Psychol Aging, Vol. 1(1), 34-40.

[20] Lindiwe M.S. (2011). The Relationship between Happiness, Creativity, Personality and Locus of Control in Ireland for Those who are employed and unemployed. Unpublished BA Thesis, DBS School of Arts, Dublin.

[21] Lao, R. C. The developmental trend of the locus of control. Unpublished paper presented at the meetings of the American Psychological Association, New Orleans, 1974.

[22] Lee, V.K. & Dengerink, H.A.(1992). Locus of Control in Relation to Sex and Nationality: A Cross –Cultural Study. Journal of Cross- Cultural Psychology, Vol. 23 (4), 488-497.

[23] Manger, T. & Eikeland, O.J. (2001). On the relationship between locus of control, level of ability and gender. Scandinavian Journal of Psychology, Vol. 41 (3), 225-229.

[24] Özerdem Ö (2003). *Ortaokullarda öðrenim gören öðrencilerin denetim odaklarýna iliskin karsýlastýrmalý deðerlendirme (A comparative evaluation on secondary students' locus of control).* Unpublished MA Thesis. Yakýn Doðu University, Institute of Educ. Sci.

[25] Pannells, Tammy C. and Claxton, Amy F.(2008) 'Happiness, Creative Ideation, and Locus of Control', Creativity Research Journal, 20: 1, 67 — 71

[26] Richmond, B. O. and De La Serna, M. (1980) Creativity and locus of control among Mexican college students. *Psychological Reports* 46, pp. 979-983.

[27] Rotter, J.B. (1966). Generalized expectancies for internal versus external control of reinforcement. Psychological Monographs, 80: 1-28.

[28] Sahin, S., Kiralp, Y. & Dincyurek, S. (2008). Denetim Odagi Farkli PDR Ogrecilerinin Empat Beceri Duzeylerinin Bazi Dezeylerinin Bazi Degiskenler Acisindan Incelenmesi",VIII. Ulusal PDR Kongresi, 21-23 Eylul 2005.

[29] Schultz, D.P., Schultz, S.E. (2005). *Theories of Personality* (8th ed.). Wadsworth: Thomson. ISBN 0-534-62402-2.

[30] Schieman, S. (2001). Age, education, and the sense of control: a test of the cumulative advantage hypothesis. Research on Aging vol. 23 (2), 153-178.

[31] Sherman, A.C., Higgs, G.E. & Williams R.L. (1997). Gender differences in the locus of construct. Psychology & Health, Vol. 12(2), 239-248. Available Online 19 Dec 2007.

[32] Slagsvold, B. & Sorensen, A. (2008). Age, education, and the gender gap in the sense of control. International Aging and Human Development, Vol. 67(1), 25-42.

[33] Tucker , G. R, Hamayan, E. & Genesse, F.H. (2006). Affective, cognitive and social factors in second language acquisition, Canadian Modern Language Review, 32, 214-26.

[34] Yasar, V. (2006). Farklý liselerde öðrenim görmekte olan 16-18 yas grubundaki öðrencilerin denetim odaðý düzeyleri ile bazý kisilik özelliklerinin karsýlastýrýlmasý (Comparison of locus of control levels and some personality characteristics of students in the 16-18 age group having education in different high schools). Unpublished MA Thesis, Marmara Uni., Institute of Educ. Sci. Istanbul.

Innovative Organizational Strategies to Engage Gen Y

Puja Khatri and Neha Raheja

University School of Management, Guru Gobind Singh Indraprastha University, Delhi

ABSTRACT

Today's workforce is composed of the cohorts of the Veterans (also called the Traditionals, 1922-1943), Baby Boomers (1943-1960), Gen X-ers (1961-1980), and the Nexters (also called Millenials or Gen Y-ers, 1980-2000) ("Managing the Clash," 2000). As Millennials become a larger percentage of the workforce, employer success will depend on Millennials' success, so it becomes imperative that the Millennials are engaged. It is therefore the employers' role to provide variety in work tasks and patterns as well as opportunities to learn the interesting aspects of even mundane tasks (Barnes). Employee engagement should be a top priority for any employer that wants to keep Millennials, as research supports common intuition: if people like their jobs, they will be less likely to leave. The purpose of this paper is to analyze various innovative organizational strategies to engage "Generation Y" as this generation forms the largest part of workforce.

INTRODUCTION

"They are the newest generation to enter the labor market, yet they already have clear ideas about what they expect from you as an employer. They are in high demand, so if you can't meet their needs, they'll find someone who can."-Stuart & Lyons, on Generation Y.

Gen Y is typically identified as being a fickle and wavering group of individuals. Here today, gone tomorrow. On to the next job. Attributed to becoming bored, seeking enjoyment or following the road, Millennials are known for moving on.

What is the cause of all of this? What are some of the reasons that Gen Y has seemingly lost their loyalty to long-term job commitment? Through experience and observation, these seem to suggest some causes:

- An unstable economy has caused Gen Y to devalue the tenure of a position. Even if you stayed with the same company for 30 years, what's the payoff for remaining when benefits, pensions and investments are not guaranteed?

- The company gets what it gives. As companies become less loyal to their employees, employees become less loyal to the companies. Gen Y especially sees disloyalty as a major red flag and a cue to exit.
- Millennials crave exploring the next opportunity to discover, create and expand. Sometimes called dreamers; this generation has an entrepreneurial nature that searches for freedom, limitlessness and fulfillment.
- Suppressive, rigid, traditional corporate cultures don't match the mindset of this generation. Gen Y workers are less tolerant of work environments that don't reflect personal values, opinions and/or feelings toward change.
- Much of this generation is still in search of the purpose of life. Either because they don't know what they want to do when they grow up or they aren't sure how to get there. Sometimes they're just passing through in search of where they fit.
- Gen Y is an entitled group. This group was raised to expect, receive and question everything. This sense of privilege has caused some in this group to lack patience in developing professionally, an unconcern with paying their dues and a different perception of how "work" should work.

Companies are having a lot of trouble recruiting and retaining younger employees, yet they will represent 3/4 of the entire workforce by 2025. It's imperative that companies keep their younger employee's engaged and motivated to do work, especially in a recession. Companies need to act fast because 56% of Gen-Y will leave their current job within a year, reports Sodexo Motivation Solutions. For millennial employees to enjoy a given job, they must find experience interesting and feel engaged beyond their office work (Thompson, Nicholas W., 2011). Therefore, organizations need to employ innovative strategies to engage Gen Y as mentioned below:

Respect

They expect and assume respect right away (Johnson, John & Smith, Jack). Gen Yers should be treated as colleagues, not as interns or "teenagers" (Bruce Tulgan). Millennials want to be respected for the contribution they can make to the job and feel they should not be treated poorly because they are young or less experienced than others (Manning, Terri Mulkins).

The culture at HDFC Life provides every individual equal respect and recognition irrespective of their designation. As a matter of fact, innovative ideas are considered irrespective of the designation of the employee who shares them, as far as they are beneficial to the organization.

- **Flexible Work Schedule:** Dianne Durkin remarks, "If a company wants to improve employee retention levels, they need to provide freedom from the walls of a cubicle and offer compensation time and flexible work schedules. Those who don't will pay the price." On the similar lines, Bruce Tulgan feels flexibility should be allowed in scheduling. Gen Yers demand flexible work arrangements (Sylvia Ann Hewlett, Laura Sherbin, Karen Sumberg)

HP India allows its employees to start their day within 2 hours from 8 am on a regular 8-hour working day. The company allows job sharing whereby any two employees could work for 20-40 hours per week on one job. Employees could work half-a-day and the other half from any location. Sameer Wadhwan, GM HR, explains rationale behind this: "The issue is not control, but facilitation, and motivating our independent, knowledgeable and creative employees."

"We provide unlimited sick leaves and flexible work options, let employees bring their own devices to work, sponsor health and wellness programmes, employee assistance and much more," says Abhinaya S Rao, head of people, ThoughtWorks India. R. Anish,

Director, HR, South Asia, Intel shares, "We believe in giving our employees adequate flexibility at work and they are actively encouraged to meet their personal commitments as they focus on their professional ones."

- **Listen to the Millennial Employee:** They had loving parents who listened to them and don't like being ignored (Healthfield). They also want their valuable contributions appreciated; they want their ideas to be heard by expert listeners who do not discount. Gen Yers outright simply because they are young (Oppel, Wayne)

Godrej Consumer Products (GCPL)'s, 'Bedhadak Bolo' is an initiative which salutes the spirit of expression and innovation. ThoughtWorks provides both online and offline forums for people to interact among themselves and with leadership teams, share information, ask questions and express their views.

'Sparsh' is an employee communication program at HDFC Life which is a town hall activity conducted annually company-wide in the month of November and December. Depending on the theme of the year, the presentations are designed to capture the industry performance, business performance, initiative updates, achievements, organizational goals etc. The entire communication meet happens at four levels to ensure people at all levels

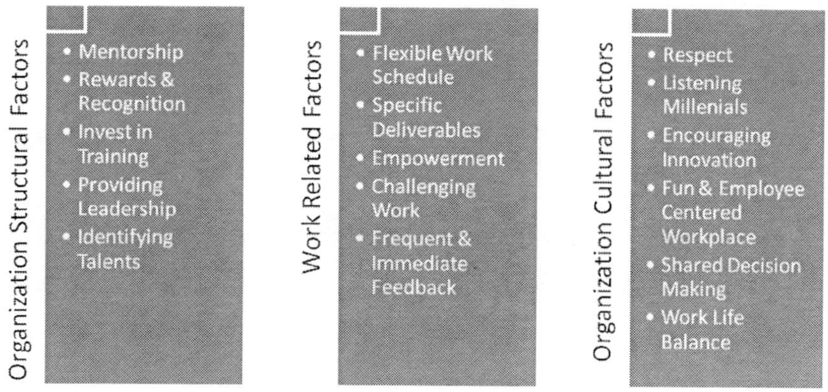

are connected in the same aspect. This year, they launched 'E-Sparsh' which is a comprehensive online query and grievance management system. This system is a one-stop-shop for all queries related to employee concerns which allows prompts attention to any employee query by ensuring it's just one click away.

- **Innovation Through People:** Gen Yers are not merely outside-the-box thinkers; they are innovative over-the-wall doers who will not settle for one-size-fits all solutions (Oppel, Wayne).

  Intel India encourages innovation and invests in it through various programs. 'Ideas to reality' (I2R) have been initiated by India Site Management which is looking at exploring the unique market opportunities India offers and tailoring solutions that leverage these needs. The team encourages employees to share their innovative business and technology ideas that are reviewed, funded and incubated by the Site Management. Intel also has an 'Intel Involved' program for employees, which is a dedicated effort at coordinating a variety of employee volunteering initiatives in support of education, environmental stewardship and safety, health and community service.

  To encourage the spirit of innovation, 'Hackathon' and 'Labrats' are competitions that PayPal hosts to filter cutting edge and sponsorable ideas.

- **Mentorship:** Establish mentoring relationships (Tulgan, Bruce). They prefer a casual relationship with their manager. Millennials value mentorship over autocracy, and they can be a key ally when relevance is clearly stated (Keif, Malcolm). For millenials, mentoring is the top priority and are very close to Gen Xers (Pekala, Nancy, 2001).

  At Walt Disney Co, everytime MD- Ronnie Screwvala gives solution to CEO, Siddharth Roy Kapoor, it is a little sprinkling of his "No Fixed Time Fixed Place Mentoring" glitter.

  Saugata Gupta, CEO-consumer, Marico has regular skip-level meetings and one-on-ones with his employees when travelling. The theory is simple. Guide them, advise them and in the process, get to know them better.

- **Provide Fun & Employee-centered Workplace:** They want to enjoy their work, make friends at work. Help long-term employees make room for them. Worry if they are not laughing, planning office events, going out to lunch with workmates, etc. (Healthfield, 2011). Create a comfortable, low-stress environment (Tulgan, Bruce).

  Intel's employee care program 'Sparsh' ensures that while we take care of some of the basic needs of employees through our core benefits, we also create an environment of fun and camaraderie." GCPL's 'Just Like That' is an informal platform for employees to celebrate occasions, and 'Monday Mania' is a campaign against Monday morning blues - an initiative aimed towards making the organization a fun place to work. The 'Ambassadors Team' across Monsanto India is the employees-in-action group, responsible for creating a fun and safe workspace environment.

- **Rewards & Recognition:** Reward Gen Yers when they have done a good job. Offer increasing responsibility as a reward for accomplishments (Tulgan, Bruce). In addition to incentives, today's workforce wants praise. "Thank you and you did a great job," goes a long way (Durkin, Dianne, 2007). Gen Yers demand more flexibility, professional freedom and higher rewards (Guthridge, Matthew, Komm, Asmus B., Lawson, Emily)

  Godrej Consumer Products Ltd's 'profit sharing' program is built around the principle of EVA (Economic Value Added) forms unifying glue which stimulates performance through razor like focus on goals.

  To engage with the Gen Y workforce, NetApp introduced a promotional referral program called 'Go For the Green' last year. The program allowed employees to receive a cash bonus for their referrals, and also the opportunity to win cash prizes or various 'environmentally friendly' transportation devices, including a smart car, scooter, or bicycle. They also run quarterly employee referral campaigns with exciting prizes like LCD television, iPhone, home theatre systems and company branded goodies.

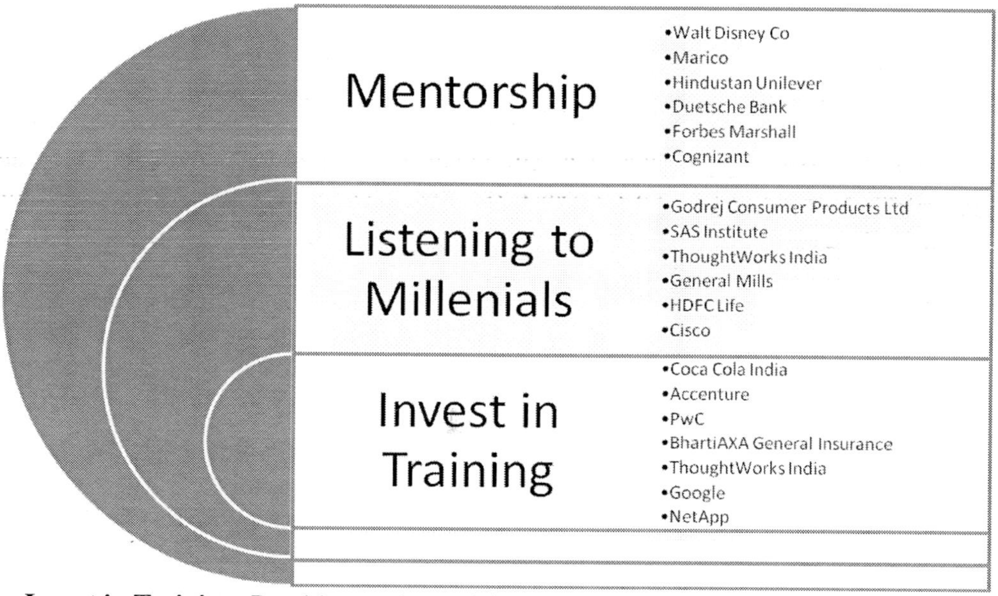

- **Invest in Training:** Provide ongoing training and learning opportunities (Tulgan, Bruce). Coca-Cola India's flagship programme 'Pegasus' develops functional experts each year, thus enhancing their skills, to take on future roles within the company. Spread over seven months, the participants are exposed to several development opportunities; a 360 degree feedback and personalised coaching for individual personal development, academic learning sessions to develop general management skills, collaborative business projects for experiential live learning and importing and exporting learning by replicating best practices.

Under the aegis of the Coca-Cola University, a special program Eagles, helps source fresh young talent ahead of demand, for our franchise bottlers. Spread across six months, the Eagles program includes classroom learning, e-learning, mentoring, coaching & feedback and fieldwork. There are several other training programs conducted by the Coca-Cola University and the Company throughout the year for skill development and capability building.

Monsanto India offers training and development opportunities through cross-functional roles and assignments, it encourages employees to build strong inter-personal relationships and maintain a healthy work-life balance. The vision fosters learning and growth opportunities, spurring innovation to create products, technologies and services that enable its farmer customers to produce more and improve their lives. This excites and engages its employees to do their best and build careers, while making a difference to the society.

- **Shared Decision- Making:** Shared decision making is an expectation of the future workforce that has potential to match well with their values once they've been supported to acquire the essential skills. Millennials have been accustomed to being part of decision making within their families. In an egalitarian way, they believe that good ideas can come from all contributors and that those ideas have equal value and deserve equal consideration (Broom, Catherine). Millenials feel they are indispensable and have high expectation of having the ability to contribute to decisions in their workplace (Kapoor, Camille, Solomon, Nicole)

  Manjunath S. R., Director – HR, NetApp, shares, "Our values and culture allows employees the freedom to express themselves candidly, feel empowered to do things which has a positive impact on the work, participate in decision making, work on state-of-the-art work and innovation, collaborate with people and teams across the globe and getting recognized for their contributions."

- **Providing Leadership & Guidance:** Leaders should harmonize individual employee goals and expertise from each generation with company objectives to ascertain that every worker puts effort into achieving the shared vision and feels responsible for the outcome (Kupperschmidt, 2000). For this purpose, management should display good leadership qualities such as fostering collaboration by communicating both good and bad news, building trust by acting with integrity and respect, and celebrating success with promotions and challenges (Kupperschmidt, 2000). Balance clearly delegated assignments with freedom and flexibility (Tulgan, Bruce). Millennials in particular don't do well with ambiguity or loose instructions. Providing clear expectations will result in clear outcomes and actually be preferred by the employee (Keif, Malcolm). Millennials want to look up to and admire their boss. They want in on the "whole" picture. Teach, coach and give them the best investment of time. They expect a relationship with their boss and are more t rusting of authority figure (Healthfield, 2011).

"Employees, who know what is going on, who feel that they are an integral part of the picture, and who have a goal to strive for, are more likely to be engaged and to stay than employees who are made to feel expendable. Conducting exit interviews also provide insights into the reasons why employees leave," states Chirag Buch, COO & HR Head, Bharti AXA General Insurance.

- **Indentifying Talent:** Spend time getting to know Gen Yer staff members and their capabilities (Tulgan, Bruce). Monsanto India has institutionalized a number of best practices to identify talent. For instance, as a part of 'People Leader Learning Series', all people managers go through an intensive training on recruitment and staffing to help identify skills from talent, performance, and potential.
- **Provide Frequent and Immediate Feedback:** One of the best retention tools to use with employees is honest communication and feedback. The lack of clear and relevant feedback can be a huge source of frustration for employees, and is ranked as one of the primary reasons for leaving a job (Keif, Malcolm). As part of the employee development approach, it is imperative for organizations to establish feedback system (Flowers, William, Hogan, Lance R.). Millenials are used to being assessed and receiving focused feedback (Elam, Carol, Startton, Terry, Gibson, Denise D.)
- **Work-Life Balance:** They do not want to work 80 hours a week and sacrifice their health and their leisure time, even for considerably higher salaries (Sweeney, Richard T). Home, family, children & friends are their life (Healthfield, 2011). Millenials needs to have more time for themselves and less structured lives (Alch, Mark L., 2000). Gen Yers are characterized for placing life over work (Dellwo, Jason C.)

  Qualcomm provides multiple programs and ways to help employees to have a rich and rewarding career. Its comprehensive work/life balance program called QLife offers a blend of activities and services, helping employees achieve balance between their lives at work, at home and in the community.
- **Offer Opportunity and Challenge with Specific Deliverables:** Millennials, with their great desire to make a difference in the world, seek opportunity for growth. If a Millennial seems impatient with the speed of advancement, give him/her responsibility over a small, but significant, project. Ask the individual to develop specific goals, identify deliverables, and set a timeline. This can be as simple as asking a roll tender to explore methods for improving movement of paper. Assigning a mentor can aid in the process, though care should be exercised in finding the right person who understands and can appreciate their differences (Keif, Malcolm). Provide clear & realistic information to potential Nexter employees on what to expect from the job (Johnson & Smith). Millenials believe hardworking and goal setting leads to achievement of their as well as organizational goals (Salahuddin, Mecca M., 2010).

At MakeMyTrip.com, Rookie Award is given to appreciate outstanding contribution made by a new employee.

- **Empowerment:** Make them feel their contribution is important to the company & empowering them by providing them freedom & trust (Johnson & Smith). At Agilent Technologies, employees are empowered to voice their feedback and suggestions.
- **Challenging Work:** Boring is bad. They seek change and challenge; they are looking for the next thing (Healthfield, 2011). Provide challenging work that really matters. Focus on work, but be personable and have a sense of humor (Tulgan, Bruce).

At Agilent Technologies India, there is also an emphasis on providing people an exposure to new jobs and skill-sets through various internal job postings to allow a learning experience. Employees are encouraged to take risk and engage in cross-functional roles for the sake of learning

Authors/ Factors	*Terri Mulkins Manning*	*Healthfield*	*Buckle, Beu, Novicevic, Sigerstad*	*Wayne Oppel*	*John Johnson & Jack Smith*	*Anita Weyland*	*Richard Sweeney*	*Dianne Durkin*	*Bruce Tulgan*	*Malcolm Keif*
Respect	√	x	X	x	√	√	x	x	√	x
Flexible Work Schedule	√	x	√	x	√	√	√	√	√	x
Listening Millenials	x	√	X	√	x	x	x	x	x	x
Creativity	x	x	√	√	x	√	x	x	x	x
Mentorship	x	x	X	x	x	√	x	x	√	√
Fun & Employee-centered Workplace	x	√	√	x	x	√	x	x	√	x
Rewards & Recognition	x	x	X	x	x	√	x	√	√	x
Training	x	x	√	x	x	√	x	√	√	√
Providing Leadership & Guidance	x	√	x	√	x	√	x	x	x	x
Frequent & Immediate Feedback	√	x	√	x	x	x	√	x	√	√
Work- Life Balance	√	√	√	x	√	x	√	√	x	x
Challenging Work	√	√	x	x	x	√	x	x	√	√
Empowerment	x	x	x	x	√	x	x	x	x	x
Specific Goals	x	x	x	x	√	x	x	x	x	√

DISCUSSION & CONCLUSION

In this paper, we analyzed various innovative strategies implemented with organization to engage Generation Y. Generation Y's attitude towards work is quite different from preceding generations. With the influx of Generation Y into workforce, organizations can attain sustainable competitive advantage by devising effective engagement strategies. The paper looked at the various characteristics as well as needs of Millenial generation which are required to be looked into by employer in order to engage them. Organizations that respect their employees, provide challenging work with specific deliverables, greater flexibility, fun and employee-centered work environment, supportive leadership and guidance, encourage continuous learning and listen to their employees are more likely to engage Generation Y.

REFERENCES

[1] Stuart, A, & Lyons, S. (2008), Millennials in the workplace – Understanding and capitalizing on the connected generation

[2] Healthfield, S. (2011), Managing Millenials

[3] Alch, Mark L, The Echo-Boom Generation: A Growing Force in American Society

[4] Manning, Terri Mulkins, What the Under 30 Generation Wants in the Workforce: What Employers

[5] Buckley, M. Ronald, Beu, Danielle S., Novicevic, Milorad M., Sigerstad, Thomas D., Managing Generation NeXt: Individual and Organizational Perspective

[6] Oppel, Wayne, Generational Diversity: The Future of the American Workforce

[7] Johnson, John & Smith, Jack, Generations in the Workforce

[8] Sweeney, Richard, Millennial Behaviors & Demographics

[9] Kupperschmidt BR (2000), Multigenerational employees: strategies for effective management

[10] Elam, Dr. Carol, Stratton, Dr. Terry & Gibson, Denise D., Welcoming a New Generation to College: The Millennial Students

[11] Durkin, Dianne, Recruiting & Retaining Generations X & Y

[12] R Zemke, C Raines, B Filipczak (2000), Generations at Work: Managing the clash of veterans, boomers, xers and nexters in your workplace.

[13] Salahuddin, Mecca M., Generational Differences Impact on Leadership Style And Organizational Success

[14] Dellwo, Jason C. (2007), Four Generations to Train: Seniors, Boomers, Xers, and Nexters Coming Together

[15] Guthridge, Matthew, Komm, Asmus B. and Lawson, Emily, Making Talent a Strategic Priority

16] Hewlett, Sylvia Ann, Sherbin, Laura, Sumberg, Karen, How Gen Y & Boomers Will Reshape Your Agenda

[17] Keif, Malcolm, Recruiting Gen X and Millennial Employees to Grow Your Business

[18] Flowers, William, Hogan, R. Lance, Employee Development Approach for Generation Yers: A Conceptual Framework

[19] Pekala, Nancy, Conquering the Generational Divide

[20] Schawbel, Dan, Why Companies Are Having Gen Y Retention Problems

[21] Broom, Catherine, Entice, engage, endure: adapting evidence-based retention strategies to a new generation of nurses

[22] Thompson, Nicholas W. (2011), Managing the Millenials: Employee Retention Strategies for Generation Y

[23] "Great Places to Work 2012"

[24] Weyland, Anita (2011), Engagement and talent management of Gen Y

[25] Kapoor, Camille, Solomon, Nicole (2011), Understanding and managing generational differences in the workplace

Changing the Game: Generation Y

Vijita Agarwal and Rajesh Sharma

University School of Management Studies, Guru Govind Singh Indraprastha University, Delhi

ABSTRACT

They're smart. They're suave. They're rational. They're confident and they are taking the world by storm. Generation Y have established that they are the new change, the new beginning.

Generation Y includes those individuals who were born roughly between 1981-2002. (Jazmine Boatman, 2011) Generation X was born around1965 to 1980. Narrowed definitions put 'Gen Yers' as those of ages 16 to 27. One of the reasons for the boom in the workforce is Generation Y which has accelerated from 14% to 35% of the total workforce in just over 30 years garnering 32 million workers. (Armour, 2005) Their procession from adolescence to adulthood has made them aware of the changes in the social and cultural landscape. Right to vote, right to consume alcohol, transition from education to employment are some of the changes that describe this procession.

With a positive winning attitude, they always aim to give in 100% in anything they do and strive to fulfil their ambitions in the long run. Recognized by their will to remain independent, and not a burden to their parents, these youngsters write their future with their own hands. They refuse to bow down before any injustice or unfairness, will fight for their rights and respect and are not afraid of challenging the existing status quo.

LITERATURE REVIEW

Generation Y has been studied in different perspectives by practitioners and academicians. Neuborne, E. and Kerwin, K. wrote in Business Week (1999) America's new generation, called Generation Y, Echo Boomers or Millennium Generation, are forcing marketers to rethink their strategies. The brands that were popular with their parents are being rejected by this generation. It is believed that behind the shift in Gen Y labels lies a shift in values on the part of Gen Y consumers. Having grown up in an even more media-saturated, brand-conscious world than their parents, they respond to ads differently, and they prefer to encounter those ads in different places. The marketers that capture Gen Y's attention do so by bringing their messages to the places these kids congregate, whether it's the Internet, a snowboarding tournament, or cable TV.

Peter Sheahan (2002) in his book describes Generation Y as Generation Y consists of the segment of the population born between 1978 and 1994. In this book, the author notes that while Generation Y people are creative and ambitious, they are difficult to manage. His intentions are to provide understanding of the Generation Y mindset and to offer practical solutions for the entire employment cycle, from attracting, motivating, managing, training and retaining Professional staff.

The Scapegoat Generation: America's War on Adolescents authored by Mike A. Males (Males, 1996)

Claims that politicians, private interests, and the media unfairly blame adolescents for social problems, this book explodes various myths about teen pregnancy, violence, and risk behaviors. "Generation Y," suggesting change strategies to reverse attitudes and policy that have abandoned youth, such as reducing child and teen poverty, and reducing age-based laws that unfairly restrict adolescent opportunity, employment, and freedom.

Karen Kueh and Boo Ho Voon in their article Culture and service quality expectations: Evidence from Generation Y consumers in Malaysia (Karen & Boo Ho Voon, 2007)examine the influence of individual-level cultural dimensions on Generation Y consumers' expectations of service quality. This study contributes to the scant research on service quality among Generation Y consumers in developing countries. It also assesses the five-factor structure of the SERVQUAL scale in a new country setting, that is, Malaysia.

Siri Terjesen and Susan Vinnicombe, Cheryl Freeman, (2007) in their article "Attracting Generation Y graduates: Organisational attributes, likelihood to apply and sex differences".

Among university students, the five most important organisational attributes are: "invest heavily in the training and development of their employees" "care about their employees as individuals" "clear opportunities for long-term career progression" "variety in daily work" and "dynamic, forward-looking approach to their business". Sex differences exist in both the importance of organisational attributes and the perceived extent of their presence in three organisations. In describing an ideal employer, women rate eight attributes as more important than do their male counterparts: "really care about their employees as individuals" "variety in your daily work" "friendly, informal culture" "employ people with whom you feel you will have things in common" "use your degree skills" "relatively stress-free working environment" "internationally diverse mix of colleagues" "require you to work standard working hours only". Compared to women, men rate just one attribute as more important: "a very high starting salary". The perception of presence of these important attributes is significantly linked to likelihood to apply.

Information-Seeking Behavior in Generation Y Students: Motivation, Critical Thinking, and Learning Theory by Angela Weiler (2006) who is Instruction Coordinator and Circulation Director has done indepth research in information-seeking behavior, motivation, critical thinking, and learning theory was explored and compared in a search for possible motivating factors behind students' dependence on television and the Internet for their information needs. The research indicates that only a very small percentage of the general population prefer to learn by reading. The students currently on college campuses, as well as those due to arrive in the next few years, have grown up in front of electronic screens: television, movies, video games, computer monitors. It has been said that student critical thinking and other cognitive skills (as well as their physical well-being) are suffering because of the large proportion of time spent in sedentary pastimes, passively absorbing words and images, rather than in reading.

It may be that students' cognitive skills are not fully developing due to ubiquitous electronic information technologies. However, it may also be that academe, and indeed the entire world, is currently in the middle of a massive and wide-ranging shift in the way knowledge is disseminated and learned.

In 2006 Yoon Jin Ma from Department of Family and Consumer Sciences, Illinois State University and Linda S. Niehm, Department of Family and Consumer Sciences, Illinois State University in the paper Service expectations of older generation Y customers: An examination of apparel retail settings highlighted the shopping orientation of Generation Y.

The purpose of this research is to examine the relationship of older Generation Y (Gen Y) customers' (18-27) shopping orientations to their expectations for retail services. It also seeks to assess the importance and impact of service expectations and perceptions on customer satisfaction and loyalty when shopping for apparel in different types of retail outlets.

Susan Gardner and Susanna Eng article What Students Want: Generation Y and the Changing Function of the Academic Library highlights the orientations of Generation Y. This article presents the results of a 2003 undergraduate library user survey as a case study of Generation Y. Survey data support four main traits attributed to Generation Y, which are discussed within the context of library use and satisfaction. Implications for future directions in academic library services based on the new ways Generation Y learn and use the library are explored.

Cathy Bakewell, Vincent-Wayne Mitchell, (2003) "Generation Y female consumer decision-making styles", International Journal of Retail & Distribution Management Points out that

Since environmental factors have influenced Generation Y shoppers (those born after 1977) to make them different from older groups, this study examines the decision making of Adult Female Generation Y consumers using Sproles and Kendall's (1986) Consumer Styles Inventory (CSI). The study uses the CSI as a basis for segmenting Generation Y consumers in to five meaningful and distinct decision-making groups, namely: "recreational quality seekers", "recreational discount seekers", "trend setting loyals", "shopping and fashion uninterested" and "confused time/money conserving". Implications for retailers and marketing practitioners targeting Generation Y consumers are discussed.

OBJECTIVE OF THE STUDY

To study the characteristics of Generation Y.

RESEARCH METHODOLOGY

In this paper I have developed and analyzed two structured-cases which have two main elements: the conceptual framework and the research cycle.

Conceptual Framework

An effective research approach involves prolonged periods in the field collecting huge amount of data. On the other hand, an efficient approach facilitates the researcher's ability to respond in a flexible manner to the themes and insights that emerge from the data. For this paper I have taken elements from both the approaches.

The relevant literature was surveyed which helped in developing the themes of the research and identified gaps in existing research. Literature review helps in formulating a range of ideas, concepts and theories. The researcher's conceptual lens acts as a lter and helps in gleaning the huge range of observations made in the eld. This helped me to clearly understand what territory I need to explore.

Research Cycle

The understanding of the research themes expressed in the Conceptual framework is accumulated through cycles of Research. For this research paper a structured-case research cycle was conceptualized in four stages, which have been adapted from practice-based models of organizational research and action and the incremental process improvement wheel. The four stages are:-

Plan: In this the research design was selected on the basis of concepts and relationships that is formulated in the conceptual framework. At this level I decided what type of cases I should look at and the methods by which I will collect record, process and analyze the data.

Collect Data: In this step the actual work of collecting the data was done. The data is collected and recorded, and is done according to the plan outlined in step-1. I collected the data from both Primary as well as the Secondary sources. Primary sources included long unstructured interviews with the two respondents. Secondary sources included mainly desk research.

Analyse: After the collection of the data, the next step was to analyze it. The two respondents were analyzed on Income/ pocket money spent on different recreational pursuits

Text messaging on mobile phones, Use of mobile phones, Music preferences, Movies preferences, Influencers of Generation Y, Influence of peers, Idea of pragmatism Core values (Clues such as a strong work ethic, respect for authority, loyalty and commitment, financial conservatism, long-term planning, and delayed gratification), Relational Connection, Consumerism experiment importance of money, Idea of Trusted Guidance, Idea of communication.

Reflect: A formal stage of reection, involving deliberate and critical thought, is performed after the data are analyzed. This involved:

Reviewing the research process, such as methods to collect and analyze data.

Evaluating the outcomes of analysis, including assessing emergent themes, challenging current interpretations and seeking conrming evidence for tentative ndings.

Reviewing the structures of structured-case. The inputs to the conceptual framework were re-examined, and the research themes rened.

GENERATION Y ANALYZED

Why Different?

Being from an entire generation altogether, their ideas and thoughts differ to a large extent as compared to their previous generation. Being young, they have different priorities as compared to the older generations. (Barna, 2001) While the older generation is more mature and spend and save money in terms of investment and future, Generation Y spends it generously on parties, food, travel etc. since they have many more years down the lane to save for their future. Another difference is the way they see the world. While the adults are more cautious, more sceptical and wary, the Y youngsters are more care-free and exuberant and do not worry about taking rash decisions since they believe that this is the time to make mistakes and to learn from them. The point is, people operate in different ways due to the difference in their age; however that is not the only differentiating factor. (Coupland, 1991)

The everyday social, economical and political conditions also draw the line. Being nurtured and pampered by technology from a young age has made them tech-savvy and adaptable to any technology within minutes. Their compatibility with technology is why employers choose them over Generation X making Gen Y quicker to respond and more reliable. A perfect example is text messaging. While most adults prefer calling up over messaging, the youngsters prefer instant messaging with their fingers literally fly over the keys typing abbreviations for various words. Armed with blackberries and iPods, Gen Y is online 24x7. (Bansal, 2012) They grew up on the internet and hence know how to launch an endeavour online. An apt example is billionaire Mark Zuckerberg, who launched Facebook from his dorm room.

Expectations and Aspirations

Since they carry out their work at top-notch level, they have high expectations from their employers and want them to recognize their work and give them their due credit without any partiality. Another trait is their need for change. Living in a fast-paced world, they crave new and innovative ways to make their life meaningful, a rationale for their continuous change in careers causing frustration among employers who struggle to retain the talent with increased incentives. They seek out challenges and promise to break them down for solutions and regard colleagues as vast resources to gain knowledge from. They seek to make an important impact from day 1 in their surroundings and they are always eager to learn about new things, whether technology or entertainment. (McCrindle, 2005) Their workplace is where they multi-task best. Juggling emails, messages on blackberry, reaching targets and research is an everyday norm for them. Generation Y seeks attention, but in a healthy way through feedback and guidance. They appreciate being kept in the loop and seek praise and encouragement from mentors who can help direct and develop their young minds and careers. The millennial generation wants real life guidance and not proverbial street directories which show the way to financial and life's achievements. (Sayers, 2011) They want real life role models giving specific directions who not only know and travel the right path, but can show them the way too.

The reduction in the geographical disparity also adds to their advantage and the boon of technology is to be thanked for it. With the vast multitude of information easily accessible over the internet, the data available to a corporate in the Big Apple is also available to a Gen Y'er halfway across the continent, which in turn leads to the development of the weaker countries by their passionate youth.

Working in groups while at school and university, Gen Y has been groomed to function in teams with cooperation and coordination to bring out the required results, giving great value to team work. (Stillman, 2011)Friendship with their co-workers is a strong motivator for them that Gen Y workers will chose a job just to be with their friends.

Gen Y has broken the chains of routine jobs and is now choosing options that test their intelligence and intellectual levels such as marketing, social media, blogging and PCR analysis.

Quality Time

However they are not to be mistaken as workaholics. They know the importance of a personal life and do not let it clash with their professional duty, thus maintaining a work-life balance. These youngsters do realize the significance of quality family and personal time and hence schedule their work accordingly, prioritizing family over work. (McCrindle, 2005)They have their own indulgences to relieve from workload and stress such as partying, music, movies, weekend vacations etc. Though their tastes in music might differ from Generation X, which prefers serene melodies of Bob Dylan and Beatles over death metal and Eminem, Generation Y defend their tunes with an explanation that even rap and metal music give out the same life's philosophies, however with a different and a quirky touch. Another characteristic worth mentioning is their sense of style. They can be smart corporates with crisp outfits and stern looks or the carefree ultra-chic at the party scene. (Great expectations: managing Generation Y, 2011) They prefer wearing flip-flops even to the workplace believing the more comfortable they are, the better they can work! Sometimes there dressing sense at the work place is looked down upon as its too casual, but the youngsters swear by the comfortable attire.

Clash of the Titans

'Gen Yers' refuse to follow hollow traditions and beliefs, in turn earning the wrath of their older generation in the process. However their actions must not be mistaken for disobedience.

They hold their elders with great respect and one of their constant efforts is to make their elders proud of their achievements and to keep them happy and safe. Generation Y opposes to only those beliefs and conventions which are being followed without any rhyme or reason. However they do adjust if it means a lot to their elders. (Generation X and Y: Who They Are and What They Want, 2008) Conflicts between generation X and Y are fairly common and happen almost in every household whether it's the way of working, solving tiffs or finding solutions and sound communication between both is the answer to bridge this gap. Generation Y must understand that they cannot expect the boomers to stay stable in this ever-changing scenario and Gen Y must also respect the older generation's sentiments.

Tech-Savvy Achievers: Generation Y grew up with technology and rely on it to perform their jobs better. Armed with BlackBerrys, laptops, cellphones and other gadgets, Generation Y is plugged-in 24 hours a day, 7 days a week. This generation prefers to communicate through e-mail and text messaging rather than face-to-face contact and prefers webinars and online technology to traditional lecture-based presentations. **:** Nurtured and pampered by parents who did not want to make the mistakes of the Generation X. Generation Y is confident, ambitious and achievement-oriented. They have high expectations of their employers, seek out new challenges and are not afraid to question authority. Generation Y wants meaningful work and a solid learning curve.

Team-Oriented and Attention Seeking: As children, Generation Y participated in team sports, play groups and other group activities. They value teamwork and seek the input and affirmation of others. Part of a no-person-left-behind generation, Generation Y is loyal, committed and wants to be included and involved. Generation Y craves attention in the forms of feedback and guidance. They appreciate being kept in the loop and seek frequent praise and reassurance. Generation Y may benefit greatly from mentors who can help guide and develop their young careers.

CONCLUSION

The fast-track has lost much of its appeal for Generation Y who is willing to trade high pay for fewer billable hours, flexible schedules and a better work/life balance. The previous work driven generations may view this attitude as narcissistic or lacking commitment, discipline and drive, Generation Y legal professionals have a different vision of workplace expectations and prioritize family over work.

While the other generations consider Generation Y as proud, pompous or arrogant, Generation Y begs to differ. They believe that they are not proud, but confident, not arrogant, but following their will to achieve their dreams. They are the new wave of change and development, promising to take the world to the next notch by doing an impeccable job and accepting their responsibilities while simultaneously respecting the older generation and supporting the younger generation Z. Generation Y with its novel ideas and optimistic attitude is here to stay.

REFERENCES

[1] Armour, S. (2005, June 11). *Generation Y: They've arrived at work with a new attitude.* Retrieved from USATODAY.com: http://usatoday30.usatoday.com/money/workplace/2005-11-06-gen-y_x.htm

[2] Angela. (2006). Information Seeking Baehaviour in Generation Y Students:Motivation, Critical Thinking, and Learning Theory. *Journal of Behavioural Sciences* .

[3] Bansal, Y. (2012, March 29). *Reliance on technology makes youth confused.* Retrieved from www.tehelka.com: http://www.tehelka.com/

[4] Coupland, D. (1991). Generation X: tales for an accelerated culture.

[5] Generation X and Y: Who They Are and What They Want. (2008). *Board Matters Newsletters , 8* (3).

[6] *Great expectations: managing Generation Y.* (2011, July). Retrieved from http://www.i-l-m.com

[7] Group, T. B. (2001). *Barna Research Group Teenage Attitude Study.* Retrieved from www.barna.org: http://www.barna.org

[8] G, S., & Eng, S. (2003). What Students Want: Generation Y and the Changing Function of the Academic Library. *International journal of Retail & Distribution Management* , 95-106.

[9] Jazmine Boatman, P. R. (2011). Generation Next, Ready to step up, or step out? *Global Leadership Forecast 2011.*

[10] McCrindle, M. (2005). 'Understanding Generation Y'. *Association of Tertiary Education Management.*

[11] J, Y. (2006). Service expectations of older generation Y customers: An examination of apparel retail settings. *Managing Service Quality* , 620-640.

[12] Kueh, & Voon, B. H. (2007). Culture and service quality expectations: Evidence from Generation Y consumers in Malaysia. *Managing Service Quality* , 656-680.

[13] Males, M. A. (1996). *The Scapegoat Generation: America's War on Adolescents.* Monroe: Common Courage Press.

[14] Neuborne, E., & Kerwin, K. (1999, February 15). Generation Y. *Business Week* , pp. 46-50.

[15] Sheahan, P. (2002). *Generation Y Encoded.*

[16] Sayers, M. (2011). Looking under the Surface of the Millennial Generation. *Christian Research Journal , 34.*

[17] Stillman, J. (2011, June 06). *Want Gen Y to Learn Faster? Combine Technology and Teams.* Retrieved from mindflash: http://www.mindflash.com/blog/2011/06/want-gen-y-to-learn-faster-combine-technology-and-teams/

[18] T, S. (2007). Attracting Generation Y graduates: Organisational attributes, likelihood to apply and sex differences. *Career Development International* , 504-522.

[19] *The challenge of Generation X and Y in PFG's.* (n.d.). Retrieved from passionistfamily: http://www.passionistfamily.org.nz

Inclusive Healthcare – A Sustainable Model for Generation Y

Saswati Tripathi

Ansal University, Gurgaon

ABSTRACT

While identifying reasons for the failure of communication technology to transform the healthcare system and constructing models of better designed technology with socio-technical integration is relatively straight forward, implementing these solutions into the rapidly changing medical world has proven considerably more difficult. From a technologist's perspective, the promise of technology remains powerful. It aims to make a significant contribution to the field of socio-technical approach to design by alluding the audience to this new generation Y phenomenon in healthcare In this paper, I note the current perspective on Indian healthcare, develop a framework for understanding inclusive healthcare business and explain a model of healthcare service provider in India that seeks inclusiveness through proximity followed by a comparison among two other healthcare providers that are focused on delivering quality healthcare at low cost so that services can be afforded by the economically poor. Based on this research I identify three dimensions of inclusive healthcare namely affordability, availability and accessibility.

Since the task of providing healthcare to the poor in India is complex and multidimensional, there is need for a variety of models to emerge that can cater to its various challenges. However, collaboration and partnerships among these various service providers following diverse business models, non- existent at present, can give rise to a robust ecosystem of inclusive healthcare.

INTRODUCTION

The healthcare workforce has grown with the addition of a new group of physicians, nurses, allied health professionals, administrators, and support staff who belong to the youngest generation now in the workforce-generation Y, or the millennials.

The common traits that define or are associated with generation Y workers are often regarded as barriers yet provide healthcare leaders with a clear guide to understanding these employees and drawing out their best qualities and performance. For the organization to fulfill its social contract to provide high-quality, cost-effective, and safe healthcare, it must satisfy the needs and manage the expectations of those who directly deliver these services. This is especially important in today's environment, which is marked by the still-fluid stipulations of the Affordable Care Act (ACA), changed consumer expectations, and public demands for transparency and accountability.

Healthcare as an industry in India has grown to become one of the most promising and progressive sectors in recent times. A variety of factors such as growing population and economy, increasing life expectancy, expanding middle class, higher income levels, rise in incidence of diseases, increased Government outlays and better awareness about health are expected to further the growth. Besides the presence of corporate hospitals, the availability of highly qualified doctors and scientists, their expertise and state-of-art technology have helped India become an attractive destination globally for medical tourists, clinical studies and research and development.

Despite this growth, healthcare delivery and services in India continue to be lacking. India houses 16% of the world population, 21% of the global diseases and the largest burden of communicable diseases in the world, yet its healthcare infrastructure is one of the weakest and not comparable with generation Y with other developing nations.

- For every 1000 Indians there are 0.9 beds; whereas countries such as Russia, China and Brazil have 9.7, 4.1 and 2.4 beds respectively.
- India's current situation of 0.6 physicians per 1000 population is not very encouraging in comparison to BRIC countries and some other South East Asian countries.

Government expenditure in India as a percentage of GDP is also amongst the lowest in the world at 0.9% and as a result, private spending is high – the share of the private sector healthcare spending is the largest among the BRIC countries.

Health insurance – both government sponsored and private – is also minimal. Only 14% of India's population is covered by insurance schemes. This makes affordability of quality healthcare a serious issue given India's low per capita income and sizable population below the poverty line.

The situation is worse for the urban poor and rural population. The growth in the healthcare sector over the last decade has been lop-sided and restricted to largely the private sector, in major metropolitan and urban areas. Only 13% of the rural population has access to a primary healthcare centre and 9.6% to a hospital. Although rural areas house 70% of the Indian population, 80% of India's doctors and 60% of hospitals are located in urban areas. This lack of inclusion with respect to healthcare is, and will continue to be, a huge barrier for India's economic growth.

A Framework for Understanding Inclusive Healthcare

In India, this concept means offering healthcare services to the entire population of nearly 1.2 billion, i.e. including those that are currently excluded from healthcare services. In order to accomplish this, critical challenges of availability, affordability, and quality will need to be addressed in a long-term and sustainable manner.

Inclusive healthcare can drive sustainable development only when everyone has access to adequate healthcare services and this entails addressing questions like:

- Are healthcare services available when and where required?
- Is healthcare affordable for every individual?
- Is the quality of healthcare delivered of acceptable quality?

One possible framework for understanding 'inclusive healthcare' in India focuses on the Availability, Affordability, and Quality of healthcare delivery and services. These form the key pillars that various initiatives must be focused on to drive long-term, sustainable and inclusive growth in healthcare.

Availability

India's challenges with respect to availability of healthcare are multi-fold. They include lack of infrastructure, weak connectivity and lack of resources. With respect to infrastructure, we already know that India has only 0.9 beds per 1000 Indians. But that's not where it ends. Often times, functionality of the available infrastructure are also a huge concern. Connectivity, both physical and virtual, is also an issue. A villager seeking healthcare services in a typical Indian village has to travel about 10 km and spend an entire day to avail care. Finally, India has a dearth of skilled human resources. On average, we have 0.6 physicians per 1000 individuals and the issue is more serious in rural areas where only 20% of the doctors, but 70% of the population reside.

Affordability

Costs of healthcare services in India have been rising for several years. The bulk of these costs are borne by consumers - 74% of all healthcare expenses in India are out of pocket, one of the highest in the world. A very small portion of the Indian population, only 14%, has some kind of health insurance that helps share the burden of these rising costs. Trends such as increasing incidence of diseases, especially lifestyle diseases, and the lack of focus on preventive care clearly indicate that the issue of rising costs will get more acute over the coming years, unless serious measures are taken to curb it.

Inroads into smaller cities by private players; Some private players have begun making forays into Tier II and III cities using differentiated models which allow them to operate at different price points vis-à-vis the big city models.	**Initiatives focused on reducing costs of healthcare services:** low cost or no frills hospitals that are functional and frugal, cost management through bigger and better economies of scale

Quality

The third pillar for driving inclusive healthcare growth focuses on the overall quality of healthcare. Although quality of care rendered in India has improved over the last few decades, it has been inconsistent across providers. Corporate hospitals offer top quality physicians and specialists with state of the art facilities, where as some public hospitals are often not equipped to handle even minor complications.

Inadequate quality of care is often the result of several inter-connected factors.

- Lack of competition in healthcare delivery services in some parts of India, particularly rural areas, reduces incentive to improve quality.
- Poor infrastructure/ overburdening of existing infrastructure and resources due to shortages in supply
- Absence of clearly prescribed national guidelines and standard operating procedures coupled with lack of accountability and monitoring mechanisms perpetuates the problem of poor quality of care.

Poor quality of care further increases the disease burden on an already stretched healthcare system.

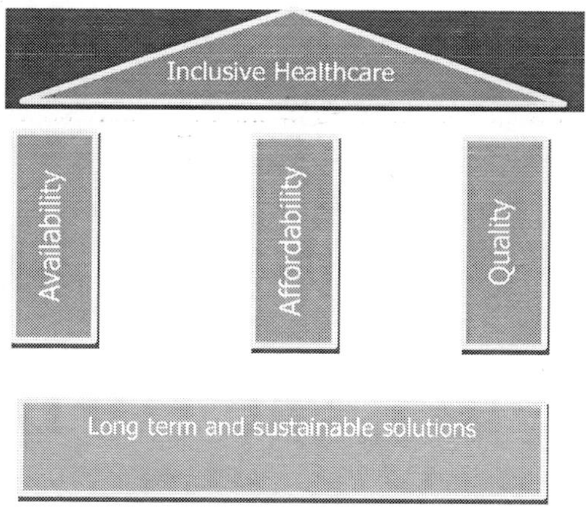

Vaatsalya-Basic Healthcare in Proximity

Dr. Ashwin Naik and Dr. Veerendra Hiremath founded Vaatsalya in 2004 to address the inadequacies of healthcare services in rural and semi urban India. Most private hospitals in India are located in large cities and metropolitans, focusing on tertiary healthcare which is most profitable among healthcare segments. However, tertiary care accounts for roughly 10% of the total healthcare demand in India with primary and secondary healthcare accounting for 60% and 30% respectively. Ashwin and Veerendra realized that in order to address the healthcare needs of the semi urban and rural population, they needed to setup a chain of hospitals so that they can significantly reduce the inconvenience and expenses their patients incur while travelling long distances to get good quality healthcare. Moreover, these hospitals needed to provide such services at low prices since the vast majority of Indian population staying in semi urban and rural India belong to the lower levels of economic strata. However, their biggest challenge in establishing good quality hospitals away from big cities would be to attract high quality medical practitioners to such locations.

Even though there is a large demand of healthcare services in smaller towns and cities, doctors faced great difficulties in establishing their practices because these places lacked the basic infrastructure and technology that doctors would need to deliver their services. If the doctors wanted to practice what they have learnt in medical colleges, they needed to build the healthcare infrastructure from ground up, as well as attract other doctors to create a team that is necessary for addressing basic healthcare needs of the target population. Thus, Ashwin and Veerendra realized that they have to create a doctor centric model if they wanted to realize their objective, since availability of dedicated and high quality doctors was essential for sustaining their hospitals.

Doctor Centricity for Generation Y

At Vaatsalya, doctors are also offered higher designations and positions of responsibility than what they would have had in urban hospitals, they also share greater managerial responsibilities and have significant autonomy in decision making. Vaatsalya makes conscious effort to maintain a flat hierarchy in the organization and retain the entrepreneurial spirit in each of their hospitals by keeping formalization to a minimum and allowing the doctors to be in charge of all operational matters.

Vaatsalya hospitals are located in areas where there is a significant unmet demand for healthcare. A new Vaatsalya hospital breaks even within a period of 12-18 months and has more than 80% capacity utilization in its steady state of operations. Such high demand implies that the average doctor at Vaatsalya hospitals get to treat a lot more patients and conduct many more procedures than what they would have done in an urban private hospital. This not only helps the doctors to develop their expertise rapidly but also gives them the satisfaction of being able to heal more number of patients, thereby creating greater impact through their profession. Thus, Vaatsalya is able to provide careers to its doctors that are financially rewarding, intellectually stimulating and professionally attractive because of the organization culture and the impact that they can create. This is a significant factor that has led to the success and sustainability of their business model so far.

No Frills Low Cost Operations

Vaatsalya caters to population residing in villages and small towns, majority of who are economically poor, having limited means to pay for healthcare, therefore the hospitals make relentless effort to reduce their costs so that they can offer healthcare services at prices that is affordable for their target segment. This is achieved by several means.

First, Vaatsalya standardizes its operation as much as possible. Vaatsalya hospitals have found fifty bed hospitals as most suitable for the kind of places they operate from and offer services in four basic functionalities that can address close to 70% of the primary and secondary healthcare needs of the population. These are Gynecology, Pediatrics, General Medicine and General Surgery. Apart from operation theatre, a basic diagnostic laboratory and intensive care facility, each of the hospitals have a pharmacy attached to them. Vaatsalya charges INR 100-300 per bed per night, while consultancy fees range from INR 25-100, both of which are substantially lower than market rates.

Vaatsalya minimizes capital expenditure by leasing its hospitals rather than buying real estate, thus taking advantage of lower prevailing rents in semi urban locations. The hospitals do not own or operate ambulances and the equipment purchase is kept to the essentials. Bed categories are designed to accommodate equal number of general, private and critical care beds. For example, a typical 50 bed hospital will have 20 beds in general ward, 20 in semi-private and private category and rest in critical care. Operational expenses are minimized by not having complementary facilities such as a cafeteria. Finally, Vaatsalya has centralized all its procurement that has resulted in cost savings of close to 20%.

In many ways, Vaatsalya is a pioneer in the Indian healthcare sector. By means of innovations on multiple fronts they have been able to bring good quality basic healthcare to semi-urban and rural India. They have established a model that is financially viable and scalable. The founders believe that if they are able to attract a dedicated set of medical practitioners as they have done so far, they will be able to setup 50 more hospitals in the next few years that would span across several Indian states, reach out to more than a million patient a year, which would in turn benefit four to five million of the Indian population living in semi urban and rural India.

However, there are other hospitals in India, and interestingly located almost in the same geography (South Indian states of Karnataka and Tamil Nadu) as Vaatsalya, who are able to address the healthcare needs of those at the bottom of the economic strata. I will compare the business models of two such hospitals, Narayana Hrudalaya which provide inclusive cardiac care by driving down costs and leveraging technology i.e. telemedicine and Aravind Eye Hospital which does it by mass servicing of eye care by increasing efficiency, conducting eye camps as a means to create steady demand and creating inclusiveness through cross subsidy.

At a broad level of analysis they might seem to be similar to one another because all of them are focused on driving down cost of operations so that they can reduce the prices of their services, make them affordable for the masses, even while maintaining their financial viability. However, this is where their similarity ends. While each of them can be called a success story, their business models are very different from one another as has been highlighted in the following table. As a consequence the challenges that they face in maintaining their growth are also very different from one another. Providing healthcare to the economically impoverished in India is a multidimensional problem. The price of good quality healthcare services is beyond the reach of a significant segment of the population, there is not enough capacity in hospitals to cater to the healthcare needs of such a large population and the market forces have made majority of the healthcare services focused on the tertiary urban market, located far away from the small towns and villages where more than 700 million Indians live.

Table 1: A Comparison Between the Three Business Models

	Narayana Hrudalaya	*Aravind Eye Hospital*	*Vaatsalya*
Healthcare Domain	Tertiary: Cardiac Care	Tertiary: Eye Care	Primary & Secondary
Key constraint that was overcome	Affordability	Availability	Accessibility
Location	Urban metropolis	Urban	Semi urban
Operating Model	Largely centralized	Largely centralized	Decentralized
Cross Subsidization	60% paying patients subsidize poor patients	40% paying patients subsidize 60% free patients	No cross subsidization
Other Subsidies	Yes, through careful tapping of external sources such as the Government	Yes, e.g., eye camps fully supported by external sponsors. 10% external support	None
Leveraging Technology	High, telemedicine for outreach	Low	Low
Backward integration	Yes, into developing the supply chain of human resources	Yes, into manufacturing of lenses	No
Diversification	High, into neurosurgery, orthopedics, bone marrow transplant (all in tertiary segment)	Limited, other areas of eye care	Selective, e.g., dialysis, physiotherapy, diabetic care

CONCLUSION

Unlike commercial endeavors, there are no easy measures of success for social endeavors such as providing healthcare to the economically impoverished. While I have compared and contrasted the three different models of inclusive healthcare, in the final analysis, there does not seem to be a 'best' model. All three models have their utilities in the niches that they occupy and a country like India needs multiple models of healthcare in generation Y if she is to make her poorest and vulnerable citizens healthy and free of diseases. However, there are possibilities of collaboration and transfer of best practices between these models in generation Y.

The institutions and infrastructure that is necessary to deliver healthcare to the economically weaker sections are poorly developed in India. The number of doctors, medical staff, hospitals as well as physical infrastructure is woefully inadequate to cater to the needs of poor patients who are often located in remote locations of this vast nation. In this generation Y given the complexity and multidimensionality of the problem a variety of activities need to be done by different healthcare service providers if the overall objective of inclusive healthcare is to be achieved. The three business models that I have discussed are fulfilling different needs and none of them can be replaced by another. However, interactions and collaboration between them might contribute further to the effectiveness of the entire system.

REFERENCES

[1] Innovating Around India's Healthcare Challenges; July 29, 2010, India Knowledge @Wharton [http: //knowledge. wharton.upenn.edu/india/article.cfm?articleid=4501]

[2] WHO Health Statistics 2011 Report

[3] Booming Indian Healthcare Industry; May 19, 2011 Overseas Indian Facilitation Centre [http://www.oifc.in/Article/Booming-Indian-healthcare-industry]

[4] "As people became more affluent, the cost of healthcare also kept going up" [http:// business.in.com/interview/magazine-extra/quot;as-people-became-more-affluent-the-cost-of-healthcare-alsokept- going-upquot;/1872/0#ixzz1RyZCnamW]

[5] oikos UNDP Young Scholars development Academy 2010– Growing Inclusive Markets, Inclusive healthcare in India.

About the Healthcare Providers in the Study

- Vaatsalya hospitals – India's first hospital network across Tier II and Tier III towns, currently has fifteen hospitals in Karnataka and Andhra Pradesh. http://www.vaatsalya.com/web/
- Narayana Hrudalaya Cardiac Hospital is a 1000 bedded facility and is situated in Bangalore. It aims to carry out heart bypass surgery at an expense of Rs 1, 00,000.
- http://www.narayanahospitals.com/centers/hospitals/?hid=6
- Aravind Eye Hospital, Madurai Tamil Nadu proves that low cost eye care can be world class. http://www.aravind.org/
- http://www.researchgate.net/publication/ 232227502_Generation_Y_in_healthcare_leading_millennials_in_an_era_of_reform

Designing Training Evaluation Using the Kirkpatrick Model: A Case Study of a Not-for-profit Organization

Abha Kapoor and Manupriya Bali[1]

Apeejay School of Management
[1]Guru Gobind Singh Indraprastha University, Dwarka, Delhi

INTRODUCTION

Training and Development

Training may be defined as the systematic acquisition of skills, rules, concepts, or attitudes that may lead to improved performance of the trainee (Aamodt, 2007; Goldstein and Ford, 2002. Training is an inherent part of an organization's working. New hires need to acquire specific skills and knowledge whereas existing employees need to improve their skills and / or adapt to changing work environment. Effective trainings convey relevant and useful information that inform participants and develop skills and behaviors that can be transferred back to the workplace. Training aims to create an impact that lasts beyond the training program itself. The aim is to create specific plan of action and commitments that focus people's attention on incorporating their new skills and ideas back at work. Training is a process of learning a sequence of programmed behavior. It improves the employee's performance on the current job and prepares them prepares them for an intended job.

The major objective of **development** is managerial effectiveness through a planned, sequential and deliberate process of learning (Toole, 1994). Development not only improves job performance but also brings about change in personality. This provides for a planned growth of managers to meet the future organizational needs.

The fact that efficient and effective training leads to improved productivity is well researched. In view of globalization and consistent changes, investment in training has become inevitable. Thus the role played by training and development can no longer be over-emphasized.

Training can help resolve a variety of manpower problems that work against optimum productivity (Stocking, 1996). Organization-wide, these problems may pertain to :

- Increasing productivity
- Improving the quality of work and raise morale
- Developing new skills, knowledge, understanding and attitudes.

- Developing knowledge of using new tools, machines, processes, programs, methods or modifications thereof.
- Reducing waste, accidents, turnover, absenteeism, and other overhead costs.
- Implementing policies or regulations or changes to them
- Improving performance levels
- Developing replacements, prepare people for advancement, improve manpower deployment and ensure continuity of leadership.

Ensuring the Survival and Growth of the Organization

The training lifecycle involves training need identification (TNI), setting training objectives, determining content, selecting participants, determining schedule, logistical arrangements and facilitator, selecting and preparing audiovisual aids, coordinating the program, and finally evaluating the program

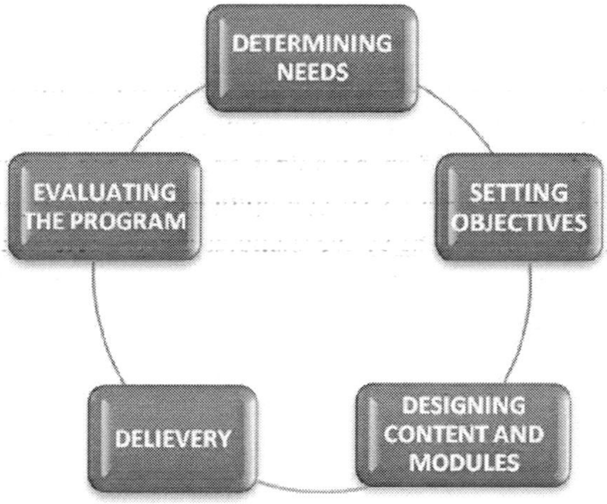

Organizations today invest significantly in training and development with the premise that the programs offer long-term returns for the organization, whether in the form improved profit, productivity, morale, loyalty, or a combination of factors. Whilst these benefits are extremely important to the company, they must be balanced against the resources which need to be used to provide this training. All training has financial costs, and while some costs like the cost incurred towards infrastructure, payment made to facilitator, etc. are obvious, others like the production loss are indirect and some may be hidden. However, all costs must be considered if training costs are to be properly assessed (J. P Pfeffer, 2006). The cost involved in training programs is not only financial but also in terms of time. Therefore, it becomes extremely important to evaluate a training program effectively to identify the areas for improvement or take decision pertaining to its continuity.

Evaluating training programs consume significant valuable time and resources. At times, training programs fail to deliver the expected organizational benefits. A well-structured evaluation process helps to determine where the problem in training lies (D. Kirkpatrick, 1994).

Considering that the business environment, technology, legislation, regulations all are constantly changing, what was a successful training program yesterday may not be so tomorrow (D. Brandenburg, 1982). Being able to measure results will not only help in adapting to such changing circumstances but will enable organizations to design more structured and competency-based training programs.

Thus, training evaluation supports the organization in a number of ways, such as:

- Determine about continuity of a training program
- Improvise training programs to support not only current but future organization requirements
- Determine value of training.

Kirkpatricks's Four-level Training Evaluation Model

Donald Kirkpatrick was the first researcher to develop a coherent evaluation strategy. He initiated his study by describing how training would lead to learning, which would lead to on-the-job application, subsequently leading to desired results. Kirkpatrick developed four-levels of evaluations which are (Kaufman, 1994):

1. Reaction (learners feeling about instruction)
2. Learning (learners performance during training)
3. Behaviour (the extent to which learners implement, or transfer, what they learned in training)
4. Results (organizational benefits, stated in terms of organizational performance or return on investment derived from the training program)

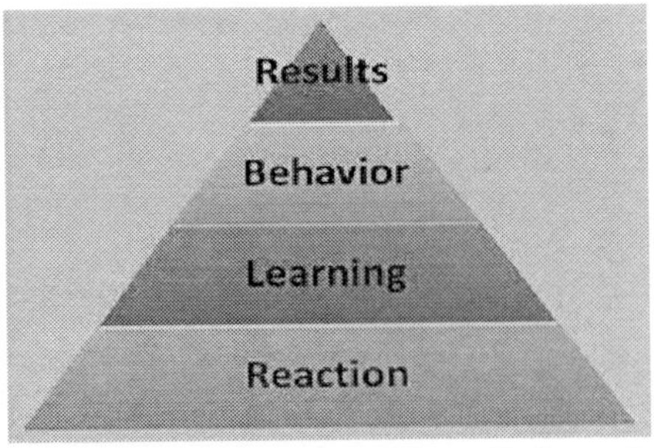

This method is widely known and understood by all those involved in the development and delivery of training, and forms the core of the systematic approach to training. The levels of training evaluation are elaborated as follows:

LEVEL 1: REACTION

This level indicates measuring participants' reaction to the training program. Every organization wants their participants to feel that the training was a valuable experience, and to feel good about the instructor, the topic, the material, its presentation, and the venue. It's important to measure reaction, because it helps to understand how well the training was received by the audience. It also helps to improve the training for future trainees, including identifying important areas or topics that are missing from the training. The participants' reactions must be measured immediately after the program (D. Kirkpatrick, 1994). However, level one evaluation should not just include reactions toward the overall program (e.g., Did you like the program?).

It is important to determine participants' reactions to the training program. Unless participants have positive attitudes toward the training program, learning (Level two outcome) and Behaviour (Level three outcome) are unlikely to occur. Also, reactions are important so as to constantly evaluate the usefulness and effectiveness of training programs. Finally, the measurement of specific aspects of the training program can provide important information about what aspects of the training program can be improved in the future. Level one evaluation broadly offers the following benefits:

- Understand participants' reaction to the training program.
- Identify areas for improvement
- Identify the level of trainees' engagement in the training program.

A detailed level one evaluation can also provide formative evaluation information that can be used to improve future versions of the training program

LEVEL 2: LEARNING

This level involves measuring the effectiveness of a training program. i.e. how much has the knowledge of trainees increased as a result of the training? A training session is planned with specific learning objectives. A training program can be measured in different ways depending on these objectives (I. L Goldstein, 2002). Level two evaluation has the following benefits to organization:

- Help trainers in promoting their training program.
- Help in interpreting the results of level three evaluation (e.g., if level three results do not occur, it may because of workplace factors and not because of any flaw in the training program).
- Detailed level two evaluation can provide formative evaluation information that can be used to improve future versions of the training program.

LEVEL 3: BEHAVIOUR

This level aims to evaluate the level of participants change in on-the-job behavior (OJB), based on the training they received. This level evaluates how the participants apply the information.

The level answers the question about training having a positive effect on job performance. Level three evaluation specifically involves measuring the transfer of knowledge, skills, and behavioral attributes from the training context to the workplace (D. Nixon, 1990). This offers the following advantages to the organization

- Measuring actual behavior on the job, rather than only measuring or demonstrating positive reaction and/or learning. This is important to have actual on-the-job results from the training program.
- Most level three results are intrinsically useful, even if level four outcomes (i.e., final organizational or business results) are never fully demonstrated
- In many situations, evidence of level one, level two, and level three outcomes will be sufficient enough of the merit and usefulness of a training program. This is especially true when all of these provide evidence of positive results of the training program.

LEVEL 4: RESULTS

The goal at this level is to find out if the training program led to final results, especially business results that contribute to the •\bottom line• a . Level four outcomes are not limited return on training investment (ROI). Level four outcomes include other major outcomes that contribute to the functioning of an organization (Plant, 1994).

Some examples of different kinds of level four outcomes:

• Improved quality of work.	• Increased sales.
• Higher productivity.	• Fewer grievances.
• Reduction in turnover.	• Lower absenteeism.
• Improved quality of work life.	• Greater job satisfaction.
• Improved human relations (e.g., improved vertical and horizontal communication)	• Increased profits.

An overview of the four-level model and its focus areas are details below:

Level	*Measurement Focus*	*Questions Addressed*
Reaction	Trainees' perceptions	What did trainees think of this training?
Learning	Knowledge/skills gained	Was there an increase in knowledge or skill level?
Behaviour	Worksite implementation	Is new knowledge/skill being used on the job?
Results	Impact on organization	What effect did the training have on the organization?

Level	*Example*	*Method*	*Implications*	*Method used in NPO*
Reaction	Did the trainees like and enjoy the training? Did they consider the training relevant? Was it a good use of their time? Did they like the venue, the style, timing, domestics, etc? Level of participation. Ease and comfort of experience. Level of effort required to make the most of the learning.	Typically happy sheets'. Feedback forms based on subjective personal reaction to the training experience.	Important to know that people were not upset or disappointed Can be done immediately the training ends. Very easy to obtain reaction feedback Feedback is not expensive to gather or to analyze for groups.	Reaction Questionnaires A. Reaction to the session including its content and design B. Trainer's facilitation and delivery C. Overall administration, facilities and logistics
Learning	Did the trainees learn what was intended in the learning outcomes?	Typically assessments or tests before and after the training. Can include trainer observation in role plays and activities Can include development of action plans	Relatively simple to set up, but more investment and thought required than reaction evaluation. Is easier for training with clear business outcomes like cost savings, service and efficiencies	HOD's/ Manager's Feedback Form

THE DESIGNING

Behaviour	Did the trainees apply their learning when back on the job? Was there noticeable and measurable change in the activity and performance of the trainees when back in their roles? Was the change in behaviour and new level of knowledge sustained? Is the trainee aware of their change in behaviour, knowledge, skill level?	Collect data from trainee and their manager and if necessary co-workers Take the most conservative data to build credibility in evaluation Review implementation of action plans	Behaviour change measurement is more difficult to evaluate and interpret than reaction and learning data Cooperation and skill of observers, typically line-managers, are important factors, and difficult to control.	Participant's Behaviour Questionnaire (180 Degree- Peer1 , Peer 2 & Subordinates)
Results	Measures would typically be business or organizational key performance indicators, such as: Output Cost Quality Time Service feedback	Many of these measures are probably already in place The challenge is to identify which measures and how they relate to the trainee's input and influence and **when** to measure. Important to agree expectations and measures up front with trainees	Assessing individual results can be achieved without too much difficulty Survey techniques can be used where no other data is available Assessing large numbers across the organization is more costly and complicated. If things improved then it was due to the training only.	Individual's Overall Performance Check

BENEFITS TO THE NPO

As many training programs are conducted in the NPO and a huge amount is invested into them, this makes it really important for them to evaluate their programs and analyze the effectiveness of the program.

On the lines of the Kirkpatrick Model and its four level evaluation, an automated software system is under the development phase in the NPO for the training feedback analysis. Questionnaires for the first three levels have been made. The automated software would require only the initial uploading of the questionnaires and the dates that are selected for them to be circulated. The training program manager would only be required to keep the track of the dates and submitting the analysis reports of the training program to the Head of Departments.

Thus, this automated software would help to maintain a cost-benefit analysis for the NPO and thus determine effectiveness of the training program.

CONCLUSION

HR as a profession is deeply concerned about issues of individual and organizational learning, change and success, and how, through its professional roles and activities, it can benefit people and organizations as they pursue various goals and interests. This intrinsic commitment means we have a driving obligation to use HR tools and processes— including the selection and use of evaluation models and frameworks—in a manner that is ethically thoughtful and sound (Reid Bates, 2004).

There is no doubt that Kirkpatrick's model has made valuable contributions to training evaluation thinking and practice. First, the Kirkpatrick model addressed the need of training professionals to understand training evaluation in a systematic way. Second, the four-level model has provided a means for trainers in organizations to couch the results of what they do in business terms. Finally, the popularity of the four-level model is also a function of its potential for simplifying the complex process of training evaluation(D. Kirkpatrick, 1960).

The data can be recorded manually, but it may be prone to errors and may become very tedious for the program manager to every time update and maintain that records. Also, the analysis of the manual data can be very difficult sometimes. With the automated system in place, these limitations can be removed. The automated system would just need the feeding of the data, in terms of employee's and their HOD's email ids. Program Manager needs to mail the questionnaires on timely basis to both of them and the feedback analysis report would be generated automatically. The advantages of this automated system would be:

1. Increased Speed
2. Safety
3. Efficient
4. Adaptable

REFERENCES

[1] Aamodt, M.G. (2007), *Industrial/Organizational Psychology – An Applied Approach*, 5th ed., Thomson Wadsworth, Belmont, CA.

[2] Al-Athari, Ahmad and Zairi, Mohamed (2002), *Training evaluation : an empirical study in Kuwait,* Journal of European Industrial Training, 26/5, pp 241-251

[3] Bates, Reid (2004), *A critical analysis of evaluation practice : the Kirkpatrick model and the principle of beneficence,* Evaluation and Program Planning 27, pp 341-347.

[4] Beets, K., & Goodman, S. (2012). Evaluating a training programme for executive coaches. *SA Journal of Human Resource Management 10*(3), Art. #425, 10 pages

[5] Bramley, P. and Kitson, B. (1994), *Evaluating Training against Business Criteria*, Journal of European Industrial Training, 18(1), pp. 10-14.

[6] Brandenburg, D., *Training Evaluation: What Is the Current Status?*, Training and Development Journal, August 1982.

[7] Digman, *How Companies Evaluate Training Programs*, Human Resource Management, Summer 1980.

[8] Dixon, N., *Evaluation: A Tool for Improving HRD*, University Associates, New York, NY, 1990.

[9] Enkuzena, Signe and Kliedere, Evija, *Management Training Evaluation: A Case Study of a Retail Store Chain*, Journal of Business Management, 2011, No.4

[10] Goldstein, I.L. and Ford, J.K. (2002), *Training in Organizations*, 4th Ed., Thomson Wadsworth, Belmont, CA.

[11] Herman Steensma, Karin Groeneveld, (2010),"Evaluating a training using the "four levels model"", Journal of Workplace Learning, Vol. 22 Iss: 5 pp. 319 – 331.

[12] Jonathan Passmore, Maria Velez, (2012),"SOAP-M: a training evaluation model for HR", Industrial and Commercial Training, Vol. 44 Iss: 6 pp. 315 – 325

[13] Kaufman, R (1994), *Levels of Evaluation: Beyond Kirkpatrick*, February, Harvard Business Review, pp. 34-54.

[14] Kaufman, Roger and Keller, John M., *Levels of Evaluation : Beyond Kirkpatrick,* Human Resource Development Quarterly, Vol, 5. No, 4. Winter 1994 ® Jossey-Bass Publisher.

[15] Kirkpatrick, Jim and Kirkpatrick, Wendy, The Kirkpatrick model : Past, Present and Future, Chief Learning Officer, November 2009

[16] Kirkpatrick, D.L. (1994), *Evaluating Training Programs: The Four Levels*, Berrett-Koehler, San Francisco, CA.

[17] Kirkpatrick, D, 1960, *Techniques for Evaluating Training Programs*, Journal of American Society for Training and Development, Vol 14 Nos 12 & 13.

[18] Kirkpatrick, D, (1959), *Techniques for Evaluating Training Programs*, Journal of American Society for Training and Development, Vol 13 Nos 11-12.

[19] Kolb, D.A. (1976), *The Learning Style Inventory: Technical Manual*, McBer & Co., Boston, MA.

[20] Pfeffer, J. and Sutton, R.I. (2006), *Evidence-based management*, Harvard Business Review, January, pp. 62-74.

[21] R.A. Plant, R.J. Ryan, (1994),"Who Is Evaluating Training?", Journal of European Industrial Training, Vol. 18 Iss: 5 pp. 27 – 30

[22] Raphael, M. and Wagner, E., *Training Surveys Surveyed*, Training and Development Journal, Vol. 26, 1972, pp. 10-14.

[23] Steve Dyer, (1994),"Kirkpatrick's Mirror", Journal of European Industrial Training, Vol. 18 Iss: 5 pp. 31- 32.

[24] Stokking, Karel M., *Levels of Evaluation: Kirkpatrick, Kaufman and Keller, and Beyond*, Human Resource Development Quarterly., Vol. 7. No 2. Summer 1995 O Jossey-Bass Publishers

[28] Warr, P, Bird, M and Rackham, N, (1970), *Evaluation of Management Training*, Gower, London.

Search Engines, the Workplace Lifeline of Gen Y: Ethics and Concerns Involved

Pratika Mishra and Swati Oberoi Dham

School of Management Studies, Ansal University, Gurgaon

ABSTRACT

Marketers today are no more dependent on trade shows consultants, peers or even print magazines for any market related information. It is the age of information sharing, and sharing it through internet. While the above mentioned sources are still important, the World Wide Web is emerging as the last and ultimate source of information. We hear maximum news and details online, if we do get to hear about any news/buyer/seller offline we go online to cross check its presence and genuineness. It is extremely common these days to have a software programmer not remember all the syntaxes, or students to not carry any books to the class or housewife not know her husband's favorite recipe by heart , all you need to do –"Just Google". Google is getting synonyms with search. There are more than 8.4 billion web pages on the World Wide Web which talk about almost every subject under the sun – weather, technology or politics. While this practice leads us into an era of "on a single click" search, it sure brings up various ethical questions to the forefront like:

- *Are these reliable sources of information?*
- *Are these sources being created for the purpose of knowledge sharing?*
- *Are these sources present because of the quality of their content?*

A lot of cases would come to light where the above questions can be answered only with a "NO". The reason behind it is a simple concept of search engine optimization and paid inclusion on the search engines. We all by now are such addicts of the information available online, that at times we are not able differentiate good information from junk. Search engine marketing is one such field which taps on the use and misuse of a search engine. It is the technique, which involves the promotion of websites by increasing their visibility in search engine results pages (SERPs) through optimization (both on-page and off-page) as well as through advertising (paid placements, contextual advertising, and paid inclusions). Depending on the context, SEM can be an umbrella term for various means of marketing a website including search engine optimization (SEO), which adjusts or rewrites website content to achieve a higher ranking in search engine results pages. The objective of this paper is to understand the search engine optimization techniques which are present in today's market, raise and discuss the ethical concerns which come along with them in the course of sustaining global competition in WebPages. It is based on secondary research from various IT Company's databases and reports.

Keywords: *Search Engine, SEM, Workplace Ethics*

INTRODUCTION

The Social media and Search engines has emerged as the most imperious tool in societal communication and information gathering in organizations and corporate employees and has as occupied the central stage in the concomitant prospective. Social Networking is the cohesive and discreet grouping of individuals or organizations who may have common objectives, interests and or activities of free expression. Social Networking facilitates social ties that link individuals who share similar values and beliefs. However Social Networking of today has reached new levels. Its growth and penetration has been prodigious. It has not only shaped the opinions across the globe but has given birth and impetus to many new revolutions. Contemporary media for societal connect, specially print and electronic have been put to notice and are compelled to re-look into their relevance in current perspective. The revolution "Gulf Spring" which shook the roots of those who ruled by fear from decades was possible by a video clip on face book by a fearless class of young connected mind. It remained invisible till it witnessed and generated the "Tahrir Square congregation and communication of gigantic proportion resulting into end of fear. The meaning or definition of Social Networking is still the same but it has acquired a 'New Avatar' and this 'Avatar' has been made possible by the Emergence of the Internet as a 'Communication Facilitator' and free expression of individual vies which has societal connotations. In 2001 Danny Sullivian coined the term "Search Engine Marketing" which covered the spectrum of activities involved in performing Search Engine Optimization, managing paid listings at the search engines, submitting sites to directories, and developing online marketing strategies for businesses, organizations, and individuals. As the number of sites on the Web increased in the mid-to-late 90s, search engines started appearing to help people find information quickly. Search engines developed business models to finance their services, such as pay per click programs offered by Open Text in 1996 and then Goto.com in 1998. By 2007, pay-per-click programs proved to be primary moneymakers for search engines. Search engine optimization consultants expanded their offerings to help businesses learn about and use the advertising opportunities offered by search engines, and new agencies focusing primarily upon marketing and advertising through search engines emerged. The more the information that was present on the web the greater is its scope for optimization.

It has been a major concern of practitioners to foster security related imperatives in the organization both at functional and delivery levels. It has gained recent momentum with the increasing awareness of security threats and there has been lot of studies going on to mitigate risks associated with malicious intents. Howard & Komili (2010) of SophosLabs studied at length the attacks made by BlackHat SEO attackers and how it was used to distribute rogue security products onto user's computers. They also analyzed the malicious SEO kits used by hackers.

Flores (2010) has worked at TrendMicro and brought out the entire progression how the onset of user friendly Google technologies are also cyber crime friendly and help attackers use SEO keywords for malpractices. Golliher (2008) in his paper on Search Engine Ranking

Variables and Algorithms discusses the various search engine-ranking algorithms in an attempt for developers to understand how to increase their visibility on the web. In an attempt to sustain the high competition on the web and duplication of common practices, McGaffin (2008) further highlighted the valuable insights that SEO can bring in terms of revalorization of the whole Marketing paradigm. He emphasizes on the synergy of SEO with public relations, traditional marketing and advertising.

OBJECTIVE OF THE STUDY

The objective of this paper is to understand the use and misuse of search engines at work place, the search engine results optimization techniques which are present in today's market and discuss the ethical concerns which come along with them. The paper dwells upon the idea of the ethical considerations of the Generation Y with respect to the search engine usage at work place.

CONCEPTUAL BACKGROUND

Search engines as the name suggest, work to search all possible pages with the given key word. This search is similar to that of a librarian. Assume you go to a librarian and as for a particular book title, the books in the library would be arranged in some sort of organized manner (alphabetically by title, author, etc) and the librarian would try to match the name suggested by you with all the categories that he/she has. Now a search engine does the same thing, its collection of pages happen to be larger and the technique of organizing these pages is not only more complex but also generated at the run-time. The pages are ranked based on their location frequency of use and presence of keywords. Based on this a huge list based on relevance is created. Search engines will check to see if the searched keywords appear near the top of a web page, such as in the headline or in the first few paragraphs of text. They assume that any page relevant to the topic will mention those words right from the beginning. Frequency is the other major factor in how search engines determine relevancy. A search engine will analyze how often keywords appear in relation to other words in a web page. Those with a higher frequency are often deemed more relevant than other web pages. Other than the above-mentioned factors, every search engine has their own technique of searching and ranking a webpage because of which each search engine has a different output for the search of same set of key words. Nobody does it exactly the same, which is one reason why the same search on different search engines produces different results. To begin with, some search engines index more web pages than others. Some search engines also index web pages more often than others. The result is that no search engine has the exact same collection of web pages to search through. That naturally produces differences, when comparing their results.

Use of Web – Crawlers / Web Spiders

Web crawlers/ spiders sometimes also know as ants, automatic indexers, bots, Web robots or—especially in the FOAF (friend of a friend) community—Web scutters, is a computer program that browse the worldwide web to get the latest up to date information from various WebPages. It can collect information of pages which have come up on the web just 4-6 hours before. A web crawler starts collecting information from the URLs, which are known as seeds. As it moves from one page/URL to another it reads various hyperlinks on each page and keeps an account of all the links. These URLs are recursively visited based on the search engine organizations priority. Based on the information gathered by these crawlers a search engine is able to get updated and latest details of all the WebPages present. An algorithm, different for different search engines, is applied to prioritize all the above mentioned factors and to produce search results relevant to the keyword entered by the user.

Paid Inclusion

It is a search engine marketing model in which a website owner has to pay to the search engine to ensure that the website's name is shown up on search engine result pages. Some search engines, means that their web spiders/ crawlers would visit these paid pages more. There are other search engines which treat paid inclusions differently and label them as advertisements. The fee structure of this paid inclusion is both a filter against superfluous submissions and a revenue generator. Typically, the fee covers an annual subscription for one webpage, which will automatically be calculated on a regular basis. A per-click fee may also apply. Some sites allow only paid inclusion, while many search engines, like Yahoo! mix paid inclusion (per-page and per-click fee) with results from web crawling. Others do not let webmasters pay to be in their search engine listing.

Emergence of the Real Time Web

In January 2009, the plane crash over Hudson River sparked a brand new trend with the help of twitter. It proved that Twitter was far more dominant than any other breaking news channels / models. The first Tweet reporting the plane crash appeared 15 minutes before any news site reported the event. Google's Hot Trends took more than an hour to show keywords related to the said crash. This triggered off the trend of real time web, where social networking sites display and publish statuses, interactions with media etc as *updates* and *blogs* of their users. In fact, performing a Google search on notable and trending events such as Brittany Murphy's death, the Haiti and Chile earthquakes, and even iPad's launch turned up BlackHat SEO pages as results.

Search Engine Optimization (SEO)

Search engine optimization is a defined as a systematic process that helps a website to build the traffic to the website from various search engines. It involves the careful maximization of visibility of corporate websites in the major search engines such as Google, Yahoo, Alta-Vista, Inktomi and many others. It makes a lot of difference between a web site that has very little visibility and one that will be seen and found by millions of people. While this all looks very simple, there is a lot about search engine optimization, which doesn't meet the eye. SEOs are put under two different categories BlackHat SEOs and WhiteHat SEOs.

White Hat SEO

White Hat SEO refers to the usage of SEO strategies; techniques and tactics that focus on a human audience opposed to search engines and completely follow search engine rules and policies. For example, a Web site that is SEO optimized yet focuses on relevancy and organic ranking is considered to be optimized using White Hat SEO practices. Those who intend to make a long-term investment on their Web site more frequently use White Hat SEO and so it is also called Ethical SEO. Some examples of White Hat SEO techniques include:

- **Keywords and Keyword Analysis:** Keyword analysis requires revisions to be made to a Website's pages so that they may rank higher in the search engine. This is "honest" SEO work and involves editing real "honest" web site pages. It is the bread-and-butter of legitimate SEO firms and is the clear winner when it comes to obtaining meaningful and long-lasting rankings.
- **Back Linking: A** back link is a hyperlink that links from a Web page, back to your own Web page or Web site. Also called an **I***n***b***ound* **L***ink* (IBL) these links are important in determining the popularity (or importance) of your Web site. Some search engines, including Google, consider Web sites with more backlink more relevant in search results pages..
- **Man Made Pages: c**ommonly a doorway-like technology (Shadow Page) that is keyword intensive and that if visited should present an honest site page. This is a labor-intensive process where a copy of a real page is made, then that copy is altered to emphasize keywords found on the main page. In some implementations, this page loads the page to be presented into a frameset, and some redirect. This is different from web design where additional content is added to the site and that is intended for human visitors. ANY man made page that is not intended for human visitors, no matter how great the content, is considered Spam by all of the major search engines.
- **Machine Made Pages:** commonly a doorway-like page where the content of the page is derived from other site content based upon keywords and compiled by a software tool. Some implementations generate pages using gibberish or templates that are easily detected by the search engines. This type of tool could literally generate thousands of additional pages in minutes. ANY machine generated page that is not intended for human visitors, no matter how great the content, is considered Spam by all of the major search engines.

- **Cloaking:** this is normally associated with sites doing IP and USER-AGENT serving where the internet server will present a page that will vary based upon the visitor characteristics. This technology is commonly used to present differing content to each search engine or browser, thus a search engine seldom sees the same content that is presented to a browser. It is true that search engines cannot crawl content like java applets and flash movies embedded on a webpage but when a human web surfer views a webpage, flash animations and java applets can create a good impact. Cloaking is used to set flash content display to humans while alternate text will be shown to the search engines. Any cloaked site that filters based upon whether the visitor is a spider or a human, no matter how great the content is considered Spam by all of the major search engines.

Insights into Ethical Concerns for New Generation Employees

Black Hat SEO

Search engine optimization, is now being extensively used by cyber criminals to promote unwanted or malicious sites. SEO has become so big that the term "**Black Hat SEO**" now usually refers to search-engine-optimized pages that lead to malicious sites rather than to the use of Blackhat methods to artificially obtain higher search result ranking. These practices actually provide short-term gains in terms of rankings, but if one is discovered utilizing these spammy techniques on their Web site, they are likely to run the risk of being penalized by search engines.

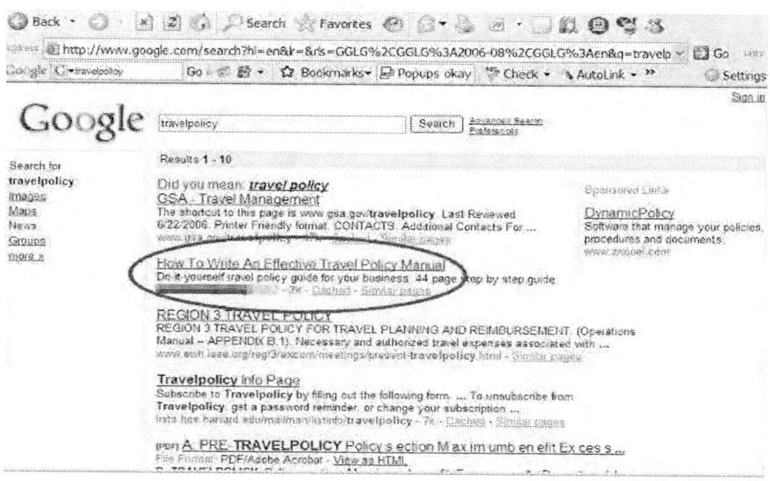

Fig. 1. Google Search for "Travel Policy" Leads to a Malicious Site

Source: Macalintal (2006) *http://blog.trendmicro.com/a-travel-policy-nightmare/* (Retrieved October 2012)

Google Trends

The popularity and user friendliness of Google allows its name to be almost synonyms with online keyword search. In May 2007 Google launched an application called Google Hot Trends, which shared with the web developers the "hottest current searches with the users in very close to real time". This tool, later renamed as Google Trends is made to help users provide insights on what people are searching for, how people are using Google, what are the latest and the hottest searched topics on the web. This helped the webmasters of various websites to build websites that would rate high on any search engine. But this also added an all-new unethical dimension to online search. From November 2007 the malicious use of SEO techniques started to sprout. All the cybercriminals by now were getting a hang of how Google or any other search engine works. This was the time when, the security industry was taken aback by the discovery of several dozen domains that hosted doorway pages stuffed with keywords specifically designed for BlackHat SEO attacks. This campaign, however, did not just stop at keyword stuffing to increase a malicious page's ranking. The cybercriminals behind it also spammed malicious links that led to doorway pages in several online forums and/or bulletin boards in order to further improve the malicious sites' ranking by way of backlinks. To ensure that the users that arrive on doorway pages do so via *Google,* BlackHat SEO pages performed a referrer check. In addition, these doorway pages also disallow *inurl:* and *site:* queries, as these advanced *Google* queries are commonly used by security researchers to look for malicious

Heath ledger. Heath ledger michelle williams picture and heath ledger roar with heath ledger gay

heath ledger 10 things i hate about you and heath ledger life livewire livewires real

Fig. 2: An Example of Keyword Stuffing at the Time of Death of Heather Ledger

Source: Flores (2010). Url: www.trendmicro.com%2Fcloud-content%2Fus%2Fpdfs%2Fsecurity-intelligence%2Fwhite-papers%2Fwp__blackhat-seo-became-big.pdf (Retrieved October 2012)

Around this occasion itself, the cybercriminals behind BlackHat SEO attacks, made one glaring mistake. They used purchased domains to host the BlackHat SEO pages. This would have worked fine for them had they been creating a valid site but they rather used it as a doorway page to lure unsuspecting users to their specially crafted malicious sites. This led to dozens of BlackHat SEO doorway pages being discovered in BlogSpot, a Google-owned free blog-hosting site.

Generation Y and Ethical Considerations

Generation Y (here in after referred to as Gen Y), born between the years 1993 to 2001 is vastly different from previous generations, especially Baby Boomers. They cut their teeth on computer keyboards, and to them, computer technology and the Internet are as natural as breathing (Coates, 2007). This generation has greater exposure to digital technology and promises to change not only the way families interact and communicate, but also how young people relate to school and learning. There is a general presumption that this young generation does not bind themselves much to the established principles of general conduct or even the law in existence even though it is evident that law and ethics serve to channel one's behavior. Awareness about the dimensions of law and ethics that may influence behavior is becoming significantly important among academia, government and the general public. With the growing interest and debate surrounding globalization, no one can underestimate or ignore the crucial role of the perception of ethical behavior of business and of exercising moral judgment (Ahmed, Chung and Eichenseher, 2003). According to Paul (2001), Gen Y has been heralded as the next big generation, an enormously powerful group that has the sheer numbers to transform every life stage it enters. This generation possesses an intuitive sense in understanding technology due to the environment in which they have grown up in and they bring a much more creative and innovative approach to solving problems than any previous generation.

But the internet has also provided the young, techno-literate consumers with a new medium to exploit businesses. There are a few studies that have considered Generation Y consumers' ethical attitudes towards internet – related misdemeanours. Since the internet transcends physical barriers like no other interactive medium before it, aberrant behaviours are multinational. The internet offers advantages of anonymity (allowing them to remain 'faceless'), a reduced chance of being detected owing to the difficulty of procuring damning tangible evidence, and convenience to perpetrators, allowing them to remain at home.

In the current era of globalization in which money is everything, Gen Y has placed unrealistically high expectations towards their chosen careers, thus causing laziness and a lack of ethics, moral values and emotional intelligence amongst the Gen Y that have joined the competitive workforce. As such, other core values such as service, respect and change are often difficult to decipher even though they are hidden way deep inside the heart of this generation (Ginchansky, 2011). According to Hansen (2011), Gen Y possesses poor work ethics as they consider the line between work and life is seamless. In other words, there is no difference between work and life as they are one. Thus, this generation prefers work to be fun and flexible because work is the means to enjoy life. Furthermore, Boyd (2010) affirms that Gen Y sees no manipulative implications in its unethical or unconventional methods because "everybody" engages in these tactics to secure a job. In such a scenario, it becomes imperative for the organizations to take a lot of preventive measures so that there is no misuse of technology in the work place by their young employees. Some of these are listed below.

Preventive Measures

Protect your PageRank: With increased awareness, about the BlackHat SEO techniques, many search engines have come up with a methodology to identify low-quality, spam links which if detected on a page, would not help in increasing the PageRank, but would instead get the page de-indexed or at the very least significantly lower its PageRank. Many organizations are desperately trying to remove low-quality links before they're penalized for them. While black hats used to offer lots of backlinks to your site for a price, now they can offer lots of backlinks to your competitor's site. So instead of using backlinks to boost your PageRank, they can now use it to hurt or eliminate the PageRank of your competitors.

Protecting Your Brand: Organizations need to take steps to protect their brand as much as possible. The first thing to do is evaluate your own SEO tactics. In case required, you can either request your WebMaster to ring down all the BlackHat SEO techniques used, or you can use Google Webmaster Tools to tell Google which links they should disregard when ranking your site. If a competitor does wage an attack against you, you don't want to give them a head start.

Monitoring Your Links: Google Webmaster Tools can be used to monitor the backlinks on a site, include more links if required or highlight if the Webmaster Tools feel that the back links on the page are suspiciously high, giving you a chance to remedy the problem before being penalized. This will give you the best chance to stop and survive a backlink attack in the event a competitor targets you.

Place limits: If search engines start placing limits on the number of keywords/ metatags/ invisible text that can be used it may reduce the problem of BlackHat SEO attacks.

Preserving Your PageRank: Using Webmaster Tools and legitimate, white hat SEO tactics, one can maintain their site's PageRank, even while they are a victim of a negative SEO campaign. As long as one continues to offer the website users a high-quality experience and excellent service on your website, it will be more difficult for a jealous competitor to hurt the brand. It is a choice of quality over quantity.

Privacy Concern for Social Media

- Social media websites using location-based services need to be stringent in terms of privacy.
- Thin Margin between advertising/marketing by companies and privacy intrusion threats.
- The privacy and security legislation ball has already started rolling in 2011, and it's likely to gain even more momentum in 2012. As people increase the amount of information they share on social media websites, the need for heightened security and privacy controls also increases.
- The big giants in the social media world possess a mind-boggling amount of personal information about the people who use their websites. Without good universal guidelines on how this information can be gathered and used, it could be misused, either intentionally or unintentionally.
- Using single access sign-on technology, users can log in once and then use multiple websites without the need to sign in again. Although the convenience of this feature tends to make it popular with users, it brings with it a whole other host of security and privacy concerns
- In 2012, it is likely that many of the smaller and up-and-coming social media websites will merge together so that they are better able to compete with the industry giants. Although websites such as Facebook and LinkedIn are currently the heavy hitters in the social media world, there are also many smaller websites out there.

CONCLUSION

The Social media and search engines has emerged as the most imperious tool in societal communication and has as occupied the central stage in the concomitant prospective. Its emergence is various shapes have given personal space for communication to a young mind in comfort of privacy without sensor of a generation passed by. They judge theme self and interact fearlessly with freedom of any societal barrier. The population of Societal media to day in Indian is estimated to be about 200 million with about 20 million on face book alone. The global population of netizens is estimated to be 500 million which may be the third largest country in world in population term if we factiously believe so. This "country" shares and cares with each other daily without print media. It is its own news editor, reporter, distributor and ombudsman. With generation Y getting addicted to getting all its information from search engines, it is an area of thought and concern as to how we can build it to be a true repository of knowledge and not just and advertising technique. A day at the office is incomplete without a visit to a search engine, whether it is for workplace related information or entertainment based movie review. This whole concept of easy access to information has also lead to easy copying, plagiarism and concerns regarding information property rights. Hence while the Google world is full of knowledge, it is a customized, profitably tweaked version and users need to beware before using such forms of knowledge.

REFERENCES

[1] Benjamin Googins., (*CA Security Advisor Research Blog*. "Blackhat SEO Demystified: Abusing *Google Trends* to Serve Malware." http://community. ca.com/blogs/securityadvisor/archive/2010/01/18/black-hat-seo-campaign-using-latest-trend-keywords-demystified.aspx

[2] The Nielsen Company, *NielsenWire*. "What Americans Do Online: Social Media and Games Dominate Activity." http://blog.nielsen.com/nielsenwire/ online_mobile/what-americans-do-online-social-media-and-games-dominate-activity

[3] Wikimedia Foundation. *Wikipedia*. "Backlink." http://en.wikipedia. org/wiki/Backlink

[4] How to prosper with the new google by Dan Thies, Search Engine Optimization Fast Start. http://www.seoresearchlabs.com/seo-research-labs-google-report.pdf

[5] How Search Engine Optimization Works, by Brian Clifton & Nikki Rae www.advanced-web-metrics.com/docs/search-engine-optimisation.pdf

[6] Top 5 concerns for Social media in 2012 http://www.reputation.com/reputationwatch/articles/top-five-social-media-privacy-concerns-2012

[7] Martin, D., Hailin, W., & Alsaid, A. (2003). Hidden surveillance by web sites: Web bugs in contemporary use. Communications of the ACM, 46 (12), 258-263. Retrieved 21st August 2012 from EBSCO Online Database Academic Search Complete http://search.ebscohost.com/login.aspx?direct=true&db=a9h&AN=25017166&site=ehost-live

[8] Freestone, O. and V.-W. Mitchell (2004) "Generation Y Attitudes Towards E-Ethics and Internet-Related Misbehaviours," *Journal of Business Ethics*, 54, 121-128.

[9] Marshall, K.P (1999). "Has Technology Introduced New Ethical Problems?," *Journal of Business Ethics*, 19, 81-90.

[10] Top 5 concerns for Social media in 2012 http://www.reputation.com/reputationwatch/articles/top-five-social-media-privacy-concerns-2012)

HR Practices for Managing Generation Y: Transformational Insights for 2013

Puja Sareen and Gunjan Mathur

Ansal University, Gurgaon

ABSTRACT

Generation Y, also known as the Millennial Generation, is the demographic cohort following Generation X. There are no precise dates for when Generation Y starts and ends. Commentators' use beginning birth dates from the latter 1970s, or the early 1980s to the early 2000s (decade).

Generation Y is the fastest growing demographic in the workforce. Organizations can no longer ignore them. They have to engage them now or lose out.

Moreover, organizations today are functioning in business environments, which have a lot of uncertainty. The uncertainty is mainly because of the unexpected and unpredictable changes. A number of challenges like pressures to reduce costs, global collaboration, cross cultural working and sensitivities, ability to engage with stakeholders, the constant drive to meet global competitive challenges and opportunities offered by advancements in information technology pose a threat to the new age HR professionals. This problem becomes more acute when business environments are faced with global economic recessions. 2012 has been no different, and 2013 could be an even more challenging year for HR professionals. However, HR professionals are always in a constant flux to predict the future and prepare for it especially when it comes to managing Generation Y.

With so much uncertainty, issues in managing Generation Y and problems surrounding corporate India today, this research paper develops an understanding of current HR Practices and tries to predicts some of the critical upcoming trends and priorities for HR professionals for the year 2013. The paper also analyses the critical HR issues facing the BPO industry today where Generation Y engagement becomes all the more critical!

Keywords: *Generation Y, HR Challenges, Uncertainty, Sustainability*

REVIEW OF LITERATURE

William Strauss and Neil Howe gave their own version of this generation in their book Generations: The History of America's Future, 1584 to 2069 (1991). Howe and Strauss maintain that they use the term Millennials in place of Generation Y because they discovered that members of the generation preferred it. Almost a decade later, they followed their large study of the history of American demographics with a book devoted to the new generation, titled Millennials Rising: The Next Great Generation (2000).

William Strauss and Neil Howe use 1982 as the Millennials' starting birth year. In later writings, they use 2004 as the last Millennial birth year. They believe that the coming of age of year 2000 high school graduates sharply contrasts with those born before them and after them due to the attention they received from the media and what influenced them politically.While managing Generation Y, organizations face a number of other challenges .Technology changes the way we work, the roles we undertake and the interactions through which work gets done. Technology affects HRM to a greater extent because of high degree of interaction between technology and HR. DeFillippi, Verkinderen and Altman (2002) argued that technology facilitates the growth of an enterprise but generates simultaneous problem of "unpluggedness" among a geographically dispersed workforce. Garavan et al. (2008) suggested that technology lies at the heart of manufacturing industry. It provides a series of business advantages. Technological developments alter the context of HR practices and the way they are implemented. Chandrakumara and Sparrow (2004) found that culture has crucial importance in organizations preferences in developing appropriate structure and methods for HR practices affectivity.

Kane and Palmer (1995) opine that external factors affecting HR practices are those pressures on firms that cannot be controlled and changed in a favorable way in the short run. These factors include economic changes. Satow & Wang (1994) found that as a result of development of the global economy, the international dimension of HR practices has become more and more significant.

So, the focus of HR practices has shifted from traditional domains such as internal selection and rewards to concepts such as globalization and international competition.

There are many ways in which companies can gain a competitive edge and effectively engage Generation Y for a lasting and sustained advantage over their competitors, among them being the development of comprehensive human resource practices Jackson et al., (1989), Kane and Palmer (1995), Poole and Jenkins, (1996).

INTRODUCTION

Today, organizations are continuously expanding across a global business environment. Companies have come to view their employees and the human resources systems and practices that support them, as the most important component of securing sustainable competitive advantage. While today's forward-looking organizations are seeking to do more with less, they also are preparing themselves to take full advantage of emerging opportunities. Essential to both goals is the effective use of their workforce investment. Business research shows that high-performance organizations prosper through all economic cycles, due in large part to their ability to leverage and apply the talents of their employees. In the short term, an organization's workforce , today's Generation Y, is critical to its ability to outperform competitors and deliver shareholder value. Over the longer term, skilled and motivated employees provide companies with a distinctive edge that resists imitation. It is now widely accepted that excellence can be achieved by bringing together individual intellectual capacity and the collective business intelligence to predict today what will happen tomorrow. Organizations today are cognizant of the fact that for achieving sustainable competitive advantage, it is imperative that they meet the challenges posed in management of their most valuable asset – People.

As organizations seek to attract, retain and develop the **Generation Y**, they are looking to their HR function to adapt in new ways. They seek better alignment between HR and expectations of Generation Y. The HR professionals need to adapt themselves to such dynamic and ever increasingly competitive environment to attain sustainability in the long run. In a scenario where businesses are also seeking to hold down the costs of the HR function itself, how the HR professionals justify their seat in the Company Boardroom.

'Generation Y' Traits

Tech-Savvy: Generation Y grew up with technology and rely on it to perform their jobs better. Armed with BlackBerrys, laptops, cellphones and other gadgets, Generation Y is plugged-in 24 hours a day, 7 days a week. This generation prefers to communicate through e-mail and text messaging rather than face-to-face contact and prefers webinars and online technology to traditional lecture-based presentations.

Family-Centric: The fast-track has lost much of its appeal for Generation Y who is willing to trade high pay for fewer billable hours, flexible schedules and a better work/life balance. While older generations may view this attitude as narcissistic or lacking commitment, discipline and drive, Generation Y legal professionals have a different vision of workplace expectations and prioritize family over work.

Achievement-Oriented: Nurtured and pampered by parents who did not want to make the mistakes of the previous generations, Generation Y is confident, ambitious and achievement-oriented. They have high expectations of their employers, seek out new challenges and are not afraid to question authority. Generation Y wants meaningful work and a solid learning curve.

Team-Oriented: As children, Generation Y participated in team sports, play groups and other group activities. They value teamwork and seek the input and affirmation of others. Part of a no-person-left-behind generation, Generation Y is loyal, committed and wants to be included and involved.

Attention-Craving: Generation Y craves attention in the forms of feedback and guidance. They appreciate being kept in the loop and seek frequent praise and reassurance. Generation Y may benefit greatly from mentors who can help guide and develop their young careers.

Generation Y is taking over the workplace and it's sooner than organizations think. By 2025, they will comprise 75% of the workforce. In light of this the HR professionals need to assume a proactive role in making the most effective use of their human capital.

Key Challenges for HR Professionals

HR and Technology Integration

Technology and HR have long been at opposite ends but over the years organizations have realized this gap and how an integrated HR & technology function can be a key differentiator for them in today's competitive landscape. Though introducing new technology into the workplace presents both opportunities and challenges, it is now widely accepted that HR Information Systems (HRIS) have the potential to transform HR into a more efficient and strategic function by allowing HR to move beyond simple administrative tasks to strategic applications (Palframan, 2002). Increasingly, HRIS is a norm rather than an exception.

Global Innovation And Knowledge Sharing in HR

As Human Resource Management evolves into an ever-increasing means of competitive advantage for multinational corporations (MNC's) greater importance is being placed on a corporation's ability to manage and share human resource innovations. Knowledge sharing comprises the processes by which the knowledge needed for an organization to succeed is created, captured, shared and utilized. It involves tapping existing knowledge in the organization (both explicit and tacit) and mobilizing it to improve the organizations performance. Knowledge Sharing is also concerned with encouraging individual and organizational learning and innovation, through collaboration where the HR professionals have to play a key role and ensure the creation of a culture of innovation & knowledge sharing in their organization.

Creating a Change Ready Workforce and Employee Engagement

Organizations have long viewed effective change management as a complex and mysterious process that can never be understood or managed effectively. Research has found that companies reporting high engagement levels achieve significantly better results, including 29% higher revenue; they are also 50% more likely to have above-average customer loyalty and are 44% more likely to turn above average profits (Izzo, John B. & Withers). Research has also shown that highly engaged workgroups are 50% more productive and 33% more profitable. Their retention rates are 44% higher and customer loyalty is increased 56%. (Weir, J. HR.com). HR Professionals need to be involved in planning, communication and facilitation of change, as people are not always prepared to successfully cope with change, thwarting the organization's ability to meet objectives. Change is often perceived as threatening and can be distracting and disruptive to your organization's ability to operate efficiently. It is here the role of HR assumes great importance, as it is their responsibility to address behaviors that create obstacles; an agile organization can be trained to handle change, not only as a one-time event, but also on an on-going basis.

Dealing with Virtual Workforce

Virtual teams are a great way to develop, deliver and grow the business. Working remotely can be a dream for professionals. It offers freedom and independence from the daily grind of commuting to work and sitting in a bland cubicle. However, as the virtual workforce grows, so do the managerial headaches. Many employees who work virtually says, they frequently feel isolated and don't know if they're valued by their companies. Others say, they don't feel like they're part of a team. Unlike managing your regular staff, virtual team management and communication require a different approach and mindset altogether. So, HR practices for managing the virtual workforce should be designed around effective communication, regular interactions, formulating a culture of trust & making the best use of technology to manage virtual workforce.

Work Life Balance

As per the HT and Synovate survey, Nov 2010 in Mumbai, maximum number of participants rated work life balance as one of the important features of a job. It is a consciously emerging trend, requiring involvement from different stakeholders (employees, bosses, employers, customers, etc). The success of any such initiative ultimately depends on employee and his/her boss's commitment and HR professionals can play a vital role in this process through a variety of interventions. There has to be clear communication from the HR professionals in any employer branding campaign about the work settings to set realistic expectations from the employee's side.

Organizations, which like to stay ahead of changes in the external world, will have to frequently fine-tune their employee benefits programs. In this direction HR professionals can introduce a variety of options, which can influence the work life balance of the employees. Only when there is a highest degree of coordination between line and HR managers, Work Life Balance (WLB) is possible. Keeping in line with such latest developments, HR managers should frame policies accordingly.

Integrated Talent Acquisition & Talent Management

It is now an essential management practice; what was once solely attached to recruitment now covers a multitude of areas. Talent Acquisition now joins the Talent Management team. There has to be a deep integration of talent acquisition (recruiting and staffing) into the talent management organization. The whole concept of talent management is to integrate the various talent processes in a company to solve problems in a more integrated and powerful way. In 2012, organizations have increasingly understood that talent acquisition belongs in the talent management function. Organizations (like JP Morgan Chase, MasterCard, Time Warner, United Health Group and others) have created a new organization, often called "talent acquisition, development and mobility" – to bring together the disciplines of recruiting and assessment into the areas of training, leadership development and succession management (Bersin & Associates, survey 2011).

For effective Talent Management, HR professionals are engaging themselves in a thorough organizational assessment to identify organizational and department trends; review strategy, challenges, opportunities & prioritize goals, work & projects and find ways to retain critical talent in organization

HRD in Cross Cultural Environment

For HR managers in the knowledge driven economy, managing a young workforce and training them on cross culture issues, has emerged as a strategic differentiator. Increasingly, for Indian companies, which are serving a diverse set of enterprises, spread across different geographies, grooming their staff on some simple and, yet, tricky culture issues, is getting increasingly institutionalized or becoming an expert outsourced option. Managing diversity well provides a distinct advantage in an era when flexibility and creativity are keys to competitiveness. HR professionals need to analyze what policies, practices, and ways of thinking within the organizational culture have differential impact on different groups. They need to focus on what organizational changes should be made to meet the needs of a diverse workforce as well as to maximize the potential of all workers.

HR Issues in BPO Industry

Each sector will have to customize its HR practices and policies to its critical needs to attain long term sustainability in an ever- competitive environment. IT-BPO is the most demanding sector in terms of evolving HR practices and the growth in this sector is tremendous. Also this is the sector where Generation Y comprises the majority of workforce. FY2012 is a year in which the Indian IT-BPO industry weathered uncertainties in the global business environment. Fortunately, this is also the year when this *Young* industry is set to reach a significant milestone – aggregate revenue for FY2012 is expected to cross USD 100 billion. The industry continues to be a net employment generator - expected to add 230,000 jobs in FY2012, thus providing direct employment to about 2.8 million, and indirectly employing 8.9 million people. As a proportion of national GDP, the sector revenues have grown from 1.2 per cent in FY1998 to an estimated 7.5 per cent in FY2012.

"The empires of the future will be the empires of the minds," Winston Churchill said these words in the year 1943. Today, India Inc is religiously following them. Even when sectors of the Indian economy like BPO are either moving towards growth or are at their prime of growth, managing Generation Y still remains a huge challenge for most companies.

When the BPO industry first started gaining traction in India, HR teams had to convince prospective employees' families and friends that the industry would provide strong careers and solid growth prospects. As the industry has matured and employees and their families welcome careers in the BPO industry, HR practices are much more focused on caring for and retaining the employee at the particular stage of employment. HR professionals in this sector need to create the HR policies for Generation Y around the key issues facing them. Some of these include

- Work life balance in a 24/7 environment
- Hiring and Retaining Talent
- Keeping the Generation Y engaged
- Enhancing employee value proposition
- Bringing down the attrition rates
- Breaking the monotony of the job
- Creating career paths and succession plans for employees
- Safety of employee's esp. during pick and drop for night shifts
- Securing data integrity and privacy, client information

Organizations which are proactive with all strategies and action plans in order to meet the above mentioned challenges will be the ones which will not only survive but emerge as winners. IBM is one such organization.

As IBM celebrates its 100th birthday, the company has initiated many strategic changes to put itself through to remain relevant amidst dramatic technological and economic change. However, one of the biggest transformations IBM went through is less about computers and more about culture. It has initiated HR practices and strategies to move away from the analog ways of the past and to embrace a variety of 21st century approaches, including some highly unconventional ones. A first step in changing its HR profile occurred back in the mid-1990s when the company dropped its famous dress code requiring a dark suit and tie in favor of "business casual." Next, the company that grew powerful in the early 20th century largely by manufacturing punch clocks got rid of "badging in" for a substantial portion of its workforce. According to the company, a full 40% percent of IBM's 400,000 global employees now work remotely. IBM has placed new emphasis on the "resources" component of HR in four directions

- First, it emphasizes equitable benefits for all, in all countries, regardless of race, gender, ethnicity, or sexual preference. By extending same-sex partner benefits, IBM earned 100% rating from the Human Rights Campaign and has received similarly high ratings from international women's labor groups.
- Second, the annual Global Pulse Survey gathers feedback from over 40% of the IBM workforce each year, on both workplace conditions and issues and on the community conditions in which IBM workers live. The company emphasizes and rewards volunteer work in its communities.

Last, and perhaps most indicative of the depths of the change at IBM, training has taken on paramount importance. The company invests approximately $1700 per IBM employee to train people to new skill areas needed by the company, including interactive and interpersonal skills.

IBM hallmarks are global teaming, crowd sourcing, mass collaboration, and endeavor-based work (where the company moves employees as needed for short periods of time, to contribute particular skills to a specific project, in the manner of a movie crew). IBM is one of the only manufacturing behemoths of the industrial age to thrive in the digital age and it has done so by redefining its company mission from business machines to global connection, data flows, and interactive human networks. It understands what most businesses — and MBA programs- — are only beginning to understand. Getting rid of the 'punch clock' and the 'sincere tie' are just a starting point.Cathy N. Davidson, (2011) " How IBM is changing HR game, HBR. Blog Posts.

So, to be successful as an interactive global network requires changing your HR game all the way down.

Transformational Insights for HR Professionals in 2013

In 2013, it appears that HR professionals will not only have to reinforce and refocus to become strategic business partners in the organizations but also satisfy their internal clients which mainly comprises of Generation Y.

HR professionals will have to build agility in their systems such that they are prepared to deal with the best and the worst at all times. Organizations will have to focus on getting their *HR metrics* right and making the most out of it to be able to better predict and make informed decisions. While outsourcing does not seem to be a priority, it appears to be catching up and will act as a major cost optimizer in the future. Organizations will have to focus on building their employer brand to attract talent. Compensation alone will not be a good retention tool. Today, employees are looking for greater stability as well as flexibility.

Social Media Policies, Top HR Challenge for 2013

For Generation Y, in many ways, social media has been a gift because it allows them to share and connect with their customers in an unprecedented way. However, it's increasingly becoming a point of contention internally for many companies. The line between what is and isn't appropriate to share online under the company name is becoming blurred. This will also lead to issues around privacy. Too much, is happening too fast with regards to social media and new technologies. Soon HR leaders will have to do find new ways for learning and development to deal with social media issues.

The mobile will take over this function. Mobile learning is a fast rage.

Predictive analytics – will be a new trend and a dominating trend (Matrix and workforce analytics). In a recent survey by BLR, social media policies were identified as the biggest challenge for human resources personnel in 2013.

Strategic Thinkers -Business Partners

2013 will be a year for HR professionals to pull up their sleeves and come up with innovative practices to deal with the challenges that Generation Y poses. It is time for HR professionals to take stock of how well equipped they are to don the role of 'Strategic Thinker ', 'Business Partners and Change Agents'.

Strategic business partner would require a great deal of change in the service offerings of HR as a function and re-orientation of HR professionals. Investing in HR professionals is a mandatory requirement for succeeding. To equip HR professionals, it is imperative that they are sponsored to 'External Training Programs' where in they can interact with expert faculty and gain knowledge. Organizational visit and co-sharing of best practices among peer organizations are a good learning forum.

Creating Opportunities

In the "good old days," when one senior staff member retired, another employee could advance. Financial crisis and recession resulted in more and more postponing retirement. This, coupled with slower business expansion, means fewer opportunities and more dissatisfied employees. Human resource professionals face the challenge in 2013 to create opportunities for their most valuable Generation Y—perhaps through cross training or continuing education, if not through actual advancement.

Managing Labor and Benefit Costs

Most companies consider layoffs a last resort—they trim benefits first and cut staff second. The employees who retain their jobs often end up working harder. This can discourage entire staffs—reducing employee productivity and leading to greater turnover. Unfortunately, economic uncertainty in 2013 may make some employers reluctant to increase staff levels or increase employee benefits.

Everything is changing and changing fast. HR professionals will be faced with a continuing challenge of shortage of talent all round. Business will need more skilled manpower with competencies that can make the business more agile and relevant. The need for competence management will be a great challenge. Being creative continuously and consistently to deal with Generation Y will be another big challenge. IT will change the face of what we do and change fast the systems; processes and may be our thoughts.

Metrics and Technological Systems

HR metrics and HR analytics is the way to go forward. Using HR metrics and analytics to their full potential will turnaround the game in favor of HR. HR metrics will not only help in building the credibility of the HR function, but it will also help HR function to build more sustainable processes and make informed decisions regarding Generation Y.

The newest HR technologies—such as those that measure hours worked more precisely and online portals for collaboration—can help companies curb costs and make optimum hiring choices.

"Technology is a huge enabler of efficiency gains," said Michael Martin, a consultant in the HR effectiveness practice at New York City-based consultancy Mercer. It helps firms improve their HR tech strategies and those without an existing framework construct strategies from scratch.

"Many of them are in the middle of making some big decisions … about buying a new HR information system. They need new talent solutions. They want various types of portals," said Karen Piercy, a principal in Mercer's human capital division. "They're looking for ease of use for their end users."

Organizations "are asking for robust dashboards and analytics capabilities. They're looking for things that are mobile and social, with proper controls built into the system to make sure people can't self-serve in [confidential] areas."

Increasingly, the consultants say, their clients are focused on cultivating HR processes and a workforce whose skills facilitate business goals, whether a company is growing and extending its international reach or recovering from a fiscal slump.

As a way forward, Mercer advises clients to zero in on these essential areas Portal integration that provides ease for employees, whether they're self-servicing around employee benefits or trying to problem-solve on a work project. Self-service that goes beyond access to employee benefits. "Push it out as far as you can," Piercy said. Use technology to record "time and attendance, leaves of absence. … Performance appraisals, career management, pay—all of that is online."

CONCLUSION

With fewer resources and growing needs, organizations need to refocus the HR elements that deliver value, and change or cut elements that don't. While it's true that dwindling resources can act as a catalyst for innovation, it's also true that cuts produce fear, anxiety, and inaction. The challenge for HR is to help build the aspects of the organization that support innovation – trust, the ability to succeed, collaboration, all which are of key concern and interest to Generation Y.

The focus of HR Managers today is on creating HR policies, which are based on openness, equity and consensus. The HR professionals agree with the challenge of creating an organizational climate in which people are willing to work with zeal, initiative and enthusiasm; and which makes *Generation Y feel like winners.* Appreciation and recognition for their outstanding contribution boosts the morale of the employee. Involvement of employees in decisions, asking for their views, suggestions, keeping a continuous and close touch with them is to be kept on priority. To maintain healthy workplace relations requires fair treatment of people and prompt redressal of grievances. To ensure that THIS generation of employees are effectively engaged, HR professionals need to treat people as resources, reward them equitably, and integrate their aspirations with corporate goals through suitable HR policies. *Commitment to quality in all aspects of human resource management will ensure success.*

HR Practitioners should try to refine recruitment and retention strategies using social media, drive new efficiency in existing processes and programs, build a robust business case for workplace wellness, develop the next generation of leaders, use social media to communicate more effectively, motivate younger workers to build their careers in organization, turn diversity into a performance driver, improve change management expertise, engage people and build a robust culture with limited resources, encourage innovation, create a succession plan that will work in different situations and communicate more effectively with the workforce.

Thus, the framework of HR practices in 2013 which focus on Generation Y should be – "Aligned, Connected and Responsive".

REFERENCES

[1] Chandrakumara, A. Sparrow, P. (2004). Exploring Meaning and Values of Work Orientation as an Element of National Culture and Its Impact on HRM Policy- Practice Design Choices, International Journal of Manpower, (6), pp. 364-389.

[2] DeFillippi R.J (2002), "Organisational Models for Collaboration in New Economy", Human Resource Planning, 25(4): 7-18.

[3] Garvan T.N. Wilson, (2008), " Mapping the context and Practice of training Development and HRD in European call Centers, Journal of European Industrial Training, 32, 612-728.

[4] Hoover, Eric (October 11, 2009). "The Millennial Muddle: How stereotyping students became a thriving industry and a bundle of contradictions". *The Chronicle of Higher Education* (The Chronicle of Higher Education, Inc.). Retrieved December 21, 2010.

[5] Howe, Neil; Strauss, William (September 2000). *Millennials Rising: The Next Generation.* New York: Vintage. pp. 3–120.

[6] Izzo, John B. & Withers , P. Values Shift The New Work Ethic & What it Means for Business. Prentice Hall Canada, 2000.

[7] Kane, B. and Palmer, I. (1995), ''Strategic HRM or managing the employment relationship?''International Journal of Manpower, Vol. 16 No. 5, pp. 6-22.

[8] Kochan, T.A., MC Kersie,R.B and Capelli, P.(1984), "Strategic Choice and Industrial Relations Theory ",Industrial Relations ,23:pp. 16-39.

[9] Milkovich,G.T. and Boudereau, J.W. (1991), "Human Resource Management", USA: Richard D.Irwin, Inc.

[10] Palframan, (2002) "HR technology strategies: What is driving them today : executive summary" (Research report)

[11] Poole, M. and Jenkins, G.(1996), "Competitiveness and Human Resource Management Policies", Journal of General Management,Vol.22,No.2,pp.1-19.

[12] "Portrait of the Millennials". *Millennials: A Portrait of Generation Next.* Washington D.C.: Pew Research Center. February 24, 2010.

[13] Schuler R.S.and MacMillan Ian C. (1984), "Gaining Competitive Advantage through Yegneah,", "An Examination of Human Resource Management Practices in Iranian Public Sector", Personnel Review, 37(2):203-221.

[14] Weir, J. HR.com. 2003. Reporting findings of First, Break All the Rules, by Marcus Buckingham and Curt Coffman and Now, Discover Your Strengths, by Marcus Buckingham and Donald Clifton.

[15] Yegneah, H. and Su, Z.(2008), "An Examination of Human Resource Management Practices in Iranian Public Sector", Personnel Review, 37(2):203-221.

[16] Zhong-Ming Wang, Takao Satow, (1994) "The Patterns of Human Resource Management: Eight Cases of Chinese-Japanese Joint Ventures and Two Cases of Wholly Japanese Ventures", Journal of Managerial Psychology, Vol. 9 Iss: 4, pp.12 – 21.

[17] Cathy N. Davidson, (2011) " How IBM is changing HR game HBR. Blog Posts.

Satisfactory Level and Work Life Balance of Women in the Information Technology Sector

Y. Lakshmi Prabha and Gnanasakthi Jagadeesan[1]

Department of Home Science, St. Joseph's College for Women (A), Visakhapatnam, Andhra Pradesh
[1]Department of Family Resource Management, Avinashilingam Institute of Home Science and Higher Education for Women, Coimbatore

ABSTRACT

The problems connected with dual roles of women may be viewed as those of burden of work, interpersonal relations within the family, and of role conflict. Women are more likely than men to bear responsibility for home chores and child care. The very nature of the work in IT sector, coupled with their own built-in beliefs, socialization trends and the widely prevalent stereotypes come in the way of IT women achieving positive work life balance. The satisfaction of women employed in IT and ITeS companies in terms of their work and family life was studied through a survey using a three point Likert scale. There was a significant difference between the two groups with relation to the satisfaction experienced in work and family.

Keywords: *Dual Roles, IT Women, Work, Life, Work Life Balance, Satisfactory Level*

INTRODUCTION

One of the striking features in 21st century India is a phenomenal increase in the number of employed women among the middle classes. While a decade back women chose careers in public sector units, banks and factories, teaching and secretarial work, women today prefer careers in hospitality, airlines, retail, Information Technology enabled Services(ITeS), media and entertainment. The Information Technology industry is perceived to be a women friendly industry. The state of Andhra Pradesh contributes to about 15 per cent of national IT exports. IT sector contributes to about 49.11 per cent of total exports from all sectors in the state. (Government of Andhra Pradesh, 2011). IT career is a dream destination for majority of youth in India today. The attractive pay package and emoluments, comfortable work environment, the prospects of foreign travel and the social prestige associated with the job are all vital factors drawing youth and even mid-career professionals to the IT sector.

The present study was undertaken with the objectives

- to study the socioeconomic characteristics of women employed in the IT sector(IT and ITeS) in Hyderabad, Andhra Pradesh, and
- to assess the overall satisfaction experienced in family life management by women in Information Technology Sector and its implications on their work life balance

The design of the study was descriptive, comprising of quantitative and qualitative data collection and compilation. A three point Likert scale was administered to understand the overall satisfaction experienced by the IT women in work and family spheres.

RESULTS & DISCUSSION: SATISFACTORY LEVEL AND WORK LIFE BALANCE OF IT WOMEN

In the modern home the intelligent use of resources is measured by the satisfaction obtained. The data pertaining to the satisfactory level in work and family arenas, overall satisfaction and work life balance of IT women are presented.

Satisfaction Level of IT Women

The satisfaction level of IT women of both groups is discussed in Table 1

In the work component, women experiencing satisfaction constituted 65 per cent in IT and 56 per cent in ITeS. Twenty three per cent of IT women and 16 per cent of ITeS women were very satisfied. The not satisfied group were more than one tenth in IT and slightly more than one fifth in ITeS. It appears that the women not very satisfied with work component are more in the ITeS sector. Work interfacing with family predicted negative job satisfaction for women adds Komarraju (2006).

The specific issues where the ITeS women were not satisfied were the work environment and pay package. More than 90 per cent of IT women from both groups were satisfied or more satisfied with relationship with co-workers. This reflects the positive team synergy in their work places. While 23.5 per cent of IT and 29 per cent of ITeS women were not satisfied with their time management, more than half of IT women and more than one third of ITeS women were not satisfied with the leisure time available. Nearly 60 per cent of IT women and 54 per cent of ITeS women were not satisfied with time spent on self. Seventy per cent of IT women and 60 per cent of ITeS women were not satisfied with time spent with children. Similarly nearly half of IT and ITeS women were not satisfied with the child care arrangements. Nearly one third and one fourth of IT and ITeS women respectively were not satisfied with the transport arrangements. It emerges that time management and child care were the crucial areas affecting the satisfaction of the IT women.

Table 1: Satisfaction Level of IT Women

Statements	*IT n=200*						*ITeS n=100*					
	Very satisfied		*Satisfied*		*Not Satisfied*		*Very Satisfied*		*Satisfied*		*Not satisfied*	
	No.	%	No.	%	No.	%	No.	%	No.	%	No.	%
Work environment	63	31.5	133	66.5	4	2.0	19	19.0	68	68.0	13	13.0
Relationship with colleagues	66	33.0	123	61.5	11	5.5	23	23.0	71	71.0	6	6.0
Relationship with boss	56	28.0	121	60.5	23	11.5	22	22.0	66	66.0	12	12.0
Pay package	20	10.0	142	71.0	38	19.0	5	5.0	51	51.0	44	44.0
Time management	25	12.5	128	64.0	47	23.5	9	9.0	62	62.0	29	29.0
Availability of leisure time	12	6.0	87	43.5	101	50.5	5	5.0	60	60.0	35	35.0
Time spent on self	9	4.5	72	36.0	119	59.5	3	3.0	43	43.0	54	54.0
Time spent with children	14	7.0	46	23.0	140	70.0	8	8.0	36	36.0	56	56.0
Division of household responsibilities	29	14.5	121	60.5	50	25.0	8	8.0	82	82.0	10	10.0
Child care arrangements (I.T: N.A=12, ITES: NA=15)	11	5.5	67	33.5	98	49.0	5	5.0	33	33.0	47	47.0
Transport arrangements	24	12.0	115	57.5	61	30.5	17	17.0	59	59.0	24	24.0
Working of paid help (I.T: N.A=28, ITES: NA=17)	17	8.5	129	64.5	26	13.0	5	5.0	64	64.0	14	14.0
Relationship with partner	105	52.5	90	45.0	5	2.5	50	50.0	44	44.0	6	6.0
Sexual life with partner	86	43.0	102	51.0	12	6.0	49	49.0	48	48.0	3	3.0
Money management	51	25.5	119	59.5	30	15.0	27	27.0	59	59.0	14	14.0
Financial freedom	63	31.5	113	56.5	24	12.0	33	33.0	56	56.0	11	11.0
Freedom in decision making	64	32.0	107	53.5	29	14.5	36	36.0	59	59.0	5	5.0
Recreational activities	36	18.0	95	47.5	69	34.5	14	14.0	55	55.0	31	31.0
Dietary intake of self	30	15.0	106	53.0	64	32.0	17	17.0	61	61.0	22	22.0
Housing	35	17.5	131	65.5	34	17.0	25	25.0	64	64.0	11	11.0

In the family life component while half of IT women were satisfied, the corresponding segment in ITeS were more than three fourths of the sample. One fifth of women from IT and ITeS groups were very satisfied with family life and nearly 30 per cent of them from IT and ITeS were not satisfied with family life component. It emerges that the ITeS women experienced higher levels of satisfaction in family life than the IT women. This might be so because of the job schedule of the ITeS women which permits them to spend more time during the day at home, since they work in shifts mostly. On the other hand, the IT women are away for most part of the day and hence experience time crunch, which in turn affects their satisfaction levels.

Satisfaction Score in Work

The information pertaining to the satisfaction score in work of IT women versus selected socioeconomic variables is given in Table 2.

Table 2: Satisfaction Score in Work of IT Women

		Group						't' value
		IT			ITeS			
		Mean	S.D	No.	Mean	S.D	No.	
Age	21 - 30 yrs	9.77	1.86	143	9.83	2.18	65	0.21 NS
	31-40 yrs	9.41	1.59	46	10.55	1.79	22	2.641**
	41-50 yrs	7.09	1.64	11	10.92	1.61	13	5.769 **
Education	Diploma/ Intermediate/ITI	-	-	-	10.64	1.74	14	-
	Graduates	10.13	1.94	24	9.9	1.96	40	0.446 NS
	Professional	9.96	1.68	27	10.91	2.27	23	1.697 NS
	Post Graduates	9.4	2.13	50	10	1.62	14	0.977 NS
	P.G Professionals	9.35	1.76	99	8.56	2.24	9	1.271 NS
Designation	Junior level	9.77	1.8	161	10.36	1.98	75	2.265 *
	Middle level	8.67	1.95	30	9.75	1.65	20	2.04 *
	Senior level	8.33	1.87	9	8.2	3.56	5	0.093 NS
Monthly Income	Up to Rs.30000/-	9.86	1.74	151	10.17	2.05	89	1.238 NS
	Rs.30001-60000/-	9.42	1.79	24	9.14	1.95	7	0.349 NS
	Rs.60001-90000/-	8.38	2.14	13	9	0	2	$
	Above Rs.90000/-	7	1.04	12	13	0	2	$
Size of family	Small	9.54	1.86	103	9.98	2.01	60	1.413 NS
	Medium	9.47	1.88	89	10.33	2.16	39	2.282 *
	Large	10.25	2.31	8	11	.	1	$
Age of youngest child	<=2 yrs	9.76	1.86	45	10.75	1.60	12	-1.689 NS
	2-4 yrs	9.93	1.72	44	11.08	1.68	12	-2.069 *
	4-6 yrs	9.96	1.57	28	10.67	1.68	18	-1.438 NS
	6-8 yrs	8.25	2.12	8	10.00	.	1	$
	8-10 yrs	7.56	1.74	9	12.00	1.73	3	$
	> 10 yrs	8.36	1.86	11	10.76	1.89	17	-3.306 **
Total								-2.482 *

*-Significant at 5% level; **-Significant at 1% level; NS-Not significant; $ fewer sample

It is observed that there was a significant difference between the IT and ITeS women with respect to satisfaction in the work arena and it was significant at 1% level in the age range of 31-40 years and 41-50 years. It was significant at 5% level among women at the junior and middle level of hierarchy, among those living in a medium size family and those having a youngest child in the 2-4 years age group. The overall 't' value indicates that there is a significant difference at 5% level between the two groups of women in terms of satisfaction in work. Rani and Rani, (2011) agree that high correlation exists between work task and employee satisfaction with a mediator variable namely work life balance. Reddy, et al. (2010) stress that there is a need to formulate guidelines for the management of work-family-conflicts at organizational level as it is related to job satisfaction and performance of the employees. Work pressures are the most powerful predictors of work family conflict which bears stronger negative relationships with job satisfaction and life satisfaction than does family work conflict (Greenhaus and Parasuraman, 1999).

Satisfaction Score in Family Life of IT Women

The data pertaining to the satisfaction in family life are given in Table 3.

Table 3: Satisfaction Score in Family Life of IT Women

Variables		Group						't' value
		I.T			*ITeS*			
		Mean	*S.D*	*No.*	*Mean*	*S.D*	*No.*	
Age	21 - 30 yrs	28.96	5.24	143	27.58	4.62	65	1.815 NS
	31-40 yrs	28.22	4.40	46	29.00	4.62	22	0.676 NS
	41-50 yrs	26.91	4.28	11	26.08	3.59	13	0.518 NS
Education	Diploma/Intermediate/ITI	-	-	-	29.71	2.89	14	-
	Graduates	28.50	4.33	24	27.90	4.52	40	0.522 NS
	Professional graduate	28.81	5.66	27	27.04	4.40	23	1.220 NS
	Post Graduate (PG)	29.52	5.47	50	29.29	4.36	14	0.147 NS
	Professional PG	28.25	4.76	99	22.89	4.37	9	3.254 **
Designation	Junior level	28.78	4.91	161	28.01	4.68	75	1.129 NS
	Middle level	27.73	5.87	30	27.00	3.63	20	0.498 NS
	Senior level	30.00	3.81	9	25.80	5.85	5	$
Monthly Income	Up to Rs.30000/-	29.00	5.09	151	27.56	4.69	89	2.176 *
	Rs.30001-60000/-	28.04	4.43	24	29.00	3.42	7	0.526 NS
	Rs.60001-90000/-	28.92	5.12	13	26.00	0.00	2	$
	Above Rs.90000/-	25.58	4.38	12	31.00	0.00	2	$
Size of family	Small	28.21	5.22	103	26.95	4.37	60	1.579 NS
	Medium	28.85	4.81	89	28.97	4.59	39	0.132 NS
	Large	32.63	2.39	8	23.00	.	1	$
Age of youngest child	<=2 yrs	30.27	5.40	45	29.17	3.27	12	0.671 NS
	2-4 yrs	29.64	5.17	44	27.58	5.74	12	1.191 NS
	4-6 yrs	30.07	4.13	28	29.39	4.58	18	0.525 NS
	6-8 yrs	24.88	5.44	8	31.00	.	1	$
	8-10 yrs	25.56	4.25	9	34.00	1.73	3	$
	> 10 yrs	28.09	2.98	11	27.18	3.96	17	0.654 NS
Total								1.636 NS

*-Significant at 5% level; **-Significant at 1% level; NS-Not significant, $ fewer sample

The analysis regarding the satisfaction score in family arena between the IT and ITeS women revealed that there was a significant difference at 1% level between the two groups among the women with professional PG degrees. The difference was at 5% level among women with a monthly income of up to Rs.30,000/-. It is observed in the work and family segments that the satisfaction experienced by IT/ITeS women is significantly impacted by the age of the youngest child. This highlights the priority accorded by IT women to their child care and rearing responsibilities and also reflects the typical mind set of a working mother. The overall analysis 't' value revealed that there was no overall significant difference between the two groups. Women continue to spend more time than men on home and family activities, even when they are employed outside the home. The negative relationship between work involvement and family involvement would be stronger for women than men. Women experience more substantial trade-offs between their work and family lives (Greenhaus and Parasuraman, 1999).

Satisfactory Level of IT Women and Work Life Balance

An analysis of the total satisfaction score in both the work and family arenas revealed that the designation, monthly income, stage in family life cycle and strained relationship with spouse contributed to a significant difference in terms of the total satisfaction score at 1% level and total work experience and availability of paid help at 5% level of significance.

It is observed that family factors like strained relationship with spouse, stage in family life cycle and availability of paid help influenced the satisfaction experienced by the IT women. Similarly work factors like the designation and monthly income which define the role and status of an employee also strongly affected the satisfaction of the women. Moreover, the role as an employee is better defined and an established process is laid out to fulfill it and hence the better prospects of achieving greater work role satisfaction. On the other hand, a woman's role in the family is abstract and bereft of any set training and behavioural module to ensure success. This is further impacted by the gender role ideology held by the family members. As a result when the homemaker who is also a career woman strives to achieve satisfaction in work and family spheres she may not succeed equally in both of them and may face work-family-conflict or family-work-conflict. This is supported by the findings of Greenhaus and Parasuraman, (1999) who agree that work and family roles can conflict with one another in some respects and enrich each other in other ways. Work-family linkages can produce conflict or integration. Attitudes that arise within one role may produce similar effect in another role. Positive relationship exists between satisfaction at work and satisfaction at home.

Work life balance is equated with the satisfaction experienced in the two major segments of one's life namely work and family. The overall satisfaction experienced is an apt indicator of the work life balance of an individual. On examining the mean overall satisfaction scores of the IT women it is seen that women in 41-50 years age group, the PG professionals, the ones at the senior level, earning Rs.60,000 and above, living in nuclear families, with 9-12 years work experience and those having paid help had higher scores. It emerges that education,

Table 4: Satisfaction Level IT Women

Variables		*Overall satisfaction score*			*'t' value*	*'F' value*	*Sig.*
		Mean	*S.D*	*No.*			
Group	I.T	38.64	6.40	200	0.073	-	NS
	ITeS	38.69	5.73	100			
Age	21 - 30 yrs	38.33	6.21	208	-	2.362	NS
	31-40 yrs	38.74	6.26	68			
	41-50 yrs	41.21	5.23	24			
Education	Diploma/Intermediate/ITI	37.64	3.08	14	-	0.669	NS
	Graduate	38.42	5.50	64			
	Professional graduate	38.34	6.22	50			
	Post Graduate(PG)	38.09	7.17	64			
	Professional PG	39.40	6.23	108			
Designation	Junior level	38.07	5.88	236	-	5.089	**
	Middle level	40.66	6.50	50			
	Senior level	41.29	7.98	14			
Monthly Income	Up to Rs.30000/-	38.18	6.11	240	-	4.305	**
	Rs.30001-60000/-	39.19	5.53	31			
	Rs.60001-90000/-	40.20	6.30	15			
	Above Rs.90000/-	43.86	6.50	14			
Stage in life cycle	Beginning	40.27	5.70	84	-	8.108	**
	Expanding	37.30	6.26	155			
	Contracting	39.85	5.90	61			
Type of family	Joint	38.10	5.18	87	-	1.408	NS
	Nuclear	39.07	6.70	192			
	Extended	37.14	4.62	21			
Total work experience	< 3 yrs	39.79	7.13	33	-	2.757	*
	3-6 yrs	38.16	6.10	129			
	6-9 yrs	37.64	5.74	74			
	9-12 yrs	40.23	6.05	64			
Work hours per day	6 hrs	38.83	5.19	6	-	0.265	NS
	8 hrs	38.95	6.47	157			
	10 hrs	38.32	6.08	112			
	> 10 hrs	38.24	5.08	25			
Have paid help	Yes	39.09	6.28	241	2.479	-	*
	No	36.88	5.44	59			
Experience strained relationship with spouse	Yes	35.80	5.55	117	6.864	-	**
	No	40.48	5.87	183			
Total		38.65	6.18	300	-	-	-

*-Significant at 5% level; **-Significant at 1% level; NS-Not significant

supportive spousal relationship and availability of adequate support system contribute substantially to work life balance. It may be concluded that women in the later expanding stage of family life cycle are able to balance their work and family life better on account of may be, their experience, access to resources and availability of support system.

Table 4 Projects the Overall Satisfaction Score of IT Women Versus Socio-economic Variables.

The findings on satisfaction score emphasize that eventhough the scores on work segment were not very satisfactory, they did not negatively impact the satisfaction in family arena and also the satisfactory scores in family could have spilled over into the work arena to ensure a comfortable level of work life balance. This finding is corroborated by Muchinsky's (2007) spillover model which explains the relationship between work and family. This model asserts that there is similarity between what occurs in the work environment and the family environment. The model propounds a notion of positive relationship between work and family variables such that an individual's satisfaction with work enhances family life and vice versa.

Kumar and Kumar (2011) hypothise that a balanced life is one where one spreads the energy and effort emotional, intellectual, imaginative, spiritual and physical between key areas of importance. The neglect of one or more areas, may threaten the vitality of the whole.

SUMMARY & CONCLUSION

The satisfaction level of IT and ITeS women revealed that ITeS women expressed higher level of dissatisfaction with work and IT women expressed greater levels of dissatisfaction with family life. It emerges that education, supportive spousal relationship and availability of adequate support system contribute substantially to work life balance.

BIBLIOGRAPHY

[1] Government of Andhra Pradesh (2011), ICT Policy Document, Hyderabad

[2] Greenhaus,J.H., and S. Parasuraman, (1999), Research on Work, Family, and Gender,In Powell.G.N (Ed.), Handbook of Gender and Work, Sage Publications, New Delhi, Pp. 391-412.

[3] Komarraju, M. (2006), Work-Family Conflict and Sources of Support Amongst Malaysian Dual-Career Employees, Asian Academy of Management Journal, Vol. 11, No. 1, January 2006, Pp. 83-96.

[4] Kumar, A.S and P.S.Kumar (2011), A Research Study on Managing Work Life Balance, International Journal of Knowledge and Research in Management and E-Commerce, Vol 1(2).

[5] Muchinsky,P.M. (2007), Psychology Applied to Work, Thomson Wadworth, US, Pp. 345-378.

[6] Rani.S. and K.Selvarani (2011), Work/Life Balance Reflections on Employee Satisfaction Serbian Journal of Management, Vol.6(1), Pp. 85-96.

[7] Reddy.N., M.Vranda, A.Atiq, B.Nirmala and B.S.Ramu (2010), Work-life balance among married women employess, Indian Journal of Psychological Medicine, Vol 32(2), Pp. 112-118.

[8] Upadhya,C. and A.R.Vasavi (2006), Work, Culture and Sociality in the Indian IT Industry: A Sociological Study, School of Social Sciences, National Institute of Advanced Studies, Indian Institute of Science Campus, Banaglore, India.

[9] Upadhya,C. (2006), Gender Issues in the Indian Software Outsourcing Industry, In Gurumurthy.A, P.J.Singh, A.Mundukur & M.Swamy(Eds), Gender in the Information Society: Emerging Issues, UNDP-APDIP ICT4D Series, Elsevier, New Delhi, Pp. 74-84.

Application of Behavioural Finance in Investment Decisions

Ashish Kumar and Sanchita Bansal

School of Management Studies, Guru Gobind Singh Indraprastha University, Delhi

ABSTRACT

Behavioural finance is a new approach which has got evolved in response to the anomalies and imperfections of the financial market in which the investors do not always behave in the rational manner.Behavioural finance is the study of the influenceof psychology on the behaviour of financialpractitioners and finally its impact on the market. It combines behavioral and cognitive psychological theory with conventional economics and finance to provide reasons for why people make irrational financial decisions and what implications such decisions have on market and make the market inefficient. Behavioural finance helps in understanding how an investor interprets and acts on an information totake an investment decision. This paper is an attempt to study the risk aversive nature of investors and relevancy of behavioural finance theory in Indian context.

Keywords: *Behavioural Finance, Loss Aversion, Anchoring, Market Efficiency*

INTRODUCTION

All of us are living in an imperfect world and with the growing imperfections in the financial markets the field of Behavioural Finance is gaining importance. Due to uncertainty in the market regarding investment decisions people became confused and emotions tend to influence their investment decisions. This sometimes results in irrational financial decisions by the investors and which further contributes to the imperfection of the market. Behavioural finance provides explanations to the question why people make irrational financial decisions. Itdemonstrates how emotions and cognitive errorsinfluence investors and the decision-making process.

BEHAVIOURAL FINANCE: MEANING

As a separate field of study it can be stated that 'Behavioural Finance' is the offspring of psychologyand economics. It is the study of the influenceof psychology on the behaviour of financialpractitioners and the subsequent effect on markets (Sherfin, 1999). Itis a fairly new field that pursues to combinebehavioural and cognitive psychological theory withconventional economics and finance to provideexplanations for the irrational financial decisions of investors. It challenges the theory of market efficiency by providing insights into why and how market can be inefficient due to irrationality in human behaviour (Sewell, 2007). Itstudies howinvestors' emotions and psychology affect their investmentdecisions. It makes an attempt to find out how people in general andinvestors in particular make common errors in theirfinancial decisions due to their emotions.

Evolution of Behavioural Finance

The evolution of the behavioural finance as a separate field of study can be attributed to the growing gap between expected and actual returns from the market because of irrational decisions on the part of investors. To recognizesuch fallacies with the intention to avoid them in future and to transformthe quality of decision-making process, slowlya need was felt regarding the impact ofpsychology in investment decisions. All these developments led to the growth of behavioural finance as a separate field of study. The conventional financial theory states that most of the participants in the financial market are wealth maximizers. Nevertheless, there are many occasions where emotion and psychology influence their decisions, instigating them to behave in impulsive or irrational ways. Behavioral finance combines behavioral and cognitive psychological theory with conventional economics and finance to provide reasons for why people make irrational financial decisions and what implications such decisions have on market and make the market inefficient. It is the study of influence of psychology on the behaviour of financial practitioners and its impact on the financial markets. Behavioural finance helps in finding answers to the questions of inefficiency of financial markets, (Sewell, 2001). At the initial stage perpetrators of traditional finance were not willing to accept the view put forth by psychologists. It was only when the evidence of the influence of psychology and emotions on decisions became more convincing, behavioural finance received some acceptance. The award of 2002 Nobel Prize in Economics to psychologist Daniel Kahneman and economist Vernon Smith is the vindication of the field of behavioural finance. It was in 1970s when the researchers began to explorethe field of behavioural finance to understand thepsychological process resulting in such mistakes. In that decade numbers of books werepublished on investors' psychology. The turning point in its development came when in 1979 Amos Tversky and Daniel Kahneman published their work in 'Econometrica'. In their research they criticizedthe "Expected Utility Theory" model and developedtheir own model known as "Prospect Theory" which showed how the people manage risk and uncertainty.After reading "ProspectTheory", Thaler linked the psychological approach towhat he believed were the shortcomings of economictheory—especially regarding the explanation ofirrational behaviour given present economic model.Tversky, Daniel Kahneman and Thaler started tocooperate, resulting in merging of psychology andeconomic and financial theory (M. Sewell, 2007).Among other prominent researchers who contributed to the advancement of behavioural finance and explain many stock marketanomalies and crashes were Shefrin and Statman(1994), Shiller (1995), Shliefer (2000).

REVIEW OF LITERATURE

A large number of studies have been executed to explore the impact of psychological factors on the investment decisions of investors. These studies have empirically identified the influential factors in investment decisions by surveying the behaviour of investors.

Tversky and Kahneman (1973) in their study described three important heuristics namely; representativeness, availability and anchoring which are employed in making judgments under uncertainty. 'A*vailability'* is a judgmental heuristic in which a person evaluates the frequency of classes or the probability of events by availability', i.e. by the ease with which relevant instances come to mind. The reliance on the availability heuristic leads to systematic biases. '*Representativeness'* refers to the tendency to form judgments based on stereotypes. While representativeness may be a good rule of thumb it may lead people astray. E.g. detecting patterns in random data, being overly optimistic about past winners and overly pessimistic about past losers, healthy growth in earnings in the past will be sustained in futures as well whereas in reality it could be by chance as well. *'Anchoring'* means after forming an opinion, people are unwilling to change it, even if relevant new information is available. **Kahneman and Tversky (1979)** in their study described how people frame and value a decision involving uncertainty which is popularly called prospect theory. In this theory they found empirically that people look at choices in terms of potential gains or losses in relation to a specific reference point which in most of the cases is the purchase price. According to this theory, people feel more strongly about the pain from loss than the pleasure from an actual gain. **Thaler (1980)** argues that there are circumstances when consumers act in a manner that is inconsistent with economic theory and he proposes that Kahneman and Tversky's prospect theory be used as the basis for an alternative descriptive theory. In yet another study **Tversky and Kahneman (1981)** introduced framing. They showed that the psychological principles that govern the perception of decision problems and the evaluation of probabilities and outcomes produce predictable shifts of preference when the same problem is framed in different ways. **Shiller (1981)** discovered that stock price volatility is far too high to be attributed to new information about future real dividends. **Fernandez and Rodrik (1991)** model an economy and show how uncertainty regarding the identities of gainers and losers can lead to status quo bias. **Grinblatt, Titman and Wermers (1995)** analysed the behaviour of mutual funds and found evidence of momentum strategies and herding. **Basu (1997)** finds evidence for the conservatism principle, which he interprets as earnings reacting `bad news' more quickly than `good news'. **Camerer and Lovallo (1999)** found experimentally that overconfidence and optimism lead to excessive business entry. **Wermers (1999)** studied herding by mutual fund managers and he found the highest levels in trades of small stocks and in trading by growth-oriented funds. **Meir Statman (1999)** in his study focused on Market efficiency as it is at the center of the battle of standard finance, behavioral finance, and the value of investment professionals. As per him "market efficiency" has two meanings. One meaning is that investors cannot systematically beat the market and the other is that security prices are rational. Rational prices are always based on the practical characteristics, such as risk and ignore value-expressive characteristics, such as sentiment. Behavioral finance has shown, however, that value-expressive characteristics are importantnot only in investor choices but also in asset prices. **Huberman (2001)** provide compelling evidence that people have a propensity to invest in the familiar, while often ignoring the principles of portfolio theory. **Harrison and Rutstrom (2009)** in their study proposed a reconciliation of expected utility theory and prospect theory by using a mixture model. **The Wall Street Journal (2009)** found that where behavioral finance comes in. Most investors are intelligent people, neither irrational nor insane. But behavioral finance tells us we are also normal, with brains that are often full and emotions that are often overflowing and that means we are normal smart at times, and normal stupid at others. **Sahni (2011)**in his study analysed the behaviour of Indian investors and came out with the findings that Indian investors are risk aversive in nature and theory of behavioural finance is equally applicable in India.

OBJECTIVES OF THE STUDY

The present study has been carried out with the objective of studying the relevancy of the theories of behavioural finance in Indian context and risk aversive nature of investors.

Hypotheses of the Study

The study tested the following two hypotheses:

H1: "Investors behaviour remains unchanged in the situations of rise and fall in the price of a share" for checking the loss averseness of Indian Investors.

H2: "Investors' perceptions towards broader stock market do not change even if there is a rise or fall in the stock market for three consecutive days."This hypothesis was developed for assessing the validity of Anchoring on Indian Investors.

RESEARCH METHODOLOGY

The research design for the present study is descriptive in nature. To assess the applicability of behavioural finance a survey of investors has been conducted in the National Capital Region of the country. The relevant information has been obtained from the investors with the help of a structured questionnaire. The sample size for the survey has been restricted to 150 and convenient random sampling has been used for the purpose. For testing the validity of the hypothesis non parametric chi-square test has been used.

RESULTS AND DISCUSSION

Loss Averseness of Indian Investors

Loss aversion means that investors are more sensitive towards the losses in comparison to gains. In other words it means investors are generally interested in reducing the amount of loss rather than expecting to increase their future profit. It can be explained by the propensity of the investors to hold on to a loss making stock while selling winning stocks at an early stage. There is a great degree of asymmetry between the values that people put on gains and losses. Out of 150 respondents 91 have stated that they would like to hold the stock in case of loss whereas 59 respondents have stated their willingness to sell the stock when it is losing. In the case of a gaining stock 103 respondents opted for selling the stocks when it was rising in the market whereas 47 respondents have showed their inclination to hold the stock. (Table 1)

The validity of role aversive nature is checked with the help of Chi-Square Test. The hypothesis being tested is that "Investors behaviour remains unchanged in the situations of rise and fall in the price of a share."

Table 1: Observed Frequency

	Sell Stock Now	*Hold Stock for a Month*	*Total*
Losing Stock	59	91	150
Gaining Stock	103	47	150
	162	138	300

Source: Primary Survey

Table 2: Expected Frequency

	Sell Stock Now	*Hold Stock for a Month*	*Total*
Losing Stock	81	69	150
Gaining Stock	81	69	150
	162	138	300

Source: Author's Calculations

Table 3: Computation of Chi Square

Observed Value (O)	*Expected Value (E)*	*(O-E)*	*$(O-E)^2$*	*$(O-E)^2/E$*
59	81	-22	484	5.975
91	69	22	484	7.014
103	81	22	484	5.975
47	69	-22	484	7.014
			Chi Square Value	25.978*

Source: Author's Calculations

* significant at 5% level

The degree of freedom in this case will be given by {(r-1)*(c-1)}, where r stands for number of rows and c stands for number of columns. Thus degree of freedom will be equal to {(2-1)*(2-1)} = 1. 5% significant level has been chosen for the purpose of testing the hypothesis. At this level the tabular value of $x2$ (Chi-Square) is 3.84. Since, the computed value of $x2$ (Chi-Square) (25.978) is greater than the tabular value, the first hypothesis (H1) is rejected. Therefore the inference may be drawn that there is a difference in investors' behavior when a stock is losing in the market and when it is gaining in the market. The risk aversion in gains leads an investor to sell too quickly into rising stock prices, thereby depressing prices relative to fundamentals. Conversely, risk seeking in losses causes them to hold on too long when prices decline, thereby causing the prices of stocks with negative momentum to overstate fundamental values.

Relevance of Anchoring in Respect to Indian Investors

Anchoring means individuals give more importance to the recent behaviour and give less importance to the long time trend. The anchor is the most recently remembered price. The tendency of the investors to use this anchor results in similarity of stock prices from one day to another. The tendency of past prices to serve as anchors may explain the observed tendency for trends in individual stocks prices to be reversed.

Out of 150 respondents 62 respondents have stated that market can't be predicted on the basis of past prices alone. Therefore their responses have not been considered for testing the second hypothesis. Out of remaining (88) respondents 34 investors believed that there would be a similar trend in case of an uptrend in the market for three consecutive days while 54 believed that it will reverse. Whereas, in the case of a downtrend in the market, 30 respondents believed that downtrend will continue in the market and 58 expected that it would get reversed.

The validity of Anchoring is checked by the Chi-Square Test. The hypothesis being tested is that"Investors' perceptions towards broader stock market do not change even if there is a rise or fall in the stock market for three consecutive days."

Table 4: Observed Frequency

Market Trend	*Increase*	*Decrease*	*Total*
Increase for three days	34	54	88
Decrease for three days	58	30	88
	92	84	176

Source: Primary Survey

Table 5: Observed Frequency

Market Trend	*Increase*	*Decrease*	*Total*
Increase for three days	46	42	88
Decrease for three days	46	42	88
	92	84	176

Source: Author's Calculations

Table 6: Computation of Chi Square

Observed Value (O)	*Expected Value (E)*	*(O-E)*	*$(O-E)^2$*	*$(O-E)^2/E$*
34	46	-12	144	3.130
54	42	12	144	3.429
58	46	12	144	3.130
30	42	-12	144	3.429
			Chi Square Value	13.118*

Source: Author's Calculations

* significant at 5% level

The degree of freedom is {(r-1)*(c-1)}, where r equals to row involved, and c is the no. of columns, so degree of freedom is {(2-1)*(2-1)} or 1. The level of significance chosen is 0.05. On this basis tabular x2 (Chi-Square) is 3.84. Since, the computed x2 (Chi-Square) value is 13.118, the hypothesis is rejected.

Thus, there is a difference in investors' perception when the index of a stock market has consequently increased or decreased for three days in a row, which shows that the anchoring theory is relevant in Indian context.

CONCLUSIONS

The study concludes that most of the investors are risk aversive in nature. They prefer stable returns even if these are moderate. Investors have the tendency to sell the stock whose price is rising at an early stage of growth. In contrast to this they like to hold a stock when it is losing in the anticipation that it will rise in the future. It shows that in case of losses investors are ready to take risk. The study also confirms that anchoring theory is relevant in context of our country as well.

REFERENCES

[1] Basu, Sudipta (1997):"The Conservatism Principle and the Asymmetric Timeliness of Earnings", Journal of Accounting and Economics, 24(1), pp. 3-37.

[2] Camerer, Colin, and Dan Lovallo(1999):"Overconfidence and Excess Entry: An Experimental Approach",The American Economic Review, 89(1), pp. 306-318.

[3] Fernandez, Raquel and Dani Rodrik (1991):"Resistance to Reform: Status Quo Bias in the Presence of Individual-Specific Uncertainty",The American Economic Review, 81(5), pp. 1146-1155.

[4] Grinblatt, Mark, Sheridan Titman and Russ Wermers(1995):"Momentum Investment Strategies, Portfolio Performance, and Herding: A Study of Mutual Fund Behavior",The American Economic Review, 85(5), pp. 1088-1105.

[5] Harrison, Glenn W., and E. Elisabet Rutstrom (2009):"Expected Utility Theory and Prospect Theory: One Wedding and a Decent Funeral", Experimental Economics, 12(2), pp. 133-158.

[6] Huberman Gur (2001):"Familiarity Breeds Investment",The Review of Financial Studies, 14(3), pp. 659-680.

[7] Kahneman, Daniel, and Amos Tversky (1979):"Prospect Theory: An Analysis of Decision under Risk", Econometrica, 47(2), pp. 263-292.

[8] Ritter, Jay R. (2003): "Behavioral Finance", Pacific-Basin Finance Journal, 11(4) pp. 429-437.

[9] Sahni, Deepak (2011): "Behavioural Finance: Testing Applicability on Indian Investors", SSIJMAR, 1(2), pp. 1-12.

[10] Shiller, Robert J. (1981):"Do Stock Prices Move Too Much to be Justified by Subsequent Changes in Dividends?", The American Economic Review, 71(3), pp. 421-436.

[11] Statman, Meir (1999): "Behaviorial Finance: Past Battles and Future Engagements"; Financial Analysts Journal, 54(5), pp. 18-31.

[12] Thaler, Richard (1980):"Toward a Positive Theory of Consumer Choice", Journal of Economic Behavior & Organization, 1(1), pp. 39-60.

[13] Tversky, Amos, and Daniel Kahneman (1973):"Availability: A Heuristic for Judging Frequency and Probability", Cognitive Psychology, 5(2), pp. 207-232.

[14] Tversky, Amos, and Daniel Kahneman (1974):"Judgment under Uncertainty: Heuristics and Biases", Science, 185(4157), pp. 1124-1131.

[15] Tversky, Amos, and Daniel Kahneman (1981):"The Framing of Decisions and the Psychology of Choice", Science, 211(4481), pp. 453-458.

[16] Tversky, Amos, and Daniel Kahneman (1991):"Loss Aversion in Riskless Choice: A Reference-Dependent Model",The Quarterly Journal of Economics, 106(4), pp. 1039-1061.

[17] Tversky, Amos, and Daniel Kahneman (1992):"Advances in Prospect Theory: Cumulative Representation of Uncertainty", Journal of Risk and Uncertainty, 5(4), pp.297-323.

[18] Wermers, Russ (1999):"Mutual Fund Herding and the Impact on Stock Prices",The Journal of Finance, 54(2), pp. 581-622.

Religious Orientation and Entrepreneurial Aspirations: A Study of Generation Y at a Metropolitan University

Anu Singh Lather, Shilpa Jain and Deepti Prakash

School of Management Studies, Guru Gobin Singh Indraprastha University

ABSTRACT

Individuals often cite religious experiences as sources of personal meaning. Numerous studies have examined religiosity as a predictor of health and psychological well-being. This study examines associations between religious orientation of students (generation Y) and their entrepreneurial aspirations. Being an entrepreneur, gives you membership to a special guild of people who share a special religion. Faith in yourself and your actions greatly impact what you achieve as a person and as an entrepreneur. This study aims to bring a relationship between religiosity and entrepreneurial aspirations that today's generation seeks. The results show that females of generation Y are more religious as compared to males. However they do not differ on their entrepreneurial aspirations. Also generation Y coming from commerce, science or humanities background, nuclear, joint or extended families, and business, service or both families does not differ on their religious orientation and entrepreneurial aspirations. The results also show that there is no linkage between religious orientation and propensity of entrepreneurial aspirations.

Keywords: *Religious Orientation, Entrepreneurial Aspiration, Generation Y*

INTRODUCTION

Religion and spirituality are amongst those few important issues which pervade every stage of human development and provides meaning to the mysteries of existence. Religion not only brings out the best in people in the form of mystics, saints, cathedrals, music and literature, but has also been used throughout human existence to rationalize and justify inhumane treatment of others, persecution, intolerance of different belief systems, exploitative labour relations and political systems (Belzen, 1996, p 23). The understanding of the religious orientation of any generation has been the best way to understand a generation in a better fashion. In recent decades there has been an explosion of religious renewals and increasing interest in the experiential aspects of religion. Spiritual inclinations are expressed in various ways, with various motivations, cognitions, perceptions and behaviors. In the past four decades there has been a rise in the study of the interactive effects between religion and various form of health. Religion has often been a variable of interest to researchers who wish to describe and understand the experience of college students. In the past, most such research has focused on religious beliefs and practices (cf. review by Parker, 1971), or has attempted to describe changes in such-beliefs and practices over the course of the college experience (Hasting & Hoge, 1976; Hunsberger, 1978). Most of the studies in this field are majorly focused on relating religiosity to mental health, physical health etc. But since it is associated to the holistic well being, building up of self esteem and individual worth, it might also relate to the entrepreneurial aspirations of an individual which requires all the qualities strengthened by the right religious orientation.

An individual's decision to engage in entrepreneurial activities can be attributed to an expansive spectrum of individual-specific characteristics, ranging from personality attributes, to risk aversion, education, and unemployment. Religious beliefs are usually not associated to economic activities such as entrepreneurship; however, scholars dating back to Adam Smith and Max Weber assert that religion plays a fundamental role in shaping economics. It has been argued that values and attitudes are as much a part of the economy as its institutions and policies. Therefore, the importance of understanding the relationship between religion and an individual's economic decision-making process helps societies unveil potential opportunities for growth and development.

Generation Y will be aged between 27 and 41 years of age in 2020. They will be playing a crucial role in how the future of any country in the world is likely to be shaped. Around the world we have seen a marked change in the lifestyles and expectations of todays over 60s compared to the same generation just several decades ago.

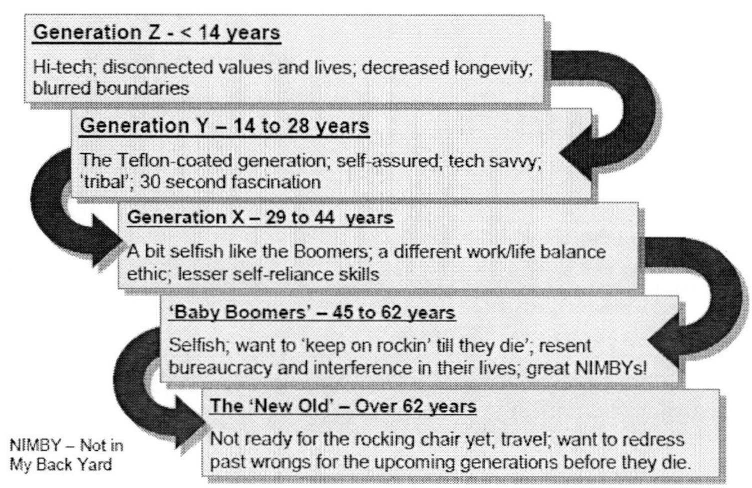

Source: Generation Y & Vision 2020: Harnessing the Innovation Potential NIHERST Global Foresight & Local Context Setting Report September 2007

Interracial and multicultural relationships have increase approximately 10 fold since the 1960s. This factor has contributed to a more open minded generation that is tolerant of differences in race, religion, culture, sexual orientation and economic status. Thus, as entrepreneurs Generation Y is less conservative in adopting change. The first Generation Y entrepreneurs with no existing background in a family business have developed their enterprises from scratch and sought to use new technologies coupled with their own original entrepreneurial thinking. This generation has immense potential to change the world economy!

Since current research on the religious interest of college students is scarce, the present study was undertaken to describe the role of religion in the life of students and their entrepreneurial aspirations at one large metropolitan university.

REVIEW OF LITERATURE

The impact of religion on the development of humanity has long been of interest to social scientists. Religious orientation typically involves discussions of belief systems, and the depth and range of personal, familial, and work related commitment to those systems. A critical theme in this work is Weber's thesis that an ethical rationality derived from religious activities significantly contributes to the development of both modern capitalism and individual economic achievement – a theme commonly folded into the dual notions of worker productivity and social contracts as illustrated by Weber's seminal 1905 work, The Protestant Ethic and the Spirit of Capitalism. Weber, of course, was not only interested in the USA, but also in the broad impact of religious institutions and belief systems on economic activity throughout the world as his less known essays on Hinduism, Confucianism, Taoism, Buddhism, and ancient Judaism illustrate.

Allen and Spilka (1967) agree and describe intrinsic religiosity as "committed religiousness," while Bergin (1991) views intrinsic religiosity as an internalized belief system that is followed "regardless of social pressure." Boadella (1998) sees intrinsic religiosity as the "the basic, simple message at the heart of a religion." It is this "intrinsic" dimension of religious orientation that is typically viewed as overlapping with the broader notion of spirituality (Scott, 1997; Harris, 2003). Or as McNeill (1988) points out, intrinsic religiosity is directly associated with "healthy religiousness." The counterpart to intrinsic religiosity is extrinsic religiosity. The extrinsic orientation is, "useful for the self in granting safety, social standing, solace, and endorsement for one's chosen way of life" (Allport, 1966, p. 455). It has been suggested that brotherhood and unity become less important to the extrinsic individual's own personal beliefs and values, while conformance to community-based norms increases in importance. In addition, from an entrepreneurial point of view there may be another positive aspects of an extrinsic orientation. We argue that the adherence to certain dogmas, church attendance, and the specific community-based parameters of behavior often associated with the extrinsic dimension of religious orientation may also be an important source of economic and social capital for entrepreneurs (Candland, 2000). Religious orientation and value-based attitudes are found to entail higher levels of entrepreneurial activity, given the importance of intrinsic religiosity for market behaviours and perceptions of market justice (Noble et al., 2007).

Religion shapes the society by giving meaning to a society's ethical structures, encouraging or discouraging certain behaviours (Dodd and Seaman, 1998). While most studies suggest a positive relationship between religious belief (and church attendance) and entrepreneurial activities (Hirschmeier, 1964; Woodrum, 1985; Kwon, 1997; Iyer, 1999; Martes and Rodriguez, 2004), other studies find no significant relationship between religious belief, church attendance, and entrepreneurial activity (Dodd and Seaman, 1998). It should be noted, however, that the studies that tend to find a positive relationship appear to be from relatively high growth economies (both developed and emerging), and/or focus on ethnic and immigrant enclaves that utilize the social capital derived from a church relationship, while the empirical studies that tend not to find a relationship are from more stagnant European economies and/or do not clearly distinguish between early stage entrepreneurs and long-term small business owners. In Muslim countries, which are usually defined as high-context cultures, people tend to be fatalist meaning that they do not believe that they have much control over events that affect them (Raven and Welsh, 2004). They strongly believe in destiny and events being controlled by fate. In Muslim culture, fatalism is characterised by the phrase "InshAllah2, which means "If God wills it" (Rice, 1999). For example, there is a widespread belief that strongly religious countries are not receptive to innovation and proactiveness (Herbig and Dunphy, 1998; Slowikowski and Jarratt, 1997; Tansuhaj et al., 1991). Dodd and Seaman (1998) argue that religion and enterprise have a complex and interdependent relationship in which religion affects a believer's entrepreneurial activities, influences the believer's decision to become an entrepreneur, enterprise management and the entrepreneur's contact network. They suggest three kinds of relationships or interactions between religion and entrepreneurship. The first relationship is between society, religion and entrepreneurship. Here, religion acts as a synthesiser of societal or national meaning systems. A national religion that provides some kind of support for entrepreneurship can be understood to make a positive contribution to the level of environmental benefit for entrepreneurship. The second relationship exists between individual faith, religion and entrepreneurship. Here, believers will be strongly influenced by the religion in which they have faith and also, use personal and professional networks within their religion. Such networks maybe less useful in situations where believers live in a very dominant religious group or a society that is relatively homogeneous in terms of religious observance. However, for minority religious groups, access to a religious network may be extremely useful. The network reinforces the behavioural norms of the faith as well as providing a primary source of contact for the individual. The third relationship exists between theory, religion and entrepreneurship. Here, dominant Protestant cultures are still often analysed through a Weberian framework. The usefulness of such a framework may or not apply now in religiously diverse cultures.

People enact rather than simply react to their surroundings (Weick, 1979), so entrepreneurship can be viewed as an example of behaviour that is socially constructed and embedded (Lavoie, 1991; Granovetter, 2000; Lipset, 2000; Jansson, 2002; Morrison, 2006). The facticity of religious constructions therefore may influence the behaviour of economic actors. Even in contexts that assume a free "market" in religions and assume a rational "consumer" choice among religious alternatives (Stark and Finke, 2000), the behaviour of adherents is constrained by these social constructions – the behaviour of adherents may also be influenced by powerful social forces of differentiation, societisation and rationalisation (Wilson, 1966). The religious "market" itself is a social construction so the observed behaviour of the market in the West is not to be taken as universal (Bruce, 1999) – particularly so in the case of Eastern religions and societies that did not undergo equivalent processes of modernisation and therefore reflect a different perspective on secularisation (Berger, 1983; Tomatsu, 1995). For example, Buddhism provides a framework by which mindfulness can be viewed as a form of entrepreneurship in the creation of socially embedded processes and structures. From this path-creation perspective, entrepreneurs are creators engaged in mindful deviation from the present (Garaud and Karnoe, 2001; Jansson, 2002). Levy (1966) described modernisation as the ratio of inanimate to animate sources of power. Berger et al. (1973, p. 8) noted that social scientists often discussed the concept of modernisation interchangeably with that of economic growth and development; they suggested that modernisation "must be seen in close relation to economic growth – more specifically, to the particular growth processes released by recent technology". McLaren (2008, p. 2) in his work Religious Foundations for Global Ethics, observes that Eastern and Western religions possess concepts of "a personal, spiritual commitment to some Ultimate, even if only mystically perceived," and that this "is often the strongest motivation for seeking and fulfilling the perceived good or virtue."

Certain ethical elements of the religious worldview under discussion have the potential not only to enrich enterprise culture, but also to justify a certain type of organizational culture. This is consonant to the fact that religious environments may indeed offer a sort of legitimization (or, in other cases, criticism) to enterprise cultures (Drakopoulou-Dodd and Gotsis, 2007, p. 99). An important aspect of Greek Orthodoxy's worldview, rooted in the Greek patristic tradition, is the deep respect, which is not confined to one's follow believers, but extended to any human being as a person with inalienable rights, irrespective of ethnicity, gender, race, etc. This emphasis on otherness reflecting God's presence permeates the monastic and anchoretic traditions of Eastern Orthodoxy as an expression of a genuine ethos incarnated in other-centered attitudes, as already discussed. Accordingly, these attitudes and stances have the potential to offer invaluable support to anti-discrimination workplace cultures, as well as to policies eliminating coercion and other abusive practices in contemporary workplaces. Religious and cultural traditions may impact upon entrepreneurial motivation, especially in the case of societies that do postulate a certain societal ethics. The latter may in fact constrain, facilitate or impede entrepreneurial activities. On the one hand, one can reasonably identify a set of differences in people's beliefs intertwined with certain cultural variables that may substantially enrich existing interpretations of economic phenomena (Guiso et al., 2006). On the other hand, culture does not only affect economic outcomes, but also gives prominence to social goals that may in turn be elaborated as the salient features of entrepreneurship (Peredo and McLean, 2006).

Studying religious values of small company leaders is particularly important. Small companies give an idea about the enterprising nature of a region. Small US businesses have an enormous impact on the American economy. Over half (52 percent) of all US employees work in small businesses. Small businesses create most new jobs, and originate approximately 55 percent of US innovations (US Department of Labor, 2006). Leaders in small businesses have much more impact on the company's values and culture than they would in large organizations, since the leader is able to engage a larger proportion of the workforce in social networks (Balkundi and Kilduff, 2006). The religious motivations of small company leaders may have particularly potent effects, influencing business contacts and business decisions (Dodd and Gotsis, 2007; Dodd and Seaman, 1998). Finally, there is some evidence that leaders of small companies tend to have stronger religious beliefs than those of larger companies (Madlin, 1986).

OBJECTIVES OF THE STUDY

- To compare the religious orientation of generation Y with respect to their gender, graduation, family type and family occupation.
- To compare the entrepreneurial aspirations of generation Y with respect to their gender, graduation, family type and family occupation.
- To find out the relation between religious orientation and entrepreneurial orientation of generation Y.

HYPOTHESES

H1. There is no significant difference in religious orientation of generation Y with respect to their gender, graduation background, family type and family occupation.

H2. There is no significant difference in religious orientation of generation Y with respect to their gender, graduation background, family type and family occupation.

H3. There is no significant relation between the religious orientation and entrepreneurial aspirations of generation Y

RESEARCH METHODOLOGY

For the study a sample of 100 was targeted out of which 74 valid responses were received with a response rate of 74%. The technique of Purposive sampling was adopted for collecting data since the research was focused on generation Y. the data was collected from the students studying in Post Graduate courses of a University in Delhi. The research design is given below:

Table 1: Showing Distribution of Sample

	Value Label	*N*
Gender	Male	36
	Female	38
Graduation	Commerce	39
	Science	31
	Humanities	4
Family Occupation	Business Family	27
	Service Family	42
	Business and Service Both	5
Family Background	Nuclear	52
	Joint	20
	Extended	2

SURVEY TOOLS

A three – part questionnaire was used for data collection.

Socio-demographic data concerning name, gender, family type (Nuclear, Joint, and Extended), family occupation (Business, Service and Both) and graduation background (Commerce, Science and Humanities).

Religious Orientation Questionnaire was designed to measure religious orientation of individuals.

Entrepreneurial Interest was picked up form Comprehensive Interest Questionnaire designed by Psycom

RESULTS AND DISCUSSIONS

The analysis of Table 1 shows that the generation Y females differ significantly from generation Y males on their religious orientation. Further the scrutiny of means table (Table 2) shows that females are significantly higher than males on religious orientation. The results are in line with the established opinions of fairer sex being more inclined to the belief in Supreme power. The results also show that there is no significant difference in the religious orientation of generation Y coming from different family types, family occupation, and graduation background. The analysis of variance and means table also shows that the females are significantly higher on religious orientation than males across all family businesses (Table 1 and Table 2a). Thus hypothesis H1 is partially accepted and partially rejected.

Table 1: Showing the Analysis of Variance of Religious Orientation of Generation Y with Respect to their Gender, Family Type, Family Occupation, and Graduation Background

Source	*Type III Sum of Squares*	*df*	*Mean Square*	*F*	*Sig.*
Corrected Model	2.983[a]	21	.142	.703	.811
Intercept	194.869	1	194.869	964.203	.000
Gender	1.134	1	1.134	5.611	.022
Graduation	.572	2	.286	1.415	.252
FamBuss	.059	2	.030	.146	.864
FamBack	.275	2	.138	.681	.511
Gender * Graduation	.182	2	.091	.449	.641
Gender * FamBuss	1.436	2	.718	3.553	.036
Gender * FamBack	.387	1	.387	1.912	.173
Graduation * FamBuss	.898	2	.449	2.223	.119
Graduation * FamBack	.006	1	.006	.028	.869
FamBuss * FamBack	.016	1	.016	.078	.780
Gender * Graduation * FamBuss	.046	1	.046	.230	.634
Error	10.509	52	.202		
Total	823.648	74			
a. R Squared = .221 (Adjusted R Squared = -.093)					

Table 2: Showing the Mean Scores of Generation Y with Respect to their Gender, Graduation, Family Type and Family Occupation on Entrepreneurial Interest

Entrepreneurial Interest	*Overall*		
Mean	3.32		
Gender	Male	Female	
Mean	3.22	3.40	
Graduation Background	Commerce	Science	Humanities
Mean	3.25	3.30	3.58
Family Type	Nuclear	Joint	Extended
Mean	3.40	3.28	2.91
Family Occupation	Business	Service	Both
Mean	3.24	3.36	3.40

Table 2a: Showing the mean scores of Generation Y with respect to their Gender and Family Business on Religious Orientation

Gender	*Family Business*	*Mean*
Male	Business Family	3.167
	Service Family	3.324
	Business and Service Both	3.145
Female	Business Family	3.305
	Service Family	3.388
	Business and Service Both	3.660

The analysis of the Table 3 shows that the generation Y does not differ on their entrepreneurial aspirations with respect to their gender, graduation, family type, and family business. However the means show (Table 4) that the individuals coming from humanities background are scoring high on entrepreneurial interest followed by science background. Also the individuals coming from extended families are higher on entrepreneurial interest as compared to individuals from joint families and nuclear family generation y is scoring the lowest. This means they are not the factors which might lead to determination of their entrepreneurial aspirations. Thus Hypothesis H2 is accepted.

Table 3: Showing the Analysis of Variance of Entrepreneurial Aspiration of Generation Y with respect to their Gender, Family Type, Family Occupation, and Graduation Background

Source	*Type III Sum of Squares*	*df*	*Mean Square*	*F*	*Sig.*
Gender	.876	1	.876	.128	.722
Graduation	13.954	2	6.977	1.018	.369
FamBuss	9.432	2	4.716	.688	.507
FamBack	9.088	2	4.544	.663	.520
Gender * Graduation	3.886	2	1.943	.283	.754
Gender * FamBuss	2.076	2	1.038	.151	.860
Gender * FamBack	9.256	1	9.256	1.350	.251
Graduation * FamBuss	10.269	2	5.134	.749	.478
Graduation * FamBack	2.049	1	2.049	.299	.587
FamBuss * FamBack	3.344	1	3.344	.488	.488
Gender * Graduation * FamBuss	2.059	1	2.059	.300	.586
Error	356.545	52	6.857		
Total	1400.000	74			
. R Squared = .267 (Adjusted R Squared = -.029)					

Table 4: Showing the mean scores of Generation Y with respect to their Gender, Graduation, Family Type and Family Occupation on Entrepreneurial Interest

Entrepreneurial Interest	*Overall*		
Mean	4.12		
Gender	Male	Female	
Mean	4.17	4.07	
Graduation Background	Commerce	Science	Humanities
Mean	3.39	4.45	5.17
Family Type	Nuclear	Joint	Extended
Mean	3.38	4.58	4.75
Family Occupation	Business	Service	Both
Mean	4.25	3.61	5.00

The results of correlations show that there is no significant correlation between entrepreneurial aspiration and religious orientation (Table 5). This shows that the religious orientation does not relate to an individual being more inclined to entrepreneurial activities. Thus Hypothesis H3 is accepted.

Table 5: Showing the correlations of Religious Orientation and Entrepreneurial Aspiration of Generation Y

		Entrepreneurial Interest	*Religious Orientation*
Entrepreneurial Interest	Pearson Correlation	1	-.105
	Sig. (2-tailed)		.373
	N	74	74
Religious Orientation	Pearson Correlation	-.105	1
	Sig. (2-tailed)	.373	
	N	74	74

CONCLUSION

Individuals often cite religious experiences as sources of personal meaning. Numerous studies have examined religiosity as a predictor of health and psychological well-being. This study examines associations between religious orientation of students (generation Y). Faith in yourself and your actions greatly impact what you achieve as a person and as an entrepreneur. Since it is associated to the holistic well being, building up of self esteem and individual worth, it might also relate to the entrepreneurial aspirations of an individual which requires all the qualities strengthened by the right religious orientation. With this premise the present study was conducted on the generation Y of a metropolitan university. The results show that females of generation Y are more religious as compared to males. However they do not differ on their entrepreneurial aspirations. Also generation Y coming from commerce, science or humanities background, nuclear, joint or extended families, and business, service or both families does not differ on their religious orientation and entrepreneurial aspirations. The results also show that there is no linkage between religious orientation and propensity of entrepreneurial aspirations.

REFERENCES

[1] Noble A D, Galbraith C S, Singh G and Stiles C H (2007), "Market justice, religious orientation, and entrepreneurial attitudes An empirical study", Journal of Enterprising Communities: People and Places in the Global Economy Vol. 1 No. 2, pp. 121-134

[2] Altinay L and Wang C L (2011), "The influence of an entrepreneur's socio-cultural characteristics on the entrepreneurial orientation of small firms", Journal of Small Business and Enterprise Development Vol. 18 No. 4, pp. 673-694

[3] Carswell P and Rolland D (2007), "Religion and entrepreneurship in New Zealand", Journal of Enterprising Communities:People and Places in the Global Economy Vol. 1 No. 2, pp. 162-174

[4] Galbraith C S and Galbraith D M (2007), "An empirical note on entrepreneurial activity, intrinsic religiosity and economic growth", Journal of Enterprising Communities: People and Places in the Global Economy Vol. 1 No. 2, pp. 188-201

[5] Valliere D (2008), "Exploring Buddhist influence on the entrepreneurial decision", International Journal of Entrepreneurial Behaviour & Research Vol. 14 No. 3, pp. 172-191

[6] Dana L P (2007), "A humility-based enterprising community: the Amish people in Lancaster County", Journal of Enterprising Communities: People and Places in the Global Economy Vol. 1 No. 2, pp. 142-154

[7] Gotsis G and Kortezi Z (2009), "The impact of Greek Orthodoxy on entrepreneurship: a theoretical framework", Journal of Enterprising Communities: People and Places in the Global Economy Vol. 3 No. 2, pp. 152-175

[8] Day N E and Hudson D (2011), "US small company leaders' religious motivation and other-directed organizational values", International Journal of Entrepreneurial Behaviour & Research Vol. 17 No. 4, pp. 361-379

[9] White A (2010), "Religious environmentalism as a vital contribution to sustainability", Journal of Enterprising Communities: People and Places in the Global Economy Vol. 4 No. 3, pp. 268-278

Author Index